JPL AND THE AMERICAN SPACE PROGRAM

Yale Planetary Exploration Series

★ JPL ★

AND THE AMERICAN SPACE PROGRAM

A History of the Jet Propulsion Laboratory

CLAYTON R. KOPPES

Yale University Press
New Haven and London

A portion of chapter 6 appeared in somewhat different form in *Journal of the British Interplanetary Society* 34 (August 1981) and is reprinted here by permission. Figure 5 is reprinted by permission of the American Institute of Aeronautics and Astronautics.

Published with the assistance from the
Kingsley Trust Association Publication Fund
established by the Scroll and Key Society of Yale College.

Designed by Nancy Ovedovitz
and set in VIP Baskerville type by The Composing Room of Michigan, Inc.
Printed in the United States of America.

Library of Congress Cataloging in Publication Data

Koppes, Clayton R., 1945–
   JPL and the American space program.
   Bibliography: p.
   Includes index.
   1. Jet Propulsion Laboratory (U.S.)—History.
2. Astronautics—United States—History.
I. Title.
TL568.J47K66   629.4'072079493   82-40162
ISBN 0-300-02408-8   AACR2

10   9   8   7   6   5   4   3   2   1

To my grandparents,
who lived from the days of the horse and buggy to the space age
with their values intact,
and to WPN

CONTENTS

PREFACE

The Jet Propulsion Laboratory in Pasadena, California, in its heyday was the world's premier space installation. It began in 1936 as the Guggenheim Aeronautical Laboratory, California Institute of Technology (GALCIT) rocket project, a loose band of six amateurs risking their meager Depression-era earnings under the aegis of an eminent Hungarian-born professor, Theodore von Kármán. During World War II the GALCIT group made fundamental breakthroughs in the theoretical and applied aspects of both solid- and liquid-propellant rocketry. These advances played an important role in converting rocketry from science fiction into respectable science and engineering. Moreover, the GALCIT researchers could plausibly claim that they—not Robert Goddard or the German V-2 experimenters—laid the foundation for the development of American rocket and missile technology. Reorganized, expanded, and renamed the Jet Propulsion Laboratory in 1944, the project developed into a full-fledged, permanent installation operated by the California Institute of Technology for the Army Ordnance Corps. The laboratory's major responsibility was basic research in missile technology and the development of the country's first tactical nuclear missiles, Corporal and Sergeant.

Space exploration was always alluring to JPL, however. In 1945 its engineers launched the WAC Corporal, the first man-made object to escape Earth's atmosphere. In early 1958 the laboratory, in collaboration with the army's team headed by Wernher von Braun, launched the first man-made satellite to orbit the Earth. Becoming part of the new National Aeronautics and Space Administration (NASA) in 1958, JPL turned primarily to space missions, with planetary exploration its particular forte. JPL's Ranger 7 was the first U.S. spacecraft to impact the moon; Surveyor, a project in which JPL supervised an industrial firm, Hughes Aircraft Company, became the first vehicle of any country to make a controlled soft landing on the lunar surface. The planetary missions were especially impressive technologically and important for a major transformation in understanding the solar system. The ten Mariners from 1962 through 1973 returned revealing pictures and vast amounts of other data from Venus, Mercury, and Mars. JPL built the orbiter portion of the Viking project, which became the first spacecraft to manage a soft landing on Mars. And in the early 1980s the laboratory sent its twin Voyagers to Jupiter, Saturn, and Uranus, in the culmination of an era of space exploration. To manage these ventures JPL grew to a peak of approximately 4,600 employees and in 1980 commanded a budget of nearly $400 million.

A history of the Jet Propulsion Laboratory is a contribution to a relatively uncharted branch of the history of science and technology—the American missile and space programs. William Sims Bainbridge has observed that "most authors who have written about the history of spaceflight felt that to string well-known facts together into unimaginative chronicles was sufficient."[1] Serious historical study of the space program is sparse, although there are some notable exceptions, such as Homer E. Newell's *Beyond the Atmosphere: Early Years of Space Science* and R. Cargill Hall's *Lunar Impact: A History of Project Ranger*. Indeed, JPL's role in the development of American missile and space technology has been neglected.[2] One purpose of this history, therefore, is to cover some of the major technological developments in which JPL has been involved. The technical side figures more prominently in the missile period, which has received less scholarly attention. During the space period the scientific implications of JPL's missions assume greater prominence. Hall provides a detailed history of the technological development of the Ranger spacecraft, the prototype for later missions. An intimate account of each iteration of spacecraft is not the purpose of this history.

Although this book pays appropriate attention to technology and science, it is not, in the end, primarily a history of science or technology per se. JPL as an institution reflects some of the central questions about the role of science and technology in modern American society, and this history attempts in particular to address some of those societal concerns. One category of issues is institutional. A recurrent theme is the complicated triangular relationship among JPL; its parent and managing entity, The California Institute of Technology (Caltech or CIT); and the chief funding agency, the army and especially NASA. The involvement of a major university in the management of a national laboratory raised important questions about the appropriate relationship between universities and the federal government and their mutual expectations. James R. Killian, Jr., who under Eisenhower served as the first presidential science adviser, singled out JPL as an example of the "enlightened spirit of partnership between Defense and the universities." He writes: "The academic institutions responded by inventing novel ways to serve government without distorting their prime functions as educational institutions. The summer study projects, the special research centers, and the large off-campus interdisciplinary laboratories such as Lincoln, the Jet Propulsion Laboratory, and the Applied Physics Laboratory, all managed by universities, are examples. It was a golden era in government–university cooperation, pioneered largely by the DOD [Department of Defense]."[3]

From other perspectives, however, the very process which Killian lauded aroused anxiety and opposition, for many persons questioned the commanding role that military purposes assumed in American research and development after World War II. The case of Caltech's JPL offers insights into the evolution and consequences of this relationship with military-oriented research. When JPL became affiliated with NASA, the direct military connection faded. A new cluster of institutional issues became important. They had to do with the degree of control NASA should exercise over the laboratory and the influence Washington headquarters should exert over a university. New programmatic issues also came to the fore. They involved the highly controversial uses of expensive space technology, in particular the balance between scientific exploration and manned ventures. This book is, then, a history of a national laboratory in relation to certain military and scientific policies in the national security state.

I use the term *national security state* to refer to the specifically American experience since World War II. During the war international conditions and American perceptions of the country's relationship with the rest of the world underwent a fundamental change. Since the United States could no longer rely on its oceanic buffer zones or on a long buildup period before fielding an expeditionary force, government planners and politicians resolved to create the capacity to confront any enemy immediately. The key to understanding the phenomenon of the American national security state lies in the recognition that the federal government forged permanent institutions to make possible a perpetual readiness to wage instantaneous warfare of great destruction. In so doing a very real, and unresolved, tension emerged between these perceived national security interests and the maintenance of the country's democratic form of government. Without attempting a full definition, I suggest the following five major characteristics of the national security state: (1) A large permanent military establishment which commanded huge resources. (2) The integration of major national institutions, such as parts of industry and universities, in pursuit of national security. Research and development establishments have been especially important because they provide the implements of massive (nuclear) and quick (missiles) warfare. (3) A centralization of authority in the executive branch and particularly in the presidency, and a concommitant reduction in congressional power. This development poses with particular acuteness the dilemma of the national security state and democracy, for vital issues—especially the ultimate decisions of the initiation of warfare—have been effectively lodged in one branch. (4) A premium on internal order and loyalty. Dissent is circumscribed for fear of its effect on national security. (5) A self-perpetuating ideology, based on a perception of an external threat potentially global in scope and implacable in its opposition, coupled with an arrogation of exclusive virtue to the United States. It is important to note that the national security state is not monolithic. Significant differences of opinion may exist, although they tend to be over means rather than ends. (I have taken the term *national security state* from Daniel Yergin, who uses it without definition.)[4]

It is also important to stress what this history is not. It is not an official history of the laboratory. The project originated when historians at Caltech and JPL director William H. Pickering agreed that the recurrent interest in a history of the laboratory would best be served by having it written by a Caltech faculty member. JPL would provide the funds through a grant to the Humanities and Social Science Division at Caltech, but the historian who undertook the task would, by virtue of holding faculty status, be assured full independence. This arrangement was bolstered when Daniel J. Kevles, a tenured Caltech historian, agreed to serve as principal investigator. After receiving my Ph.D. in 1974, I joined the Caltech faculty and completed the bulk of the research and writing by 1978. At that point I joined the history faculty at Oberlin College, where, without external funding, I finished the manuscript. True to the intent of this arrangement, JPL management did not exert pressure about matters of interpretation. The laboratory was in fact very good about allowing me unrestricted access to its files, except for a very few areas which could not be declassified; in the course of my research large blocks of material were declassified. In short, this history is an independent interpretation based on substantially free access to JPL's files.

In the course of a project of this nature, I acquired many debts, which I can only imperfectly acknowledge. First and foremost, I am especially obligated to Daniel J. Kevles, who gave of his time and knowledge generously and beyond the call of duty, to plan the project, run interference for it, and sustain its author. Without his skill as planner, counselor, and reader, this book would have been impossible. At JPL two persons were invaluable—Leo Lunine, who was my contact in the laboratory management and cheerfully provided many services, and R. Cargill Hall, who wrote the history of the Ranger project and offered many insights into the laboratory. William Pickering, the late Frank J. Malina, and James D. Burke improved the technical accuracy of the manuscript through their careful reading. Any remaining errors of fact or interpretation are of course my responsibility. Colleagues at Caltech—Judy Goodstein, Robert Huttenback, J. Morgan Kousser, Roger Noll, Rodman W. Paul, and Robert A. Rosenstone—were supportive in many ways. This was also true of colleagues at Oberlin, in particular Geoffrey T. Blodgett, William Norris, and Benjamin Schiff, and of Donald R. McCoy and William Tuttle of the University of Kansas. My friend Phyllis Bixler suffered through more than her share of JPL. The records staffs of various institutions assisted me in many ways; they include the JPL Vellum and Records Centers and Library, Washington National Records Center, Modern Military Branch of the National Archives, NASA History Office, Dwight D. Eisenhower Library, and Harry S. Truman Library. The staff of Yale University Press—particularly Edward Tripp and Charles Grench— were patient, pleasant, and very helpful to work with. Sandra Wendel performed ably as copy editor. Finally, an array of secretaries made sure the manuscript got typed. I thank Rita Pierson, Irene Baldon, Karen Wales, and particularly Lynne Schlinger and Barbara Turek. All photographs are courtesy of JPL.

Clayton R. Koppes
April 1982

1 ★★

GALCIT: SEEDBED OF AMERICAN ROCKETRY

Spaceflight seemed in the 1930s to be an impossible dream—a realm reserved for science fiction novels, comic strips, and movies like Fritz Lang's *Woman in the Moon.* In scientific circles rocketry languished in the nether region of alchemy, psychokinesis, and similar activities beyond the pale of respectability. Representative of this opinion, Forest Ray Moulton's widely used astronomy text of 1933 patronizingly claimed to understand the appeal of space-flight "romances." The Chicago astronomer assured his students, however, that there was "no hope" such wishes would ever be realized. "The difficulty of escaping the earth's gravity is insuperable; the problem of directing a journey through the celestial spaces and that of descending gently to rest on the surface of another gravitating body are equally formidable," he wrote. "Only those who are unfamiliar with the physical factors involved believe that such adventures will ever pass beyond the realms of fancy."[1]

The performance of rockets certainly offered little encouragement. Rockets were used in China at least as early as the twelfth century. Europeans later adapted them for warfare—Francis Scott Key scribbled "The Star Spangled Banner" in the immortal red glare of Congreve's incendiary rockets. But these nineteenth-century specimens were inaccurate and dangerous and fell into disuse when improved artillery became available. Rockets would have to be much more reliable and have longer and more powerful thrust before they could regain military roles, to say nothing of space exploration.[2]

A handful of scientists, to be sure, were studying the problems of rocket propulsion. Three stood out. In Russia, K. E. Tsiolkovsky published a theoretical article on space travel as early as 1903. In Germany, the Rumanian Hermann Oberth brought out an extensive theoretical analysis in 1923. And in the United States, Robert H. Goddard, a reclusive Yankee physics professor from Clark University published a classic paper in 1919, "A Method of Reaching Extreme Altitudes," which forecast the feasibility of building rockets propelled by successive impulses from powder engines that might reach the moon. In 1926 he tested the first successful liquid-propellant rocket at a farm in Massachusetts; it flew for 2 ½ seconds and reached an elevation of 41 feet. Another rocket reached a height of 90 feet in 1929. But in the ensuing public outcry, scientists and journalists ridiculed his ambitions, and the commonwealth branded his rockets a public nuisance. Like Puritan heretics fleeing to the wilderness, Goddard and his wife left Massachusetts for a solitary experiment station on the Staked Plain near Roswell, New Mexico.[3]

Rocketry suffered from a similarly low reputation in the 1930s among the very proper academics at the California Institute of Technology's Guggenheim Aeronautical Laboratory (GALCIT), one of the leading aerodynamics research establishments in the world. They studied such topics as the wind resistance of aircraft and improvement of airplane propellers to boost speeds above 300 miles per hour. The key element for the establishment of the Jet Propulsion Laboratory (JPL) was present, however, in Theodore von Kármán, the brilliant aerodynamicist who served as director of GALCIT. Born in Hungary in 1881, he received a Ph.D. from Berlin University, taught briefly in his homeland, then moved to Aachen, Germany. Robert A. Millikan, the dynamic Nobel prize-winning physicist who headed the California Institute of Technology (Caltech or CIT), lured Kármán to Pasadena in 1926. The suave, cultured Kármán became a naturalized American citizen in 1936, an indispensable credential for his cherished role during and after World War II as adviser to the United States Air Force. Often impatient with engineers, who seemed to him tied to conventional thinking, the strongly theoretical Kármán was receptive to ideas that struck others as bizarre. In the 1920s he listened sympathetically to some of Germany's pioneer rocket experimenters, and he recommended that rocket propulsion be investigated as one of the unsolved challenges of aerodynamics.[4]

Kármán's involvement in rocketry began in the late 1930s through his graduate students, in particular Frank J. Malina. Besides aerodynamics, Kármán and Malina shared interests in the arts and world affairs, and the grand old Hungarian became Malina's "second father." Although intermittently interested in rocketry, Malina did not harbor a sense of space exploration destiny. He was not a Robert Goddard who, at age seventeen, ensconced in a cherry tree at his home, had seen a vision of a spaceship whining slightly above the Earth then hurtling toward Mars. Goddard always noted the day of the vision as "anniversary day" in his diary and spent the rest of his life possessed by, and possessive of, rockets. At age twelve Malina read Jules Verne's *From the Earth to the Moon*, the fecund novel that had lured so many persons into rocketry, and continued to read sporadically on rocketry. As a senior at Texas A & M, Malina reviewed the difficulties of spaceflight in an essay and hinted that he agreed that "what man can imagine he can do." These latent curiosities pushed to the front of his mind as experiments he conducted at the GALCIT wind tunnel in 1935 and 1936 demonstrated the inherent limitations of propeller-driven aircraft.[5]

Malina listened intently, therefore, when William Bollay, a Kármán assistant, reported in early 1936 on Eugen Sänger's promising rocket-motor experiments in Vienna. A rocket plane was not so fantastic after all, Bollay explained; it might even become a stratospheric passenger carrier. Malina pushed deeper into the scientific literature on rocketry and soon proposed to Clark Millikan, a GALCIT professor and son of Robert Millikan, that he write his doctoral dissertation on problems of rocket propulsion and flight characteristics of sounding altitude rockets. The dubious Millikan advised him to enter industry. This response might have deflected Malina from rocketry altogether, but he carried his idea to Kármán, who thought it over and told him to go ahead.[6]

The first stirrings of rocketry at Caltech also attracted two enthusiasts, John W. Parsons and Ed Forman. Intrigued by Bollay's talk, they presented themselves at GALCIT and were referred to Malina. Parsons and Forman mingled deeply with the unconventional. Parsons's house on Orange Grove Avenue was the scene of various occult practices, including black and white magic. Rocketry was perhaps but a natural expression of those whose interests lay beyond the orthodox. Though neither man had gone to college, they offered important skills to Malina's budding thesis. Forman was an expert mechanic; Parsons, who worked intermittently for powder companies, possessed an encyclopedic command of explosives and similar chemicals. Parsons and Forman wanted to shoot off rockets. Impatient with theory, they had the inventor's zeal for tangible experiment by trial and error. Malina also wanted to fire rockets, but, his professional background reinforced by Kármán's stern emphasis on the primacy of theory, the doctoral candidate recognized the need to conduct theoretical analysis before rushing ahead with power and fuses. The balance was often difficult to maintain.[7]

Deciding where to start was the first problem. Disputes raged over virtually every aspect of rocketry: design of the rocket, method of launching, use of the payload parachute, and so forth. In February 1936 Malina, Parsons, Forman, and Bollay reviewed the literature of the pioneers. They were particularly impressed by Sänger's claim of having produced an exhaust velocity of 10,000 feet per second with a mixture of light fuel oil and gaseous oxygen. But none of the literature seemed to promise a rocket capable of reaching altitudes higher than the 100,000 feet (20 miles) of which balloons were capable. After much argument the group decided that considerations of rocket shells, parachutes, and the like were irrelevant until a workable motor could be designed. The group therefore set two initial goals: "theoretical studies of the thermodynamical problems of the reaction principle and of the flight performance requirements of a sounding rocket" and static tests of elementary experiments with rocket engines in order to measure such things as thrust and duration accurately. Parsons and Forman chafed under the postponement of rocket firings, but Malina hewed to his mentor's emphasis on theoretical understanding before experiment.[8]

Despite its long history the rocket engine was one of the least understood means of reaction propulsion. The basic idea behind propulsion by propeller, thermal jet engine, and rocket engine is the reaction principle. "For every action there is an equal but opposite reaction," declared Isaac Newton as his third law of motion. The reaction principle is at work when a rifle kicks against the hunter's shoulder as the bullet speeds out the barrel, or when the canoeist leaps ashore, pushing his canoe back into the stream. In these cases the reaction is unwanted, but with a rocket, the reaction is the desired means of propulsion. When the propellant in the rocket engine's combustion chamber is ignited, gases rush out through a nozzle and thrust or "kick" the rocket on its way.

For rocket experimenters of the 1930s interest always turned to Goddard, for both his achievements and his mystery. Robert Millikan, who thought rockets might be useful for his research on cosmic rays, wrote to Goddard for information in 1931. Goddard replied that his research was not yet ready for publication. It never would be. Goddard preferred filing patents to publication. In 1936 Millikan tried to interest the New Mexico experimenter in cooperative work with Caltech but Goddard again declined. Malina visited Goddard at Roswell in the summer of 1936. Beneath the surface cordiality ran tensions laden with long-term implications. Malina found Goddard unnecessarily secretive. Goddard felt Malina was trying to pluck the fruit of his twenty years' hard labor for a thesis. Two years later Harry Guggenheim, who had helped finance both GALCIT and Goddard, tried to arrange a cooperative venture between the two. But the lone wolf could countenance only limited disclosures, while Kármán insisted on full cooperation. The Clark professor probably would have exercised great influence over the Caltech group, but he seemed unable to abandon the solitary pursuit of his private vision.[9]

By the time he visited Goddard, Malina felt he grasped the theoretical dimensions of rocketry well enough to begin experiments. The GALCIT group brought little to their quest but enthusiasm, nascent knowledge, and strong backs. No GALCIT funds or facilities were available. Malina, Parsons, and Forman squeezed their experimentation into odd hours between classes and jobs. They pooled their sparse earnings to buy supplies and spent weekends scouring greater Los Angeles for secondhand equipment. Sometimes they came to the brink of giving up, as in late June 1936 when it seemed impossible to find the $120 needed for two instruments. At one point Malina and Parsons considered writing a movie script about flight to the moon which they hoped to sell to Hollywood to raise funds.[10]

Finally they were ready for their first test. Committed to doing first things first, they had built a motor, which would be tested on a stationary stand. Flight equipment lay far in the future. In late October 1936 they picked up the last bits of equipment, worked until 3:30 in the morning getting it ready, and retired for three hours of sleep. Since no campus facilities were available, at dawn they began transporting the rocket gear to an isolated spot in the Arroyo Seco about three miles above the Rose Bowl. They dug trenches to hide in, piled sandbags in front of them, and scrupulously checked their equipment. By early Saturday afternoon the gleaming duralumin rocket motor, with a water jacket for cooling and a nickel-steel nozzle, stood ready on its test stand (see figure 1).[11]

All four tests failed. The gaseous oxygen and methyl-alcohol mixture was to be ignited by a split power fuse. On the first three tests combustion ceased after ignition; each time the fuse was blown out. For the fourth they tied the fuse to the chamber. This time the motor ignited and burned for about 3 seconds, then suddenly the oxygen hose caught fire, broke, and swung around on the ground, not 40 feet from the panicked experimenters, who lit out across the canyon. Fortunately the check valves shut off the fuel lines, and the men warily returned to the scene. They began to understand why Goddard had worked for nearly twenty years "without achieving what many would call success."[12]

The testing took a turn for the better, however. On November 28 the motor ran for about 15 seconds before anything went wrong. The experimenters crawled out of the trenches and let out a cheer. "Very satisfactory," said Malina. "Now I must convince the department that we should have a laboratory on the campus." Kármán was impressed, but he first insisted on a detailed analysis of the motor's operation. Meanwhile he allowed them ten hours a week of student help for the tedious process of transporting, setting up, and taking down the equipment at the arroyo. On their last test at the arroyo on January 16, 1937, the motor ran for 44 seconds.[13]

The trio's modest success attracted some support. Two other GALCIT graduate students signed on—Apollo M.O. Smith, with whom Malina collaborated on several papers, and Hsue-shen Tsien, a Chinese-born research engineer who combined brilliance in applied mathematics with extraordinary perseverance. Weld Arnold, a graduate student in meteorology, also expressed interest and then astounded everyone by volunteering to obtain $1,000 for the project. A few days later the financial angel bicycled the five miles from Glendale to Caltech with the first installment—$100 in $1 and $5

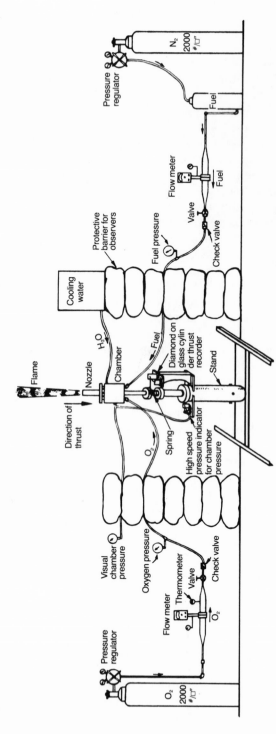

1. Schematic diagram of proposed test setup for rocket propulsion units research. Drawing by Frank J. Malina, August 28, 1936.

bills wrapped in an old newspaper. Arnold did not volunteer his source nor did the rocket enthusiasts inquire too closely. Malina and Smith began an analysis of sounding-rocket performance which soon produced paper flights of several hundred thousand feet. His interest piqued, Kármán allowed the group to start small-scale rocket-motor tests at GALCIT in the spring of 1937.[14]

The Caltech campus greeted the rocket group warily. The tests were noisy and dangerous. The group had no more than moved into the laboratory when misfortune struck. They mounted the motor and the propellant on the bob of a fifty-foot pendulum suspended from the third floor of the laboratory; the swing of the pendulum would measure the thrust produced. But the first test misfired, and a cloud of methyl alcohol and nitrogen dioxide permeated the building, leaving a thin layer of rust on much of the permanent equipment. The group, now dubbed the "suicide squad," was ordered out of the laboratory. Kármán allowed them to mount another apparatus on an outside wall of the building to continue testing. The group made the device five times stronger than they thought necessary, but two years later it exploded and hurled a piece of steel into the wall in front of which Malina had been standing. He escaped serious injury only because Kármán had called a few minutes before the test and asked him to bring a typewriter to his home. Parsons and Forman were dazed but uninjured. Despite the dangerous work, none of the original group was injured in rocket testing.[15]

Theoretical studies continued along with the testing. By December 1937 Smith and Malina had distilled hundreds of hours of work into a paper, "Flight Analysis of the Sounding Rocket," which they nervously handed to Kármán and Clark Millikan, who was showing more interest in rocketry. The two professors approved of the paper, got Malina a slot on the convention program of the Institute of Aeronautical Sciences in New York City in January 1938, and came up with $200 for Malina to make the trip—Caltech's first direct financial support for the rocket project. The paper was published two months later in the *Journal of the Aeronautical Sciences*. "If a rocket motor of high efficiency can be constructed," Malina and Smith said, "far greater altitudes can be reached than is possible by any other known means." They cautiously foresaw heights of 1,000 miles.[16]

That dramatic conclusion excited the journalists. The Associated Press (AP) wanted Malina's picture; *Time* and the *New York Herald-Tribune* reported the speech; the *Los Angeles Times* lauded the rocket effort in an editorial; and an imaginative Hollywood radio station wanted to broadcast the sound of the rocket motor. Several reporters descended on the rocket test stand that spring, and a long story on rockets was distributed nationally by the AP. Trying to go barnstorming pilots one better, a New York stunt man volunteered to be shot up by rocket at county fairs and then float down by parachute; the scientists replied that they were sorry but they could not oblige just yet. "Such fuss!" a worried Malina exclaimed. Goddard had been "almost blasted away" by publicity in the 1920s. If someone called him a "crackpot," he considered "the donor of the compliment a very mild human being," Malina noted. Hoping to avert this turn in publicity, he and Kármán insisted that they aimed for nothing more than a rocket that could reach 100,000 feet or so in altitude and return data for the study of meteorology and cosmic rays. But "the reporters seem to have better imaginations than we do," Malina sighed. They continued to file fantasy stories of moon voyages, complete with five-column sketches of passenger-carrying rocket ships blasting off from the Los Angeles Civic Center.[17]

In May 1938 the group obtained their best results yet. They built a new motor that featured a graphite lining and copper nozzle, both designed to withstand the extreme heat the motor generated. The motor operated successfully for a full minute or longer. But the project drifted into the doldrums. Smith took an engineering job, Arnold left for New York, and Tsien devoted all his time to finishing his Ph.D. dissertation. Frustrated with standstill tests, Parsons and Forman launched some black-powder rockets, which made very short flights. But they were pinched for funds and took jobs with Halifax Powder Company in the Mojave Desert. Malina became increasingly busy with a study at the GALCIT wind tunnel on the effectiveness of shelterbelts in reducing soil erosion. The rocket project seemed about to become dormant.[18]

World events were changing, however, to create the conditions in which the Pasadena enthusiasts' work would assume undreamed-of importance. The deterioration of peace, symbolized by the Munich crisis in the fall of 1938, heralded a buildup of American military strength. Kármán and his disciples at first discounted military applications for their rockets. "Army ordnance, we were led to believe, had no use for rockets whatever," he recalled. Interest developed, however, from another source—H. H. "Hap" Arnold, commanding general of the Army Air Corps, who was always alert to scientific applications for the military. He paid a surprise visit to the GALCIT laboratories in the spring of 1938 and found himself fascinated by the rocket work. His visit suddenly placed the project in a new light. That fall Arnold asked the National Academy of Sciences (NAS) Committee on Air Corps Research to start research on a number of projects, among them rocket-assisted takeoff of aircraft. The committee, of which Kármán and Robert Millikan were members, decided to fund rocket research, but not without skepticism. Jerome Hunsaker, head of the Guggenheim Aeronautics Department at the Massachusetts Institute of Technology, passed over that in favor of something he thought more serious—work on the deicing of windshields. "Kármán can take the Buck Rogers job," he said.[19]

Caltech accepted eagerly. Kármán and Millikan asked Malina to present a paper to the NAS committee on the application of rocket propulsion to aircraft. In December 1938 Malina reported that, while use of rockets as a sole means of power appeared to be limited, they were particularly adaptable to use in conjunction with propellers. Rockets might assist aircraft in taking off, climbing to operating altitudes, and achieving high speeds. Considerable theoretical knowledge had been amassed; now it was time to begin experimentation. He proposed to investigate both liquid- and solid-propellant rockets with particular attention to the difficulty experienced in supplying the propellant to the combustion chamber at high pressure and to design a motor able to withstand the intense heat.[20]

Malina's report paid off in January 1939 with a $1,000 grant from the NAS committee to GALCIT for study leading to a research proposal for rocket-assisted takeoff for aircraft. Malina had mixed emotions about the interest the group's work was receiving. "My enthusiasm vanishes when I am forced to develop better munitions," he confided to his parents. He also enjoyed the soil conservation study. But at the same time, Malina, who had actively supported the Spanish republic, was concerned about the plight of the democracies. Kármán, who was Jewish, transmitted increasing alarm about anti-Semitism in Germany. Moreover, there was a question of career, for Malina would soon finish graduate school. He had to make, as he put it, a "good guess" on the future, but he also recognized that the views of his "second father" would probably be decisive. When Malina reported to NAS again in June 1939, the committee granted GALCIT $10,000 for additional work. His anxiety about military-oriented research largely quieted by the political climate and more solid career prospects, Malina turned to rocket work full-time. The GALCIT rocket group, which had once been stymied for $120 worth of instruments, found itself awash in money. The future belonged not to conservation but to rocketry.[21]

Maj. Benjamin Chidlaw was skeptical. An aide to General Arnold, Chidlaw stopped at Caltech in late 1939 to discuss the contract the rocket enthusiasts had received. "Kármán," demanded the major, "do you honestly believe that the air corps should spend as much as $10,000 for such a thing as rockets?" Kármán was convinced. He had shepherded the funding request through the NAS committee and had lent his eminence to the proposal by becoming the project director. But skepticism remained rampant, and Kármán and his students still had a lot of persuading to do. Nothing was so important now as solid experimental results.[22]

The goals of a high-altitude sounding rocket—to say nothing of spaceflight—were set aside for the substantial challenge of developing a rocket motor that would be "immediately applicable to aeronautical purposes."

The group found that major problems had to be solved in both liquid- and solid-propellant engines. Because of their ease of handling, solids were preferable for military purposes. But they proved especially intractable to the researchers. To be effective in helping boost propeller-driven planes at takeoff, rockets would have to burn for perhaps 10 to 20 seconds. But no solid-propellant engine then known burned for more than about 3 seconds. It couldn't be done, most of the experts advised. The conventional wisdom held that once the propellant was ignited, pressure would build rapidly in the chamber and cause the engine to explode. Repeated explosions with almost every version Parsons tried seemed to prove the experts right. He tried innumerable combinations of black powder in several configurations, most designed to burn slowly from one end, like a cigarette. The experimenters clung to the hope that the difficulties were mechanical, not fundamental. They surmised that somehow the walls of the powder charge were ignited or that the charge cracked when the pressure in the chamber rose. But by spring 1940 the explosions and expert advice had driven the group to the point of giving up on solids.[23]

Kármán then turned to an old friend, theoretical analysis. He and Malina worked out four differential equations which proved that it was theoretically possible to build a restricted-burning, solid-propellant engine. The key was to maintain a constant chamber pressure, which would be possible so long as the ratio of the area of the throat of the exhaust nozzle to the burning area of the propellant charge remained constant. Encouraged, the group resumed the battle with the mechanical problems. Their report to the NAS was encouraging enough that on July 1, 1940, the air corps took control of the GALCIT grant and doubled its funding to $22,000 for fiscal year 1941.[24]

That decision infuriated Goddard. "The student work," as he termed it, was fifteen years behind his, he scoffed. But time was catching up with him. The manifold complexities of building a rocket lay beyond the abilities of the lone inventor, however hallowed that tradition may be and however brilliant Goddard was. As Homer Newell, the longtime associate administrator for space sciences and applications at the National Aeronautics and Space Administration (NASA), has pointed out: By his secrecy Goddard not only dissipated most of the influence he might have had, he also deprived himself of the engineering expertise that he sorely needed to achieve his dream. The future of rocketry belonged to the team approach—it was, indeed, inextricably tied to the massive funding sources and particular purposes of the national security state. These political and sociological factors in no way diminished Goddard's creativity. In 1960 NASA awarded his estate $1 million in recognition of the many patents the space agency could scarcely avoid infringing. But most of what Goddard discovered was either rediscovered independently or discarded by others taking a different approach. A pioneer but not a father, he continued his work in obscurity at a naval research station during the war while the future of American rocketry passed into other hands.[25]

With the air corps' $22,000 the GALCIT rocket group made a welcome exit from the Caltech campus. They negotiated with the city of Pasadena for a lease on seven acres in the Arroyo Seco, six miles from the campus, where they had first tested rockets. The city was reluctant, since some upper-middle-class homes overlooked the canyon, but Pasadena at last agreed, provided that the lease would be terminated and the facilities removed at the end of the war. In late summer 1940 the cost-conscious researchers pitched in to help build the first structures of the present-day Jet Propulsion Laboratory. The small frame and corrugated-metal structures were unheated and drafty. Crammed with rocket plumbing, the buildings had no room for a desk; Martin Summerfield, a former roommate of Malina's who had just joined the project, used the back seat of his car as an office. "It was a pretty lonely start out there in the bleak arroyo, with my new Ph.D. in hand," Summerfield recalled. Malina, Parsons, and Forman stayed in the comparative luxury of a small office on the campus until 1941, when they moved into a building at the arroyo site. By that summer, as American entry into the war looked increasingly likely, the project's funding shot up to $125,000 for fiscal year 1942.[26]

The expanding GALCIT group was making steady progress. By the summer of 1941—about a year after the possibility of long-duration, solid-propellant rocket engines was theoretically proved—they developed an engine in which they had enough confidence to suggest flight tests on an aircraft. The 2-pound propellant charge, designated GALCIT 27, was a type of amidic black powder that burned for 12 seconds and produced 28 pounds of thrust. The powder was pressed into a cylinder 10 inches long and 1.75 inches in diameter, which had a blotting-paper liner, in 22 increments at a pressure of 18 tons. Fewer increments or less pressure resulted in erratic burning that too often culminated in explosions.[27]

The group hauled the rockets to March Field, near Riverside, for tests on the petite Ercoupe, a low-wing monoplane weighing just 753 pounds. It was outfitted with a pod under each wing into which three bottle-shaped solid-propellant engines, known as JATOs for jet-assisted takeoff, were inserted. Prudence suggested phased tests. For the first, a static test, the plane was anchored to the runway, and the rocket engines were fired. In the first test one popped a nozzle, which bounced off the runway and tore a hole in the thin skin of the tail end of the fuselage. "Well, at least it isn't a big hole," one of the experimenters joked feebly. In the next test the JATOs were ignited after the plane had assumed level flight; all but one fired successfully. The climactic moment arrived on August 12, 1941, when Lt. Homer Boushey, a

Kármán student, taxied down the runway and threw the ignition switch. Smoke billowed from the plane. It soared into the air, climbing rapidly and steeply. Boushey completed his climb, circled the field, and returned to a beaming ring of comrades. For the first time in the United States, a plane had taken off assisted by rocket power. The JATOs cut the distance required for takeoff nearly in half, from 580 feet to 300 feet; the time required to become airborne was reduced almost as much, from 13.1 seconds to 7.5 seconds, or 42.8 percent. The plane's structure suffered no ill effects; in fact, Boushey reported, it was easier to handle the plane with the rocket thrust.[28]

For an unplanned climax the experimenters attempted the first takeoff of a plane in the United States using rocket power alone. Twelve JATOs were attached to the Ercoupe, its propeller was removed, and a safety poster pasted on the nose read: "What about tomorrow if I meet with an accident today?" A truck towed the plane until it reached a speed of about 25 miles per hour, then Boushey ignited the rockets, and the plane climbed about 20 feet into the air. It was a small first.[29]

The experimenters' exhilaration was short-lived, however. The August tests were carried out soon after the JATOs were made. The researchers now discovered that storing the rockets for more than a few days caused them to deteriorate to the point that explosions resulted upon ignition. If the JATOs were not storable, they would have little use in combat situations, so the project members began a frustrating search for a solution. The JATO design was modified, different types of blotting paper were used, and various chemicals were investigated as propellants. None worked. The situation, meanwhile, grew more urgent, for the United States plunged into war on December 8, 1941. Early in 1942 the navy, intrigued with the possibility of using rocket-assisted planes on aircraft carriers, offered the GALCIT project a contract to develop rockets of 200 pounds thrust and 8 seconds duration. The researchers' anxiety deepened into desperation.[30]

Parsons, the project's chief chemist, kept turning the problem over in his head. All the variants of conventional black powder seemed to have the same drawbacks. Then his unconventional mind made an intuitive leap. Why not abandon black powder altogether? Instead of charcoal, use a less brittle fuel—common paving asphalt; instead of saltpeter, use potassium perchlorate as an oxidizer. How Parsons imagined this switch has not been clarified. One version holds that it occurred to him while he watched a roof being tarred. Malina has pointed out that Parsons knew of "Greek fire," the asphalt-based material used by the ancient Greeks. Parsons was killed in an explosion in 1952, after leaving JPL, before historians could ask him. Ready to try anything, the GALCIT team heated the asphalt to 350° F, where it became liquefied, and mixed it with the potassium perchlorate. When the mixture cooled, the researchers scooped it into the combustion chamber, bounced the container a few times for uniform settling, and set it aside to harden. The finished product resembled stiff paving tar.[31]

This radical departure, designated GALCIT 53, proved successful almost at once. Further refinements in 1943 led to GALCIT 61-C, which, when burned at a chamber pressure of 2,000 pounds per square inch, had a specific impulse of 186 and an exhaust velocity of about 5,900 feet per second. The asphalt-based propellants had several advantages, and the navy used them extensively in the last two years of the war. They could be stored indefinitely within wide extremes of temperature, from −9° to +120° F. They were easier to produce and used more common ingredients. Aiming at a small rocket engine for immediate use, the GALCIT project had managed to make a fundamental breakthrough in solid-propellant rocketry.[32]

Although the project recorded its first breakthrough with the solid propellant, it devoted more effort to liquid propellants. On July 1, 1940, the GALCIT rocket project established a liquid-propellant section headed by Martin Summerfield. They hoped to produce an engine that delivered 1,000 pounds of thrust for about a minute for possible use as a JATO on air corps bombers. The odds against a rapid breakthrough were formidable. Most researchers had focused on liquids because they promised both greater thrust per unit weight of propellant and better engine control. After a dozen years of work with liquid oxygen and gasoline, Goddard had achieved a thrust still much smaller than a thousand pounds. Some top chemical engineers advised that there were fundamental barriers to this objective. A thousand pounds of thrust would require a furnace the size of a small house, one combustion expert said. But Summerfield, rummaging through the Caltech library, turned up an old English chemistry text that claimed a hydrocarbon fuel could be made to burn completely in a thousandth of a second in a small volume. He worked out elaborate calculations that suggested a small compact chamber would allow enough burning time to provide the desired thrust. Gambling that Summerfield was right, the GALCIT researchers began their quest for the right propellant combination.[33]

Military requirements circumscribed their choices. For fuels they focused on gasoline and kerosene, which were readily available and which armed-service personnel were used to handling. For an oxidizer the researchers replaced liquid oxygen, which Goddard and the Germans used as an oxidizer, but which the military objected to for practical reasons, with another Parsons inspiration—red fuming nitric acid. Tests on motors delivering 200 and 500 pounds of thrust were generally successful, and so in October 1941 the project prepared its first 1,000-pound-thrust unit. But then one of those unexpected quirks of experimentation cropped up as the scale of the unit increased. Combustion in the 1,000-pound model was unstable; sometimes it was delayed; sometimes it failed completely. Moreover, a disturbing new phenomenon appeared. Once combustion occurred, the motor often began to pulse, gathering in intensity, until, if not shut off after the fourth or fifth throb, the motor exploded. "Now we had a real unknown and there were no experts to call in," Kármán recalled. "We weren't sure we'd ever come up with a practical solution."[34]

After a series of discouraging tests, Summerfield proposed a stimulating hypothesis. Stability in the engine depended, he theorized, on reducing the delay between ignition and the start of combustion to the absolute minimum. With the combination of red fuming nitric acid and gasoline, the delay was too long to insure stable burning. Kármán, taken with the idea, began to analyze it. The resulting "instability theory of burning" became a part of rocket-engine combustion theory. But the immediate problem remained: how to translate this theoretical advance into practical results.[35]

Malina had this problem uppermost in his mind when he conferred with fellow rocket enthusiast Lt. Robert C. Truax at the Naval Engineering Experiment Station at Annapolis in February 1942. Truax's chemical engineer, Ray C. Stiff, had found in the scientific literature that aniline would ignite spontaneously with nitric acid and suggested adding aniline to the gasoline in an attempt to overcome the throbbing. As Malina turned the idea over in his mind on the train that night, he wondered: Instead of adding aniline to the gasoline, why not substitute aniline as the fuel entirely? The next morning he telegraphed his suggestion to Pasadena. In the Arroyo Seco Summerfield tied a glass beaker of aniline to the end of a stick, stood back, and poured the substance into a container of nitric acid. "There was a big fire," recalled Walter B. Powell, a GALCIT project engineer, "and from then on we were acid-aniline people." The aniline discovery not only ended the throbbing, but made it possible to dispense with an auxiliary ignition system.[36]

For several hectic weeks the GALCIT project labored over its engine. On April 15, 1942, two of the new JATOs were mounted on a Douglas A-20A bomber at Muroc Field in the Mojave. Maj. Paul H. Dane, a former Kármán student, raced the engines, then ignited the JATOs. The 20,000-pound plane took off "as though scooped upward by a sudden draft." The distance required for takeoff was shortened from 2,320 feet to 1,570, a saving of 32.3 percent; the time of takeoff from 25.1 seconds to 16.8 seconds, a reduction of 33.1 percent. "We have been struggling for this event for six years," Malina exulted. "We now have something that really works and we should be able to help to give the Fascists hell!" That event—the first time a plane had taken off in the United States with a permanently installed rocket power plant—marked, in Kármán's words, "the beginning of practical rocketry in the United States."[37]

The growth of the project from inspired lunacy to wartime respectability brought with it changing institutional forms. Funding grew from $125,000 in fiscal year 1942 to $650,000 in fiscal year 1944. The work force mounted to eighty-five by mid-1943. They used a small office building, two laboratories, and several miscellaneous structures. All looked like what they were—an improvised wartime venture. A string of test pits, cut into the side of a hill and lined with railroad ties, bore the appropriate nickname "the gulch." Employees reached the site by driving over a bumpy dirt road that washed out in the rainy season. When Eugene M. Pierce, a Pasadena architect, reported for work as an administrative assistant on a memorable New Year's Day in 1943, he had never seen the laboratory before. "I took one look at those half-a-dozen nondescript, corrugated-metal and redwood-tie and stone buildings and thought, my God!—what have I gotten myself into? There's no future for an architect here." A look inside the office building was hardly reassuring. The corridors were so narrow that "you were liable to lose your teeth" if someone opened a door when you were walking down the hall. He shared an eight-by-ten-foot office—it was "no bigger than a throw rug"—with Malina and a secretary, Miss Dorothy Lewis. They looked out on the biggest liquid-propellant test pit, and whenever a test was run, conversation stopped.[38]

If an architect doubted he had a future there, so did many engineers. Convincing qualified people to leave established laboratories for the GALCIT rocket project was hard. Physicist Howard Seifert recalled that it took a heavy selling job to get him to embark on so suspect a field as rocketry. The Caltech connection helped. Some engineers who shied away from the project because they thought it was government-run decided to sign up when they learned it was part of the Institute. Others decided that, appearances to the contrary, if the place bore CIT's imprimatur, they were willing to take a chance too. Keeping young men, particularly draftsmen, out of the talons of selective service was hard. But the project also attracted its share of men who looked upon it as a contribution to the war effort. A surprising number stayed on—Seifert into the 1950s, Pierce until he retired in the late 1960s.[39]

The pressure was intense, as at other wartime research operations. By fall 1940 the project was veiled in secrecy. "We have to suspect spies under every piece of paper," Malina said with distaste. Few persons knew what the noises and odd buildings in the arroyo were until after the war. Project members generally worked from 7:30 A.M. to 5:30 P.M. Monday through Friday and at least half a day on Saturday; unpaid overtime was common. Under these conditions tempers sometimes flared; for example, one day an engineer, angered by regulations, charged after Malina with an ax. Yet this wartime environment contributed to an esprit and informality. Most employees gathered at noon under a giant oak tree to share the lunches they had brown bagged to the arroyo. Problems of one section would be aired generally among the project's leaders; a solution to a problem in the solid-propellant section might come from someone researching liquids. The project was on its own and getting along with some disdain for structure. When Malina, who had become chief engineer in 1941, showed up wearing a necktie, a mechanic cut it off because he thought it was too formal for the place. Kármán attended conferences from time to time and participated in most major decisions. But even though the project was formally a part of GALCIT, the Institute administration did little except pass routinely on contracts.[40]

Wartime pressure and informality figured importantly in one of the most important decisions reached by the project's leaders—to set up a company to produce JATOs commercially. Some university laboratories produced items for the military during the war. A separate Caltech project, headed by physicist Charles C. Lauritsen, turned out more than two million short-duration artillery rockets by 1945. The GALCIT rocket researchers sensed, however, a chance to profit from their work. They reasoned that since GALCIT was not a profit-making institution, it should limit itself to research and development. In late 1941 Kármán tried to interest several aircraft firms in producing JATOs, but without success. These firms, already bulging with war orders, thought JATOs were too specialized and had an uncertain future.[41]

In March 1942 several members of the GALCIT rocket project formed their own company, Aerojet. Kármán, Malina, Summerfield, Parsons, Forman, and Andrew Haley, Kármán's attorney, each put up $200 and assigned any patents they had to the firm. Though it was destined to become a big defense contractor, Aerojet spent an anxious infancy. The Army Air Force (AAF), to whom Aerojet had intended to sell JATOs, found that bulldozers could often carve out runways long enough to obviate the need for rocket-assisted takeoff. The original incorporators kept the firm afloat through personal loans and deferred salaries. In 1943 Aerojet reached takeoff as the navy gave it large contracts for JATOs to be used on carrier-based aircraft in the Pacific.[42]

The founders of Aerojet devoted much of their time in 1942 and early 1943 to getting the company functioning. A virtually interlocking relationship characterized the GALCIT rocket project and Aerojet as employees shuttled back and forth between the two. Summerfield, Parsons, and Forman left to join the company; Kármán and Malina spent large amounts of time as Aerojet consultants. Many Aerojet products were tested at the GALCIT station. Malina conceded that they might justly have been accused of conflict of interest because they were wearing three hats: advising the military on JATOs, conducting research on them, and then sharing a financial interest in their production. But rocket expertise was in short supply, and, under wartime conditions, no one bothered to look very closely. Although some of the original incorporators were induced to sell their stock at relatively low prices after the war, those who held it profited handsomely indeed.[43]

By 1943 the GALCIT project, having overcome its shaky origins, had converted American rocketry from the realm of fantasy to practicality and even profitability. The importance of GALCIT and later JPL in the evolution of American rocketry has been neglected as historians and journalists have been drawn to the human interest dramas of Robert Goddard and the German rocket program.[44] The GALCIT researchers, however, were not influenced by either one—Goddard because of his secrecy, the Germans because the Pasadena researchers were not aware of them when they made their initial discoveries. The GALCIT rocket project made fundamental breakthroughs in the theory and development of both solid- and liquid-propellant rocket engines. Their work on solid propellants was particularly important, for it represents the distinctive American contribution to rocketry. The first to demonstrate both theoretically and experimentally the feasibility of a long-duration solid-propellant rocket, the GALCIT project was the seedbed of American rocketry.

Solid propellants, which are safer to handle than liquid propellants, were destined to play a central role in American military technology after World War II with such missiles as the Polaris. The intimate links among the GALCIT project, the military, and Aerojet also foreshadowed the postwar triad sometimes known as the scientific-military-industrial complex. These developments were at best dimly anticipated in 1943. At this point few persons realized the potential of rockets for either military purposes or for space exploration. It was, in any case, a long route from JATOs to ICBMs (intercontinental ballistic missile) and planetary spacecraft. The long-term prospects of the GALCIT project were highly uncertain. Then came news of the German rocket program.

2 ★★

THE WARTIME ROOTS OF A PERMANENT JPL

In midsummer 1943 Theodore von Kármán, director of GALCIT, received some top secret photographs of what looked like concrete ski jumps on the north coast of France. What did he think they were? the Army Air Force wanted to know. After deliberation Kármán concluded that they were some kind of rocket launchpads, but he had never seen any so large. Soon the air force sent him three British intelligence reports on suspected German rocket activities. These reports, though vague and exaggerated, made clear that the Germans were developing large rocket missiles whose range and payload far exceeded anything previously known. The missiles' size led Kármán to suspect incorrectly that the Germans were using means of jet propulsion different from his group's little chemical JATOs, most likely a ramjet, in which the engine is operated by the injection of fuel into a stream of air compressed by the forward speed of the aircraft. He also surmised that the Germans were using a rocket stage to boost the ramjet into flight.[1]

Enjoying air superiority, the Allies had shown little interest in rocket missiles, but these intelligence reports aroused apprehension. In September 1943 army ordnance formed the rocket development division in its research and development service. The two army liaison officers at Caltech, Col. W. H. Joiner of AAF and Capt. Robert Staver of ordnance, thought action was needed. Joiner asked Frank Malina, the GALCIT rocket project's chief engineer, for a study of the possibility of using their engines to propel long-range missiles. The United States could not then approach the Germans' reported range of 100 miles, Malina and Hsue-shen Tsien told Joiner in November 1943. The rockets the project had developed for aircraft super-performance could, however, serve as the basis for the design of long-range missiles with a large explosive load, they said. The ramjet, moreover, held promise of equaling the German claims.[2]

Kármán used the Malina-Tsien analysis as the basis for a proposal to expand the project's fundamental rocket-engine research. He suggested a four-stage research program: (1) tests of a 350-pound, restricted-burning, solid-propellant rocket missile, designed to carry a 50-pound explosive load for 10 miles; (2) design of a 2,000-pound, liquid-propellant rocket missile to travel 12 miles with an explosive load of 200 pounds; (3) theoretical studies of ramjet engines; and (4) construction and tests of a 10,000-pound missile with a range of 75 miles. The first two phases, utilizing motors already available, would have "immediate military usefulness," Kármán pointed out, but he considered them primarily research instruments to support the fourth phase. All four phases would furnish basic information in the largely unexplored realm of supersonic flight, which would be useful to designers of both missiles and high-speed aircraft. The Kármán-Malina-Tsien report of November 20, 1943, bore the designation JPL-1, the first use of the term *Jet Propulsion Laboratory.*[3]

Malina rushed copies of the report, still damp and reeking of ammonia from the copier to Joiner and Staver. Both officers, though skeptical that usable rocket weapons could be developed before the war ended, were fully convinced of their long-term importance. Staver predicted in January 1944 that a remote-controlled missile capable of carrying an atomic warhead and possessing a range equal to aircraft of the time could be developed in a few years. They wanted Caltech to become the national center for missile research, and they felt the GALCIT project had to be established in that role before the war ended, when funding might be cut and personnel dispersed. But the AAF material command turned down the JPL-1 proposal because it did not promise enough immediate results.[4]

Anticipating that rejection, Joiner, a former ordnance officer, had urged Staver to forward a copy to the army ordnance research and development office with a strong recommendation. Army ordnance had tried to interest the Office of Scientific Research and Development in guided missile research. Director Vannevar Bush had rejected the idea, however, because he felt missiles would be inaccurate and would divert too many researchers to a project that was unnecessary during the war. The JPL-1 proposal took; it gave army ordnance the opening it had been seeking for a long-term rocket-research project. Col. Sam B. Ritchie of ordnance flew to Pasadena, toured the facilities, conferred with the GALCIT group, and returned to Washington visibly "starry eyed" about what JPL could mean for American rocketry. In January 1944 Col. G. W. Trichel, chief of the ordnance rocket branch, urged Caltech to submit a more comprehensive program. He wanted the laboratory to assume responsibility not merely for research on a power plant but for research and development of all aspects of a guided missile, including prototypes for production. This would carry the project into areas it had not touched, particularly the complicated electronics of missile guidance and control. What seemed like a staggering amount of money was available—$3 million for one year.[5]

Trichel's request "threw us into a proper dither" Malina recalled. But they were excited by the scientific and engineering challenges and what success would mean for the war effort. The Caltech Board of Trustees approved the new venture in February 1944. The army authorized expenditures of $1.6 million in June 1944 followed by a cost-plus-fixed-fee contract for $3.6 million for eighteen months in January 1945. The GALCIT rocket project began to recruit more staff and to reorganize for the new thrust.[6]

The trustees made clear that they were authorizing only a wartime program, not committing the Institute to postwar operation. Nevertheless, the circumstances of JPL's birth would heavily influence its future course. Kármán and Malina had attempted to use the army request as a springboard for a permanent jet propulsion laboratory integrated within Caltech. "Our main objective would be to have the scientific leadership in the whole field of jet propulsion, including those branches which are more important for peace application," Kármán told the trustees in February 1944. The armed forces would stress research and development of military devices, he feared, and, since the military owned the research facilities, Caltech could not count on using them for its program. Kármán therefore recommended that CIT appropriate $50,000 to $80,000 to establish the nucleus of its own jet propulsion laboratory on Institute-owned land adjacent to the army project. He thought the independent laboratory could be self-supporting, as the campus wind tunnel had been. The trustees declined his proposal, however, probably because of the school's budget deficit and their wariness about making a long-term commitment in the heat of war. Whatever the reasons, the decision represented a lost opportunity, for the sheer presence of the army facilities and program would heavily influence postwar decisions.[7]

Guided missile work began officially on July 1, 1944, under the new name *Jet Propulsion Laboratory, GALCIT. Jet* was a broader term than *rocket* and avoided any stigma still attached to that word. JPL was divided into eleven sections, analogous to university departments. A section, such as that for liquid propellants, did basic research and worked on missiles simultaneously. Each section reported to the chief engineer, who held weekly research conferences of all section heads. Kármán had used a similar format at GALCIT on campus, and he chaired the JPL meetings when he was in Pasadena. The laboratory organization showed its academic origins instead of the project-oriented structure of an industrial laboratory. The Caltech connection was vital to staffing the organization, which counted 385 employees by late 1946. About one-third of the professional staff had been trained at CIT, and Institute faculty members headed most of the sections. One section chief, William Pickering, a professor of electrical engineering at Caltech, who oversaw guidance and control, became director of JPL in 1954—a position he held until 1976.[8]

Complementing the expansion of personnel, the army poured $3 million into new facilities by late 1945. This included several test pits, two laboratories, an administration and office building, and a supersonic wind tunnel. These "unique and highly specialized" facilities, while barracks modern in style, were a far cry from the original "gas house" the GALCIT rocket enthusiasts had helped build. Indeed, the new structures looked all too permanent to the city of Pasadena, which had agreed to let GALCIT use the site only for the duration of the war. When the army pressed for renewal of the lease, the city balked. The laboratory's noise and unsightliness violated "the first principle of proper zoning in residential territory," declared city manager I. W. Koiner. But when the army threatened condemnation proceedings, the city capitulated and signed a twenty-five-year lease in November 1945. Wartime tolerance was wearing thin, and the laboratory's community relations were clouded for some time thereafter.[9]

Just as the new JPL acquired momentum, Theodore von Kármán, who had been indispensable in nurturing the rocket research activities, began an extended leave of absence. He left Caltech in December 1944 to organize the air force's scientific advisory board. Although he kept a titular connection with GALCIT until 1949, he visited Pasadena only for brief periods. Kármán's departure left a vacuum that the Institute administration attempted to fill by creating a JPL executive board. Clark Millikan, the new acting director of GALCIT, became acting chairman of the board. Malina was elevated to acting director of JPL, and Louis Dunn, another Kármán protégé, took over the new position of assistant director of JPL. Malina and Dunn, who had inherited some of the coolness between their mentor and Millikan, often found relations with the board difficult. Although the board's influence diminished sharply after the formidable Dunn became director of JPL in 1946, it provided an important link between campus and laboratory during a key transitional period. By the last months of the war the project, which only a year earlier had seemed a candidate for extinction, was acquiring the trappings of permanence.[10]

The growing JPL activities were divided among four areas: the original AAF aircraft laboratory's engine research program (JPL-1); the AAF armament laboratory's hydrobomb research program (JPL-2), an effort originally aimed at testing solid-propellant, underwater rocket missiles; and the AAF power plant's ramjet research program (JPL-3). Most work was devoted, however, to the new JPL-4 contract, known as ORDCIT (from Ordnance/California Institute of Technology). The first ORDCIT contract called for research and development of a guided missile, including one capable of carrying an explosive load of 1,000 pounds for 150 miles and accurate within 3 miles of the target. In effect JPL had undertaken a crash program to make a lighter and more accurate version of the V-2, which had undergone thousands of tests since the German research began in 1929. JPL first planned to develop the Private, a small, short-range unguided missile with a solid-propellant engine. That would be followed by Corporal, a heavier, long-range, more complicated guided missile with a liquid-propellant engine. The missile ranks would stop at colonel, because that's "the highest rank that works," said Kármán, to the amusement of the ordnance research chief, Maj. Gen. Gladeon M. Barnes. As it turned out, there were problems enough even before the lower ranks worked, and a decade and a half would elapse before JPL completed development of a Sergeant.[11]

The inaugural venture, Private A, was based on Tsien and Malina's calculations in their report JPL-1 and was designed to be as simple as possible. It was powered by an existing Aerojet engine which used the asphalt-based propellant known as GALCIT 61-C and provided 1,000 pounds of thrust for 34 seconds. The 8-foot-long missile was set between the four guide rails of a 36-foot-long launcher; four standard armament rocket engines that produced 21,700 pounds' thrust in less than one-fifth of a second boosted Private A at launch. Four 12-inch tail fins provided the only in-flight guidance. During twenty-four test rounds at Camp Irwin in the Mojave, Private A met JPL's objectives handsomely, recording an average range of 10.3 miles. As JPL engineers hoped, they provided data on the effects of sustained thrust on a missile and proved the soundness of using boosters at launch. The 530-pound Private A marked the laboratory's first success with real rocket flight.[12]

Private A's success and the wartime urgency encouraged the military to press for rapid improvement in its range. Tsien and Malina had pointed out in 1943 that a missile's range could be increased by 50 percent if wings were added to the body. Payload would probably be reduced, however, and the guidance and control of such a missile raised formidable problems. With many misgivings JPL personnel opened a new series of tests on April 1, 1945—all too appropriately, April Fools' Day. The missile, dubbed Private F, was essentially a Private A with two of the three aft fins extended to form 5-foot wings and two stubby wings added to the fore part. The missiles were transported to Hueco Range, Ft. Bliss, Texas, where the army had cameras and radar to track the Private's flight. All seventeen rounds were launched successfully. After a short flight, however, each round went into a tailspin and etched a corkscrew trail of white smoke against the sky. Although some useful technical data were obtained, the observers hardly needed radar to confirm that Private F was, in Malina's words, "a fiasco." Besides the dangers of rushing into premature experimentation, the chief lesson derived from Private F was the rather negative evidence that a missile with lifting surfaces needed guidance equipment for satisfactory performance. JPL now began to devote more effort to that objective.[13]

Before moving up to the complex Corporal, however, JPL took an intermediate step to achieve the dream of the original GALCIT group—a sounding rocket. Reliable solid and liquid motors were now available, and relatively modest goals were set: transporting a 25-pound payload to 100,000 feet in altitude. The project would be a small test version of the Corporal, Malina argued, when he proposed the idea to Colonel Trichel in fall 1944. In three intensive days Malina, Homer Stewart, and some assistants forged a detailed proposal for the project—a commentary on how small an investment of time could produce results at that stage of technology. By early 1945 JPL had the army's approval. Laboratory males dubbed it WAC Corporal, from Women's Auxiliary Corps, because they considered it the "little sister" of Corporal. The acronym WAC also had a technological meaning—without attitude control.[14]

Two main decisions faced the JPL staff in designing WAC Corporal—choice of an engine and guidance. Since solid-propellant motors were then too heavy, they settled on Aerojet's modified version of a JATO engine using red fuming nitric acid (RFNA) and aniline, originally developed by the GALCIT project, that delivered 1,500 pounds' thrust for about 45 seconds. The staff considered using a gyro-stabilization scheme to guide the vehicle, but the weight was excessive. Instead Malina and Stewart calculated that if WAC were launched at high enough speed, deviation from vertical flight would be unimportant. A small engine, known as Tiny Tim, was added as a booster stage to give WAC a speed of 400 feet per second when it left the launching tower. Tests of the components and a one-fifth-scale model, Baby WAC, looked promising. The pencil-shaped WAC Corporal stood just over 16 feet in height, measured a little more than a foot in diameter, and weighed 655 pounds when fueled.[15]

With thirty-seven JPL staff members accompanying it, the WAC was transported to the ordnance department's new White Sands Proving Ground in New Mexico. Their presence suggested how quickly war-born technology had grown complex. By contrast Robert Goddard had carried out his lonely research not far away. White Sands offered a suggestive forecast of the evolution of technology and the national security state, for the range lay near the site of the first atomic-bomb test. On October 11, 1945, the test crew set the WAC in the launching tower's three guide rails and fueled it. JPL and armed forces personnel threw back their heads and watched the WAC ascend into the brilliant sunshine. They lost sight of it before the engine shut off at about 80,000 feet, but the primitive radar tracked it to a height of about 230,000 feet, more than 40 miles. After a flight of 7 ½ minutes WAC slammed back to Earth about 3,500 feet from the launcher—perilously close to the launch team. The crew was exuberant nonetheless, for no man-made object had ascended so high. Subsequent tests confirmed the first round's success. WAC Corporal had the distinction of being the first man-made object to "escape the Earth's atmosphere."[16]

After eleven test rounds JPL ran out of WAC Corporals, so it paused to redesign the vehicle. The new version, known as WAC Corporal B, incorporated several innovations. Through the use of lighter metals and various design changes, the weight of the motor was reduced from 50 pounds to 12. The missile's structure was modified so that almost all the weight was born by interior trusses instead of by the skin; this facilitated manufacture and maintenance. A rude telemetry system was planted in the nose cone, which would transmit data on the operation of the missile and its environment via a five-channel radio signal to the control center on the ground. Although it was elementary, the telemetry contained the seed of the control and data transmission systems of intercontinental missiles and spacecraft. One of the descendants of WAC was the Aerobee, constructed by Aerojet for use by the Johns Hopkins University's Applied Physics Laboratory, which played an important role in upper atmospheric research in the 1950s and helped lay the foundation for the scientific and peaceful uses of rocket technology.[17]

Even before the WAC Corporal tests, the army and Caltech began negotiations which would in large measure determine the continuation of JPL and the nature of its program. The JPL decision was important and illuminating for the larger question of the relationship between science and the military after World War II. The army's interest in JPL was clear. It ranked guided missiles second only to nuclear weapons as a military priority, and the ordnance department's research branch considered JPL its most important project. Ordnance decided initially to rely mostly on contracts with scientific and industrial institutions for "integrated projects," which involved both basic research and actual development. General Electric had a contract for Hermes, in both ground-to-air editions, and for firing the captured V-2s that were being shipped to the United States. Bell Laboratories was working on Nike, a ground-to-air missile. On September 26, 1945, scarcely a month after the war ended, General Barnes asked Caltech to operate JPL on a permanent basis. He emphasized that the laboratory would focus on basic research and enjoy substantial autonomy, but he also indicated that these fundamental studies were to be "closely coordinated" with development of "specific rocket units."[18]

Barnes's approach reflected the military's new awareness of the importance of civilian basic research, because of its contribution to military technology. Col. Leslie Simon, who would head ordnance research in the early 1950s, explained the relationship in 1947: During the postwar period "weapons research . . . should increase in earnestness and intensity as basic problems are undertaken which are worth their while for science's sake." Basic scientific and engineering research was ineluctably bound up with military objectives. The most dramatic products of wartime science—the atomic bomb and the missile—obliterated prewar American ideas of security; Americans had never faced destruction so complete and so immediate. By the same token the bomb and the missile illustrated scientists' new reliance on expensive equipment and big laboratories. Only the national security state commanded the financial resources to pay for this type of research. Science, in turn, was essential to the realization of the military's insatiable demand for technological devices. Since the middle of the war, for reasons of both ideology and interests, many leading scientists and military figures had favored a continuation of the alliance that had proved so fruitful to both. They were reinforced by leading industrialists such as Charles E. Wilson, head of General Electric and executive vice-chairman of the War Production Board, who proposed an ongoing three-way partnership of science, industry, and the military in the postwar period. What emerged was sometimes termed the scientific-military-industrial complex.[19]

If science represented, in Vannevar Bush's words, "the endless frontier," the national security establishment had a seemingly unlimited agenda. As the first Secretary of Defense James Forrestal put it: The military services should have "the free field of their own initiative to develop all the things they think are useful." This carte blanche, which relied on scientific and basic engineering research and development for its realization, made credible the incipient notion of deterrence through massive destruction. That doctrine, perhaps implicit in the conventional and atomic bombing strategies of World War II, found expression as early as 1946 in the report of the War Department Equipment Board: "The best defense appears to be to convince the entire population of enemy countries that this country is prepared to retaliate immediately on any aggressor and will answer any unprovoked attack by wholesale devastation produced by atomic bombs, biological agents, and lethal gases of great intensity."[20]

An emerging community of scientists/research engineers and national security advisers vowed to exploit technological development for military purposes fully. The main question concerned the institutional arrangements to make this possible. Edward L. Bowles, science adviser to Secretary of War Henry Stimson, called for "an effective peacetime integration" of military and civilian resources, particularly in higher education. He told Lee DuBridge, the new president of Caltech: "Not only is there a great opportunity to underwrite research for its direct contribution to the nation's welfare, and thus our security, but the opportunity exists to encourage the training of brilliant minds and to instill in them a consciousness of their responsibility to the nation's security." Many universities responded readily to Bowles's prescription. Some schools permitted classified work to go on at supposedly open campuses and even allowed classified Ph.D. theses. Some institutions set up special organizations with heavily military orientations, such as the Lincoln Laboratory at the Massachusetts Institute of Technology (M.I.T.) and the Applied Physics Laboratory at Johns Hopkins; the University of California managed laboratories for the Atomic Energy Commission. Many universities veered away from the prescript Harvard president James Conant laid down in 1946: "All such [secret] research in peacetime should be done in government establishments or by contract with industry." Caltech banned classified work on campus, although it made some exceptions at the height of the cold war, and many professors engaged in classified research on a personal basis.[21]

The question of special laboratories for military research off campus, however, presented another question for the Institute. Caltech first considered the question of postwar military research in mid-May 1945 when the navy asked it to continue operation of the testing stations at Morris Dam and China Lake. A specially formed committee on government contracts declined to do so. Many faculty members were tired of wartime projects, particularly the work on applications. "We wanted to get back to science," recalled Fred C. Lindvall, longtime chairman of the Caltech engineering division and a member of the committee. Significantly, the panel decided the issue with little consideration of the general problem of military research. It framed its decision by applying two criteria—institutional structure and basic research. Continuing a long-standing Caltech pattern, it ruled against the establishment of special organizations "outside of the regular academic organization, for carrying on special projects." The panel accepted military-funded research, so long as it was of a fundamental nature. In that case, however, the work would probably be of use to more than one service and should be sponsored by a successor to the Office of Scientific Research and Development. Stations operated by one service branch would probably emphasize the application of known principles, the committee suspected. Caltech faculty might serve as advisers or consultants to such installations, but that should remain a personal rather than an institutional relationship. The Morris Dam/China Lake case was relatively easy to decide, since the work was mainly applied and was peripheral to the interests of most faculty members.[22]

The JPL case was more complicated. Caltech's continued operation of the laboratory received strong support from Clark Millikan, acting chairman of the JPL board, in October 1945. Acknowledging the military implications, he recommended that the Institute operate JPL "as a special national defense laboratory supported by government funds." The ideological underpinnings of a conservative cold warrior no doubt influenced his position. Like his father, the recently retired Caltech president Robert A. Millikan, Clark Millikan encouraged close ties between CIT and large industrial firms. Both men enthusiastically integrated scientific resources with the military in two world wars and the cold war. Clark Millikan commuted between Pasadena and the Pentagon for advisory committee meetings on military and scientific matters in the 1940s and '50s. He read the Institute's approval of JPL in 1944 as constituting "a certain moral commitment" to continue operation. The trustees had specifically withheld consideration of postwar operations at that time, but for Millikan and others the sense of national obligation continued undiluted as world war merged into cold war.[23]

Malina countered with an elaboration of the plan he and Kármán had presented to the trustees in 1944. Caltech should continue to operate JPL for the army, the acting director said, although declassification "should be continually pressed." But Caltech should establish its own rocket laboratory, staffed by faculty members, where "completely unfettered research" could be carried out. The two laboratories should maintain close contact. This proposal would have diluted the importance of the military laboratory somewhat and strengthened the momentum toward scientific and peaceful uses of the emerging rocket-missile technology. Malina had become increasingly concerned about the connection between academic institutions and military research, particularly after seeing the atomic-bomb test site on his way to the WAC Corporal trials. He believed that limits on national sovereignty had become imperative.[24]

In the climactic decisions in early 1946 institutional interests stood out. The JPL executive board, with Kármán and Malina present, decided on March 22, 1946, to recommend that the trustees accept the younger Millikan's plan largely intact. A social peer of the Institute's trustees, Millikan was an unusually influential faculty member. Speaking for the board, he emphasized the importance of JPL to Caltech: The laboratory would help the Institute maintain its international reputation in aeronautics, and especially jet propulsion; CIT should not lose JPL's unique facilities to other institutions; able scientists and engineers could be employed at JPL without burdening the regular payroll; and, finally, General Barnes had stressed the primacy of basic research and promised that "most" work would be unclassified.[25]

The committee on government contracts was deeply concerned about the inroads of military contracts and had urged the Institute to cut back on such work. Faced with the contention, however, that institutional needs—particularly those of the engineering division—dictated keeping JPL, the committee could find "no alternative" to its continued operation. On April 1, 1946, the board of trustees approved Millikan's plan in principle.[26]

The army's fait accompli of 1944—converting the GALCIT rocket project into a full-fledged missile research and development institution—proved decisive. The army had skillfully appealed to the faculty's interest in basic research with a minimum of classified work. Most importantly the ordnance department offered cash in hand. The high cost of operating an alternative laboratory made it hard to imagine a university funding it from its own sources, and no alternative funding agency which would underwrite peaceful rocketry was on the horizon. Barnes's beguiling assurances about unclassified basic research stood little chance of fulfillment when rocketry remained dominated by weapons applications until the 1960s. Cornell physicist Philip Morrison might have had JPL in mind when he predicted in late 1946 that before long the "now-amiable contracts" would tighten up, specify results and weapons applications, "and science itself will have been bought by war, on the installment plan."[27]

The discussions of the future of JPL underscore Joseph Haberer's point that science is characterized by a "strong methodological ethic" but a "weak institutional ethic." He argues: "The history of modern science is predicated on a disjuncture between power and responsibility." The Caltech discussions examined how institutions should be organized to conduct research, but they did not assess the propriety of that research. For people such as Edward Bowles and Clark Millikan, a particular view of national security answered any questions about propriety or, indeed, imposed an affirmative obligation to do military research. Others, less certain of this view of the cold war and scientific involvement, applied the standard of basic research—at best an elusive criterion. Since basic research presumably aspired only to the advancement of knowledge and since this research was divorced from specific applications, these scientists believed they had absolved themselves of the question of responsibility. Yet in a field such as rocketry in the 1940s, basic research took place within the context of eventual military applications. However one evaluated the merits of those applications, in a field dominated by weapons considerations, the argument of basic research represented an evasion of the issue of responsibility.[28]

World War II had indeed been a boon to science. But the chief beneficiaries were those fields of science that related most closely to military concerns. This should scarcely occasion surprise, in view of the objectives of the agencies that funded the research. The continuation of such funding patterns and institutional patterns into the postwar period helped insure the continued dominance of research related to national security. From 1946 through 1960 the Department of Defense and the Atomic Energy Commission accounted for 90 percent of national funding for research and development. Some military funds went for basic research, to be sure, but that elusive demarcation tended to overlook the context in which basic research took place and the ultimate interest of the funding agency. These patterns stirred anguished soul-searching for some researchers and in some cases profound dissents. The mathematician Norbert Wiener had both the vision and the professional security to eschew work on projects that had likely military applications. The dominant perspective, however, lay closer to the example of mathematician John von Neumann, who combined basic research with extensive applications to weapons systems through his influential service to the Pentagon. In a field like rocketry the ideology of national security and the interests of the research community merged to create the "effective peacetime integration" that men like Bowles had sought. As JPL soon learned, basic research had a direct bearing on applications and created an impetus toward the actual development of weapons systems.[29]

3 ★★

FROM BASIC RESEARCH TO WEAPONRY

The winds of the cold war brought an increasing tightening to the Jet Propulsion Laboratory in both personnel and program. Despite their contributions to victory in World War II, scientists came under intense security scrutiny after 1945. As early as 1947 President Truman established a new federal employees loyalty board; during the McCarthyism nightmare, the investigation of scientists reached a climax when J. Robert Oppenheimer was stripped of his security clearance. For JPL personnel suspicion focused on a prewar political discussion group in which a number of Caltech personnel had participated. Frank Malina, Martin Summerfield, and other participants insisted that the group, while tinged with the left-wing politics that had been representative of much intellectual opinion of the 1930s, had been in no sense subversive. During the cold war, however, sensitivity to such gradations evaporated. Summerfield, who moved to Princeton University after a decade at JPL, lost his security clearance, although it was reinstated when calmer times returned. One member of the discussion circle was convicted of perjury and served a jail sentence for denying he had been a member of the Communist party.[1]

The strangest episode concerned H. S. Tsien, the brilliant Chinese applied mathematician who had been instrumental in theoretical work since the early days of the GALCIT rocket project. Tsien, who denied ever having been a Communist, decided to return to his homeland after the Maoist takeover, apparently for personal reasons. At first the federal government denied him permission to leave the United States, on national security grounds. But then the Immigration and Naturalization Service stepped in and, after a loosely conducted hearing, decided he was an undesirable alien who should be deported. Since his knowledge was too hot, however, Tsien was forced to remain in California under conditions that amounted to preventive detention. Barred from classified material, restricted in his movements, Tsien continued to teach at Caltech until 1955. Then the Immigration Service decided that his information was no longer current. With his family he sailed to the People's Republic of China, where he received a hero's welcome and reportedly went on to become the guiding spirit behind that nation's intercontinental ballistic missile program. Through the bitter, bizarre case of H. S. Tsien, the JPL circle thus played a major role in the development of missiles for both the United States and the country it once branded its bitterest enemy.[2]

In the cold war atmosphere, acting director Frank Malina decided he had had enough. Some people were suspicious of his involvement in the discussion circle, although nothing was ever proved or even formally charged against him. Malina in any case had grown tired after the intensive war years and was increasingly concerned about the combination of rocketry and atomic warfare. Since Kármán, his mentor, stayed in Pasadena only about one month a year, Malina's resignation was perhaps inevitable. He allowed his security clearance to lapse and in 1947 accepted a position with UNESCO (United Nations Educational, Scientific, and Cultural Organization) in Paris.[3]

The new director was Louis Gerhardus Dunn, JPL's assistant director and another former Kármán student. Born in 1908 on a ranch in the Transvaal, South Africa, he left for the United States at age eighteen, intending to become an airplane pilot. What he missed most were the servants, who had been "thick as fleas" on the ranch. At Caltech he sped through an undergraduate and doctoral program in six years, then became an assistant professor at the Institute. Dunn was a strong figure. Though shy, he could be the picture of bonhomie in small groups, and he particularly enjoyed interminable poker games. The epitome of the decisive, orderly executive, Dunn elicited strong responses from his associates. One engineer described him as a "suave J. Edgar Hoover" but nevertheless preferred his formality and candor. The conservative South African, who had become a naturalized American citizen in 1943, brought more structure and order to JPL.[4]

Under Dunn the administrative link between JPL and Caltech grew tenuous. The JPL executive board, still headed by Clark Millikan, lost most of its influence. The board met only twice between April 1947 and April 1949, and thereafter seldom convened more than twice a year. Dunn met periodically with Caltech president Lee DuBridge to inform him of JPL activities, but DuBridge had little role in setting policy and none in JPL's day-to-day operations. The Caltech Board of Trustees rendered few decisions about JPL except to approve pro forma pay increases and to pass on major financial arrangements such as the overhead rates the campus received for managing JPL. The Institute business office continued to approve JPL contracts, which was largely a routine matter; but by mid-1948 the JPL business operations were mostly self-contained, with the campus business connection characterized more as liaison than supervision. The JPL personnel office hired nonprofessional employees, and Dunn rendered final decisions on the professional staff.[5]

Dunn continued to hold faculty rank, but he gave up teaching and devoted his full time to running the laboratory. Several other men held joint campus-JPL appointments, but of ten section chiefs in 1948, only three (Homer Stewart, W. Duncan Rannie, and William Pickering) were faculty members. Unlike the laboratory of 1944 to 1946, which had leaned heavily on the campus for talent, JPL was developing its own core. The laboratory roster mounted steadily, reaching 785 employees by 1950. Of those, 192, or almost one-fourth, were professional staff, 30 of whom held the Ph.D. Caltech remained a favorite recruiting ground; Dunn estimated that 30 to 40 percent of the professional staff had received degrees from the Institute. The low wartime salaries, which had been as much as 20 percent below prevailing commercial standards for all types of employees, advanced rapidly so that by 1949 division chiefs received as much as $12,000 per year and section chiefs as much as $10,000. This pay scale often outstripped faculty salaries and led to the anomalous situation in which the same man received a higher rate at JPL in the afternoon than he did as a Caltech professor in the morning. The distinction was justified on the grounds that JPL professionals did not enjoy tenure or some of the other Institute perquisites.[6]

JPL's ties with Caltech were often a powerful recruiting device. The chance to be part of one of the world's premiere scientific institutions was attractive. Some laboratory staff members occasionally taught classes on campus, chiefly in jet propulsion, just as a few Caltech faculty and students at times used specialized JPL facilities, particularly the supersonic wind tunnel, for research. Yet the expectations of both the laboratory and the campus for interaction often went unfulfilled. The physical separation of the two locations created a barrier. Moreover, a far higher percentage of JPL was classified than many had anticipated; in 1950, for instance, 90 percent of the laboratory's reports were classified. And all too often, pejorative attitudes got in the way. Campus faculty tended to look down on JPL for doing too much applied work, and laboratory personnel often felt Caltech professors condescending. Attempting to bring some of the campus advantages to the JPL "peasantry," some laboratory engineers formed Hirsutus Longus (long hairs), a lecture and discussion group. But overall, from 1946 through 1950, the link between the campus and JPL began to atrophy.[7]

The changing relationship between the laboratory and the campus contributed to a reexamination of one of the principal links between the two institutions, the overhead payment Caltech received from the army for managing JPL. How much the Institute should receive had already become a perplexing question by the late 1940s, although it was not yet as vexing as it would become. Decisions were difficult, since much of the connection was intangible and involved elements difficult to define such as the degree of Institute prestige refracted on JPL. The overhead payment in the original contract of 1945 had been calculated at 12.5 percent, which yielded $358,000 on JPL's $3-million budget in fiscal year 1948,* the equivalent of more than $7 million in endowment. But by 1948 some of the fat was being trimmed from wartime contracts. A navy audit, for instance, suggested a rate as low as 7.5 percent. The new trend emphasized approval of only direct expenses, not the indirect costs the Institute liked to include.[8]

Caltech toyed with the idea of recovering the difference between direct and indirect costs by charging a management fee. Such an arrangement would have required an industrial type of contract, which usually entailed much stricter accounting procedures, including prior armed forces approval of purchase orders and pay scales. The overhead rate would probably be cut to 3 to 5 percent, and the best fee Caltech could negotiate would probably approximate 6 percent, for a total reimbursement of 9 to 11 percent. The Institute ran the risk, moreover, that such a fee might be construed as a profit and be subject to taxation. George Green, the Caltech business manager, recommended instead that the campus accept a cut in overhead rate to 8.5 percent, with the proviso that payments be made monthly instead of at year's end; the effective rate would thus approximate 9.5 percent. The army accepted the 8.5 percent figure and the advance-payment idea in mid-1949. The Institute's recovery dropped to $246,000 in fiscal year 1950, on a JPL budget of slightly more than $3 million, but the revised contract stabilized the overhead problem for the next ten years. Even at the lower rates the JPL contract remained a boon to the Institute, particularly as the laboratory budget grew and as campus involvement declined in the 1950s. In this cozy financial relationship, however, lay the seeds of a bitter dispute between Caltech and the National Aeronautics and Space Administration in the 1960s.[9]

If Dunn's JPL operated rather independently from the campus, it also enjoyed considerable freedom from direct army supervision. The general subject area of the laboratory's research—various aspects of missilery—was determined by its relationship with army ordnance. But within that broad spectrum, the ordnance department, which had relatively few technically trained officers at that time, relied heavily on JPL's own advice on what research program it should follow. The contract between JPL and the army was reviewed and renewed annually, but it identified research tasks only in

*This overhead rate did not quite equal 12.5 percent because part of the budget contained contracts for construction on which the Institute received no overhead.

the broadest terms. JPL received the exact amount of money it asked for: $2 million in fiscal years 1947 and 1948 and $2.4 million in fiscal years 1949 and 1950. (In fiscal years 1946 through 1948 army ordnance spent a total of $130 million on research and development, of which $29 million went to guided missile research.) A two-man liaison office supervised JPL for the ordnance department and usually championed the laboratory to the Pentagon. Documentation of decisions and of technical developments was often loose or elusive. Twenty years later many JPL staff members would look back with nostalgia on the army days, when funds flowed readily and technical supervision was virtually nonexistent.[10]

In the wake of the technological strides of World War II, some people imagined that push-button, split-second warfare had arrived. Most military men and their scientific advisers recognized, however, that years of basic research would be necessary before advanced weapons, such as guided missiles, would qualify as on-the-shelf items. During the war, development had proceeded rapidly. Although a particular thing might work, its underlying principles were often poorly understood; moreover, alternatives were seldom fully investigated because of the demand to produce something that worked and to produce it quickly. In 1946 to 1947 JPL thus reoriented its research program toward more fundamental studies.

Propulsion still demanded much research. Beguiled by the German V-2, most American researchers worked on liquid propellants. JPL's WAC Corporal had used liquid propellant, and much of the laboratory's propellant research focused on liquids. A bewildering array of oxidizers, fuels, and monopropellants (containing both fuel and oxidizer in one substance) had been advanced since the 1930s. The confusion reminded physicist Howard Seifert of the profusion of spirituous beverages: The variety of flavors was confusing, but the fundamental ingredients and effects were similar. An ideal liquid propellant would have several traits: It should provide the maximum thrust for its weight, ignite and burn rapidly, have high density to permit small storage tanks, and be relatively immune to shock and to temperature changes. Moreover, it would be nontoxic, noncorrosive, and cheap. A propellant meeting all these criteria was almost impossible to come by, so compromises were necessary. As with spirits, the application determined the choice of ingredients.[11]

Two classic, if still somewhat youthful, combinations remained the standards of measurement. Liquid oxygen (LOX) and alcohol had powered the V-2. This propellant had a high specific impulse; however, liquid oxygen had a high vapor pressure, and it was unreliable as a fluid to cool the motor, which remained a major problem. By contrast the two components of the propellant JPL had developed during the war—red fuming nitric acid

(RFNA) and aniline—worked well as coolants; moreover, they ignited spontaneously upon contact. The major disadvantage of the combination was that the fumes were quite toxic and the acid highly corrosive.[12]

The JPL chemistry division investigated more than fifty other propellants. Typically the division analyzed the physical and chemical properties, computed their specific impulses, and operated them in static motor tests. Data were acquired on each combination's ignition characteristics, heat transfer behavior, variations with temperature ranges, and handling problems. None matched the LOX-gasoline or acid-aniline propellants. Hydrogen peroxide, for instance, was safe and easy to handle; but it had a low specific impulse, easily became contaminated, tended to explode if used as a coolant fluid, and had a narrow temperature range. Nitromethane, on the other hand, had a high specific impulse, but presented grave handling problems. Although no striking breakthroughs resulted from this methodical survey, it represented an addition to the understanding of the characteristics of various propellants unsurpassed by any other single research group.[13]

The complex and mysterious phenomena of rocket combustion attracted much interest. "What goes on in a rocket chamber is just nobody's business," a British investigator said. The propellant shot into the combustion chamber of a typical liquid rocket in several streams at a speed of about 100 feet per second. The reaction began the instant the liquids met, and the fluids soon evaporated from the heat of the flame. The reaction was completed in the vapor phase as pressure soared to several hundred pounds per square inch and temperature as high as 5000° F. Reliable measurement and interpretation of results proved difficult under such conditions of high temperature, high pressure, and rapid reactions. JPL scientists attempted various techniques of analysis including photographing the combustion process through a window built into the side of a rocket chamber and extracting gas samples. They provided such data as the temperature of the reaction and the time needed for combustion to be completed. Yet in this complex and difficult field of research much investigation still lay ahead.[14]

Dealing with the tremendous heat generated in the combustion process presented a tall order requiring both fundamental and applied research. The combustion chamber of a rocket was at least as hot as any ordinary furnace, but if the rocket was to be light enough to fly, the chamber walls could not be nearly so thick as those of an industrial furnace. The throat of the nozzle was an especially vulnerable area. Sending the exhaust gases through the throat was like "asking a snowman to swallow a cup of hot coffee," Seifert observed. Some of the propellant was circulated outside the chamber to cool it, and JPL heat transfer specialists did much research to determine the best means of cooling and to gather data on the effects when the cooling fluid boiled.[15]

Another area of research concerned refractory materials, particularly titanium and titanium alloys. Part of a national effort to rapidly advance knowledge of refractory materials, JPL's work dealt only with those likely to have applications to missilery. One of the most ingenious outcomes of this research, headed by Pol Duwez, who later moved full-time to the Caltech campus, was "sweat cooling." This name derived from metal traversed by connected "pores" through which a coolant fluid could be circulated. Controlling the production of such metals was difficult but when successful made it possible for a small amount of fluid to cool a chamber satisfactorily. These studies resulted in a series of pioneering reports documenting the laws of heat transfer and liquid and gas flow through porous metals.[16]

Although JPL devoted less attention to solid propellants than to liquids, the laboratory recorded a major conceptual breakthrough with solids. The prevailing opinion in the late 1940s was that solid propellants could never equal liquids for big rockets. As G. Edward Pendray, a founder of the American Rocket Society, put it in 1944: solids would "never give the power and sustained performance needed for high-altitude sounding rockets . . . or long-range military or trajectory rockets." By breaking through this paradigm, JPL opened the realm of large, solid-propellant rockets, which has been the distinctively American contribution to rocketry.[17]

Besides the usual characteristics of a good propellant, a good solid propellant should burn slowly and at a relatively low temperature, should permit the use of internal-burning grains, and should be operable within wide temperature ranges. The smoky little asphalt-based JATO that JPL had developed during the war could not meet all these criteria. The first step was to find a substitute for asphalt. C. E. Bartley, a young JPL engineer, had demonstrated by late 1945 that a rubberlike polysulfide developed by Thiokol Chemical Corporation possessed most of asphalt's desirable features with few of its drawbacks. But a major problem then appeared. Shortly after ignition the propellant charge's burning rate began to accelerate then stabilized but at a level higher than desired. The Kármán-Malina theory indicated that acceleration in the burning rate meant the burning area was increasing. Bartley found that a cone was forming inside the propellant charge. Efforts to correct the coning phenomenon continued for more than a year with little success.[18]

As JPL wrestled with the burning-rate problem, the army and navy became interested in using solids for small booster rockets. Army ordnance contracted with JPL to develop a 6-inch-diameter rocket known as the Thunderbird. One of the main purposes of the Thunderbird was to test whether the rubbery polysulfide could withstand the stress of launching that reached 120g, or 120 times the acceleration of gravity. Bartley and two other JPL engineers, J. I. Shafer and H. L. Thackwell, Jr., seized on the Thunderbird as an ideal vehicle in which to test a new concept: the internal-burning star. Rocket researchers in Great Britain and at the Allegheny Ballistics Laboratory in West Virginia had conducted extensive tests on small-scale solids using a star-shaped charge but for various reasons had abandoned the star idea. JPL researchers learned of the star almost by accident, through an appendix to another report being circulated among military laboratories. For the Thunderbird motor the engineers applied a thin liner to the wall of the combustion chamber, then mounted a ten-point star-mold core in the center of the chamber. They poured the polysulfide propellant into the chamber and, when the propellant began to harden, removed the star. The design was simplicity itself. When the Thunderbird motor was ignited, the charge burned slowly from the inside, and the star gradually formed a cylinder. The burning-rate problem was solved, and the polysulfide proved it could withstand the acceleration.[19]

Even before the Thunderbird's successful tests in early 1948, Shafer sensed that the star and the polysulfide could be scaled up to sizes equaling the largest liquid-propellant rockets. Shafer performed theoretical calculations that demonstrated that a solid-propellant rocket the size of the WAC Corporal could reach an altitude of 810,000 feet—more than three times the WAC's record flight. It seemed possible, moreover, to cast a solid rocket motor as large as the V-2 that could have a theoretical range of 300 miles, more than double that of the German vehicle. The army agreed to a JPL proposal to develop a large solid rocket, known as the Sergeant, which was designed to boost a 50-pound payload to an altitude of 700,000 feet.* Static tests began in February 1949 on a 15-inch-diameter motor, about twice the size of the largest existing solid motors. Since one of the advantages of the star-shaped charge was that the propellant insulated the chamber walls from the intense heat, JPL engineers attempted to use an unusually thin steel case measuring just 0.065 inches. But JPL's solid-propellant promotors had leaped too far too fast. Twelve consecutive static tests of the motor ended in explosions. By the summer of 1950, as the laboratory geared for converting the Corporal into a tactical weapon, Dunn consigned solid-propellant research to the back burner.[20]

Angered by Dunn's decision, Thackwell left the laboratory for Thiokol, which showed great interest in following up JPL's breakthrough. Thackwell convinced General Electric (GE) to use the star-shaped charge and the Thiokol propellant in the RV-A-10, a 31-inch-diameter, solid-propellant vehicle that would deliver a 1,500-pound pay-load to 75 nautical miles. Although much larger than the Sergeant test vehicle, the GE motor more cautiously

*This missile is usually known as the Sergeant test vehicle to avoid confusion with the Sergeant weapon system developed by JPL in the mid-1950s.

used a 0.2-inch-thick steel case. The thicker case overcame the cracking problem that had caused the explosions at JPL, and the RV-A-10 enjoyed an almost trouble-free development. By 1953, JPL would return to large-scale solids and begin development of the Sergeant missile, the first large solid-propellant weapon. Solid-propellant missiles, such as the Minuteman, Polaris, and Poseidon, were also developed at other laboratories during the 1950s using JPL's basic concept of the marriage of the internal-burning star with the Thiokol propellant. The solid-propellant research at JPL in the late 1940s constituted the fundamental breakthrough that made possible the massive solid rockets of the missile and space eras, thus opening an entire field that many experts once had branded impossible.[21]

Whatever the inherent value of JPL's basic research, Army ordnance's interest lay in eventual development of guided missiles. The actual application of particular techniques provided an indispensable test of the laboratory's discoveries and frequently contributed to solving basic research problems. Moreover, because the various components of a missile interact with each other in complex fashion, actual flight tests of a vehicle were necessary for research and development of a missile system as a whole. Thus many of the laboratory's basic and applied research activities converged in the flight tests of the Corporal E, the surface-to-surface test vehicle which had been proposed in JPL's first report in 1943. The Corporal E was doubly important. As the chief of rocket research for army ordnance, Col. H. N. Toftoy, noted in 1947, it was the only American-originated rocket that could be quickly turned into a missile weapon.[22]

Aerodynamics showed both the importance of applied and basic research and the interrelationship of a missile's components. Missiles operate under extreme conditions. Unlike an airplane, which travels at a relatively uniform rate of speed, a missile is constantly accelerating or decelerating; much of its flight occurs at supersonic speed. The density of air during a flight may vary from standard sea-level value to zero. The vehicle's weight may decline to one-fourth its original value, altering its center of gravity. The eggshell fragility of a missile entails further problems. A rocket with 10 percent of its weight devoted to payload has "the same ratio of liquid-propellant weight to solid skin as an egg to its shell." Because of the newness of missilery, there was little actual data to use in design work. In figuring drag coefficients, for instance, JPL engineers relied on theoretical calculations and on data from artillery shells and airfoils. Laboratory researchers performed elaborate paper studies and tested scale models in the supersonic wind tunnel. When the configuration or weight of the Corporal changed, the aerodynamic data had to be recalculated. Finally there came a time when theory had to be translated into metal and the missiles test-flown to return data under actual operating conditions.[23]

The first Corporal E, the full-size, surface-to-surface liquid-propellant missile, was ready by May 1947. The heavy 39-foot-long Corporal weighed 4,963 pounds empty and 11,700 pounds when fueled and was designed to carry a 300- to 500-pound payload 62.5 miles. The Corporal's power plant—essentially a WAC Corporal motor scaled up to produce 20,000 pounds' thrust for 60 seconds—propelled the missile skyward at White Sands on May 22, 1947. The first American-designed and -fabricated surface-to-surface missile exceeded expectations. It appeared that Kármán's research outline would be easily fulfilled. But the first-round success was a fluke. The next two rounds failed dismally. In the second test the motor failed to develop enough thrust, and the missile rose only about one-half inch then dropped back to the launcher. After about 90 seconds enough fuel had been burned to "equalize the weight of the vehicle to the thrust," and the missile rose briefly, tilted over, and skittered through the underbrush for a few hundred yards before it blew up. A wag dubbed it the "rabbit killer." The third round, in November 1947, started well, but the motor died after 43 seconds, and the vehicle traveled only 14 miles. In both rounds the motor's throat area had burned out; the helical cooling coils simply could not keep the unit cool enough. JPL had suffered a major setback in the area where it seemingly had made the most progress, the propulsion system.[24]

For the next year and a half JPL engineers worked to design and test a new motor. The original unit had had a thick inner shell around which a thin outer shell composed of a helical cooling coil was wrapped. The burnouts tended to occur in the areas where the coil joined the inner shell; in addition, the temperatures rose very high within the inner shell, seriously weakening it. The solution lay in turning the chamber inside out so that the coolant passages formed the light inner shell and the outer shell could be kept cooler and thinner. Since helical passages were too rough for the interior of the chamber, JPL engineers apparently modified the idea of axial-flow passages on the V-2. The new axial-cooled motor proved an immediate success. The burnouts were eliminated, and the empty motor weight was cut from 450 pounds to 125. Design changes in other parts of the missile, chiefly the tanks and plumbing, cut the Corporal's weight still more so that round four weighed 4,353 pounds empty, compared to an average of 5,356 pounds for rounds one through three, a reduction of nearly 20 percent. The lighter vehicle could hurl a 1,000-pound payload 200 miles, compared with 113 miles for the earlier version. After lengthy static tests, the new motor underwent its first test flight at White Sands on June 7, 1949, in which it performed superbly.[25]

The axial-flow design represented the culmination of nine years of work on liquid-propellant motors and provided an example of how applied engineering testing might influence design concepts. The axial-cooling breakthrough was a major step in missile engineering; it solved the most basic requirement of a missile—a reliable propellant system. The Corporal E, although borrowing some ideas from the V-2, successfully demonstrated a new propellant system and deserved recognition as a distinctive development in rocketry.

But now that the Corporal could fly, controlling and guiding it raised another batch of complex problems. The aerodynamic conditions of a missile increased the difficulty of threading a needle at long distance—dropping a missile within a circle 1,000 feet in diameter from 75 to 150 miles away. The electrical engineering concepts and devices needed for such precision were "on the bench, not on the shelf," noted William Pickering, then the Caltech professor of electrical engineering who headed the JPL electronics section. Radar, for instance, had been developed only during the recent war, and television was still in its infancy.[26]

The first four Corporals were equipped with rudimentary control and telemetry systems. The telemetry apparatus transmitted to ground control much useful data on the behavior of the missile in flight and its environment. The control system, which had been adapted from an airplane automatic pilot, was not designed to guide the vehicle toward a target but simply to keep the Corporal from straying from White Sands to Las Cruces or El Paso. Nonetheless, on the first test, Corporal E impacted within two miles of its predicted spot. On the first test the ground crew also radioed a signal ordering the missile to turn left, and it responded. On the second and third tests, however, the control system proved unsatisfactory. On the fourth it failed completely. Shortly after takeoff the missile veered toward Las Cruces, and the range safety officer destroyed the bird. JPL began a fundamental reevaluation of the control system.[27]

In addition to testing the Corporal at White Sands, JPL staff collaborated with the German rocket team on a project which eventually marked what some termed the opening of the space age. The German researchers, headed by Wernher von Braun, were stationed at nearby Ft. Bliss after they were brought out of Germany. Some sixty V-2s were also shipped to the United States; rather than fire them empty, the army allowed scientists researching the upper atmosphere to load them with instruments. The White Sands exposure gave JPL personnel a good chance to look over the V-2s, from which they concluded there was relatively little they wanted to apply to their projects. The most noteworthy event was the launch of Bumper-WAC, a WAC Corporal mounted on a V-2, on February 24, 1949. Taking off from the V-2 at the high point of the big missile's trajectory, WAC Corporal reached a record height of 250 miles in altitude. It was the "first recorded man-made object to reach extraterrestrial space." Bumper-WAC was perhaps a harbinger of missile technology's turn toward space.[28]

The immediate problems of weaponry took precedence, however, in the summer of 1949. Top army officers thinking about missiles felt a sense of both urgency and opportunity. Nuclear weapons had once seemed so large and expensive that they would be reserved for strategic use by the air force. But the atomic testing in the Pacific in 1947 and 1948 indicated that nuclear weapons could be made much smaller and lighter and would become relatively cheap. They could then be used on tactical missiles for the army. This promised to enhance the diminished position of the army, the only military branch thus far excluded from having nuclear weapons—the sine qua non of the modern military. A nuclear-tipped army was in keeping, moreover, with the American military strategy of substituting technology for manpower and thereby reconciling military power with economy. To military planners tactical nuclear weapons seemed essential in Europe. These missiles could counter the Eastern bloc's armies and swarms of tanks. The fledgling North Atlantic Treaty Organization (NATO) could implement its "forward strategy" of extending its lines as far eastward as possible. From its birth NATO relied on the doctrine of the first use of nuclear weapons, regardless of whether such instruments were used against it.[29]

Such thinking entailed great drawbacks. If the deterrent failed, the West would bear the moral and political onus of the introduction of nuclear weapons. Furthermore, many people feared that once the nuclear firebreak was crossed—even with tactical atomic weapons—a general nuclear exchange would ensue. As George F. Kennan pointed out, basing the American military structure on this assumption put the United States in a position where, if war came, "we would presumably not be able to afford *not* to use" nuclear weapons.[30]

These objections carried little weight, however, in Washington in 1949 and 1950, where a sense of dread and urgency mounted. The Soviet's detonation of an atomic bomb in August 1949 ended the United States' short-run policy of an atomic monopoly and shook the easy confidence in the country's scientific superiority. "We are in a straight race with the Russians," argued budget director James E. Webb in September 1949. In this atmosphere the ferment of policy led to a military buildup, highlighted by Truman's decision to start development of the hydrogen bomb in January 1950 and by the famous staff paper NSC-68 of April 1950 which outlined a strategy of military expansion and political initiative. To some a Soviet attack seemed ominously close. NSC-68 defined 1954 as the "year of maximum peril," and the Joint Chiefs of Staff refused to rule out the possibility of war in 1951 or 1952.[31]

Reflecting the army's institutional interests and the alarmist atmosphere in the capital, Colonel Toftoy turned to JPL for help. General Electric's Hermes, which he had counted on for the first production versions of tactical missiles, was badly bogged down in research problems. The propulsion problems of the JPL Corporal had been solved. Now Toftoy wanted to know whether the Corporal could be controlled and guided reliably. Summoned to the Pentagon on September 22, 1949, Louis Dunn and William Pickering allowed, not a little rashly, that it could. They followed with a formal report in March 1950 outlining how a control and guidance system could be developed reasonably quickly from existing components. "Careful consideration of the Corporal E as a possible tactical weapon is justified," Dunn concluded. But in essence the decision to go ahead was made that afternoon in the Pentagon when Toftoy got the answer he had hoped for.[32]

Dunn and Pickering knew they were gambling on a venture much larger than anything on which JPL had yet embarked. But they did not realize the manifold complications that lay ahead in making the transition from a research vehicle to an assembly-line production item and even training troops in how to use the weapon. Nor did they realize the vast changes that weaponization—as the process was known in Pentagon jargon—would bring to the laboratory and its relationship with the army and Caltech. By 1950 JPL, while working largely under the rubric of basic engineering research, had become an almost completely secret institution and stood poised to begin the very weapons applications work that the Institute faculty had wanted to avoid.

4 ★★

WEAPONS FOR THE COLD WAR

The enthusiasm of army ordnance for converting JPL's Corporal into a tactical weapon proved less than contagious. The army's proposal threatened the air force's and the navy's hold on missiles and atomic weaponry, and it ran counter to the still dominant idea that the American nuclear stockpile should be reserved for strategic not tactical use. The Joint Chiefs of Staff accordingly turned down the army request early in 1950. Convinced he was following the right course, Colonel Toftoy of ordnance nevertheless moved the Corporal closer to weaponization under the protective cover of research on the propulsion system, although the axial-cooling breakthrough of the summer of 1949 had essentially completed this phase. The new goal was to implement full-scale research on control and guidance of the missile, with the hope of demonstrating precision guidance by July 1951. When the time came to present the army's case again, the ordnance department would then be able to point to a missile system in which both propulsion and guidance were well along. In March 1950 JPL filed a progress report which argued that propulsion and guidance developments made conversion of the Corporal to a tactical weapon feasible.[1]

As JPL finished the report, events began building toward just such a conclusion. Underscoring its interest in missilery, the army activated Redstone Arsenal at Huntsville, Alabama, in April and put Wernher von Braun and his fellow German V-2 scientists to work there. In spring 1950 defense and foreign policy analysts put the finishing touches on an epochal National Security Council study, NSC-68, that called for a vast rearmament program as part of the U.S. global strategy for the next decade or more. The outbreak of the Korean War on June 25, 1950, seemed to validate the premises of NSC-68 for the Truman administration and made it politically possible to implement its program. President Truman appointed former Chrysler Corporation president K. T. Keller to head a new office of guided missiles in the Department of Defense and to review urgently and expedite the national missile program. Keller began his review with the results of Corporal round-five tests on July 11, 1950, freshly before him. Although the round's performance was weak—a malfunction in the air tank caused the Corporal to fall short of the expected range—it augured well for the principles of the guidance and control systems JPL had chosen.[2]

In planning its approach to guidance and control, the laboratory faced three major constraints imposed by the army. First, the Corporal missile should be "fail-safe" and fall near the target despite ordinary malfunctions. Second, the missile should follow a "zero lift," or nonmaneuvering, trajectory; this reduced weight and structural requirements and afforded the tactical advantage of relinquishing control earlier. Third, existing techniques and even existing equipment should be used wherever possible; moreover, only minimal modifications should be made in the Corporal's propulsion system and airframe. We could see many ways "to do better, cheaper," recalled Caltech-JPL systems analyst Homer Stewart, "but the pressure of providing a useful weapon at an early date was the overriding thing that controlled almost all system considerations."[3]

Making a missile fly an accurate course from launcher to target required guidance and control systems. Control, which meant keeping the missile stable in flight, was relatively easy. JPL had adapted and improved autopilots similar to those used in piloted aircraft for its early Corporals, and in 1949 the laboratory had made an important step by developing some pneumatic components in place of the existing hydraulic units. Although further refinements lay ahead, the autopilot operated successfully in round five and validated the principle of Corporal control.[4]

The guidance system proved a good deal more complicated. Here JPL was influenced by the lessons of the only missiles hitherto used in combat, the German V-2s, but the demands for greater accuracy necessitated new ideas as well. In combat the V-2 used a simple, self-contained, inertial guidance system. When the guidance signals indicated the missile had reached the proper point in its flight, the motor was shut off; this point was analogous to the moment an artillery shell leaves the muzzle of a gun. The missile coasted ballistically toward the target. If no disturbances occurred, the missile would fall close to the target; but many uncertainties, particularly air density and wind currents, frequently caused major errors. The V-2s that were successfully launched—about 60 percent of the attempts—had a circular probable error (CPE), if it could be called that, of 25 to 35 miles. Army ordnance wanted the Corporal CPE reduced to at most a half mile. JPL electronics experts pondered more comprehensive systems, particularly an all-inertial system that would guide the missile all the way from the launcher to the target. Such a system's potential simplicity, reliability, and invulnerability to enemy countermeasures made it attractive. But JPL estimated that its development would take at least three years. The army did not want to wait.[5]

Instead the laboratory adopted some of the ideas the Germans had used only experimentally, a radio-command guidance system. A ground-based radar and a Doppler system, similar to but more sophisticated than the Germans', would track the position and velocity of the missile. This information would be fed into computers that would then issue commands to keep the missile generally on course. To refine the system beyond the German concepts, JPL added a tracking radar, which, in conjunction with its computer, would make more precise measurements and corrections. These units guided the missile to its apogee, but drag uncertainties late in flight could cause a target error of as much as two miles. JPL therefore added a range-correction system that measured deviations near the apogee and maneuvered the missile as it reentered the atmosphere to eliminate much of the uncertainty.[6]

These techniques and the equipment were essentially modified World War II surplus. For the Doppler set, JPL adapted existing equipment that had been developed by the ballistic research laboratory. For the tracking radar the laboratory utilized a World War II SCR-584 set that no longer existed as a production item plus some added components under development by General Electric for its Hermes missile. The radar, the basic communication and tracking device, "was clearly not quite adequate to . . . the problem," Stewart pointed out. But instead of redesigning the radar or going inertial, time pressure dictated adding the Doppler in order to achieve the required precision quickly. The basic radar and Doppler equipment flew on round five, although they were not yet operational, and the pattern for the Corporal guidance system was established.[7]

The Corporal, bearing a proved propulsion system and promising guidance and control, was alluring to Keller and the military. The missile expediter wanted to emphasize ground-to-air missiles for antiaircraft use and accordingly ordered the Nike system speeded. Basically he and the military wanted to put into production any missile that showed promise of quick availability; in all, twenty-six separate missile projects were approved for research or development. According to some estimates—overly optimistic, as it turned out—Corporal could be ready for mass production in 1951 and deployment in 1952, more than a year before Nike. Keller recommended the Corporal as a weapons project in October 1950, and the Defense Department agreed. By late December the Corporal had received approval as a carrier of atomic weapons. There was little to indicate the decision to weaponize Corporal reflected new agreement among the services or that it fit into an integrated tactical scheme. Since the air force and the navy received authorization for several missile projects, they muted their objections to the army's one prize. Corporal fulfilled the desire for any guided missile that could be available soon. The demand for speed would bedevil JPL, the army, and the contractors for the next six years of Corporal's weaponization.[8]

Under normal conditions as much as a decade might elapse before a missile completed the journey from the research phase to mass production. JPL saw no chance of meeting Keller's desire for a production prototype in mid-1951, but the laboratory devised a schedule it hoped would make production possible by spring 1952. Rounds six through ten were intended to prove out the propulsion, autopilot, and guidance system, except for postburnout guidance by June 1951. Rounds eleven through eighteen would complete the rest of the system by March 1952. Twelve more tests would follow to provide statistical performance data and to allow for minor improvements in components.[9]

The round-six Corporal firing on November 2, 1950, cast gloom over this schedule. Round six crashed after a flight of 36 miles, about 34 miles short of its target. The primary cause of the error, malfunctions of the air tanks in the propulsion system, was solved quickly, and in subsequent rounds the propulsion system functioned reliably. More discouraging was that the radar and Doppler beacons, the flight-beacon transmitter, and the telemetric equipment—all the electronic equipment on board—failed because of the extreme vibration in flight. On two subsequent rounds the missile struck within 5 miles of the target. By round eleven, on October 10, 1951, the basic configuration of the missile had been set. But a major malfunction caused the round-eleven bird to fly vertically and then drift west, toward the city of Las Cruces. Impact was on the desert, about 15 miles from the launch site. Thus although the basic configuration had been set, the problem of reliability required extensive work before Corporal could be considered a satisfactory weapon.[10]

The round-eleven test at White Sands in October 1951 marked the end of the era when fundamental engineering research dominated activities at JPL. A trek to the desert had been an important feature of JPL activities since the early 1940s, first to the Mojave for the Private tests, then after the war to the newly established White Sands in New Mexico. Conditions had been hard on the blistering, windy desert. At first everyone lived in tents, and rations sometimes dwindled to beans and cheese. But by 1950 White Sands boasted such comforts of permanence as a swimming pool and handsome quarters. Testing new and expensive things under a demanding timetable meant hard work and tension; relief was found in hard play. All-night poker games quickly became a staple of White Sands weeks. JPL director Louis Dunn particularly liked to gather intimates together for a day-and-a-half train ride—despite, or perhaps because of, his background in aeronautics he preferred the train—from California to El Paso. Visits to Juárez took the chill off desert evenings. Missiles and Mexico made White Sands perhaps the ultimate in machismo for JPL males. The White Sands experience reminded Homer Stewart of the stories of oil exploration gangs in the outback. But more importantly, the White Sands expeditions performed an important moral function for the laboratory. "You learned who you could trust," said Stewart. Away from home distractions, concentrating on work in a tense environment, playing hard, the two dozen or so top JPL officials formed an elite communication group that tended to cut across formal lines in the laboratory.[11]

By mid-1951 the nature of JPL's White Sands operation had changed. Indicative of the laboratory's growing specialization and formality, Dunn stationed a group of JPL engineers at the test base full-time. Since the fundamental engineering research on Corporal had been largely finished, this test crew would carry out a long series of flights of production versions of the missile to gather data on reliability. The permanent contingent at White Sands reflected overall changes in the laboratory under the impact of weaponization. By mid-1951 the JPL budget, which had averaged about $200,000 per month in the late 1940s, had climbed to $400,000 per month; the number of employees increased from 546 on January 1, 1950, to 742 on June 30, 1951. The ratio of one scientist-engineer to three nontechnical personnel held, and particular efforts were made to strengthen the electronics staff.[12]

Louis Dunn, innately cautious, feared the laboratory was growing too fast. The Caltech emphasis on small groups of top men reinforced his natural inclination toward cautious expansion, and with missile activity booming nationally, top men were increasingly hard to attract. JPL's facilities, despite some new construction, were also strained. But there was no turning back. By 1953 the JPL budget reached more than $11 million annually, and its employees numbered 1,061. To cope with the increasing size and complexity, Dunn inserted a second tier of management between his office and the various sections. Instead of each section reporting to him directly, the sections now reported to one of three division heads. One of those division chiefs, William Pickering, functioned as a project manager in all but name, able to make demands across sectional and divisional lines to bring whatever talents were needed on the Corporal project. Organization along disciplinary lines that had reflected JPL's academic origins yielded increasingly to the project format of an industrial or arsenal laboratory.[13]

One of the consequences of these changes from 1950 to 1953 was a decline in the relative importance of basic research, which had once been JPL's raison d'être. The army continued to acknowledge the importance of fundamental studies, but it left no doubt that Corporal hardware had to claim priority. Thus basic research held approximately steady, but its $3 million total in 1953 represented less than a 30 percent slice of the laboratory budget.[14]

The accelerating tempo at JPL in 1950 and 1951 refueled the controversy which had been simmering over the laboratory's location. What was supposed to have been solely a wartime operation showed signs of becoming permanent. In 1951 more than 400 residents in areas of Altadena and Flintridge signed a petition denouncing continued operation of the laboratory adjacent to their upper-middle-class residential areas. They objected to the noise of the static-motor tests and to the laboratory's unsightliness. The army had built no permanent buildings, and the minimal landscaping and standard army paint left the place looking like a combination of an army base and an industrial yard. The residents also claimed JPL was unsafe. Rumors circulated that the flashing red lights that sometimes woke residents early in the morning heralded ambulances taking out the bodies of JPL personnel killed in tests. The laboratory tried to meet some of the objections by moving large-motor tests to the desert, installing noise suppressors, and trying to get more funds for landscaping. And the flashing red lights, JPL officials explained, signaled the departure of test crews and their missiles for White Sands under military escort. The army meanwhile abandoned plans to buy some additional property adjacent to the laboratory. Although satisfactory to some persons, these cosmetic touches could not satisfy the hard core who felt, as had the Pasadena city manager at war's end, that JPL was simply out of character in a residential area.[15]

The location controversy was a large headache for Caltech president Lee DuBridge, who prided himself on the Institute's unusually good town-gown relations. He adopted a familiar cold war defense. "It seems to me that possibly you are blaming the wrong people for this situation," DuBridge told one protester. The necessity for continuing weapons development programs was "not the fault of Caltech or of the military services but the fault of one Joseph Stalin." DuBridge called in heavy artillery for reinforcement, Maj. Gen. E. L. Ford, chief of ordnance, who said in a letter that the obstacles to moving the laboratory were "insurmountable." Fifteen million dollars would be needed to duplicate the facilities, and the connection with the Institute probably would be lost; moreover, any attempt to move such a "key center" of research would interrupt the work and cause "a grave hiatus in the future armament of the nation." At a press conference in Pasadena, Brig. Gen. Leslie Simon, Ford's assistant, ventured that JPL would remain in place for the duration of the cold war. The conciliatory gestures plus the patriotic appeals succeeded in calming the controversy, although it did not end until well into the NASA era.[16]

The furor over the location was ironic, for the strains of weaponization had all but severed the already weakened ties between the laboratory and the campus. Faculty members found it increasingly hard to keep a foot in both camps, especially if they worked mainly on Corporal. Pickering, professor of electrical engineering at Caltech, taught his last class on campus in 1950 and moved full-time to the laboratory. By 1952 of the dozen section chiefs and administrators at JPL only three held joint CIT-JPL appointments. Only sixteen Caltech graduate students worked part-time during the year at the laboratory. JPL's growth and its expansion into new fields, instead of increasing cross-fertilization with the campus, tended to retard contact. Louis Dunn exaggerated only slightly when he said a quarter century later: "The Caltech connection was of no importance whatsoever." Missile czar Keller was also skeptical. He told Caltech trustees in 1952 that he did not think educational institutions managed applied research efficiently. Although the military disagreed with him, Keller felt that eventually JPL should be transferred to nonacademic management.[17]

But giving up JPL was exactly what the Caltech administration did not want. The Institute apparently never formally authorized the weaponization decision. The JPL board, composed of both JPL and CIT members, acknowledged in August 1950 that the cold war emergency had "resulted in certain departures from the basic policies which were . . . to guide the laboratory's operations during normal times." But the consensus of the board was that the emergency made weaponization "justified and desirable." That informal acceptance conformed with the general outlook of Caltech officials. In common with probably a majority of American scientists and engineers, they felt they had an obligation to bend their talents to weapons development. Instead of conflict between weapons secrecy and university's free inquiry, they tended to see military research and university activities as complementary. Caltech, for the most part, barred classified work on campus. These objections "vanished" if the work were performed off campus, DuBridge noted. "Our only criterion is that such work should be a proper part of the Institute's activities and an important contribution to national defense." Such projects, he believed, contributed to both governmental and institutional prestige. The Caltech president thought, furthermore, that military laboratories were inefficient and advocated transferring all of them to private, though not necessarily university, control. (In 1951 and 1952 several Institute administrators and leading professors conducted a Defense Department study, Project VISTA, which analyzed possible use of tactical nuclear weapons in Europe. The deliberations took place off campus but consumed considerable faculty and administrative time under official institutional auspices.) While philosophical ideas probably were adequate to insure continued CIT management, the administration could scarcely overlook the mounting overhead funds the Institute received—an issue that would draw added attention in a few years. Far from seeking to disengage from JPL, DuBridge attempted unsuccessfully in 1950 to interest army ordnance in a long-term contract.[18]

The faculty and the trustees exhibited more reservations about JPL's direction than did the laboratory board and the Institute administration. Some felt, in fact, that a majority of the faculty would have favored disengaging from JPL. The trustees concluded in 1952 that, because of the emergency, the Institute had "no alternative" but to continue to operate JPL. But the overseers noted that, despite some basic research, Corporal had thrown the laboratory's research program "somewhat 'off the track.'" JPL was not, however, interfering with the campus program. When the Corporal reached completion, the research program should return to normal; if not, the trustees should again review JPL's status. For the most part the arguments for retaining the laboratory were framed in negative terms: cold war assumptions admitted no alternatives, and the laboratory at least did not interfere with the campus. A resounding affirmative statement of the interaction and mutuality of Institute and laboratory interests remained noticeably absent.[19]

While the campus connection waned, the threat of army control increased. In mid-1952 army ordnance notified Louis Dunn that JPL was to be designated a class 2 army facility, the official status of a government-owned, contractor-operated facility. The ordnance executive officer assured JPL that this was purely a bookkeeping arrangement that would "validate, but . . . in no sense alter, the present operating status." Nor would the designation entail appointment of a commanding officer or military administrative staff. His misgivings allayed by these assurances, Dunn accepted class 2 status without talking to DuBridge. But soon standard military forms, dealing mainly with personnel and property, began to arrive at the laboratory, and at one point an arsenal representative exerted pressure on JPL to change its publication policies.[20]

Then the bombshell hit. Brig. Gen. Simon telephoned Dunn on November 28, 1953, and informed him that the ordnance corps wanted to appoint a commanding officer for the laboratory. DuBridge and Dunn found the idea "wholly unacceptable." A major reason for JPL's success lay in its civilian management, DuBridge told the new chief of ordnance, Maj. Gen. E. L. Cummings. The laboratory could not operate under two sets of rules, civilian and military. If ordnance were dissatisfied with Caltech-JPL operations, the Institute would immediately begin negotiations looking toward full army control. Ordnance backpedaled hurriedly, lauding the present management. Laboratory operations continued much as before, the army presence confined to liaison officers and occasional inspection visits.[21]

What lay behind the ordnance gambit was unclear. Perhaps it was bureaucratic juggling or simply a trial balloon. Whatever the reason, the possibility of a commanding officer suggested how far JPL had drifted into the army weapons network. An ordnance liaison officer at JPL, Maj. G. E. Parsons, Jr., had described the laboratory's role in the Corporal program as "practically identical to the function of an ordnance arsenal." Indeed, since mid-1951 JPL had increasingly assumed such a role, as its work with contractors and the army made clear.[22]

Having proved the soundness of the Corporal concepts, the JPL "arsenal" faced the overriding problem of making the missile reliable. This sort of work did not present the challenges and exhilaration of arriving at the initial designs; it was not glamorous, merely essential. Reliability of the missile was difficult to insure, for the failure of some minute component could jeopardize an entire flight, and the extreme environments in which missiles operate made testing and data retrieval difficult. But a weapon system could be no more reliable than the personnel who operated it, and so troop training assumed equal importance. From mid-1951 through 1956 JPL's Corporal activities focused on reliability of both materiel and personnel.[23]

In a logical, efficient scheme for weapon systems development and production, William Pickering pointed out, "right from the very beginning there must be a clear concept of what the weapon system is supposed to do." If the development program were properly conducted, "the weapon should be ready for production, completely documented, properly designed, consistent with all the requirements of the weapon system, training programs ready to go, maintenance programs established, manuals written, and supply channels ready to be activated; so that when the first production devices come off the line, a complete weapon system is in being." Some changes would still prove necessary, of course, but they would be minor and probably possible "to effect in the field." But neither the development nor the production of the Corporal conformed to this plan. The design of the prototypes was incomplete when production began, the need for training programs and instruction manuals was but vaguely conceived. Indeed, the military characteristics, which laid down the requirements Corporal should meet, were not ready until thirty-six missiles had rolled off the assembly line. Under such conditions the chaotic development and production of Corporal resulted in a weapon of dubious utility.[24]

The army had begun campaigning for production authorization almost as soon as Corporal was converted into a weapons project. Test-round seven in January 1951 had given added assurance that the concept of the guidance system, though unwieldy, was sound, but the round also suggested that extensive development remained before a satisfactory prototype would be ready. Undaunted, missile-expediter Keller not only accepted the army's request for 180 missiles in March 1951 but raised it to 200. He hoped to have a facility capable of turning out twenty missiles per month by May 1952, with deployment possible by the end of the year. The low bid came from Vendo Company of Kansas City, $10,972,100; Firestone Tire & Rubber Company of Los Angeles submitted the next lowest bid, $13,044,512. Firestone had wanted badly to get into missile work, and, acting on the advice of JPL, the military selected Firestone over Vendo. JPL advised that Vendo had under-bid the actual cost of the job in order to get the contract, that it showed too little engineering skill and too few subcontractors, and that its location would make liaison with JPL difficult. Firestone received a letter of intent in July 1951 and a definitive contract in December 1951. With the round-eleven test in October the aerodynamic configuration had been frozen, and Louis Dunn agreed that it was now possible, if costly and risky, to telescope development and production.[25]

A production firm normally would have the benefit of extensive production engineering in which the newly designed articles were refined for ease of manufacture and detailed engineering documents drawn. Some items, such as the radar command beacon, had not been frozen even by the time production began. And since testing continued in an attempt to improve reliability of already established designs, innumerable smaller changes might still be introduced. JPL could not simply turn over engineering drawings to Firestone and perform minimal liaison work. The laboratory became intimately involved in production details, primarily through a production planning section composed of top personnel who worked closely with Firestone engineers. But a constant tug-of-war continued between the researchers' desire to incorporate the latest changes into production versions and the manufacturer's need for fixed specifications. Telescoping development and production cut time but interfered with both orderly production and testing. Many items were manufactured that would subsequently be discarded, and some tests would take place without fully incorporating previous modifications. Telescoping entailed "a certain amount of waste," army ordnance acknowledged in its understated way, but we "must be prepared to defend this approach on the basis of the 'crash' nature" of the program.[26]

Relations were often strained between JPL and the factory. Laboratory drawings were often incomplete, owing to the sense of urgency and to JPL's inexperience in working with contractors. The laboratory, in turn, complained of contractors' poor performances. Some problems lay beyond the contractors' grasp. Some materials were in short supply in the early 1950s, and the booming missile market made it hard to recruit qualified personnel. In some cases, as with some components Motorola produced for the airborne guidance system, the necessary standards were not known when production began but had to be determined by further testing. All too often, however, the high volume, relatively low-cost firms found themselves ill prepared to meet the demanding standards missiles dictated. JPL rejected the first fifty gyroscopes one subcontractor produced because of poor workmanship, mainly dirt (including metal chips, filings, dust, and even extra screws and nuts) in the units. The laboratory gave the firm technical help, chiefly in setting up a clean room, but rejections continued to run as high as 60 percent. The laboratory remained skeptical of Firestone's engineering talent, particularly in electronics. As Firestone production slipped far behind schedule in 1954 and the Department of Defense threatened to intervene, Colonel Toftoy called company officials in and talked to them like a Dutch uncle. Army ordnance had originally anticipated that Firestone would be the prime contractor for all phases of production, in line with the corps' typical practice. Acting on JPL's recommendation, however, ordnance in 1952 gave Gilfillan Brothers, an experienced Los Angeles electronics firm, a prime contract covering the ground guidance system. Gilfillan performed good work and assumed a large degree of control over the Corporal when JPL phased out in 1956. But for the first several years the system development had in effect three prime contractors—JPL, Firestone, and Gilfillan—who worked together erratically with too little overall coordination.[27]

Production problems were aggravated because no one knew for sure what standards had to be met, either for components to perform properly or to satisfy military desires. While the contractors cranked out parts, JPL continued extensive testing of components. The laboratory organized a reliability group whose job was to accumulate enough quantitative information, through actual test flights and simulations, to establish safety margins for Corporal components and the system as a whole. One of the chief problems, not merely for Corporal but for most contemporary missile projects, was failure of electronic components because of in-flight vibration. The high cost of test flights and the difficulty in gathering information led the laboratory to set up shake tables that simulated the vibrations encountered in flight. After electronic components endured countless hours on the shake tables, JPL formulated rigid specifications, many of them a good deal more stringent than terrestrial manufacturing firms were used to. Wind tunnel testing remained important, especially for calculating drag upon reentry into the atmosphere. These simulations stood in a reciprocal relationship to the continuing test flights at White Sands, as data from the simulated tests were continually revised according to "real world" conditions.[28]

The urgency and lack of overall system planning had particularly serious consequences for the design of ground-handling equipment. Ground handling of a liquid-propellant missile, which had to be fueled at the last moment, would always be awkward and would necessitate extra trucks to carry propellant and air for the pumping system. Time pressure dictated that the missile not be redesigned; the ground-handling equipment would have to fit around it as best it could. "The major emphasis on design was to get something that worked," JPL reported. "No particular stress was put on making the design work well." Because of inadequate personnel, the laboratory did not design ground equipment but did exercise a review over the models proposed by subcontractors. The final system was arrived at only after changing some subcontractors and after searching among existing equipment. Each Corporal required eight major pieces of equipment: four trucks, two carrying propellants, one an air compressor, and one a conventional air supply; a shipping container for hauling the missile; an erector, a self-propelled vehicle that transported the missile to the launcher and hoisted it to a vertical position for firing; the launcher; and a special platform to service the nearly 40-foot-long missile when it was erected.* When a Corporal battalion took to the road, it stretched over sixteen miles.[29]

These equipment items were not integrated with each other or with the missile. As a result, even in so simple an item as the missile-handling rings, two sets of rings had to be provided to be compatible with the varying types of equipment. The erector, adapted from a Hi-Tender used in apple orchards, was a headache. The erector was fairly reliable, but when something went wrong, it was so foreign to the types of equipment the army was used to that repairing it proved almost impossible. This array of trucks and cranes served just to get the missile ready for firing; it did not include a separate tentful of ground-guidance equipment or the command center. The limitations of the ground-handling equipment would seriously compromise Corporal's usability in tactical situations. Pickering received a graphic demonstration of the Corporal's cumbrous logistics several years later when he was traveling in Italy. His tourist bus and all the other traffic had to pull off the road to let a Corporal battalion squeeze past.[30]

The final element of the Corporal system was the warhead. The army envisioned and tested several types of warheads: chemical, biological, radiological, fragmentation cluster, and general purpose (high explosive). But Corporal's primary role was as an atomic carrier. The Atomic Energy Commission and Sandia Corporation developed the actual warhead. JPL's task came in developing a command arming system to insure that the probability an armed warhead would fall on friendly troops was less than 1 in 10,000. The decision to arm would be made by computers on the ground, the

---

*Each battalion required 18 propellant trucks (5 ton) with hoist, plumbing, and tanks; 13 air supply trucks with tanks and plumbing (5 ton); 4 air compressor trucks (5 ton); 4 air compressors; 4 trucks, fire and pumper (2 ½ ton); 60 dry-powder fire extinguishers; 36 emergency personnel showers; 18 300-gallon collapsible tanks; 18 water trailer prime movers (2 ½ ton); 18 electric pumpers; 41 two-piece glass fabric suits; 41 leather-covered-with-glass-fabric, plastic face-piece hoods; 82 protective overboots; 82 protective gloves; 41 cooler suits (for use over acid suit); 41 cooler hoods (for use over hoods); and 41 masks with speaking diaphragm.

Pasadena laboratory decided, based on the measurements of the trajectory at the last possible moment, just before the missile reentered the atmosphere. To minimize possible errors, a decision to arm had to be transmitted over both a radio command channel and a Doppler command channel. The system also incorporated a manual override, but under normal conditions the computer made the decision. The arming system, like the guidance system, had limitations. Under certain conditions the missile might impact within the specified distance from the target but not receive a signal to arm; under other circumstances an arming signal might be transmitted even though the missile missed the target by as much as two miles. The warhead thus added another element of uncertainty in the Corporal system performance.[31]

The final determination of the diverse elements fused into the Corporal system came in a series of 105 test firings at White Sands begun in August 1952 when JPL launched the first Corporals produced by Firestone. These missiles had emerged from the factory in May 1952, when Keller had hoped to see a production capacity of twenty per month. By year's end Firestone fabricated 30 missiles, compared to 200 called for in the contract; the firm reached its best average, 13 per month, in 1955. Firestone turned the missiles over to JPL, where they were dismantled, inspected, modified, and reassembled. Many elements of custom work remained, as the JPL modification center corrected manufacturing flaws and replaced parts with new designs based on the latest tests. From August 1952 through August 1953 skilled JPL field crews at White Sands fired fifty-six production vehicles, recording an average system reliability of 43 percent. Subsequent tests eventually attained an overall reliability rating of 47.1 percent.[32]

This record, JPL learned in November 1952, fell far short of the stiff military characteristics the army had finally formulated. The Corporal should be operable within a range of 25 to 80 nautical miles. At least half the missiles launched must impact within 150 yards of ground zero: the remaining half must land within 300 yards of the target. The missiles that were launched were to have in-flight reliability of 95 percent. All Corporal system equipment was to be mobile. Not more than four hours could elapse from the start of the emplacement of ground-control equipment and launcher to the firing of the first missile. After firing, this equipment must be ready to go into traveling position within an hour. Corporal must perform satisfactorily under these weather conditions: air temperatures from 125° to −25° F, surface winds as high as 35 miles per hour with gusts to 50 mph, and relative humidity as high as 100 percent at all temperatures below 90°. These standards represented an ideal the army knew was probably unattainable with Corporal. The question now became how much of a shortfall it would accept.[33]

The military characteristics seemed almost utopian when the other half of the reliability equation was considered: personnel. The army chafed to get its hands on the missile and telescoped the engineer tests (normally an ordnance corps function) with the user tests (ordinarily a field forces operation after the engineers had finished with the system). Fourteen engineer-user tests were fired in 1953 and early 1954, using JPL-modified production missiles. One missile impacted within 300 yards, another within 600 yards, and the remainder more than half a mile away; the reliability rating was 28 percent. But even worse, when the field forces, who would use the missile in war, began test firings by themselves in 1954, they had almost no success. One battalion commander revealed that his troops had not managed even a successful mock firing. General Mickelsen, commander of Ft. Bliss, where the field forces had been practicing, suspended the tests.[34]

In desperation the army called a secret two-day meeting of top JPL and contractor representatives in June 1954. The army chief of staff had decided to deploy one Corporal battalion in Europe by the end of 1954, but that seemed seriously jeopardized now. "Things I would like to say I can't here, they are too highly classified," Mickelsen told the missile builders. "We are placing great dependence on the . . . Corporal design, and we can't afford to do anything less than our utmost to get it working." Many problems surfaced, particularly about training. JPL had been training troops since mid-1952, but a combination of high soldier turnover, often inadequate technical backgrounds, and delays in providing operation manuals and training equipment undermined instruction. In one case only one-third of the students completed the class. The frequent changes in equipment made it doubly hard to keep troops current. JPL had concentrated on the technical aspects, leaving the tactical questions mainly to the army; too many things fell through the cracks because of poor coordination. Operational procedures had been built up "almost out of opinion," with little overall review, JPL representative Bob Rypinski said. The opinion spread around JPL that the military used a ruler when the missile needed a micrometer and that when the Corporal was turned over to the army, reliability dropped to zero.[35]

The upshot of the conference was a still larger role for JPL. The army established a Corporal Technical Consultants' office (CTC), composed of Firestone, Gilfillan, and JPL members, with JPL as the dominant party. The CTC office facilitated liaison between the contractors and the military, cutting delays in exchanging information that had sometimes reached nine months. JPL appointed a technical coordinator with authority to decide on any changes in operating procedures. The laboratory assumed a larger role in troop training, including writing dozens of detailed procedural manuals. As the agency most familiar with the overall system, the Pasadena laboratory was the logical place to assign these responsibilities; indeed, this step was overdue. In 1952, when JPL had just begun its liaison with contractors and training of troops, an army officer stationed at the laboratory remarked that the Caltech offspring had assumed responsibilities "undreamed of" in the early stages of the Corporal program. In 1954, when a development laboratory's role would normally be ending, JPL found itself most deeply involved.[36]

Reassured that Corporal was being straightened out, the army moved forward with its plans for deployment. The first Corporal battalion, composed of troops who had fired the missile four times at Ft. Bliss, was sent to West Germany in February 1955. This was the first U.S. guided missile outfit to be deployed abroad. The decision, which reversed an earlier army position against sending type 1 Corporals abroad, raised serious questions. Ordnance acknowledged that "the probability of successfully attacking a given target with this system under field conditions is marginal at best." Type 1 Corporals were not deployed "for strictly operational purposes" but for training and logistical experience. It also seems likely that the army calculated the Corporal would awe the Soviet Union, a consideration which may have lain behind General Mickelsen's sense of urgency. One top JPL official reported an army general as being interested almost solely in the Corporal's psychological effect on the Russians. Placing Corporals in Europe coincided with the voguish attention Secretary of State John Foster Dulles and Harvard professor Henry Kissinger and other academic strategic thinkers paid to limited nuclear war from about 1955 through 1957. Tactical nuclear weapons such as Corporal seemed briefly to offer a putative middle path between massive retaliation and conventional warfare. Under such considerations the first Corporal battalions made their debuts in the tense European theater.[37]

Whatever hopes the army had for an operational missile were pinned on Corporal types 2 and 2A, which were basically the same as type 1 but incorporated many refinements of components. Troop training with type 2, which began in late 1954, improved to a reliability rating of 60.6 percent. The improved missile claimed part of the credit. Faithful following of JPL-formulated standard operating procedures was at least equally important; in fact, the troops, going by the book, surpassed JPL engineers, who, like experienced cooks, sometimes erred when they went simply by approximation. The 60-percent rating appeared to exhaust the Corporal's capabilities, short of a major redesign. The system still fell far short of the military characteristics. A weapons evaluation board of the Continental Army Command in November 1956 pronounced Corporal type 2 still "only marginally suitable for use." The chief problem continued to be the unreliability of components—something for which no solution seemed to exist within the compromises that had undermined the system from the start. Other worrisome problems included the system's vulnerability to detection and electronic countermeasures by an enemy, occasional failure of the warhead to arm, and the system's inability to function in rainy weather. Evaluations such as this worried the field commanders who would have to use the product. One American general in Europe asked for the short-range Honest John missiles over Corporals, and others were said to prefer to stick with conventional artillery because they feared the Corporal would reduce their capabilities. Sometimes nothing was better than something. But the army high command, reasoning basically that since there was nothing like Corporal, it therefore represented an American advantage, succeeded in having nine battalions deployed in Europe in 1956 and 1957.[38]

If war came, Corporal would operate in this manner (see figure 2). The missile, housed in a large, cylindrical metal container, arrives on a flatbed trailer. Two wreckers swing the trailer onto the ground, and the troops erect a tent over it. Tracks are attached to the cylinder and the missile is rolled out of the "can." Each working part of the missile is checked out, as is the guidance equipment some distance to the rear. Checkout completed, the erector picks up the 3,074-pound missile and moves it to the launching area, where 6,566 pounds of the highly toxic propellants flow from two trucks into the missile tanks. The 1,500-pound warhead is mated, the erector booms the missile to the vertical, and the crew attaches the missile to the launcher. The final data are fed into the guidance computers, the firing crew takes cover, and the commander in another tent begins the countdown: "Three, two, one, FIRE! Missile Away!"[39]

The Corporal rises slowly, stabilized by its autopilot. After 4 seconds a programmer in the missile tilts the vehicle toward the target. After 25 seconds radar acquires the missile and guides it on the standard trajectory. When the Doppler system senses that the Corporal's velocity is high enough—from 43 to 69 seconds after launch—a radio signal from the ground shuts off the motor. The missile approaches the zenith of its trajectory after 100 seconds of flight, and ground computers measure position and velocity and quickly calculate range errors. A range correction signal is sent to the missile, where it is stored until the bird reenters the atmosphere, at approximately 200 seconds, and the missile executes the command. After another 20 seconds of flight, the missile strikes the target. If the decision to arm has been given, the area is devastated by the force of an atomic bomb possibly three times as powerful as the one dropped on Hiroshima.[40]

Whether Corporal could fulfill this carefully wrought scenario under tactical conditions at even a 60 percent reliability rate remained in doubt. Operations procedures, as well as shipping and storage conditions, were

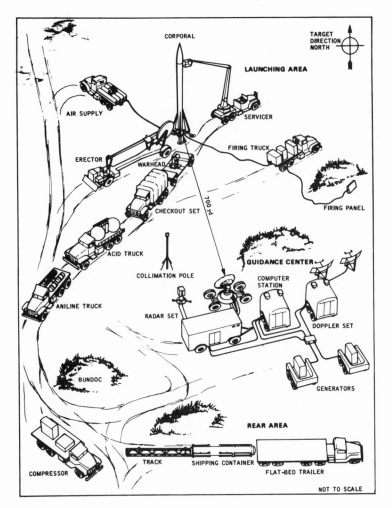

2. Corporal tactical field test.

bound to vary from carefully controlled test patterns, Brig. Gen. G. C. Eddy pointed out, with adverse effects on reliability. The answer—an actual battle test—never came during the decade or so of Corporal's deployment. Tactical atomic war games, such as the mammoth Exercise Sagebrush in Louisiana in 1955, revealed many shortcomings. A JPL observer at Sagebrush, H. J. Wheelock, was seriously concerned whether "army commanders would use the Corporal missile properly." Troops deviated from operating procedures, components continued to break down and replacements proved hard to get, the big and unique equipment presented major problems of concealment, and vulnerability to countermeasures remained disturbingly high. F. W. Mulley, a member of the British Parliament who later became defense minister, reported after observing a test firing in Europe: "My own impression . . . was to doubt whether such weapons could ever be really effective under conditions of active service." A trip to visit Corporal battalions in Europe in 1956 left JPL engineer Bob Terbeck feeling "they would be unable to fire if called upon to do so."[41]

Given these doubts about Corporal's reliability, the question arose whether the missile project had been worth its development and production. JPL defended it. "In a strict sense, the Corporal program was the pioneering missile program of the United States," JPL's final report on the Corporal pointed out. As such the program produced some important advances in the state of the art, particularly in propulsion and electronics. The Corporal propulsion system ranked at the time as the most efficient liquid-propellant version in the United States. The missile also incorporated the first successful, all-electronic radio-guidance system and introduced the idea of range correction. The testing program resulted in a much improved design of electronic components for "ruggedness, reliability, and miniaturization." Missile builders also learned much about missile structures and ground-handling problems. These achievements were undeniable results of the Corporal program. But virtually all of them could have been attained—probably more efficiently and possibly more rapidly—in a strict research and test program. The more troubling question Corporal raised was whether it should have gone into production and deployment. Approximately 1,090 missiles were produced at a total cost of about $226 million; of this about $42 million represented research and development funds, and $26 million went to JPL. The system's reliability under tactical conditions remained highly suspect, and its cumbersome logistics constituted, as JPL acknowledged, a serious drawback. Deployment of Corporal in Europe seemed calculated to produce, as the *London Times* said of some other NATO decisions, "the maximum amount of provocation with the minimum amount of deterrent effect."[42]

Even Corporal's staunchest supporters couched their defense in such terms as "first," "there is nothing else like it," and "the best that could be achieved under the circumstances." Corporal was at best an interim weapon. The army's demand for speed, research uncertainties, and contractor problems had produced a system Pickering characterized as a lash-up of existing equipment and designs: "A modified Corporal E rocket, an all-electronic autopilot derived from the Sergeant test-vehicle project, modified Signal Corps 584 radar, a Doppler link for velocity measurement," and ground-handling vehicles modified from construction and agricultural machines.

That system, in turn, attained at best marginal accuracy under test conditions and probably would have been highly erratic in time of war. Hastily conceived in the atmosphere of NSC-68 and Korea, the Corporal seemed to be more useful for psychological display than usable as a weapon.[43]

Some of Corporal's backers, notably Gilfillan Brothers, thought a thoroughly redesigned Corporal type 3 could alleviate most of these problems. But the laboratory argued that the better approach was clearly to start over with a new product, engineered as a weapon from the beginning with complete systems integration. By 1956, when JPL at last managed to disengage from Corporal, it was already far along on the next rank: Sergeant.

5 ★★

MATURATION OF THE MISSILE PROGRAM

JPL's first major advance in rocketry had come through the solid-propellant JATO units in 1940. Within a decade the laboratory pioneered the first large-scale, solid-propellant motor in the Sergeant test vehicle. Although this Sergeant was shunted aside in favor of the Corporal, JPL knew solid propellants well. Since many of the Corporal's drawbacks as a tactical weapon stemmed from its liquid-propellant system, the laboratory happily shifted its emphasis back to solid propellants when interest developed in Corporal's successor.

In the early 1950s JPL kept a finger in the solid-propellant stream through work on the Loki. An antiaircraft missile based on the Germans' World War II Taifun, Loki was the Army Ordnance Corps' backup in case the Nike failed. Ordnance originally contracted with Bendix Corporation for a liquid Loki, but as research on that project faltered in 1950, the army asked JPL to consider developing a solid-propellant version. Director Louis Dunn put aside most of the work on the Sergeant, which was of a more fundamental nature, to accommodate the immediate applied goals of the Loki weapon.[1]

Loki was a quixotic antiaircraft weapon but a sweet research project. The small rocket measuring about 6 feet long and 3 inches in diameter had a package of high explosives strapped on the end. The Loki was unguided—a direct hit would be lucky—and so it was shot in supersonic barrages. "The theory, I guess," recalled laboratory systems analyst Al Hibbs only half in jest, was that "when it exploded the quantity of shrapnel raised the density in the air so that the airplane's drag would increase so much it would fall to the ground." JPL fired thousands of barrages of Lokis from 1951 through 1956, eventually getting the speed up to 4,500 feet per second. But Nike worked, and the army one day cancelled the Loki, to JPL engineers' disbelief and consternation. "We've got solid propellants burning faster than any other solid propellants ever built," they protested. "Look at the work in dynamic stability, look at the work in aerodynamics." But finally the question was put to John Small, who in effect headed the project at JPL: What could Loki be used for? Small "leaned back, looked up at the ceiling and said 'Fourth of July!'" Loki eventually enjoyed considerable use as a cheap and reliable high-altitude sounding rocket. And it kept JPL current in solid propellants.[2]

The laboratory moved more deeply into solid propellants in 1953 as it pondered a successor to Corporal, which was still undergoing development and testing. JPL broadened a half-million-dollar study of the optimum characteristics of surface-to-surface missiles for army ordnance to include solid-propellant vehicles. Laboratory researchers reported in mid-1953 that solids could equal or exceed liquids in performance, if, as they expected, a satisfactory means of range control could be devised. Ordnance granted JPL $675,250 for a theoretical and experimental study of a solid-propellant missile system. The corps also gave Redstone Arsenal and General Electric smaller amounts for similar studies.[3]

JPL, GE, and Redstone presented their solid-propellant proposals to a special Sergeant evaluation committee in spring 1954. William Pickering, the Corporal project manager, was one of the six members, all of whom came from ordnance research organizations. The committee reaffirmed that the Corporal's deficiencies, particularly its cumbersome ground handling and its susceptibility to countermeasures, precluded even an improved edition's meeting army requirements. The board also briefly considered and then rejected modification of the Nike for surface-to-surface use. Of the proposed new systems, GE's Dobbin, with a marginal radio-guidance system, was the least complete and sophisticated. The arsenal concluded that either of two all-inertial guidance schemes would prove satisfactory.[4]

The JPL proposal showed the advantages of greater ordnance funding, extensive theoretical and experimental analysis in many fields, and the invaluable experience of the Corporal shakedown cruise. That pioneering weapons project especially underscored for the laboratory that "future guided-missile weapons must be considered as true system problems." JPL's proposed Sergeant was accordingly the most detailed, particularly in its consideration of ground-handling equipment to obviate one of Corporal's most nettlesome problems. The laboratory's guidance system, which combined both radio and inertial guidance, also marked an important advance. The radio portion resembled Corporal's but boasted the addition of features that generated pseudorandom noise that could only be decoded by the Sergeant ground system; the system thus was virtually immune to enemy countermeasures. JPL felt that, compared to an all-inertial plan, the radio-inertial system promised quicker development, better accuracy, and lower cost.[5]

The evaluation committee accepted JPL's proposal intact, except for some minor alterations in the propellant. Sergeant development would cost $30 million to $50 million, the committee estimated, and take four to six years. Allowing time for manufacturing and troop training, the Sergeant system should be ready for action by about 1960. Corporal's successor should have a life of about five years.[6]

The army ratified the committee's decisions and gave JPL a new contract for the Sergeant system, beginning in the fall of 1954. Director Dunn proposed a three-step program. The first phase embraced purely research and development goals in which some of the components might bear little resemblance to the final items. In the second phase experimental versions of every major element of the prototype system would undergo testing. The final stage entailed tests of engineering models approximating as closely as possible the final tactical system. He estimated that at least fifty test rounds would be necessary before production began. Suffering daily the trials of the telescoping of Corporal, Dunn sternly warned against the inevitable temptation to "crash" the Sergeant. "A properly planned development program," he argued, would "pay for itself many times over" by avoiding changes in the most expensive areas, production and field modification. Dunn concluded: "It may take a year or two longer to produce the final engineering models, but it will take no longer to deliver the first production of the system elements that really satisfy the desired military characteristics and accomplish the objective of a workhorse missile representing a significant improvement on the Corporal."[7]

These words might have served as Dunn's swan song. In August 1954 he suddenly resigned to take charge of the budding Atlas missile project, the first U.S. intercontinental ballistic missile, at the newly formed Ramo-Wooldridge Corporation. JPL contributed importantly to this turning point in centuries of weaponry in which the destructive power of nuclear weapons was combined with a lightning-quick delivery system across vast distances. Atlas had grown out of the recommendations of the "Teapot Committee," chaired by John von Neumann, the brilliant mathematician, important weapons adviser, and sometime advocate of preventive nuclear war against the Soviet Union. The blue-ribbon committee, which was composed of two future presidential science advisers (George Kistiakowsky and Jerome Wiesner) and influential academics and aerospace industrialists, included three men associated with the laboratory: Dunn; Clark Millikan, chairman of the JPL board; and Allen Puckett of Hughes Aircraft, a former director of wind tunnel research at JPL. Dunn found the laboratory a good training ground for his new role in the expanding missile industry for which his style of management was perhaps better suited. During his eight years as director, JPL had nearly tripled in employees and more than quadrupled in budget. The laboratory changed from an institution devoted chiefly to basic research, albeit in a weapons context, to an intimate link in military research, weapons development, and training.[8]

Dunn's abrupt departure gave Caltech president DuBridge a moment of panic, for the Institute had to find a new director quickly. Dunn suggested William Pickering. The nomination at first surprised DuBridge, since the nominee specialized in electronics, not propulsion; but Pickering had gained broad experience as Corporal project manager. After scanning the country for other possibilities, Caltech administrators appointed Pickering. Du-Bridge extracted a pledge that the new chief would not use JPL as a stepping-stone to industry but would stay at least until the Sergeant project was finished. As it happened Pickering stayed until 1976. Pickering's background reflected and reinforced the deepening involvement of what had once been strictly a jet propulsion laboratory in electronics, and he encouraged JPL to move solidly into science and space a few years hence.[9]

The new director, the laboratory's third foreign-born chief administrator, was born in New Zealand in 1910. Attracted to Caltech by an uncle, Pickering took a Ph.D. in physics in 1936 and joined the Institute faculty in electrical engineering. His early research interests included the cosmic-ray studies that Caltech's Nobel prize-winning president Robert A. Millikan and Victor Neher conducted using balloon-borne sensors. Pickering maintained and broadened this interest after World War II when he sat on several national committees charting research in the upper atmosphere and beyond. The new director had begun work on telemetry and guidance at JPL in 1944 and moved full-time to the laboratory in 1950, although he retained the rank of professor at the campus. More personable and less of a martinet than Dunn, Pickering also was less rigorous as an administrator. He reorganized the laboratory along the lines of disciplines one would find on campus, somewhat de-emphasizing Dunn's project-oriented setup. Some interpreted Pickering's more laissez-faire attitude toward management as indecisiveness and complained that "the last man in got the decision." The managerial diffuseness stemmed in part from the laboratory's rapid growth in size and in fields of endeavor that took place under Pickering. When he returned to the campus as a professor in 1976, he seemed to many observers still a scientist.[10]

The increasing importance of electronics at JPL, which would become most apparent in the space era from 1958 onward, was gathering force during the Sergeant project. Although JPL had chosen a radio-inertial guidance system for the new missile, the Pasadenans' continuing studies indicated that the uncertainties that originally had surrounded the all-inertial system could almost certainly be overcome. They concluded in mid-1955 that an all-inertial system, though somewhat less accurate, warranted parallel development with the radio-inertial format. The laboratory sub-contracted for an all-inertial development with General Electric, which had worked on such a system for its now-defunct Hermes. The booming military interest in longer-range missiles, however, drained funds away from Sergeant in 1955. The army decided that the all-inertial system offered many advantages in tactical use, cancelled the GE contract, and concentrated all-inertial work at JPL. This decision added a year to Sergeant development, pushing the projected production start-up date to 1960.[11]

Turning the Sergeant to all-inertial guidance freed the JPL engineers who had worked on the radio-guidance portion and created an imperative to keep them occupied. The laboratory sensed an opportunity in the notorious competition between the army and the air force to develop an intermediate-range ballistic missile (IRBM). JPL suggested to its friends in the army missile center at Huntsville, Alabama, that it modify the Sergeant radio-inertial system as a backup for Jupiter's all-inertial scheme. The Sergeant format offered virtual immunity to countermeasures, while the radio-guidance system for the air force's Thor was vulnerable enough that 500 to 600 miles of its range could be denied. JPL's proposed system was possible—indeed, it had been largely proved on specially modified Corporals. The laboratory proposed, in essence, that the radio scheme the army had rejected first for Sergeant and then for Jupiter, and which JPL had agreed to abandon in favor of Sergeant's all-inertial, should serve as a Jupiter backup. Maj. Gen. John B. Medaris, the commander at Huntsville, liked the scheme. Intrigued by the idea of combining JPL's guidance ability with the Army Ballistic Missile Agency's propellant research, he wanted the laboratory to become part of his operation. Pickering insisted, however, that JPL retain its autonomy. JPL began work on the radio-guidance backup early in 1956 and continued until 1958, when Jupiter lost out to Thor. This work gave the laboratory's radio section experience which they could capitalize on in long-distance space communication.[12]

The army's interest in Jupiter, thought observers such as Herbert York, could be traced to the space-flight ambitions of Wernher von Braun and his colleagues. JPL also found the space bug infectious. The laboratory participated in the proposal for Project Orbiter, the army's unsuccessful proposal for an earth satellite for the International Geophysical Year (IGY) coming up in 1957. The Pasadena group also collaborated with the Huntsville corps on the reentry test vehicle (RTV), which demonstrated the feasibility of an ablation-type nose cone (one which peels away as the missile undergoes the terrific aerodynamic heating upon reentry into the atmosphere). These efforts—important preliminaries to space ventures—would bear fruit and markedly alter the course of the laboratory in the late 1950s.[13]

By 1956 the Jet Propulsion Laboratory reached a crossroad. It had committed itself to two major missile projects simultaneously, Sergeant and Jupiter, plus scattered other research. That volume of work demanded a budget of more than $24 million for fiscal year 1957, an increase of 75 percent over the $13.7 million in 1956. Most of that went directly to weapons development; $6 million was programmed for supporting research, much of it related to missile problems. The laboratory predicted the number of employees would increase from 1,300 to about 2,000. Caltech, by contrast, had a budget apart from JPL of $11.6 million in fiscal year 1957. The child was outgrowing the parent. Some Institute trustees decided the time had come for a closer look at JPL.[14]

The budget hike spurred the chairman of the trustees, Albert B. Ruddock, of Santa Barbara, to question the Caltech-JPL connection. Ruddock, who had just succeeded Los Angeles lawyer James R. Page who had headed the board for thirteen years, was more attuned to faculty opinion than most trustees. Ruddock drafted a proposed policy statement in which he emphasized the nature of the university. Caltech's primary responsibility lay in offering first-rate scientific education and in performing basic research which in themselves represented notable patriotic contributions. "Except under the most stringent conditions of emergency, this service should not be diluted or complicated or endangered in any respect," he said. JPL, however, possessed "a most limited educational value" for CIT. The Institute had agreed to operate JPL and then to move into weapons development because the military needed help in the perceived cold war emergency. But enough time had now elapsed so that the federal government should have developed its own scientific and technical staffs. If the government had not done so, it should take corrective steps to progressively diminish JPL activities. "Service in emergency, yes, by all means," Ruddock said, "but perpetually spells to me something drastically and radically wrong."[15]

Lee DuBridge vigorously defended the JPL tie in two long letters to Ruddock and in a formal statement to the board. The laboratory no longer was a drain on Caltech, he argued. "JPL has become a completely separate operation," he said. "Two or three individual faculty members" still spent time at JPL, but all "the others have withdrawn to the campus." JPL provided some small assets, chiefly the high-speed wind tunnels, but DuBridge did not argue that there was any substantial overlapping of interest or intertwining of programs between the campus and the laboratory. Then why should Caltech continue to lend its name to JPL?[16]

"Yes, we are holding the government's elbow in a field where the government is not fully competent to stand on its own," the Caltech president said. As a spokesman for the national scientific elite, DuBridge stood in the tradition of Vannevar Bush and similar figures who had attempted at the close of World War II to give the most prestigious universities a substantially free hand and dominant role in federal research. A decade's experience had not changed DuBridge's mind. "I doubt if a government ever can be a good research manager," he said. "The government should not attempt to run its own research facilities, but should contract out all of them." Nor did Du-Bridge, a veteran cold war science organizer, doubt the value or necessity of JPL weapons projects. He felt that CIT, like other leading universities that managed military research centers, fulfilled a patriotic obligation. To him the army "beyond question" needed Caltech to manage JPL. The only alternatives he could envision—government or industrial management—would not work. Civil service status would entail too much red tape, salaries too low to attract good people, and a mass exodus from the present staff. Industrial firms would not want to operate a research facility unless they received production guarantees, which would compromise JPL as a source of "unbiased" advice to the government.[17]

DuBridge argued the army's case so vigorously that Ruddock wondered whether he was speaking from the viewpoint of the government or the Institute. Might they not say with Priscilla, "speak for yourself, John," the chairman parried. "I think it is a little bit of both," DuBridge replied. "Those of us who have been connected with JPL and with government affairs" were proud both of the laboratory's service to the government and of the credit it had reflected on Caltech. DuBridge liked to have the JPL staff "as a part of the 'family' even though they are possibly cousins rather than brothers."[18]

The JPL prodigy, moreover, had "never failed to carry his share of the family budget," the CIT president noted. Indeed, a cash nexus helped undergird John Alden's advocacy. Caltech received an overhead sum for its management of JPL, which in 1955 amounted to $500,000 on the $12.5 million laboratory budget. That sum, the equivalent of income from an endowment of about $10 million at contemporary interest rates, represented almost 5 percent of the Institute's budget, not including JPL, in 1956. Even more important, this money fell in the category that universities desired most: unrestricted income that could be used at the school's discretion. A divorce from JPL would mean a "serious, though not disastrous" loss of annual income, DuBridge continued. Financial reasons should not dictate continuation, he said, but it was "financially easier to continue." Getting the Institute's services at 4 percent of the laboratory budget was a "bargain" for the government.[19]

This presented an anomaly: As JPL grew, and the overhead Caltech derived from the laboratory increased, the connection between JPL and the campus declined. The cost formula Caltech used, in common with most other university contracts with the federal government, followed the principle of "no profit and no loss." No problem arose with costs for staff, building, and services on the laboratory premises, which were charged directly to the government. If JPL were closed down, the government would be liable for all termination costs; Institute costs would be minimal. The question became sticky with the funds Caltech received for campus overhead charged to the laboratory. Some argued, as DuBridge knew, that the Institute in effect turned a profit on the laboratory. JPL costs to the campus were computed on a basis similar to other grants and contracts; each was supposed to bear its pro rata share of university overhead. "We like to think of it in terms of a sharing of essential costs rather than in terms of making a profit," the president said.[20]

But the very size of the JPL budget in relation to the Institute's, and the laboratory's separation from the campus physically and programmatically, put consideration of CIT-JPL finances in a separate class from normal contracts. If the Institute's overall budget were $19 million, and JPL's portion of that were $12 million, the JPL contract would bear twelve-nineteenths of the cost of operating the business office. This formula overstated the JPL burden, for while the CIT business office exercised general oversight, the laboratory had maintained its own large business office since the late 1940s. If JPL were terminated, the campus business office, DuBridge conceded, would not shrink by twelve-nineteenths. Other services were less plausible than the business office. General Institute operations, such as the library, president's office and its auxiliary functions, and deans' offices, would operate in substantially the same form whether or not JPL existed. Some of these, such as the library, felt some effect from JPL. But many of these services, such as the deans' offices, felt no impact. Even the president's office had but minimal involvement. DuBridge visited the laboratory at widely separated intervals, and both Dunn and Pickering confirmed that the president during the 1950s dealt with JPL only on the most important policy questions, generally those having to do with relations with the government and the community.[21]

The pressure of time cut short the first significant dialogue in a decade on the CIT-JPL relationship. At least one trustee, Leonard S. Lyon, favored the Institute's withdrawing from the laboratory because it did not enhance campus educational efforts. Some other trustees favored continuing the relationship on grounds of its contribution to national defense. DuBridge felt the increased budget had to be accepted or rejected in toto; no tapering off or compromise approach seemed possible to him for 1957. He indicated, however, that future budgets would probably drop to $15 million to $20 million annually. The Jet Propulsion Laboratory board, in one of its infrequent meetings, recommended approval of the new budget. The trustees agreed, allowing Pickering to complete budget negotiations with the army a few days later.[22]

The board of trustees appears likely to have voted for continuing the campus-laboratory relationship in any case. It was unfortunate, however, that the issues Ruddock raised had not received more thorough discussion. The ramifications of JPL's importance to national defense received uncritical acceptance. The ordnance corps almost always praised JPL's work highly. The value of JPL's projects, while of undoubted importance to the army, occupied a less obvious position in the realm of national defense and global policy. The shortcomings and dangers of Corporal were clear in 1956, and the Jupiter radio-inertial guidance system was only a backup; Sergeant's value remained to be assessed as its development progressed and the strategic environment changed.[23]

If one supported these weapons projects, it did not necessarily follow that only a university-affiliated laboratory could develop them. Some industrial firms, such as Ramo-Wooldridge, conducted research effectively. Alternatively, JPL might have been converted into a nonprofit corporation, such as RAND. Moreover, the military services boasted a better research record than men like DuBridge perceived. The Naval Research Laboratory received high marks, and the Naval Ordnance Test Station at China Lake, California, developed an effective antiaircraft missile, the Sidewinder. The army's Huntsville contingent, while enjoying an inflated reputation, pioneered in many aspects of missilery and ran the Redstone and Jupiter projects capably. Furthermore, government laboratories, which functioned as updated arsenals, provided an essential yardstick to measure the cost performance of industrial contractors. National defense needs, however they might be assessed, could have been fulfilled had JPL adopted different institutional arrangements.[24]

For half-a-million dollars a year the army enjoyed the prestige reflected by being able to say that one of the world's premier scientific institutions worked for it. The army was also paying for a historical accident; the legal arrangement continued to raise a protective umbrella analogous to the status of a nonprofit corporation even though the original rationale no longer held. The army was paying partly for keeping JPL within its orbit and for not allowing an attractive research institution to drift into a rival camp. JPL and Caltech administrators had acknowledged in 1952 that weapons development had deflected the laboratory from its appropriate course and had pledged that JPL would return to its proper role after Corporal. But the temptations of further weapons work and the dangers of disengagement proved difficult to resist. JPL and Caltech were to a degree captives. So long as the laboratory not merely performed classified work but was integrated into the army weapons system, neither Caltech nor JPL could offer or receive the benefits that both should have derived from their affiliation.

The Jet Propulsion Laboratory was able to run the Sergeant development more smoothly and much closer to schedule than it had Corporal. Ample problems harassed the laboratory, of course, but they were more managerial than technical. External influences made a heavier impact on the Sergeant program than on Corporal. The army, having built up its in-house guided missile capabilities since the early 1950s, exercised much more supervision over technical and contract affairs than previously. The paperwork got so bad that even the chief or ordnance felt moved to complain. Complicating things still more, the army's guided missile operation at Huntsville underwent two major reorganizations and several minor ones during the life of the project. Erratic funding, reflecting Sergeant's relatively lower priority than the expensive ICBM and IRBM projects, probably delayed the tactical missile by about half a year. The funding shortfall in 1958 proved especially serious, as JPL feared for a time it would have to furlough some Sergeant engineers.[25]

Mindful that Corporal's transition from development to production had been what Pickering termed a "miserable mess," the research institution tried a new co-contractor arrangement. Under this plan the army selected the production contractor early in the development phase; the firm then sent a cadre of engineers to work shoulder-to-shoulder with JPL staff during the design process. The company also would do some of the more routine engineering on its own. Pickering felt that the arrangement would perhaps slow development, but he willingly adopted the idea in the hope that it would ease the transition and perhaps speed production. On JPL's recommendation the army chose Sperry Gyroscope Company of Great Neck, New York, as the contractor. The firm, which had considerable experience in guided missile electronics and production, set up a special division, Sperry Utah Engineering Laboratories (SUEL) in Salt Lake City, for Sergeant. SUEL's aggressive actions encouraged JPL, and the co-contractor relationship began harmoniously. But as the Sergeant entered the engineering model stage in 1959 and 1960, growing animosity between the laboratory and the firm seriously impeded the smooth transition the arrangement should have fostered.[26]

JPL had organizational problems of its own. Pickering succeeded Dunn as laboratory director just as Sergeant got underway, so JPL faced a shakedown cruise with a new director and a new project at the same time. Robert J. Parks, a former Pickering student, followed him as chief of the guidance and control section and became Sergeant project manager. Pickering's research-oriented reorganization of the laboratory may also have impeded project management somewhat. Of greater importance, however, was the increasing fragmentation of JPL as its activities diversified. During the period of the Sergeant development, 1954 to 1960, the Pasadena institution also found itself heavily committed for a time to the Jupiter program. Moreover, JPL plunged into its new environment, space. This entailed a succession of large projects, such as Explorer and Pioneer, a shift from army cognizance to the new NASA, and rapid institutional growth. Sergeant, a major project for JPL in 1954, was gradually displaced in importance.[27]

On balance, however, the development of Sergeant moved efficiently. JPL's phaseout in mid-1960 was only two months late, and part of the delay was attributable to managerial troubles with the contractor. As innovative in concept as Corporal, Sergeant enjoyed the great advantage of succeeding Corporal. The development of the liquid-fuel missile had returned a store of data that benefited Sergeant designers. Corporal also yielded plenty of valuable negative information; it told JPL how not to build a missile system. The need for sophisticated systems engineering came through strongly. With Sergeant JPL acquired essential experience in systems engineering that helped show the path for spacing technology.[28]

The considerations surrounding JPL's design of the solid-propellant motor afforded a good example of how trade-offs may have compromised the performance of a particular component but produced a better overall system. The laboratory's design was based on the principle of the case-bonded internal-burning star it had pioneered in the late 1940s. Knowledge of propellant characteristics had expanded considerably during the 1950s through such programs as Loki at JPL, Hermes at GE (which had been augmented by disgruntled JPL engineers), and various projects at the solid-propellant manufacturer Thiokol Chemical Corporation. The laboratory's studies indicated that long, thin missiles performed better than short, thick ones; the optimum diameter of the motor lay in the range from 28 to 36 inches. JPL settled on 31 inches, primarily because that was the size of the atomic warhead. Since the motor case formed the outer shell of the bottom half of the missile, the motor necessarily followed the warhead's dimensions. JPL and Thiokol experimented with various propellant refinements in an attempt to improve performance. A regressive-thrust motor had to be abandoned because it caused too much aerodynamic heating; a progressive-thrust design induced axial acceleration beyond the capability of the guidance system. JPL thus returned to a constant-thrust motor. The burning time did not meet the optimum, but it was chosen to insure satisfactory range. As development progressed, the motor's length declined from 171.5 inches to 141 inches and the weight by nearly 20 percent. The final JPL design ranked as a moderate-performance rather than a high-performance motor because of the system compromises, but it was adequate for its task.[29]

During the motor work an important managerial principle was also established. When JPL and Thiokol disagreed over who would make final decisions on motor design, the Huntsville supervisers ruled in favor of the laboratory. Armed with this authority, JPL could exercise an overall system judgment it had not enjoyed until the last days of Corporal development.[30]

The elements of the Sergeant system began to come together in the series of eight feasibility flight tests in 1956 and 1957. The series began in January 1956, about six months late, because of a funding shortage and problems in fabricating a strong yet light motor case. Extensive static testing of motors and hundreds of computer simulations and wind tunnel firings of Sergeant scale models had preceded the feasibility series. JPL also flew some Sergeant components on Corporal tests. The 1956–57 series gave assurance that the propulsion system, airframe, and drag brakes provided an adequate foundation for further system development. Many refinements remained, of course; for instance, the Sergeant's nose gradually took on a finer, longer shape. But the final configuration closely resembled the feasibility test models.[31]

Various improvements over Corporal facilitated development. To reduce vibration JPL packaged subsystem units in nearly solid blocks formed of hollow shells instead of flimsy internal skeletons. Transistorized electronics were used throughout, and automatic checkout equipment permitted quick verification of circuits' readiness for launch. One of the principal innovations was the drag brake system. Drag brakes were necessary for range control because, unlike liquid propellants, a solid-propellant motor could not be shut off quickly to insure accurate range. At a signal from the guidance system, the drag brakes, located about midway on the missile body, were actuated. Four paddle-shaped flaps, weighing a total of several hundred pounds, clicked out from the missile body with camera-shutter speed. Creating a drag force of sixteen tons, they slowed the missile to the proper velocity so that it would impact near the target. The drag brakes presented some developmental problems, such as vibration levels higher than anticipated and a balky hydraulic actuating scheme. When Sperry seemed stymied by these challenges in 1957, JPL brought the drag brake development back to Pasadena and completed it satisfactorily.[32]

The feasibility tests were encouraging enough that they threatened JPL's philosophy of orderly development. Secretary of the Army Wilbur Brucker visited the laboratory in August 1957. Worried by Corporal's approaching obsolescence, he pressed for an earlier availability date than October 1962. He seemed to feel that JPL was "off in their ivory tower engineering the Sergeant to perfection and was not being realistic about the compromise between the availability date and the quality of the product." The JPL staff rejoined that they aimed for perfection not for its own sake but to meet the military characteristics. Any shortening of the development schedule would preclude meeting those standards. No one wanted a repetition of the Corporal experience. As a result of these discussions and further ruminations, the army left the development schedule essentially intact but compressed training and production to call for readiness by August 1961.[33]

The flight tests of the experimental model in 1958 and 1959 brought JPL's

Sergeant participation close to completion. During the first part of this block, the final feasibility testing took place. During the second, testing of the missile as an integrated system and tests for reliability took precedence. By now the all-inertial guidance system was well advanced. Details of the system remained shrouded in security classifications twenty years after its development, but the principles were clear. A special type of dead-reckoning system, the inertial format needed no ground link. Three mutually perpendicular accelerometers were mounted on a platform in a compartment between the warhead and the drag brakes. Velocities were computed from the accelerations, and positions were derived from the velocities. These data were fed into a computer mounted in the missile, which, in turn, calculated corrective maneuvers. For the computer to interpret the data properly, two things were necessary: the accelerometers' orientation had to be known precisely, and the effect of the Earth's gravitational force had to be accounted for, which could be accomplished only on the basis of prior estimates of this force. This posed one of the chief problems in designing an all-inertial system: stabilizing the platform with respect to a known frame of reference, such as the Earth, by means of gyroscopes and servomechanisms. Parks and some associates made an important stabilization breakthrough which speeded the system's development. Although the inertial system had the obvious advantage of immunity from countermeasures, JPL still felt that troop safety required that the decision to arm the warhead should be made on the ground. The Sergeant thus retained a special secure ground link over which the arming decision was transmitted.[34]

With the inertial system and other components promising higher reliability than Corporal, JPL's reconsideration of tactical ground-handling equipment bore fruit by improving mobility. The choice of a solid propellant greatly simplified ground-handling equipment and procedures; for example, equipment worth one million dollars, ranging from forty-three trucks to eighty-two pairs of protective gloves, could be eliminated from a typical Corporal battalion.[35]

Sergeant also had an advantage over Corporal in that ground-handling equipment could be designed from the start of missile engineering instead of being adapted after the fact. Originally the laboratory planned to transport the missile much like the Corporal, intact except for the warhead. But the 34-foot-long, 11,400-pound Sergeant would require special equipment and could not be transported by air as the military characteristics dictated. JPL therefore decided to transport the missile in four sections—warhead and fuse, guidance, motor, and fins—that could ride on standard army cargo trucks. Besides vastly improving ground mobility, the four-section concept exceeded the air-transportation guidelines the army sought and made camouflage much easier. When the sections arrived at the launching site, they were quickly joined on a specially designed erector-launcher. JPL originated the concept of this piece of equipment, based on a 2 ½-ton tractor-trailer, and then turned it over to Sperry for improvement and production. The erector-launcher raised the missile automatically to the 75-degree elevation for firing. Two separate vans near the launching site automatically checked out electronic circuits before launch and controlled the firing. By contrast with Corporal's clumsiness, the Sergeant could go into action as quickly as one hour after a road march—a capability that exceeded the military characteristics. Thus by the completion of the twenty-two experimental rounds in late 1959, Sergeant seemed well on its way to fulfilling the army's hopes for a second-generation missile.[36]

But then managerial problems struck that threatened to undo the technical progress. By 1959 JPL found itself virtually the odd man out in the army-Sperry-JPL triangle. The initially good relations between JPL and Sperry had seriously deteriorated. Sperry apparently could not persuade some of its top management to move to the Utah plant. The firm also had serious organizational problems (for example, it lacked a Sergeant project manager with overall authority until spring 1960), tried to use plants spread thirty miles apart, and relied too much on engineers just out of school. JPL also felt Sperry tended to completely redo laboratory designs even when simpler refinements would have been adequate. By 1958 JPL engineers were complaining vociferously of SUEL's poor workmanship and "woefully incompetent" management. JPL engineers repeatedly pointed out problems. But as the official army history of Sergeant put it: "Sperry managers stubbornly insisted that the company was completely capable of running the program without JPL's help and proceeded to cover up the existence of major technical problems and system deficiencies in verbose, sales-brochure-type progress reports."[37]

Whatever Sperry's own problems, JPL was not blameless. The laboratory engineers' abilities tended to encourage a condescending attitude on their part toward their counterparts in production firms. "JPL never had anybody they considered to be a good contractor," JPL business manager Val C. Larsen, Jr., recalled. "They all turned out to be S.O.B.'s after the first one or two jobs." JPL attitudes stemmed in part from a natural pride in their work on Sergeant and particularly when the laboratory, along with the Huntsville group, had pulled American chestnuts out of the fire with Explorer 1. But pride sometimes crossed the line into hubris. The JPL commitment to Jupiter and the glamorous Explorer and Pioneer also distracted the laboratory from full attention to Sergeant. Partly because of this competition, JPL was three to six months late getting completed designs to Sperry. The laboratory's tendency to go it alone, reinforced by a sense of prerogatives due it by virtue of its systems authority, bred what the army termed an "inherent exclusiveness" that sometimes impeded cooperation with other contrac-tors.[38]

The co-contractors' woes were exacerbated by the heavy hand of the army. The ordnance corps, particularly the industrial division, displayed an in-creasing volition to substitute its designs for those of the systems contractor it had chosen. After JPL had spent three years engineering a container in which to transport the missile, Picatinny Arsenal abruptly began work on a completely different model. Ordnance replaced the suspension system of the erector-launcher with one that soon proved less satisfactory than the JPL model. When the army forced the laboratory to accept a subcontract for the launcher from American Machine & Foundry (AMF), which had submitted the lowest bid but could not promise the standards the laboratory outlined, Pickering and General Medaris engaged in a testy exchange. Pickering: "If AMF is the selected contractor, the laboratory will assume that it is [in] fact relieved of the accountability for schedule, quality, and compatibility for this portion of the Sergeant system." Medaris: "I deeply regret the fact that you felt compelled to write [as you did] . . . and I cannot agree." The army's "breakout" plan added to Sperry's woes. Three arsenals in diverse parts of the country got SUEL engineering data which they then used to seek com-petitive bids for Sergeant production in case war broke out and put the Utah plant hors de combat. Implemented before Sperry completed its engineer-ing, the breakout plan amounted to a premature invasion of proprietary rights and contributed to the firm's demoralization.[39]

On the whole, however, Sperry and the army drew closer together. JPL stood in a different relationship to the army after it was transferred to NASA on January 1, 1959. Army ordnance resented losing the laboratory, whose technical successes now became in a sense an irritant. SUEL's long-range interest lay with the army, particularly the industrial division. In spring 1960 the industrial section at Huntsville assumed cognizance of the Sergeant project, over the objections of the research and development division, which had been JPL's mainstay within the army. Brig. Gen. John G. Shinkle, the army officer who had the most direct supervision over Sergeant, seemed especially anxious to prove that the army-Sperry team could stand on its own feet without the JPL crutch. The laboratory had planned to reduce the number of engineers assigned to Sergeant in 1960 from 110 to 40 during the year. Sperry insisted, however, that it could handle the project after June 30 without any JPL assistance. Shinkle agreed. Pickering acknowledged that SUEL had improved in 1960, but he still doubted they could handle the entire project. Nonetheless, he reaffirmed his faith in the design of the system, wished Sperry and the army good luck, and put all his Sergeant engineers to work for NASA.[40]

During the next year the Sergeant program seriously deteriorated. The experimental flight tests slipped behind schedule and yielded alarming re-sults. The large range errors would "hit the fan at DA [Department of the Army] level," said the chief of ordnance, Lt. Gen. J. H. Hinrichs, "we will have to have some good answers." "JPL should be in the act," he said. But the former Sergeant engineers were immersed in NASA projects. Production began haltingly at Sperry in 1962. The Sergeant continued to be listed as a limited production version until 1968, when enough of the wrinkles were ironed out to make it finally qualify as a shelf item.[41]

In Sergeant JPL gave its sponsors a tool with which to implement the strategic theories of the 1950s. Sergeant battalions were deployed in the two tactical fields where the United States extended its nuclear umbrella, West-ern Europe and South Korea. As a more reliable system than Corporal, Sergeant etched with new clarity the dilemma of American reliance on nuclear weapons, whether strategic or tactical. Echoing George Kennan, Eisenhower worried privately that "the more the services depend on nuclear weapons the dimmer the President's hope gets to contain any limited war or to keep it from spreading into general war." In the NATO war games of 1955—aptly named Carte Blanche—simulated atomic bombs were em-ployed for the first time. Within 48 hours 335 such blasts were reported across western Germany, the Lowlands, and eastern France, thereby obliter-ating any meaningful distinction between tactical and strategic nuclear war-fare. This exercise brought home the truth of French Premier Henri Queuille's observation of 1949: if America again liberated Western Europe, "you probably would be liberating a corpse." Under these circumstances Western Europeans were torn between two fears—that in the event of a Warsaw Pact invasion the United States would not come to the nuclear rescue, or on the other hand, that it would. By the late 1950s tactical nuclear war no longer seemed so fashionable to American nuclear theorists, and some of them, such as Henry Kissinger, recanted their earlier enthusiasms for the doctrine. But neither Eisenhower nor his successors, despite notions of "flexible response," were able fully to resolve the dilemma of the nuclear tripwire.[42]

The Sergeant program gave JPL invaluable experience in system en-gineering that underwrote its future eminence. But the headaches and lim-itations of weapons development convinced Pickering that Sergeant should be the laboratory's last weapons system. He feared that further such work would reduce JPL to little more than a "job shop" for the army. The labora-tory needed a program that would enable it to stay in the technological vanguard. Thus, not out of dissatisfaction with its role in engineering weap-ons for the cold war but from reasons of perceived institutional necessity, JPL took a momentous turn in its history. The new scene of technological challenge was in space.

6 ★★

WINDOW TO SPACE: EXPLORERS AND PIONEERS

Although most of JPL's research and development activities in the 1940s and 1950s were devoted to terrestrial missilery, space exploration still haunted many of the laboratory's scientists and engineers. Frank Malina and Martin Summerfield calculated in 1945 that it was possible to build a rocket that would "escape earth's atmosphere." Summerfield joined Howard Seifert and Mark Mills on a more detailed study of the physics of long-range rockets in 1947. And JPL personnel teamed with the German V-2 group at White Sands in 1949 to launch the Bumper-WAC, the "first recorded man-made object to reach extraterrestrial space." Passing the time between test flights at White Sands in 1950, some JPL engineers scribbled back-of-the-envelope calculations that showed it was possible to cluster some Loki rockets on a Corporal missile and land an empty beer can on the moon. JPL director William Pickering was active throughout the 1940s and '50s on the Upper Atmosphere Research Panel, which sponsored research using high-altitude sounding rockets.[1]

Earth-orbiting satellites, whose principles had been known since Isaac Newton, had approached technical feasibility with the development of rocketry during World War II. Any object set moving outside the Earth in a proper direction and at a proper speed will travel around the Earth in an elliptical orbit, where centrifugal force exactly balances the pull of gravity. The first requirement for orbiting a satellite was attaining the proper speed. Intercontinental missiles attained speeds of about 4 miles per second and went out into space about 800 miles before falling back to Earth. Satellites require a speed of 5 miles per second. (To escape the Earth's gravitational field and travel to the moon requires an initial speed of 7 miles per second, planetary flights only a little more.) Some scientists at the RAND Corporation and the navy had proposed building satellites in the late 1940s. By 1954, as the United States initiated a crash program to develop intercontinental ballistic missiles and the scientific and military uses of satellites became apparent, satellite proposals neared the hardware stage.[2]

Scientists won approval for a satellite as a U.S. contribution to the International Geophysical Year coming up from July 1, 1957, to December 31, 1958. JPL became involved in the venture when the Army Ballistic Missile Agency (ABMA) and the Office of Naval Research (ONR) sent their proposal for the joint effort, Project Orbiter, to Pasadena for review in late 1954. Orbiter's first stage would be an uprated Redstone missile. The remaining stages would consist of Lokis, the small, solid-propellant antiaircraft rockets developed at JPL; the second stage would use twenty-four Lokis; the third, six; and the fourth, one Loki and the 5-pound payload. If any one of the thirty-one Lokis failed, however, the satellite would not attain orbit. Homer Stewart, the Caltech aerodynamics professor who also supervised systems analysis at JPL, suggested that Orbiter use instead a smaller number of the more powerful and more reliable Sergeant rocket motors, scaled down from 31 inches in diameter to 6 inches in diameter. Revised accordingly, the Orbiter proposal presented a strong case based on proved propulsion technology. It almost certainly would have made possible a launch by August 1957, and possibly earlier. This date assumed importance in retrospect, for Sputnik was launched in October 1957.[3]

Technology was not the only consideration, however; Eisenhower wanted the program to be nonmilitary. The former general consistently stressed the peaceful and scientific uses of space in contrast to the military and prestige-grounded arguments advanced in some quarters. Eisenhower's announcement gave a strong advantage to Vanguard, a dark-horse entry from the Naval Research Laboratory, despite its smaller rocket which was still under development. Vanguard, however, boasted superior electronics technology and therefore could return more sophisticated scientific data. JPL and ONR scrambled to improve Orbiter, which had offered only optical tracking, with beefed-up tracking and telemetry components. But too late; Orbiter succumbed to Vanguard. Ironically Stewart had to preside over the demise of the ABMA-ONR-JPL proposal which he had been instrumental in formulating. He chaired the Ad Hoc Committee on Special Capabilities, a subgroup of the Defense Department's guided missiles committee, which refereed the competition between Orbiter and Vanguard. In addition to concern for a nonmilitary rocket instead of an adaptation of a military missile, the committee members reached differing technical judgments that reflected in part interservice rivalries. The two army-designated committeemen—Stewart and Clifford C. Furnas, chancellor of the State University of New York at Buffalo—strongly supported Orbiter. But the other six members voted to make Vanguard the first American satellite program. When Sputnik upstaged Vanguard while Orbiter waited in the wings, the decision became one of the most controversial of the space age. It also provided an early glimpse of some of the competing objectives of the space program, in particular the frequent conflict between scientific and national security goals.[4]

JPL and the other Orbiter backers chafed under the decision and tried to get it reversed. But Orbiter remained moribund. Yet through personal and institutional connections in the communications aspects of missilery, JPL remained near the center of action. Pickering was a member of the technical panel for the earth satellite program that was organized by the U.S. IGY committee in October 1955, and he chaired the working group on tracking and computation. The JPL director thus found himself in the anomalous position of promoting a competing technical proposal but organizing operational support for Vanguard.[5]

JPL and ABMA found an institutional outlet for their Orbiter studies in the reentry test vehicle (RTV), which, by a circuitous course, eventually produced the first American space triumph. ABMA, led by Wernher von Braun and General Medaris, was developing the Jupiter, a medium-range ballistic missile that was engaged in a notorious competition with the air force's Thor. To counteract the intense heat the Jupiter encountered as it reentered the atmosphere at high velocity, ABMA planned to use a blunt ablation-type nose cone, in which the various layers burned away during reentry. The nose-cone test missile (RTV) was extraordinarily similar to Orbiter; indeed, the missile needed only a fourth-stage rocket and payload to create a satellite. JPL's Orbiter electronics proposals proved readily adaptable to the RTV program. The laboratory's telemetry could send data back to ground control on the heating effects of the missile during flight, and its tracking mechanism made it possible to recover the nose cone at the end of the flight.[6]

The main JPL electronic contribution was Microlock, a phase-locked loop tracking system. The innovation in Microlock was its ability to lock to a very low-level signal; under ideal conditions it could lock on a signal as low as a milliwatt nearly 6,000 miles away. The origins of Microlock could be traced to some of the early guidance and information theory research for the Corporal. Researching the high-frequency properties of transistors, JPL engineers discovered they operated well but could put out only 50 milliwatts. Such low power at first seemed to be useless, but paper calculations followed by experiments demonstrated that, if an appropriate phase-locked receiver were used, the signal might be received from as far as 1,000 miles in free space transmission. As adapted for the RTV, Microlock would also extract information from five minimum-weight telemetry channels. Microlock was an interesting example of how advances in hardware sometimes led to a string of conceptual innovations.[7]

The RTV also incorporated JPL's skills with solid propellants in the upper stages of the launch vehicle. The first stage employed a modified Redstone missile, which was designated Jupiter C.* For the second stage, eleven small-scale Sergeant motors were mounted annularly inside a tub; the three motors of the third stage fit inside the second stage, and the fourth-stage motor and payload sat in the center of the two outer rings. When each stage fired, it broke the shear pins that attached it to the previous assembly and let that stage fall back to Earth. For greater accuracy the upper stages were enclosed in a spinning tub that was powered by two battery-driven electric motors. The tub began spinning at 550 rpm before takeoff; about 70 seconds into the flight, the speed gradually increased to about 750 rpm. This procedure eliminated "resonance between the spin frequency and the natural bending frequencies of the missile," which increased as the first-stage propellants were consumed. The spinning tub imposed severe vibration and centrifugal force on the second stage. Extensive ground testing under simulated flight conditions showed the motors performed well, but small changes in the nozzle design were necessary. Throughout the design of the upper stages, highly accurate positioning and balance were necessary to curb vibration and deflection.[8]

The lash-up seemed somewhat "Rube Goldbergish," in the words of Eisenhower's second science adviser, George Kistiakowsky of Harvard University. But it worked. The first RTV was fired on September 20, 1956, from Cape Canaveral, Florida. Some Pentagon officials watched nervously because they feared the RTV was a ruse for a clandestine satellite launching. The first RTV set records for American missiles to that point: an altitude of 682 miles and a distance of 3,350 miles. All the test objectives were met. The motor demonstrated the desired power, the aerodynamic design worked satisfactorily, and the Microlock system performed very close to theory. Since the army was interdicted from attempting a satellite, the fourth stage was loaded with sandbags. Had the RTV contained a small Sergeant motor for just a little extra kick, JPL and ABMA would have put a satellite in orbit— a year before the Soviet Union.[9]

*The Jupiter and Jupiter C nomenclature is often confusing, owing to bureaucratic sleight of hand used as weapons in the interservice missile rivalries. The key point is that the RTV, Orbiter, and Explorer all used the Redstone missile as a first stage. In these series the Redstone was designated Jupiter C by Medaris because they were therefore accorded a higher priority at the cape. The actual Jupiter, an intermediate-range ballistic missile, was used to propel the Pioneer satellites of 1958 and 1959. The common denominator in these series was that JPL's spinning cluster of high-speed stages was mounted on both the Redstone (or Jupiter C) and Jupiter missiles. The entire enterprise bore the designation Juno, with Explorer being Juno 1 and Pioneer being Juno 2. (See John B. Medaris with Arthur Gordon, *Countdown for Decision* [New York, 1960], p. 119.)

In the second RTV test, May 15, 1957, the missile took an erratic course because of a guidance malfunction shortly before the fuel cutoff. The nose cone was tracked to its point of impact but was not recovered. (The missilemen suspected sharks beat them to the cone since on some subsequent tests jaws had ripped open the balloons that kept the cones afloat.) The third firing, on August 8, 1957, succeeded brilliantly. All major systems worked satisfactorily, and the nose cone was recovered at a range of 1,160 miles. The ablation-type nose cone proved superior to other techniques and was subsequently adopted in the other American missiles. The design of the Jupiter had been validated, and the tests ended with several sets of flight hardware in various stages of fabrication left over. Indeed, the successful culmination of the program appeared to thwart the efforts of ABMA and JPL personnel, particularly Homer Stewart, who wanted to keep the RTV series going as a backup to a Vanguard they expected to fail. With the RTV terminated, ABMA and JPL did the next best thing. Medaris and von Braun put the extra hardware in controlled storage, from which it could be made flight-ready in less than four months for "more spectacular purposes." JPL project manager Jack Froehlich assigned the remaining Sergeant scale motors to long-term life test, which had the same effect.[10]

As the RTV series concluded in the summer of 1957, JPL found itself in a period of self-analysis and frustration. The Sergeant missile program was moving along well but more weapons projects were unattractive to JPL. Fearing that JPL might become just a "job shop" for the army, Pickering and Caltech president DuBridge had agreed in 1954 that the Sergeant would be the laboratory's last major weapons development. The radio-inertial guidance program the laboratory had undertaken on Jupiter ranked as a backup to a backup in an interim development. Satellites seemed the best new direction for JPL. As Pickering noted in mid-1957, "the whole trend of rocketry is in this area." The problem for the Pasadenans was to "find the right way to begin." That seemed to mean working through the army, but the air force's lock on military satellite planning to that point seemed to leave the army with only the marginal activity of reconnaissance satellites limited to tactical uses. Indicative of the uncertainty at the laboratory, as late as the summer of 1957, it seemed that primary attention over the next three years should be given to extending the RTV flights. Then, on Friday night, October 4, 1957, JPL personnel who were scattered across the country discovered that a red light was orbiting the Earth and that its name was Sputnik, Russian for fellow traveler.[11]

Pickering had gone to Washington, D.C., five days earlier for a week of IGY meetings. On Monday he had heard a Russian scientist announce that the USSR would launch a satellite "in the near future," as the translator rendered the phrase; but an American scientist who knew Russian leaned over to Pickering and whispered, "That's not what he said—he said 'imminent.'" Even so, the JPL director was not prepared for what he heard at a party at the Soviet embassy the night of October 4. Walter Sullivan, the *New York Times* science writer, bustled into the room and asked Pickering what he knew about the satellite the Russians said they had just launched. It was the first that Pickering—and probably anyone else in the room, including the Russians—knew about Sputnik. Pickering hurriedly conferred with several others including Lloyd Berkner who hushed the room and proposed a toast. Amid successive torrents of celebratory vodka and caviar, Pickering and his IGY colleagues slipped out to the IGY offices a few blocks away. There they pieced together what information they could to see whether Sputnik really was in orbit, calculated when it would pass over New York, relayed the information to the press, and went to sleep—only to be awakened after an hour when their calculations proved mistaken. They had to recalculate the time of passage and call the press again. It was a long night that left indelible impressions. JPL personnel could remember years later where they were when they heard the news, what they first thought, and what they did, much as other people could recall how they felt when they heard of the deaths of presidents or of the bombing of Pearl Harbor.[12]

The night of Sputnik 1, von Braun and Medaris were chatting with the new secretary of defense, Neil McElroy, who by coincidence was visiting Huntsville. "Vanguard will never make it," cried von Braun. "We have the hardware on the shelf. For God's sake turn us loose and let us do something. We can put up a satellite in sixty days, Mr. McElroy! Just give us a green light and sixty days." As von Braun kept repeating "sixty days," Medaris cautioned: "No, Wernher, ninety days." McElroy returned to Washington noncommital.[13]

The Eisenhower administration took the news of Sputnik in stride. At his first meeting to consider a response to the Russian satellite, on October 9, the president asked Donald Quarles, assistant secretary of defense for research and development, if it was correct that the United States could have orbited a satellite more than a year earlier by using a Redstone. Quarl s said yes. But Vanguard had two advantages, he continued. It stressed the "peaceful character of the effort," and it avoided "the inclusion of material, to which foreign scientists might be given access, which is used in our own military rockets." The army still felt it could launch a satellite within four months, a month earlier than Vanguard. Eisenhower demurred. The need for military classification of the rocket still impressed him. The satellite had been tied to the IGY and had never been a crash program, he recalled. "To make a sudden shift in our approach now would be to belie the attitude we have had all along," he pointed out. The administration soon agreed to advance Vanguard's first launch date, and on October 31 the president cautiously accepted McElroy's suggestion to use the army backup to Vanguard. Eisenhower also beefed up his science advisory system by appointing his first adviser on science and technology, James R. Killian, Jr., president of MIT. On November 8 Eisenhower delivered a nationally televised address designed to reassure citizens that their security was not endangered and that the presumed humiliation of Sputnik was only temporary. Among his props was the recovered nose cone from the ABMA-JPL reentry test vehicle.[14]

Public recrimination was centered in Congress, in the military, and in certain sectors of the scientific and technical communities. The metaphor of Pearl Harbor was invoked frequently, although no attack on American soil had been observed. Berkeley physicist Edward Teller, "father of the H-bomb," informed a television audience that the United States had lost "a battle more important and greater than Pearl Harbor." Senate majority leader Lyndon B. Johnson, Democrat of Texas, asserted that "we do not have as much time as we did after Pearl Harbor," and became a lifelong space enthusiast. The Sputnik syndrome represented varying proportions of wounded pride, a domestic political weapon, a genuine international challenge, and an opportunity for promoting institutions' self-interest. Brig. Gen. Homer Boushey, who had piloted the plane bearing the first JPL JATOs in 1940 and was now deputy director of air force research and development, warned: "Who controls the moon controls the earth." Pickering remarked sourly: "It is pretty obvious that very few people in this country had any appreciation of the political significance of the Russian satellite," and that included the politicians "in a position to make decisions." It was an "obvious fact" that the Russians were "well ahead" in weapons technology, he continued. To "recover national prestige" the United States did not need dramatic scientific breakthroughs but "good management and good engineering on programs which already exist." Not coincidentally, this meant using the capabilities of ABMA and JPL on Jupiter and perhaps on a more daring attempt to leapfrog the Russians.[15]

The laboratory staff hastily drew up Project Red Socks, a plan to launch nine rockets to the moon in a hurry. The laboratory used the full cachet of its parent in the proposal, dated October 25, 1957: "The California Institute of Technology believes that it is essential for the United States to initiate an immediate program for the scientific exploration of the moon." Sputnik implied the Russians could send flights to the moon, said the proposal. "National interest appears to require the United States to demonstrate as soon as possible that U.S. science likewise has this capability." The first rocket, which would use the RTV hardware, would be scheduled for June 1958 and send 15 pounds around the moon. The remaining eight flights would consist of scaled-up RTV equipment and send 120-pound payloads to the moon from January 1959 through the end of 1960. The first flight would carry instruments to measure temperature, pressure, and light intensity. The remaining flights would expand on these experiments, and the last several rounds might incorporate more sophisticated guidance to refine the orbit around the moon. In the quest for spectacular science, JPL officials flirted with even bolder ideas. Pickering and other scientists toyed with the idea of exploding an atomic bomb on the lunar surface, which would "shower the earth with samples of surface dust in addition to producing beneficial psychological results."[16]

These schemes seemed audacious, even bizarre, for a space program that had yet to get off the ground. Pickering and DuBridge peddled the Red Socks proposal through the corridors of the Pentagon. Lt. Gen. James Gavin, head of army research and development, liked it immensely and told the Californians he would consider its approval the crowning achievement of his career. Assistant secretary Quarles seemed interested, but he wanted to involve the air force. Back in the corridor, Pickering turned to DuBridge and said, "Well, that kills that." Red Socks never got into the race.[17]

Through October and November, however, the pressure built for Jupiter. A few days after Sputnik 1, the audacious Medaris told the crews at ABMA to take the RTV hardware out of storage and begin readying it for launch. Medaris lacked higher authority for this action; in fact he issued his instructions at the same time the president reaffirmed his intention to stick with the nonmilitary approach. Medaris figured the amount of money was relatively small and that he could bury it somewhere, if necessary. He was banking, too, on the long-held conviction in army-JPL circles that Vanguard would falter. The Soviet Union bolstered his plans when, on November 3, it orbited Sputnik 2 with a dramatic payload: 1,100 pounds in weight and a live dog, Laika. On November 8 the Department of Defense at last gave the army and JPL authorization to prepare their satellite. Eventually known as Explorer, it remained a backup, but it was the moment the two agencies had sought since 1954. Then, on the night of December 6, Vanguard was readied for takeoff, was fired, exploded, and sat burning on its launchpad in the hot glare of international television. After "flopnik" Orbiter's moment had arrived.[18]

When von Braun blurted to McElroy that the hardware was on the shelf he was correct except for one detail: the satellite itself had yet to be built. Von Braun confidently assumed his team would get that plum, but Pickering was determined to shake it free for JPL. The laboratory had earned the job because of its work on Orbiter and the RTV, and the payload logically fit with JPL's communications work, particularly Microlock. Just prior to the meeting at which the roles would be assigned, Pickering asked Medaris for a few minutes alone. He argued that JPL should build the satellite; Medaris agreed. The general probably felt the laboratory could handle the electronics work better than Redstone, and he wanted to keep JPL actively in the army's orbit. Von Braun's jaw dropped when Medaris and Pickering walked into the meeting and informed him of the decision, but the collaboration proved fruitful, and there was more than enough work for both teams. The quarter of an hour Pickering spent with Medaris was momentous. If Redstone had built the Explorer 1 satellite, it would have had a lock on both the missile and the satellite. JPL would have been relegated to a minor supporting role, chiefly in its tracking network, from which it would have been highly unlikely to develop into a major space laboratory. Electronics, which had begun shouldering propulsion aside as the laboratory's dominant activity during the Corporal weaponization, opened a window to space for JPL.[19]

Laboratory personnel worked intensively on what was code-named at JPL Project Deal. Project manager Jack Froehlich, a formidable poker player, had bestowed the name in the aftermath of the Sputniks with the remark: "When a big pot is won, the winner sits around and cracks bad jokes and the loser cries, 'Deal!'" The next round was coming up even sooner than the ninety days Medaris had promised, for scheduling conflicts at the cape dictated that the vehicle be ready for launching by January 29, 1958, just eighty days after the go-ahead. Although Vanguard had promised a 25-pound payload, JPL more cautiously elected to limit theirs to 20 pounds. The payload structure weighed 30.8 pounds, including just 18 pounds for the instrument compartment. Three relatively simple experiments were chosen to investigate the satellite's environment, about which little was known. The first two, although having some scientific merit, were designed primarily to furnish information for future satellite design. The first experiment tested the extreme temperatures the satellite would encounter as it passed from full sunlight to the complete shade of the Earth. A thermistor measured the internal temperature of the high-power transmitter and the satellite's skin temperature. Resistance thermometers performed a second skin measurement as well on one of the nose cones. The second experiment measured the impact of micrometeorites on the satellite's surface by means of an impact microphone, an amplifier, and a circuit of eleven wire grids. The third experiment was primarily scientific and resulted in the most dramatic findings of the early satellite programs. This was the cosmic-ray experiment of James Van Allen of the State University of Iowa and involved placing a Geiger–Müller counter and associated equipment in the satellite to measure radiation. Originally programmed for Vanguard, the Van Allen experiments were added to Explorer at Pickering's suggestion.[20]

JPL's work on Explorer was relatively straightforward and surprisingly informal. Two considerations—shape and temperature—were among the main design constraints in designing the fourth stage. At first JPL engineers considered but rejected a spherical shape. A sphere probably could not be made rugged enough to survive launching through the atmosphere without either adding too much weight for strengthening or adding a protective cone. A cylindrical shape seemed preferable. This shape was consistent with the last-stage rocket motor and with the instrumentation to be carried. The final stage measured 80 inches long and 6 inches in diameter. The easiest and most reliable way to counteract the extremes suggested extensive insulation and a careful ratio of bare steel, which provided a relatively high temperature, and aluminum exide, which furnished a low temperature.[21]

Three typical JPL approaches to design characterized the plans and fabrication. First, simple, reliable components were used instead of more complicated ones which might have yielded higher performance but presented more design risks. The booster stages, for instance, used the relatively small 6-inch scale Sergeant motors. These units had undergone more than 300 static tests, 50 flight tests, and 290 ignition-system firings without a failure. Second, the laboratory used the experience its engineers had derived from the minute details of manufacturing to the maximum. For instance, it was very difficult to determine misalignment of the components because the relatively simple instruments could not measure the misalignment precisely. JPL engineers thus precalculated the misalignment of all components "with only experience as a guide"; this made possible field assembly of the large rotating second stage with a misalignment of less than a thousandth of an inch. In another case a structural engineer checked the strength of a motor case by standing on it until it was deformed the maximum amount and observing that it suffered no apparent ill effects; these informal findings were later confirmed by sophisticated spin tests. Such techniques had contributed to JPL's problems in preparing drawings and insuring reproducibility when dealing with contractors in its missile programs, but for producing a limited edition prototype under severe time pressure, experience proved a trustworthy guide.[22]

Third, dual or triple systems were used wherever possible so that a malfunction would not endanger a system or the entire mission. The igniter, for instance, might have to be fired in a vacuum; its failure would abort the mission. Three safeguards were employed: the igniter was designed to fire in a vacuum, the motor was sealed to hold atmospheric pressure, and the igniter was sealed in a container holding atmospheric pressure. The last two considerations added slightly to the weight, but the added weight purchased much greater reliability at low cost. The concept of dual or triple systems, known as redundancy, came to play a vital role in space missions.[23]

Besides work on the Explorer itself, JPL had to quickly expand the tracking network. Two primary Microlock stations already existed from previous experiments, Earthquake Valley near San Diego, California, and Air Force

Missile Test Center in Florida. JPL designed equipment for new stations, which were set up in Nigeria and Singapore in cooperation with the British IGY committee. These stations were to snare telemetry data from the experiments. The orbital calculations would be handled through the Florida and California stations, and since Explorer 1 was launched eastward, an hour and forty-five minutes would elapse before confirmation of orbit would be possible.[24]

By early January JPL had finished its booster stages and satellite and moved them to Cape Canaveral under extraordinary secrecy. After the Vanguard failure the army had clamped maximum security restrictions around Explorer, which was known even in highly classified cables between Redstone and JPL as "Missile 29." Medaris wanted to make the preparations for launch appear to be just another Redstone missile test. Any JPL personnel who could be obviously related to a satellite launch, particularly project director Jack Froehlich, moved under elaborate decoy plans. Secrecy during the erection of the missile and mating of the upper stages was particularly sensitive. The upper stages were to be covered with canvas for the hurried predawn movement to the launch pad. Then the launching structure was brought up, and the bird cages surrounded the missile so that the top section was not visible away from the launching area. Missile 29 could then be "identified as a Redstone since the part in view will appear the same as a standard Redstone booster." Medaris warned: "I cannot overemphasize the importance of these decoy plans and the absolute necessity of covering this launching as a normal test of a Redstone missile, and I desire it well understood that the individual who violates these instructions will be handled severely."[25]

The preparations moved smoothly, and by January 29 Missile 29 sat ready for countdown. The secrecy had to end somewhere, of course, and by then a crowd of VIPs and newsmen had journeyed to the cape but under an agreement whereby no news was released until after the launch. Missile 29 perched on the pad for two days while flight personnel consulted weather forecasts as anxiously as General Eisenhower did before D day. On the 29th and 30th high winds from the jet stream forced postponement; the engineers feared the missile could not stand the force. But on the 31st the winds, while still strong, subsided enough to justify the risk. The countdown proceeded normally and was only twenty-five minutes behind schedule. At JPL engineers clustered around the teletype hookup to the cape and watched anxiously as a nervous operator tapped out the events of the last minute of counting:[26]

X-1 AND COUNTING
2247EST

K
NO TIME WILL BE GIVEN FROM HERE ON IN
45 SECONDS
20
15
10
9S
^{7} 6 54 3 2 1
BLAST OFF
PROGRAM STARTED
LIFT OFF

Inside the blockhouse at the cape, Medaris listened intently to the principal indicator that the rocket was climbing steadily: a whining signal transmitted from the nose cone. Then it stopped. "I've lost my signal!" cried Medaris. A signal going dead usually meant missile failure. "Oh, oh . . . Too bad . . . This doesn't look good," murmured crewmen. An army captain ran to a phone, dialed the central recording station: "Signal lost at the blockhouse. How's yours?" The reply: "Noisy but legible." After forty anxious seconds of seeming failure, the crowd pressed into the blockhouse was reassured.

STILL GOING AT ONE MIN NOW
STILL GOOD
90 SECONDS
GOT THROUGH THE JET STREAMS
EVERY THING NORMAL   LOOKS GLO XX GOOD
110 SECOND NOW   115
R140   SECONDS
145
APPROACHING BURN OUT[27]

After 155 seconds the first-stage rocket burned out and fell into the Atlantic. As the vehicle coasted upward past 200 miles, the guidance system tilted the assembly into a horizontal path. At 225 miles and 403.7 seconds, when the missile's position paralleled the surface of Earth, a ground signal ignited the second and third stages. The velocity increased quickly, from 5,520 miles per hour to 17,680 miles per hour. After 428.6 seconds of flight—9 more than predicted—Explorer 1 reached an altitude of 228 miles, 10 miles higher than forecast. The fourth-stage rocket ignited and gave the final stage a kick that should have sent the satellite into orbit. At the Pentagon, where another watch party was going on, von Braun turned to Pickering and said, "It's yours now." JPL took control.[28]

The Associated Press moved a story from the cape:

THE ARMY'S JUPITER-C MISSILE BLASTED OFF FRIDAY NIGHT,
CARRYING A SATELLITE INTO SPACE. ARMY OFFICIALS SAID IT
WOULD NOT BE KNOWN FOR ABOUT TWO HOURS WHETHER
THE MISSILE HAD SUCCEEDED IN PROPELLING THE FIRST
AMERICAN 'MOON' INTO ORBIT AROUND THE EARTH.

JPL personnel in Pasadena felt helpless. There was nothing to do but wait
and be poised to pick up Explorer's signal, if it was in orbit.

GEN MEDARIS SAID HAVE A CUP OF COFFEE—SMOKE A CIGARETT
SWEAT IT OUT WITH US
K
OK TNX LXX ALOT   DAY   WILL DO
K
DE JPL
WE ARE BEING NONCHALANT AND LIGHTING UP A MARJAUNA
HA[29]

The laboratory crews were anything but relaxed. At the cape Medaris and
other officials kept popping into the JPL data analysis room for assurances
Explorer was in orbit. Froehlich, Stewart, Al Hibbs, and other laboratory
personnel were poring over the telemetry from the downrange stations, in
order to send their West Coast colleagues a prediction of when the bird
should pass. The velocity seemed adequate for orbit, but they had no data on
the angle of inclination. "The thing could be pointing up too high or pointing down so low from the horizontal that it would have been a disastrous
launching," Stewart recalled. As best they could figure, Explorer should pass
within about 105 minutes, or certainly by 110 minutes. But Explorer did not
show. Seven minutes late: Everyone throughout the organization was "really
getting pretty upset." Eight minutes late. Finally the San Gabriel Valley
Amateur Radio Club near Pasadena, followed quickly by the Earthquake
Valley Microlock station, picked up the signal. The satellite was late because
the jet stream had given it an extra kick of about 100 feet per second, which
sent it into an orbit with a higher peak and hence a longer transit time than
JPL trackers had thought possible. When injected into orbit, the object
enjoyed ample margin for error. Its position was only about 0.8 degrees
from the horizontal, but a satisfactory orbit would have been possible with a
deviation as great as 4 degrees. Explorer 1's apogee was 1,580 miles, its
perigee 223 miles, and the time for one orbit 113.2 minutes. Explorer 1 was
in orbit, and JPL was jubilant.[30]

When the Microlock snatched the signal from space, it also turned the
international limelight on JPL. No longer an obscure army laboratory
known chiefly to missile cognoscenti, JPL basked happily in the warm glow
of favorable publicity. Pickering, Van Allen, and von Braun hoisted a model

of the Explorer 1 satellite over their heads at a Washington news conference at 2:00 A.M. the next day, and a wire-service photograph of the occasion appeared in hundreds of American newspapers. The *New York Times* ran a sidebar on the laboratory, and *Time* included a profile of Pickering with those of Medaris and von Braun. Most of the attention focused on von Braun and his colleagues; preoccupation with the more dramatic and more easily understood rocket booster and with the human-interest story of the former Germans working for America was perhaps understandable. No matter. JPL was bursting with pride and already dreaming of a major role in space exploration. In triumph, and in defeat, JPL would not return to its former obscurity.[31]

JPL and ABMA continued to collaborate on a series of Explorers through July 1958. They were designed to exact quickly the maximum mileage from existing technology, and they focused on the intriguing cosmic-ray data returned from Explorer 1. Although basically similar to the first satellite, they introduced some refinements in the payload. Explorer 2, launched on March 5, 1958, did not achieve orbit when, because of a structural failure, the fourth stage failed to ignite. Explorer 3 placed the second successful American satellite into orbit on March 26, 1958. Meteorite and temperature measurements resembled those on Explorer 1. The major innovation was a tape recorder that made it possible to transmit much fuller cosmic-ray data. Because of the small number of tracking stations, much of the orbit could not be observed. Just as this had caused an anxious two hours on January 31, it also meant that much of the telemetric data was lost. Explorer 3 contained a miniature tape recorder. Moving at a very slow rate of 0.005 inches per second, the recorder needed less than three feet of tape to freeze the data from an entire orbit. When the satellite neared a tracking station, a ground signal switched on the playback head and the high-power transmitter. In less than five seconds all the data from the orbit was sent, and the tape was erased and reset.[32]

The returns from Explorer 3 continued to astound scientists. Pulse rates at the apogee of the orbit registered at least a thousand times what had been expected; counts exceeded 35,000 per second at the highest altitudes, over South America, and saturated the Geiger–Müller counter. The data from Explorers 1 and 3 enabled Van Allen to announce on May 1, 1958, the discovery of "a very great intensity of radiation about altitudes of some 500 miles over 34 degrees north and south of the equator." He theorized that these phenomena, ultimately known as the Van Allen belts, consisted of charged particles trapped in the earth's magnetic field.[33]

These extraordinary findings led JPL, ABMA, and IGY scientists to devote Explorer 4 entirely to radiation studies, in conjunction with the novel

Argus experiment. The satellite was launched successfully on July 26, 1958, and carried almost twice the weight of instrumentation of the previous vehicles. Van Allen developed new instruments that could record 60,000 particles per square centimeter per second, several thousand times that previously measured. Explorer 4 recorded data from areas not sampled previously. Its predecessors had ranged between 35 degrees north and south latitude; Explorer 4 covered most of the Earth's surface, with extremities at 51 degrees. The Argus experiment provided data never present before. In late August and September the navy sent three rockets to an altitude of 300 miles over the South Atlantic where small atomic bombs were exploded in brilliant pyrotechnic displays. Explorer 4's instruments recorded the radiation from the explosions that was trapped in the atmosphere and made possible considerable refinement of the knowledge of the Van Allen belts and related phenomena. Explorer 5 failed to achieve orbit. The radiation experiments of the three successful Explorers had scored a scientific coup with what Van Allen aptly termed "the most interesting and least expected results" of the probes.[34]

The last major phase of the program to adapt existing technology to quick and easy projects bore fruit in Pioneers 3 and 4. These ventures were essentially simplified revisions of the ill-fated Red Socks proposal. ABMA substituted a modified Jupiter missile, which developed 150,000 pounds of thrust, for the 78,000-pound-thrust Redstone. JPL's three spinning upper-propulsion stages remained basically the same. The payload contained the familiar temperature sensors and Geiger–Müller counters; the laboratory added a shutter-trigger mechanism that was supposed to be tripped by the reflected light of the moon. The 12.95 pounds of instruments were housed under a striped conical hat that somewhat resembled the canopy of a merry-go-round.[35]

Two Pioneers, designed by the air force and Space Technology Laboratories, preceded the JPL-ABMA combination in the fall of 1958. Neither worked, and the laboratory and the army again had a chance to upstage a rival service. Pioneer 3 was launched from Cape Canaveral on December 6, 1958, but it did not achieve escape velocity when the first stage cut off prematurely. The payload rose to a height of 63,500 miles, about 7,000 miles short of the previous Pioneer. Nevertheless, two of the flight objectives were partially met; the new Goldstone station tracked the probe without a hitch, and the radiation counters returned further refinements of data on the Van Allen belts.[36]

Before JPL-ABMA had a chance to try again, the Soviet Union sent Luna 1 toward the moon on January 2, 1959. Later renamed Mechta, or "dream," Luna 1 passed within 3,728 miles of the moon's surface and passed on into orbit around the sun—the first vehicle to escape Earth's gravitational attraction. The flight of Pioneer 4, launched on March 3, 1959, therefore seemed anticlimactic, although it was by far the most successful of the Pioneer series. The probe passed within 37,200 miles of the moon 41½ hours after injection. The light mechanism stayed dark because it had been programmed to operate when Pioneer came within 20,000 miles of the moon. The tracking system worked superbly, however, and received Pioneer's signals until the spacecraft's batteries failed about 407,000 miles from Earth. Pioneer 4 followed Luna 1 into orbit around the sun, becoming an artificial planet that completed a circuit every 395 days.[37]

Pioneer 4 augmented JPL's sense of accomplishment and feeling of superiority; the laboratory and ABMA had again bested its American rivals. Existing technology, hastily modified, had put the United States on the board. But the Soviet successes continued to rankle and encouraged JPL officials to press for a more vigorous space program. Modifications of existing technology had reached their limits. JPL engineers had recognized early in 1958 that the Explorers and Pioneers represented a string of improvisations—useful for the moment, perhaps, but not at all what they believed a credible U.S. space program demanded. The laboratory's ambition for international leadership in space already made it a dynamic, abrasive presence in a new civilian space agency.

7 ★★

THE TERRESTRIAL POLITICS
OF OUTER SPACE

The Jet Propulsion Laboratory brought to the space program a tradition of tackling big problems. In both propulsion and communications JPL had aimed at major advances in the field instead of merely making refinements in existing knowledge. From the earliest days of rocketry the laboratory had felt the lure of space, particularly planetary exploration. John Small, a senior engineer at the laboratory, once explained the JPL ethos as wanting "to do the final far-out things." It would rather reach for Saturn's rings than land on the Martian surface, would rather make the life measurement on a planet than set down a capsule, and would rather land a capsule than build the spacecraft. But aiming for the "final far-out things" first required negotiating the political mazes on Earth.[1]

The laboratory initially continued its alliance with the Army Ballistic Missile Agency. The research and development areas of the two organizations complemented each other, and Wernher von Braun's overpowering interest in building a giant booster rocket dovetailed with JPL's interest in deep space. ABMA's ambitions were nothing short of breathtaking. A plan it put together early in 1958 contended that a four-man experimental space station was feasible by 1962, a manned lunar expedition by mid-1966, a permanent moon base by 1973, and a manned expedition to a planet by 1977. The first step was to provide a more advanced vehicle than Juno 2 had used for Explorer. Medaris proposed that by spring of 1959 an interim vehicle known as Juno 3 could swing past the moon with a 120-pound payload at a distance of 5,000 to 10,000 miles and photograph the back side, never seen by man. By late 1959 a Juno 3 could manage a hard landing with an instrumented payload on the lunar surface. (Medaris's timetable was hopelessly optimistic. The first U.S. spacecraft to achieve a hard landing on the moon would be Ranger in 1964, and Soviet spacecraft would easily beat American cameras to the back side.) JPL felt, however, that Juno 3 fell between two stools: It was too big for minimum probes, which Juno 2 could handle, but not big enough for more advanced missions that would be guided and fully instrumented. Juno 3 was thus a "closed-end development" that was "not really compatible with the expected course of developments in the guidance field."[2]

Juno 3 had been devised to meet a Department of Defense request for readily available technology for military satellites. JPL soon concluded that it wanted to push beyond existing technology and deeper into space. It was time, the laboratory argued in April 1958, to embark on a "really integrated propulsion system with growth potential and broad usefulness in other programs." The basis of this departure, billed as Juno 4, would be the familiar Jupiter. In place of the three unguided, solid-propellant upper stages of Junos 1 through 3, however, Juno 4 would use two more powerful and more sophisticated guided, liquid-propelled upper stages. JPL argued that it should develop both the 45,000-pound-thrust second stage and the 6,000-pound third stage. The laboratory insisted, moreover, that it exercise responsibility for space missions. ABMA would continue development of Jupiter and of satellites and lunar probes. The army at first demurred but then accepted JPL's ambitions.[3]

The fate of the Juno 4 proposal rested with the Advanced Research Projects Agency (ARPA), which the Eisenhower administration had established in the Department of Defense in February 1958 to handle the military space program and to act as a caretaker for any eventual civilian space projects. ARPA made two decisions which had highly significant long-range implications for JPL. First, it cut back the laboratory's role in propulsion. Instead of JPL's second-stage unit, ARPA selected the 45,000-pound-thrust engine that General Electric was developing for Vanguard. The laboratory was left with just its 6,000-pound upper stage, known as the 6K. Even that project would meet its demise before long, thus eliminating JPL from work on launch vehicles altogether and rendering its name somewhat anomalous.[4]

ARPA's other decision laid the foundation for a command and tracking system that grew into the Deep Space Network (DSN). Providing support for all aspects of American civilian spaceflight, the DSN became a vital part of JPL's activities. The problems of tracking the Explorers had called attention to the need for a worldwide tracking system, and ARPA authorized JPL to set up such a network. The system's cornerstone was located at Goldstone in the Mojave Desert, where ambient noise was minimal. On the bed of a dry lake some 100 air miles northeast of Pasadena, a huge revolving antenna 85 feet in diameter began to take shape. As spacecraft ventured deeper in the late 1960s, this remote outpost was upgraded with a 210-foot antenna. Foreign stations were readily approved for Australia and Spain in 1958, but the African location was another story. Liberia or Nigeria made the most sense from the standpoint of the spacing of the stations. JPL communications experts ruled against those countries, however, because of their heavy rainfall and "lack of available Caucasian raw material." Dry, white, politically reliable South Africa got the nod instead, even though the long hop made it harder for Goldstone to acquire the signal.[5]

The ARPA decisions suggested that JPL's future did not lie with the army but with the proposed civilian agency which was gaining increasing support. The military would retain a satellite role and perhaps something more, but the air force, not the army, would run the military space program. JPL officials were divided on the advisability of hitching their destiny to the civilian star. Many persons at JPL found the military grooves, classified documents, and closed doors comfortable. Some JPL technical staff members had worked happily in early space intelligence gathering activities. Some favored setting up a space program within the Atomic Energy Commission, which boasted a reputation for skilled scientific work under tight deadlines and also had a long-range interest in applying nuclear propulsion to rocketry. But by spring 1958 JPL found the idea of a civilian agency increasingly attractive. As one of Director Pickering's aides, J. W. McGarrity, put it: JPL and Caltech had "almost . . . a moral obligation to see that the assets in a unique organization like JPL . . . are not restricted to serve only the military." President Eisenhower proposed the civilian agency in April 1958. On July 29, 1958, he signed the bill, which an eager Congress had broadened and strengthened, that created the National Aeronautics and Space Administration. If JPL wanted to see its idea of a space program develop, the laboratory needed to find a home in NASA.[6]

JPL executives feared, however, that certain political and economic forces militated against a successful civilian space program. Senior engineer Clifford I. Cummings articulated these misgivings in an insightful analysis based on his wide exposure to the aircraft and missile field. Cummings thought Congress had to create a new agency because of the failure of the organizational setup for extreme-range ballistic missiles. The army had the competence, chiefly through ABMA and JPL, but the air force and the navy had the mission. Ideally NASA should have control of both competence and mission. Cummings believed this would not materialize, however, primarily because of opposition from the aircraft industry, which was facing severe economic straits. Guided missiles were replacing military aircraft, and military emphasis was shifting from aerodynamics and structures to electronics. The firms claimed, however, that their failure, even temporarily, would be disastrous for the economy. "They also argue," he said, "that our country is plagued with being too efficient in its production for its own economic good, and hence that inefficient production such [as] is generated by making planes or missiles that will in all probability never be used is essential to economic stability."[7]

The space program promised to rescue the industry, Cummings continued, as some aircraft company executives acknowledged. "It is certainly possible to spend large sums of money in inefficient production in this area," he observed dryly. The industry would try to assert control over NASA politically, financially with open-ended contracts that would yield notorious overruns, and through personnel. The results could be disastrous. Aircraft companies were "hopelessly inefficient" places to carry out advanced development, he said. Their engineers, however well intentioned, had "little understanding of research and advanced development at reasonable cost produced at a quoted time—they have never seen any."[8]

The organizational basis for NASA lent credence to JPL's fears. The core of the new agency was the old National Advisory Committee on Aeronautics (NACA), a federal research establishment dating to 1915. Although NASA had a hunting license to pick up other organizations, such as JPL and ABMA, the Pasadenans feared the results if NACA officials dominated the new agency. The NACA fraternity would probably favor research at their own civil service centers, augmented by extensive outside contracting, mostly with aircraft firms. To be sure, NACA had done important early work in aeronautics; Pickering credited the agency with development of the modern airplane. But JPL staffers, who tended to be disdainful of civil service science generally, thought NACA by the 1950s had a severe case of tunnel vision. To them, NACA was an unimaginative bureaucracy composed of "jellyfish-type individuals" who were most interested in pushing known principles to the next decimal point. Loaded down with wind-tunnel research, NACA seemed to have become little more than a service bureau for the air force and aircraft firms. To make matters worse, NACA's space planning focused on satellites. Its early reports did not include lunar or planetary missions—JPL's main interests.[9]

Cummings's analysis was a prescient forecast of many of the problems the space program would encounter in the next two decades. The close political ties between the firms and NASA, the troubled contracting history, and the very choice of missions and assignments of research and advanced development—all would be focuses of controversy. JPL as an anomalous organization both inside and outside of NASA would be constantly buffeted by these forces. In the end, the laboratory found its role much reduced from its early ambitions—in part because it threatened that very alliance between NASA and the aerospace firms.

Pickering moved quickly in a bid to establish JPL as the dominant force in NASA. The JPL-Caltech hierarchy sensed an institutional opportunity; they also believed—not a little arrogantly—that the laboratory had a mission to set the new space agency on the proper course. Pickering told Killian, Eisenhower's science adviser:

> it is essential for the new agency to accept the concept of JPL as the national space laboratory. If this is not done, then NASA will flounder around for so long that there is a good possibility the entire program will be carried by the military with NASA providing only some research support and perhaps helping with scientific payloads. If JPL does become the national space laboratory on the other hand, then not only does a complete experienced laboratory knowledge-able in all phases of the problem become the key asset of NASA, but there is assurance that a realistic program will in fact be established and pursued. As you well know, one of the problems in the present space program is the multiplicity of committees and groups which are planning programs. It is essential for some competent group to be given a clear-cut responsibility and told to draw up a realistic long-term program which they can successfully complete on schedule.

Perhaps renamed "National Space Laboratories," as some JPL engineers suggested, the Pasadena laboratory would dominate NASA.[10]

Pickering and Caltech president Lee DuBridge responded eagerly to the first NASA overtures in the fall of 1958. From the start of NASA operations on October 1, 1958, sentiment grew within the organization for a more ambitious program than what NACA had outlined. This view reflected in part the ideas of members of the Naval Research Laboratory (NRL), which NASA absorbed on October 1. Although JPL had tended to diminish the navy laboratory's capabilities because of its civil service connection and its misfortunes with Vanguard, NRL personnel displayed competence and imagination that would surprise and sometimes confound JPL. The first NASA administrator, T. Keith Glennan, president of the Case Institute of Technology in Cleveland and a former commissioner of the Atomic Energy Commission, also favored a more aggressive program. Glennan wanted to snatch both parts of the army's space package—ABMA and JPL—so that NASA could "acquire at the earliest possible date a developmental and operational capability for large space vehicles." The NASA chief did not want to depend on the military services for vehicles. ABMA boasted experi-ence in complete space vehicles. "JPL has strong capabilities relating to small payload packages, guidance, electronics and to upper-stage booster systems, and high-energy rockets, thereby complementing ABMA's limited experi-ence in these fields," a NASA staff report noted. To develop facilities equiv-alent to JPL would require a capital outlay of $60 million, entail the recruit-ment of 2,000 to 3,000 people, and take three or four years.[11]

The Department of Defense did not want to lose JPL. Assistant secretary of defense Donald Quarles argued that the laboratory, particularly its work on the Sergeant missile, was too important to national security to allow the changeover. But the army wanted desperately to keep ABMA to maintain its toehold in long-range missilery. A compromise was reached quickly. NASA would get JPL; the army would keep ABMA for at least another year. In three short negotiating sessions NASA and the Defense Department worked out the arrangements for transferring JPL property and personnel. The laboratory would see the Sergeant program to completion, which was expected in 1960, and it would continue to do some research for the army. Eisenhower signed an executive order approving the transfer on December 3, 1958, and the bulk of JPL efforts came under NASA jurisdiction on January 1, 1959. The space agency contract paralleled the one JPL had enjoyed with army ordnance, thus allowing the laboratory to retain wide discretion in its operations. The second NASA administrator, James E. Webb, said he would never have written the contract that way, but any doubts that surfaced in 1958 were submerged by the desire for a smooth transition in a time of urgency.[12]

JPL brought not only ability but hubris to NASA. The laboratory intended to take the lead in the space program, and it had space-flight missions planned to match its outsized ambition. DuBridge told the Caltech trustees that "JPL will be NASA's major space-flight laboratory." But NASA officials had more modest ambitions for their acquisition. A draft outline of JPL's mission in October 1958 by NASA headquarters pointed first to "supporting research in communications, telemetry, guidance and control, rocket propulsion utilizing both solid and liquid propellants and in related fields—all subject to coordination with other centers to avoid undesirable duplication." Secondarily it sketched "specific interplanetary mission assignments together with related research and development including, in some cases, technical direction." The vast gap between these two concepts of roles would fuel controversies for years.[13]

One of the first products of JPL's relationship with NASA was a long-range program for space exploration. As Pickering had told Killian, planning for space exploration had heretofore been haphazard, even schizophrenic. Program sketches had veered from NACA's penchant for cautious incremental advances to ABMA's excessively exuberant plans for manned vehicles to range throughout the solar system in the next decade. Both extremes had in common the assumption that almost anything, whether small or large, could be justified in the space program. NASA agreed to fund a $1.3 million study at JPL in October 1958, even before negotiations to add the laboratory to the new agency had been completed. JPL officials felt they were outlining not only the laboratory's future program but NASA's major space program. From November 1958 through January 1959 several top staff members of the laboratory devoted considerable time to what would prove to be a revealing study.[14]

The first flight, a circumlunar probe, would take place in July 1960. Two Mars flights would follow in October, when the red planet made its nearest approach to Earth. A pair of flights to Venus would occur in January 1961. During the next eighteen months, when Venus and Mars were too far away for favorable launching conditions, JPL would practice with an escape out of ecliptic orbit in September 1961 and a lunar satellite in April 1962. Venus satellites would follow in summer 1962 with Mars flybys late in the year. With the planets again out of position in 1963, three lunar flights were scheduled. The planners listed flights after 1963 as tentative. They consisted of Venus landings in the spring of 1964, a manned circumlunar flight in August 1964, and a manned flight around Mars and return in January 1965. The JPL timetable of eighteen flights in five years was exceedingly optimistic. The Mars probes scheduled for 1960 represented a big jump over the Pioneers the laboratory was engineering at the time of the planning study, and some of the flights outlined have yet to be attempted. But some JPL participants felt the sketch might be criticized as too conservative, and they pondered "spicing it up with 'spectaculars.' "[15]

As the first systematic look at space exploration by a NASA agency, the plan revealed much about early thinking on space even though it was not implemented. Other studies had tended to look first at technology and try to find a mission to fit; JPL decided instead that missions should come first, and then vehicles, tracking, facilities, and the like could be built to fit. The plan revealed, first, JPL's commitment to planetary exploration. The lunar flights, while of some intrinsic merit, played a role primarily as test runs for the planetary voyages. Second, the leading criterion that guided the choice of missions was technical feasibility. The timetable took advantage of every opportunity when Mars and Venus assumed the best positions for launches. Feasibility was linked, thirdly, to dramatic impact. "The public demands sudden and spectacular achievements from their [sic] space program," the final report concluded. JPL ranked "public reaction" second only to feasibility in the scale of criteria for mission choices; scientific and technical merit ranked third. Indeed, scientific objectives were sketched only in general terms, and they were made to fit around the missions; the choice of missions was not based on a survey of the key scientific questions to which the space program might address itself. Pickering told Medaris that through mid-1962 "scientific experimentation would be carried along when space and time permitted." Fourth, the laboratory did not at this point anticipate the gap that eventually arose between proponents of manned and unmanned spaceflight, with scientific advocates usually favoring the unmanned segment. "Certainly, a manned landing on another planet is one of the most important objectives of a long-range program," the report said. "Regardless of how clever we become with remote measuring devices, one hard-rock geologist landed on the moon, for example, would be worth many tons of automatic equipment."[16] The writers did not anticipate that most of the astronauts would be pilots, not scientists.

In the course of the study the JPL planners sometimes worried how space exploration might be justified and considered drawing on the Caltech humanities division for help. In the report, however, possibility became its own rationale. The laboratory did not so much answer the question of justification as assume that public demand for firsts in the space race provided one. To JPL, early planetary missions offered the best route for fast, dramatic bursts in the space race. Perhaps these were the sorts of rationales to be expected from engineers immersed in international technological competition. Certainly many politicians and pundits were equally alarmist and just as enamored of hardware. Such an approach promised immediate payoffs for the space program. But the long-term consequences might prove less happy for these advocates. What space planning needed most was an orderly incremental program with a strong intellectual and scientific rationale. Born in a moment of national anxiety, the space program would be inextricably identified with international rivalries and quasi-military applications. If those foundations of the space program were challenged, its support would splinter.

Once JPL had selected the missions, it began to fit the hardware around them. The main technical problem in NASA's first several years was building reliable first-stage boosters. James D. Burke, who headed the propulsion segment of the study, outlined a plan for a "unified vehicle family." He hoped to see NASA select a minimum of basic designs and stick with them so that they would develop maximum experience and reliability. IRBMs were considered but discarded in favor of the larger ICBMs. The laboratory proposed three classes of vehicles. Providing an escape payload of 150 to 300 pounds, vehicle A would consist of an ICBM and appropriate upper stages; vehicle B would be similar but larger and provide 300 to 1,000 pounds payload. The third class, the giant Jupiter 5, was tagged as the deep-space workhorse vehicle. ABMA thought it would be ready in 1962. In JPL's outline the first-stage boosters of the early years would become the second-stage vehicle of the Jupiter 5. The laboratory tried to preserve its role in propulsion by emphasizing the importance of the 6K rocket it already had under development for the final stage. NASA accepted the vehicle plan largely intact, for it seemed to offer a rapid, reliable way out of the forest of conflicting rocket designs. JPL also outlined major expansions of tracking and other facilities that its program required. These remained to be hammered out with NASA as actual program and budgetary decisions materialized.[17]

An initial attempt to come to grips with these questions took place in Pasadena on January 12 and 13, 1959, when JPL and NASA officials held their first full-dress meeting. Although there was some agreement, the meeting was most memorable for its adumbration of the theme that would bedevil JPL-NASA relationships for the next decade: the relative independence of the laboratory. The JPL minutes emphasized the Pasadenans' point of view. Pickering argued for a long-range, balanced program overall that entailed supporting research, development, and advanced development for his shop. "A strong 'in-house' capability is necessary to maintain technical competence," he said. "The Laboratory expects to give support to NASA, but it is hoped that technical supervision of programs other than those in which the Laboratory has a direct interest will be kept to a minimum." For Pickering, program was central. JPL should be a "doer," immersed in actual research and development; monitoring of outside contractors should be minimized. And the laboratory should have substantial independence in formulating and carrying out its program.[18]

Abe Silverstein, director of NASA's Office of Space Flight Development, countered with the agency position. He acknowledged the need for a long-range program and for the maintenance of in-house expertise. But he took a different emphasis from Pickering, as was reflected in the NASA version of the meeting found in notes by Homer Newell, head of its space sciences office: "Longer range developm.—of course. But must build up confidence of Congress so that they will provide the support." Silverstein stressed that NASA had "a rugged job monitoring nat'l program." He envisioned JPL playing a big role as monitor. NASA wanted broad support from JPL. He foresaw a laboratory that would be more responsive to headquarters, which meant substantial curbs on the independence Pickering sought. In short, NASA wanted JPL to operate as an insider, like other agency centers, rather than as an outsider, like a contractor.[19]

Insider or outsider? It was perhaps significant that the NASA bureaucracy thought of the laboratory in those dichotomous terms. The answer seemed to be that JPL was part insider, part outsider. The laboratory's anomalous status gave it a unique value as a yardstick institution but also placed it in political peril. Vast amounts of time and energy would be consumed in resolving the question of insider or outsider throughout the next decade.

JPL pressed NASA hard early in 1959 for authorization to take the first step in its space program, Project Vega. Three early rounds were programmed in accordance with the JPL five-year plan—lunar and Mars probes in the second half of 1960 and a Venus flight in 1961. (The fourth would be a new meteorological Earth satellite; two to four more flights would be determined later.) The vehicle for these flights consisted of a payload and a three-stage rocket. The first-stage Atlas would be developed by Convair Astronautics, the second would employ the Vanguard rocket designed by General Electric, and the third would use the 6K segment JPL had been working on. Vega was only an interim vehicle, whose usefulness would extend only until the Centaur was ready in 1962; but Pickering told Glennan in 1959 it ranked nonetheless as "one of the most important actions which NASA must take this year." Vega promised a quick planetary capability, and some of the program's segments would become building blocks for later developments. As the first vehicle system NASA would build under its own direction and for scientific and civilian purposes, Vega would free the agency from its dependence on military vehicles. If NASA did not inaugurate Vega at once, Pickering pointed out on March 24, 1959, two serious consequences would follow. First, the Mars flight in 1960 would have to be scrapped, "with consequent loss of prestige to both the U. S. and NASA." Second, any slippage in development would endanger Vega's lead time over Centaur and give force to the argument that NASA should just wait for Centaur. The desire both to start a planetary flight program quickly and to free NASA from its military dependency induced JPL to cast its lot with Vega.[20]

After long delays in its chaotic early months, NASA finally authorized the Vega program at JPL on March 26, 1959. From the start a host of problems—budgetary, organizational, and technical—plagued Vega. The project never received the financial support it needed but had to operate under serious budgetary and manpower restrictions, especially in the areas outside propulsion. By 1959 NASA had assigned priority to Project Mercury, the first U. S. man-in-space venture, which left Vega constantly underfunded. JPL faced continual organizational woes. The laboratory had the role of project manager to supervise and integrate the whole effort, but it did not have the authority to match. Unlike the Sergeant missile project, where JPL had enjoyed technical control and considerable contract authority, the Vega operation left open virtually two lines of authority to the contractors—one from the laboratory, the other from NASA headquarters. JPL felt the contractors sided with the agency holding the purse, NASA headquarters. The agency's Washington office seemed continually confusing to the laboratory. Instead of one central project office, as had been set up for Mercury, Vega efforts required time-consuming and sometimes contradictory coordination with each of the major branches in NASA. Finally, the schedule for launchings slipped badly. There simply were not enough launch stands available in the country to wedge in Vega firings, and NASA was slow in contracting to build additional stands. By November 1959 the first launching, originally slated for summer 1960, had slipped to March 1961. Vega's margin over Centaur had diminished to a critical point.[21]

The technical difficulties and high costs of space technology, moreover, added to doubts about the possibility of meeting Vega's ambitious schedule. Consider guidance, one of JPL's prime responsibilities. No American space probe launched through the summer of 1959 could boast of guidance into or after the injection phase. The most advanced spin-stabilized vehicle was estimated to have no better than an even chance of impacting the moon, and some estimates ranged as low as 10 percent. True space-mission capabilities required guidance not only through injection, however, but also the capability both to perform mid-course corrections and to complete terminal maneuvers, whether for orbit or soft landing. JPL engineers began to think that the sensible course would be to use lunar flights as the proving ground for developing all the elements of a spacecraft system. The shorter distance to the moon made possible more economical development, and the more frequent launch opportunities promised faster progress. Without question the lunar emphasis weakened the planetary program that JPL desired. But as a laboratory report pointed out in October 1959: "It is impossible, in a six-vehicle program having the current manpower and funding limitation, to mix equally lunar and interplanetary programs without seriously jeopardizing the *whole* program." It was also impossible, the report concluded, "to adequately disguise an interplanetary program as a lunar program." The laboratory thus argued for "a strong lunar program in which the interplanetary capability is less than optimum."[22]

JPL was in part making a virtue of necessity, for by the fall of 1959 Vega little resembled the scenario of a few months earlier. Aiming at the most difficult problems first, JPL engineers had pitched their initial designs at the Mars 1960 probe. They soon decided that a Mars mission posed too many technical barriers for so new a program. The Mars mission, which Hibbs had once termed "of the utmost importance," faded out in June 1959. A more realistic Mars attempt was sketched for October 1962. Glennan got cold feet about the Venus mission also in the summer of 1959. He pointed out to Eisenhower that the proposed launch, in January 1961, would be only the first or second firing of the Vega vehicle, "and the chances of full success seem[ed] quite low." The NASA administrator deferred the Venus venture until 1962, when it would again assume an approachable position. By the fall of 1959 the first four Vegas had been cut back to lunar missions, the first of which would take place in March 1961. The planetary probes would have to wait until 1962. If the schedule slipped much more, Vega would become an example of the very problem it was supposed to correct: a short-term vehicle that would be used for too few missions to assure much reliability and then would be discarded.[23]

Despite these problems Vega might have survived had not a competitor surprisingly emerged from the murky waters of the military-space bureaucracy. The rival was Agena B, a clandestine air force project which had capabilities similar to the second and third stages of Vega. NASA and military officials had traded information on their vehicle plans in December 1958 and had formalized them in "A National Space Vehicle Program" on January 27, 1959. Agena had not been mentioned, even though the air force apparently began its development about that time. The air force used the Agena as the injection stage in its Discoverer satellite program—a role Vega could easily have assumed. NASA did not learn of the interloper until late summer 1959. The duplication could not be justified; President Eisenhower reacted angrily when he heard of the air force's maneuver. But NASA bowed to force majeure; Glennan recognized the political clout the air force wielded in Congress. Even though Vega had prior rights to development and its abandonment lost $17 million, he decided to cancel it and adopt Agena B in early December 1959.[24]

"Quite a bombshell you threw at us," Pickering told NASA assistant administrator Richard Horner on December 8. The JPL head had learned of the cancellation only the day before; laboratory documents as recent as December 3 had still assigned Vega prominent roles. Glennan had informed Pickering of the decision but had not sought JPL's consent. The cancellation caused consternation at the laboratory. JPL had pinned most of its early space dreams on Vega; Pickering had expected that half of the laboratory's effort in 1960—almost everything except for the Sergeant missile—would be devoted to Vega. The 6K propulsion development project was reduced to research status. This marked a historic turn in the laboratory. Never again would propulsion, the field in which the laboratory had first gained fame, assume prominence at JPL.[25]

"I look at this and get concerned over the whole plan of the Lab's part in NASA," Pickering told Horner. "The implication is pretty heavy as to reorientation of JPL." Horner agreed that the decision "must be disturbing in many respects to you and your staff." It would entail "a major reorientation" of the laboratory's work, he acknowledged. But the cancellation, he continued, contributed to sorting out the roles of the NASA centers that Glennan had desired for some time. The space agency had finally wrenched ABMA from the army. Renamed Marshall Space Flight Center, it would assume responsibility for launch-vehicle systems. The new Goddard Space Flight Center in Beltsville, Maryland, would supervise Earth satellites and sounding-rocket payloads. JPL would take over the development and operation of spacecraft for lunar and planetary exploration. Although it meant abandonment of work on vehicle systems, this was an ample assignment. Pickering acknowledged later that the laboratory probably could not have maintained its propulsion and vehicle work along with the spacecraft assignment. In the short run, however, JPL officials had to determine where their space role would lead over the next few years.[26]

By the end of December JPL and NASA officials hammered out a revised space program for the laboratory. The solution blended headquarters' preference for lunar flights with JPL's designs for planetary exploration. Seven flights were planned. Five lunar reconnaissance missions were scheduled from spring 1961 through fall 1962; known as Rangers, these would use the Atlas-Agena B. Venus and Mars probes would follow in the second half of 1962; carrying the name Mariners, they would be propelled by the Atlas and the new Centaur. Both NASA and JPL agreed that it was "technically possible and highly desirable to fly early." This posed a high-risk decision. Since the Vega spacecraft had been targeted for planetary missions, it was more complex and potentially raised more problems than necessary in a lunar reconnaissance object. On the other hand, by making use of the design to that point, a continuation of the Vega plans had the appeal of potentially faster and more economical development. The Vega spacecraft thus became the basis for both Ranger and the early Mariners.[27]

In the aftermath of the cancellation of Vega, JPL's program for the next several years had been basically determined. The lunar program expanded rapidly in 1960. That summer the laboratory let contracts to four industrial firms to study the next phase of its lunar program, the softlander eventually known as Surveyor. As the Sergeant missile work was phased out, the Mariner projects, a formidable competitor to the lunar work, began moving up from the inside. By the end of 1960 Ranger spacecraft were nearing the assembly stage, and Mariner design concepts were approaching the first attempts at hardware.

During the program reorientation of late 1959 and early 1960, the laboratory organization, which had been fairly informal, began to become more bureaucratized. Pickering appointed Brian Sparks as the first deputy director in 1959 and gave him considerable authority over day-to-day affairs. Two other staff engineers, J. W. McGarrity and J. I. Shafer, provided limited staff assistance to the director. Planning support came from a four-man planning staff headed by assistant director J. D. McKenney. Assistant director Frank E. Goddard, who had been detailed to NASA headquarters for a time after the agency was formed, handled JPL-NASA relations. Business administration continued to be headed by Val C. Larsen, Jr., the third assistant director. Two program directors rounded out the director's office:

Cliff Cummings, who headed the Ranger effort, and Robert J. Parks, who ran the Sergeant missile program until the JPL portion was phased out on June 30, 1960, when he became head of the Mariner program. Pickering also made increasing and more formal use of the senior staff, a group of twenty to thirty executives including the director's office staff, the division chiefs, and some administrative and other selected personnel. The weekly senior-staff meetings were a significant forum for discussing laboratory policies.[28]

The technical work of the laboratory was organized in accordance with the matrix concept. The matrix would remain the laboratory's basic organization pattern for the next two decades, although it was subject to criticism and severe strains. Based on a study by the management analysis firm of McKinsey & Company, the JPL matrix resembled forms in use at Argonne Laboratory, Marshall Space Flight Center, Hughes Aircraft, and other industrial firms. The line organization of the technical staff was divided among seven technical divisions, somewhat analogous to university departments; then a small project organization would form a thin overlay across the divisions.* The rationale behind the matrix concept was that the technical divisions carried the ongoing work of the laboratory, while project offices were finite and subject to dissolution. Since several similar projects would be going on simultaneously, the best technical talent would presumably be applied to any or all of the projects as needed; scientists and engineers would not be pigeonholed on one project when their talents might be needed elsewhere. The division chiefs wielded great authority. They exerted considerable influence on the programs the laboratory undertook through their relationships with the director's staff and program offices. Within their satrapies the division chiefs planned and directed all the laboratory's activities; approved all personnel actions, except for hiring and firing section chiefs, which required the approval of the deputy director; shifted funds

---

*The divisions and the sections under them were:
1. Systems: Program Support, Systems Analysis, Systems Design, Systems Test and Operation.
2. Space Sciences: Research Analysis, Space Instruments.
3. Telecommunications: Communications Systems Research, Communications Engineering and Operations, Communications Elements Research, Telemetering and Command Systems.
4. Guidance and Control: Electronic Devices, Sergeant Guidance Engineering, Guidance and Control Engineering, Electro-Mechanical Devices.
5. Engineering Mechanics: Materials Research, Missile Engineering, Professional Services, Engineering Research, Spacecraft Engineering, Design.
6. Physical Sciences: Chemical Physics, Gas Dynamics, Physics.
7. Propulsion: Solid-Propellant Rockets, Solid-Propellant Chemistry, Liquid-Propulsion Research, Liquid-Propulsion Development.

within programs; and controlled the facilities and equipment the divisions used on a long-term basis.[29]

The program director had responsibility for the end product of a given program, such as the lunar program, after the general design approach had been settled by the senior staff. To accomplish this he had to rely on the technical divisions, and much of his time involved coordination with the division chiefs to insure they provided the work required. The program director tried to iron out jurisdictional disputes between divisions, although they could appeal to the deputy director. The program director also established liaison with contractors. His authority extended to programs, not personnel. His personnel authority reached only his immediate staff, which he was expected to limit "rigorously." For instance, Cummings had only his deputy, James Burke, and two other engineers on his staff in mid-1960; but he drew on 600 professionals divided among the divisions. The interface between the program directors and the division chiefs posed potentially the most serious problem in organization. The matrix concept had considerable validity, especially as a means of insuring continuity of research and advanced development efforts, cross-fertilization of ideas, and the recharging of the staff through rapid integration of new talent. As the laboratory became more heavily committed to programs with specific objectives and tight schedules, however, serious doubts emerged as to whether the program organization was strong enough.[30]

While JPL's internal reorganization took place, the laboratory also faced a difficult shakedown cruise in its external relations with NASA. McKinsey & Company had warned that the "operation of a large laboratory, under contract with a private institution, presents problems unprecedented" in NACA's experience with its research centers. Glennan at one point confided to his assistants that "constant misunderstandings, accusations and arguments" had marked the first phase of NASA-JPL relations. JPL officials felt equally frustrated, with complaints that ranged from too much NASA interference in technical minutiae to the direction of the space program as a whole. The conflicts focused on five areas.[31]

First, the most basic problem was what role JPL would play in NASA. Did the laboratory really fit inside? "You have at JPL an eager, able and enthusiastic group," Glennan told Caltech president DuBridge in August 1959. "Given unlimited funds, they would be happy to solve all of our problems." He cautioned DuBridge, however, "that everything in this field will not be done by Goddard, by JPL, or any other single group." But having given the laboratory the impression it would operate from the inside, NASA had failed to follow through, the administrator admitted to his deputies. The Washington office had encouraged JPL to draw up long-range studies, such as the five-year plan, but then it had not attempted to formulate programs in response to them. Pickering had detailed some of his top staff members to headquarters, but, said Glennan, "we have failed to make a conscious effort to make JPL a real part of NASA management." Glennan wondered whether the inside approach had been wise or whether JPL should be treated like a special contractor, such as the Los Alamos laboratory of the AEC.[32]

JPL chafed under the programmatic, budgetary, and manpower restrictions NASA imposed on it. The measure of autonomy JPL had enjoyed under the army seemed neither possible nor desirable to the space agency. The personnel ceiling was perhaps the most irritating to JPL. Because NASA imposed a ceiling of 2,400 employees in 1959 and 1960, when laboratory employees numbered approximately 2,650, JPL had to terminate about 100 persons in addition to normal attrition. The personnel limit seemed arbitrary to Pickering, but headquarters defended it as a concomitant of budget control. It was also something more: NASA used the ceiling as a device to limit JPL's in-house capability by forcing tasks to be contracted out. This issue touched the JPL status question and therefore remained a focus of dispute between Washington and Pasadena for some time.[33]

JPL found some amelioration of lines of authority, however, during the months before Glennan resigned in January 1961. Although the laboratory's technical activities on Ranger had made great strides during 1960, the project had been bogged down in organizational chaos. NASA headquarters had been reluctant either to decentralize authority or to set up a special project organization. Under the ad hoc arrangement that ensued, JPL, Marshall Space Flight Center, Lockheed, and the air force each had slivers of authority. Conflicts were bucked to a bickering, slow-moving coordination board for resolution. After most of 1960 was consumed in an organizational ordeal, Ranger was reorganized in January 1961 with Glennan's promulgation of a major organization change called Management Instruction 4-1-1.

The core of 4-1-1 was a project development plan, which set up specific project organizations for NASA undertakings and spelled out the rights and duties of the NASA centers. The project development plan amplified an important agreement Caltech and JPL had reached with NASA in August 1960. Headquarters had explicitly agreed to give the laboratory a voice in the determination of its program and to allow JPL virtually free rein in technical matters unless major reprogramming was needed. The August understanding assumed major importance for JPL as an interpretation of its basic contract with NASA. It embodied the concept of mutuality, meaning that actions were to be undertaken after both JPL and NASA agreed; NASA would not issue unilateral directives. This agreement gave the laboratory much of the freedom it wanted. Now it had to perform.[34]

Despite these improvements in relations, NASA cast an increasingly skeptical eye on JPL in a second area: management. Glennan found the laboratory's staff as "bright and undisciplined" a group as he had seen. "It lacked any real sense of the management techniques" which NASA programs needed. JPL had gotten its way previously because it had more technical competence "than the army ever thought of having." The story would be different with NASA, which outshone the army, and, in Glennan's opinion, boasted a staff "substantially more competent" than JPL in some areas. Headquarters personnel attributed many of JPL's problems to top management, which did not provide "full-time direction of a decisive nature." Decisions made at the top were often upset by the technical decisions, NASA complained. The gap between JPL and government practice appeared, too, in such areas as the laboratory's weak financial management and procurement processes, lack of staff assistance for Pickering, imprecise lines of authority, and splits between the technical and nontechnical sides of the house. NASA's fears were warranted. JPL eventually performed admirably—indeed, by the mid-1960s it was giving management lessons to aerospace firms. But the learning process, which included several conspicuous failures in the Ranger project, was agonizing.[35]

Third, NASA began to show an attentiveness to the connection, or lack of it, between the laboratory and Caltech that had not interested the army. Glennan realized CIT did little to earn its management fee. He felt significant advantages could accrue from having a laboratory aligned with Caltech, but he wanted to see some tangible evidence. Glennan praised his fellow college president, DuBridge, for his expressed "determination to bring the 'resources' of the Caltech campus into a more positive and productive relationship with JPL. This seems to me to be the very essence of the reasoning behind the involvement of an educational institution of high quality in the management and operation of an activity such as JPL." One perhaps unexpected by-product of JPL's joining the civilian space effort was the opportunity, and the expectation, of greater campus involvement.[36]

Fourth, Pickering tried to carve out a dominant role for JPL in space science. He proposed that the laboratory, and the other NASA centers for that matter, act as the principal liaisons with the scientific community. Headquarters would rely on the centers, rather than independent boards, for advice; this would effectively allow the centers to decide which experiments and experimenters would get aboard the spacecraft. From NASA's point of view this scheme had two problems. First, it surrendered too much authority. Second, since the centers would be competing with outside scientists for places on the spacecraft, the plan raised obvious questions of conflict of interest. Caltech provost Robert F. Bacher, a perceptive science politico who had been an AEC commissioner, underscored this objection. He noted that the University of Chicago had encountered this very criticism in its operation of Argonne National Laboratory. JPL's gambit failed; headquarters would select experimenters. This decision, however necessary, may have had a negative side effect. It stifled the laboratory's development of a strong scientific capability and contributed to the dominance of project engineering.[37]

Finally, JPL and NASA continued to differ over the pace of the space program. Within the Eisenhower administration were two contending schools of thought, neither of them aggressive enough for JPL. For his part, Eisenhower doubted the value of sending a man to the moon, and he particularly opposed the notion of a space race with the Soviet Union. When the president's science advisory committee reported that a crash program for a manned lunar landing could cost $35 billion, the cabinet greeted the idea with derision. "Well, let's come back to reality," Eisenhower said. He suggested an annual budget of $1 billion to $1.5 billion. The administration's approach to the space program, though fiscally conservative, was not that of a crabbed accountant. The president insisted the United States should conduct "a scholarly exploration of space." In his final budget message to Congress, in January 1961, he was prepared to say that manned spaceflight should stop after the Mercury program. He chose less categorical language and put science first: "Further testing and experimentation will be necessary to determine whether there are any valid scientific reasons for extending manned spaceflight beyond the Mercury program."[38]

As head of NASA Glennan came to believe that putting a man on the moon was worthwhile, although not "a matter of prime importance." But he too thought the space race was a delusion. He did not believe the United States could avoid competition with the Russians, but it could and should establish the terms of competition. Glennan urged a long view. Sputnik had been first—there was no undoing that. The two countries competed on many fronts, and international leadership entailed much more than a space derby. "When one starts to talk about the prestige of the United States resting on the question—'When do we get a man on the moon?'—it seems clear that all sense of perspective has gone out the window," Glennan confided to his diary. Indeed, the American preoccupation with a race gave the Soviet Union a golden opportunity. After leaving office, Glennan suggested to Nikita Khrushchev that, "if he were as smart as I think him to be," he would stage "a barrage of propaganda and successful spaceflights until he had the U. S. committed to a costly program"—and "then withdraw from the 'race.'" By the end of 1963 there was evidence that Khrushchev had done just that.[39]

No "space cadet," Glennan favored a program that would reach a level of $2 billion to $2.5 billion per year and land a man on the moon by about 1975. Not only would such a pace keep scientific objectives uppermost, by avoiding the heavy costs of trying to develop new technologies concurrently, it would also keep the budget in line. He warned that the alternative—a race to the moon as was undertaken with Apollo—threatened "in the long run . . . [to] work strongly to our detriment."[40]

In retrospect one could see that under Glennan the foundations of two decades of NASA programs were laid. The agency's budget reached $915 million in fiscal year 1961 and climbed over a billion the next year. At this point, however, directions were not yet clear, and NASA institutions vied with each other for their portions. After probing the diffuse NASA programs, presidential science adviser George Kistiakowsky, a Harvard chemist, returned the mordant verdict: the agency "did not have a space program but only one to feed the many hungry NASA mouths."[41]

JPL was one of those eyeing a larger platter. When the Ranger budget fell short and the laboratory had to terminate nearly 100 employees in May 1960, Pickering sent Glennan a plaintive letter. Ranger was resembling Vega. "It appears that once again we are saddled with an interim project which will gradually slip to the point where it is no longer justified and must be cancelled," Pickering fretted. More than fourteen months had passed since JPL had conducted a space experiment, and at least eleven months would elapse before the first Ranger flight. "We would like to believe that we are doing something important for the nation," he said. To most of JPL's senior staff that meant beating the Russians. "It is the U. S. against Russia," said Pickering in early 1960, "and its most important campaign is being fought far out in the empty reaches of space." But if one asked, "'Do we now have a space program?' the answer must be 'No.'" JPL looked to the incoming Kennedy administration for new impetus. But few persons at the laboratory anticipated the chastening experience that lay ahead.[42]

Improbable beginning. Members of the GALCIT rocket research group lounge on the floor of the Arroyo Seco before a motor test in 1936. They are, from left, student assistant Rudolph Schott, Apollo M. O. Smith, Frank J. Malina, Edward S. Forman, and John W. Parsons. One hose feeds propellant, the other oxygen to the rocket motor, the small cylindrical chamber mounted on the top of the test stand. The squarish glass container atop the sandbags contains cooling water that is piped to the motor's water jacket. The GALCIT experimenters sought relative safety behind the sandbags during the tests.

The Kármán aegis. Theodore von Kármán, patron of the early GALCIT rocket project, performs last-minute calculations before a JATO test at March Field in August 1941. With the great aerodynamicist are, from left, Clark Millikan, his successor as head of GALCIT; Martin Summerfield, who played a key role in early discoveries; Frank J. Malina; and Captain Homer Boushey, the test pilot, and later head of air force research and development.

Wartime foundation. The first permanent facilities of the GALCIT rocket research project, hard by the muddy bed of the Arroyo Seco, in 1942.

National laboratory. JPL in 1975. The bed of the Arroyo Seco is to the right.

Romantic rocketry. Malina and the WAC Corporal at White Sands in November 1945.

Toward space. Bumper WAC—a WAC Corporal riding atop a German
V-2—blasts off from White Sands on April 25, 1949. Attaining a record
altitude of 250 miles, the WAC Corporal became the first man-made
object to reach extraterrestrial space.

Corporal tests. Nattily turned out for a round of
testing of the Corporal missile at White Sands
are Louis G. Dunn (left), JPL director
1946–1954, and one of his confidants, senior
engineer Paul Meeks.

Sergeant mating. Army troops attach the warhead to the Sergeant missile during a practice
round in 1960. For firing the missile was positioned at an angle of about 75 degrees on its
mobile launcher.

A satellite at last. A jubilant William Pickering (left), James Van Allen, and Wernher von Braun hoist a model of Explorer 1 at a news conference after the confirmation that it had become the first American satellite to attain orbit.

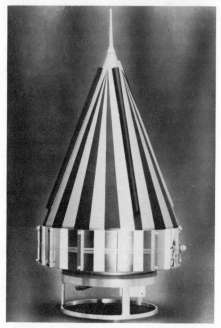

Earth escape. Pioneer 4, launched on March 3, 1959, became the first American spacecraft to escape earth's gravitational pull. It passed the moon at a distance of 37,300 miles.

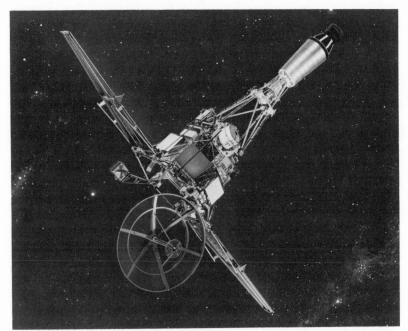

Planetary prototype. Ranger 1 established the basic configuration out of which JPL's lunar and planetary spacecraft evolved.

Mariner culmination. Looking like a galactic frog, Mariner 10 represented the culmination of the Ranger-Mariner series. Just as the Model T could be sensed beneath the skin of the streamlined automobile, so too the basic Ranger 1 could be imagined in the repackaged and simplified Mariner 10.

Director and friend. William Pickering, director of JPL 1954–1976, with a Mariner spacecraft.

Caltech connection. Lee A. DuBridge, president of Caltech 1946–1969, and a firm supporter of the CIT-JPL link, with Pickering.

Political ritual. Space officials present pictures of Mars from Mariner 4 at the White House in August 1965. From left, William Pickering; Oran Nicks of NASA; J. N. James, Mariner project manager; President Lyndon B. Johnson; and James E. Webb, NASA administrator 1961–1968, and sometime JPL nemesis.

Lunar panorama. Once the troubled Surveyor finally made a soft-landing on the moon, it revealed a solid surface safe for Apollo. This photograph, part of a circular mosaic of hundreds of television photos taken by Surveyor 7 in January 1968, shows a perilous 20-foot boulder in the right background. The hills in the center background are about 8 miles away.

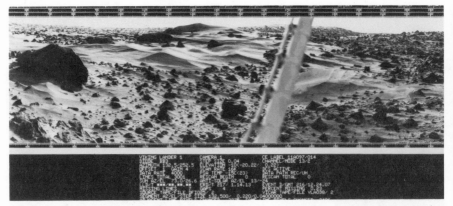

VIKING LANDER 1   CAMERA 1   CE LABEL 118097 014
AZIMUTH 132.5-252.5   TIC RATE 0.04   CHANNEL MODE 13/2
                      ELEVATION 10K-20.22   0.22
                      YAW   20K 283
DATA RATE 4000   DIA TEMP 283
LIN 62 EL = -73.0 26.6 BIT LEN 13
MISSING LINES   AZ 1.1 1.14.13
                                          SHOT 9 GMT 216 12.34.07
CURRENT TAPE FILE 8 PTS
                      49.500 0.220 0.04000000

Mars as Mars. By the time of the Viking 1 lander, which took this picture in August 1976, scientists had ceased to think of Mars as moonlike. The rocks and sand dunes shown here resemble desert panoramas on Earth, such as Death Valley. The object bisecting the photograph is the boom of Viking's miniature weather station.

Scientist as director. Bruce C. Murray, director of JPL 1976–82.

Facing page: By Jupiter. Voyager 1 photographed Jupiter and its four planet-size moons, known as the Galilean satellites, in March 1979. Assembled into this collage, they are not to scale but are in their relative positions: reddish Io (upper left), Europa (center), Ganymede, and Galisteo (lower right).

8 ★★

JPL'S FALTERING START IN THE PRESTIGE RACE

The period from John F. Kennedy's election in November 1960 through May 1961, when he called for a manned landing on the moon by the end of the decade, ranks as one of the most crucial in the history of the space program. A national debate took place which raised many of the critical questions about the pace and content of the space program. On one side were those who thought science should play a paramount role; while by no means oblivious of the program's importance for national prestige, they argued for a broader perspective both on the proper ends of space activity and on what constitutes national greatness. On the other side stood those who pressed the national security argument; to them the paramount goal of the space program should be enhancement of American prestige and military capability. JPL staff members lined up solidly in the national security camp. Having taxed the National Aeronautics and Space Administration under T. Keith Glennan for "a lack of dynamic, informed technical and administrative leadership," they hoped that Kennedy's campaign pledge to "get the country moving again" would translate into a bigger and faster space program.[1]

The broadly based scientific position received a thoughtful exposition from James Killian, Eisenhower's first science adviser and the president of M.I.T., in December 1960. Killian's speech was a companion piece to Eisenhower's valedictory warning about the dangers of the military-industrial complex. The M.I.T. head agreed that science and technology played a vital role in foreign policy, particularly as an influence on the third world, which assumed increased importance in the late 1950s and early 1960s as the scene of competition between communism and capitalism. "Status seekers in the community of nations" (that is, the Soviet Union) had used spectacular science and technology "to build their prestige," Killian acknowledged. The

Facing page: The Saturn system. A montage of images taken from photographs by Voyager 1 in November 1980. Saturn rises behind Dione (foreground). Tethys and Mimas are fading in the distance to the right; Enceladus and Mimas are off Saturn's rings to the left; and Titan is in its distant orbit at the top. (The orbs are in their relative positions but are not to scale.)

Russians' expensive space program could not maintain an image of strength over the long pull, however. "True strength and lasting prestige will come from the richness, variety, and depth of a nation's total program," he said. Not content to be second best, the United States should build its own balanced space program instead of copying the Soviets. "In the long run we can weaken our science and technology and lower our international prestige by frantically indulging in unnecessary competition and prestige-motivated projects." Killian supported a cautious man-in-space program but reminded his listeners that "the really exciting discoveries in space can be realized better by instruments than by man." The costs of manned space would be "startling," and should be balanced against other urgent national needs. "The image of America," he pointed out, "may be shaped by the quality of its inner life more than by its exploits in outer space."[2]

From within the Kennedy administration Harvard economist David E. Bell, the former marine who was director of the Bureau of the Budget, offered a similar admonition. He pointed out that the space program would impinge on other, probably more worthwhile, federal activities. Within the space program he questioned the focus on "full-scale participation in the 'weight lifting' and manned space-flight competitions." He preferred a "strong scientific and technological program," as well as space applications such as meteorology and communications. These would be at least as effective as prestige builders, for they were "a specific token that we are more concerned with the problems of *men on earth* all over the world than we are with placing *men on the moon*."[3]

This position was seconded by no less a spokesman for science and national security concerns than Vannevar Bush. He contended that the Apollo program misled the public on what was "really worthwhile in scientific effort" or what science was all about. The National Academy of Science's report favoring Apollo had been weak on the scientific returns in proportion to the huge cost and had based its justifications on national prestige. The elder statesman doubted that a moon race was in fact going on—a position which NASA indeed admitted in 1973, long after that justification had served its purpose. In any case, Bush argued, national prestige was "far more subtle" than NASA's "immature" concept. He concluded: "Having a large number of devoted Americans working unselfishly in undeveloped countries is far more impressive than mere technical excellence."[4]

Proponents of the national security argument, such as President Kennedy, gave precedence, however, to the space program's contribution to technological superiority. The United States followed a strategy of technological hegemony from World War II forward. The Corporal and Sergeant missile programs had reflected this policy. Technological superiority reduced military personnel needs and at the same time laid a foundation for nuclear credibility. The arcane practice of deterrence was heavily based on technological superiority. The United States tried to demonstrate its readiness to use the nuclear arsenal without actually precipitating the disaster of setting it off. Of the various ways the United States tried to demonstrate its credibility, technology was a central means of indicating resolve short of actual use. Technological defeats, such as the presumed damage of Sputnik, demanded repair. Believing American credibility had to be restored in many areas, John Kennedy favored a technological demonstration through the space program. To him the "space gap" symbolized "the nation's lack of initiative, ingenuity, and vitality under Republican rule," recalled one of his closest advisers, Theodore Sorensen. "The President was more convinced than any of his advisers that a second-rate, second-place space effort was inconsistent with this country's security." Kennedy and Vice-President Lyndon Johnson agreed with the aggressive new NASA administrator, James E. Webb, who contended that "the viability of representative government and of the free enterprise system" was being "tested in our space program."[5]

The Kennedy administration built what Sorensen termed "the most powerful military force in human history—the largest and swiftest buildup in the country's peacetime history." The New Frontier's military package ranged from counterinsurgency forces, as epitomized by the Green Berets, to a massive expansion of the ICBM fleet which even Secretary of Defense Robert McNamara decided went too far. An aggressive man-in-space program emerged ineluctably as a key component of this military buildup, for reasons not only of prestige but of direct military capability. NASA administrator Webb approvingly quoted Gen. Thomas S. Power, commander-in-chief of the Strategic Air Command, who praised NASA's "close cooperation with the Department of Defense [which] will not only further . . . the peaceful conquest of space but also help create the building blocks for the future military systems which may be required." Webb estimated that three-fourths of the cost of Apollo went toward the development of near-Earth orbital capabilities, which were essential for possible military missions, such as interception of "hostile space vehicles." (Apollo's military payoff became clearer in the 1970s and '80s as the Defense Department moved into activities such as "killer" satellites and figured heavily in the development of the space shuttle.) Other building blocks included large launch vehicles and complex ground facilities, which Webb termed "vitally important" for military missions.[6]

Moreover, NASA was "picking up the slack" in order to maintain a basic industrial sector—the aerospace industry—as aircraft production declined."[7] Clifford Cummings's analysis of the relationship between the industry and the space program was borne out. The space program, particularly its manned component, was a godsend for the aircraft firms. As would become clear, Webb ran NASA with great solicitude for those politically powerful foundations of the military-industrial complex—sometimes to the disadvantage of JPL.

The national debate on the space program took on particular urgency from two events in April 1961. First, on April 12, Yuri Gagarin orbited the Earth in a Soviet spaceship; he was the first human in orbit. Second, on April 15, the Bay of Pigs invasion began. By April 19, the disastrous consequences of the incursion became apparent, and that day Kennedy called Lyndon Johnson into the oval office and told him to find a "space program which promises dramatic results in which we could win." Under the vice-president's goading, NASA planning quickly crystallized in favor of putting a man on the moon, a program eventually known as Apollo.[8]

In this crisis atmosphere Pickering established a new JPL committee on April 25 to come up with a space plan to retrieve national honor. Laboratory engineers were especially perturbed by the Soviet planetary launches. Two Mars missions were launched in October 1960, both failed; and two Venus flights were launched in February 1961, one failed but the other sent Venera 1 on its way. These were the missions JPL had wanted the United States to attempt in its 1959 report; moreover, the Soviets used a big, new upper stage. To JPL the Russian program was both a political setback and a professional affront. Rationalizations based on scientific exploits or the overall national space record would not do, Pickering said. The new study should "take into account the primary importance of the propaganda and geopolitical aspects of space achievements, as well as the value of missions having scientific merit."[9]

Accordingly the authors of the study in May 1961 based their program on the assumption that "the USSR has chosen to win the 'space race' in order to prove to the people of the world that the Communist system is more virile than the Capitalistic system." In evaluating the desirability of missions, national prestige scored 45 points on a 100-point scale. Technology (space capability and practical nonmilitary applications) received 35 points, and science weighed in with just 20. (This weighting contrasted with the 1959 study in which JPL had ranked feasibility first and "public reaction" second; scientific and technical merit had ranked third then too.) American space goals should be putting a man on the moon in early 1967, establishing a manned lunar base in 1969, and landing a man on Mars in 1973. The main purpose was to be first, not to do "a better engineering job or obtain . . . more scientific data," the study committee said. Scientific data could be obtained on a "piggyback," or space available, basis. In keeping with the sense of urgency, the report called for greater freedom in business and contract procedures and more secrecy before launches, including if necessary a new launch base other than Cape Canaveral.[10]

Many JPL senior staff members eagerly endorsed the study. Robert V.

Meghreblian thought it cut through the mistaken notions on which the existing space program was based, which he believed emphasized primarily the quest for scientific knowledge. "To my mind, a billion-dollar-a-year space program programmed at gaining purely scientific information about outer space is a waste beyond comprehension," he said. "To discard a modern instrument of international competition which has been so brilliantly exploited by the Soviets is to jeopardize the security and prestige of the nation." The leaders of the space science division, Al Hibbs and Manfred Eimer, argued for an all-out manned race to the moon, even though it would curtail most of that division's activities. Believing the Americans' chances of beating the Russians were slim, they wanted all projects not directly related to man-on-the-moon halted and the project conducted with maximum secrecy and elaborate cover stories. Pickering endorsed the report. When he visited NASA headquarters in mid-May, he was encouraged to find the planning for Apollo well advanced. "In general, the Lab's ideas and views are in conformity with these plans," he reported.[11]

On May 25, 1961, Kennedy addressed Congress on "urgent national needs" and called for putting a man on the moon by the end of the decade. Taking "a clearly leading role in space achievement" was essential "if we are to win the battle that is going on around the world between freedom and tyranny," he said. The president's decision, followed by congressional endorsement, rippled throughout the space establishment. The day Kennedy made his speech, NASA issued a new flight plan in which it listed JPL's lunar missions, Ranger and Surveyor, as ventures in "direct support" of Apollo. National security considerations—prestige objectives most of all—had displaced the scientific, peaceful rationale. JPL lunar programs director Clifford Cummings explained the effects of the decision to Lyndon Johnson when he visited the laboratory on October 4, 1961: "Originally our lunar program had been oriented toward scientific and technological objectives," Cummings said. "Now . . . the emphasis has been changed so that support of the manned operations is the primary objective, and space technology and lunar science are secondary. We believe, however, that we can accomplish the space science and technology objectives as planned, while at the same time providing essential support to the manned effort." Apollo's goals were not necessarily compatible with lunar science or planetary exploration, however. When choices had to be made between them, as they surely would, Apollo's top priority threatened to distort or curtail scientific activities.[12]

One such impact was evident in the obsession with schedule on Project Ranger. Its director, James Burke, believed the laboratory had to learn to produce by a schedule. "The planets do not wait," he liked to point out. But the greatest fear was that the Russians would not wait either; this was what seemed to give particular lunar and planetary windows an extraordinary urgency. Burke pasted a picture of a Soviet Venera spacecraft to his wall and wrote beneath it: "The better is the enemy of the good." Laboratory engineers filed papers headed "Beat the Russians" and decorated them with doodles that showed clocks with hands at the eleventh hour, swinging pendulums, and the words "FLY SOON" cascading in block letters across the page. To the difficulty of doing new things was added the complication of doing them rapidly.[13]

The scope and pace of the space program through the 1960s was primarily the result of the Kennedy administration's approach to the cold war and, more particularly, the perception of crisis in early 1961. The administration's abrupt expansion of the space program, and especially its Apollo decision, was encouraged by the institutional needs and political perceptions of men like the senior staff of JPL. Space was important to them intellectually, but in 1961 it was important primarily as a new arena of competition in national security technology. JPL was still building weapons systems during the early years of the space program, and in a symbolic sense space missions were a new phase of weaponry in the early 1960s. The laboratory staff, like many other Americans, readily transferred the technological urgency of "Beat the Russians" from missiles to space. This position failed to recognize, however, that prestige entailed more than the projection of power. By 1963 the State Department was encountering opposition from other countries to renewing some space program agreements because of their military overtones. As Robert Packard of the department's Office of International Science Affairs explained: Emphasis on Apollo as a crash program reduced "the credibility of our program as a balanced, rationally-paced undertaking for essentially scientific and beneficial purposes."[14] National prestige, as men like Killian, Bush, and Bell realized, was subtler and more multifaceted and required fidelity to ideals, not primarily displays of national security technology.

They also deplored the diversion of science by nationalist motives. The space program owed its impetus to nationalist rivalries, but the realization of its full potential called for an international perspective. Science, however grievously compromised, aspired to a global outlook. The space program offered a chance to turn the fruits of science from weapons to the broadening of human understanding. JPL would eventually play a leading role in making possible a transformation in understanding of the solar system but only as the cold war ethos of the space program diminished.

JPL faced three critical problem areas in the development of Ranger in the context of the space race—the design and fabrication of the spacecraft, laboratory management, and the unclear and sometimes contradictory objectives of the project. The design problem was particularly important. The

Ranger concept had been inherited from Vega, which, in turn, had had its origins in Juno 4. This concept was to lay the foundation for planetary spacecraft, which necessarily were more complicated than lunar machines. Although this promised a long-term payoff, using the lunar Ranger to prove out planetary design concepts added to the project's short-run pressures. Communication from planetary distances was one of the principal problems. It necessitated a high-gain antenna that would point continuously at the Earth, which, in turn, required that the spacecraft have full attitude stabilization in all three axes—roll, yaw, and pitch. JPL engineers also decided that the longitudinal axis should usually point toward the sun because they were uncertain whether the onboard sensors could detect the Earth from planetary distances. This further complicated guidance and control, but it offered as a by-product that solar cells on fixed panels could be used as the main source of electrical power. Ranger also required an onboard sequencer. For a 66-hour lunar flight, battery power would have sufficed instead of solar panels, and a high-gain antenna was unnecessary. The complex guidance and control system represented a big step over the Explorers and Pioneers, which had been stabilized simply by spinning the vehicle along its roll axis. The added complexity placed a heavy strain on JPL's electronics division. Burke, who had little background in guidance and control, relied on one of his deputies in this area. The strain told particularly when Mariner's guidance and control demands siphoned many key people away from Ranger in 1961 and 1962. In many cases unsupervised junior engineers and technicians were designing and fabricating Ranger's guidance and control assemblies.[15]

Like Vega, Ranger tended to be an all-or-nothing machine. Mission success depended on a long train of items working satisfactorily in sequence. The failure of any one component, particularly at the beginning or in the middle of the sequence, could abort the entire mission. There was little provision for partial mission success, and little backup or redundant equipment that could function if the primary unit failed. The Vega design had utilized the expected allowable weight to the fullest, and when Ranger's weight was cut, the stress became severe. Everything had to work right for the mission to be a success.[16]

This design characteristic necessitated engineering excellence in every detail—something the Ranger management structure could not provide. The detailed design and actual fabrication of the spacecraft devolved on the technical divisions, where the ongoing work of the laboratory was carried out. But these divisions found their attention divided among several projects at once in 1962: Ranger, Mariner, Surveyor, and perhaps other smaller ventures. Engineers were responsible to their division chiefs, not to the Ranger project manager. He had to rely on the divisions to assign and supervise the personnel. With their attention divided, division chiefs and their subordinate section chiefs seldom had a detailed grasp of the needs of a particular project. Burke had little power to demand; he had to rely on negotiation with the powerful division heads. If they could not provide detailed engineering guidance, it had to come from his undermanned project office. The harried project director exerted little influence on the design of the spacecraft. Burke estimated that he spent as much as 60 percent of his time dealing with NASA headquarters. His two deputies were spread too thin to provide detailed supervision. Some of this responsibility devolved on the systems division, but it had neither the personnel nor the clout to follow through. Design and fabrication quality depended chiefly on whether the individual who did it was satisfied; changes in design could often be made with inadequate consideration of the effects on other components; and there was no central clearinghouse to collect and evaluate failure reports. Supervision of outside contractors was lax.[17]

Under the best of circumstances this organization would have had problems, but other factors taxed the structure as well. One was personnel. The planetary Mariner was a more alluring project and attracted many JPL personnel away from Ranger. The laboratory simply did not have enough experienced personnel to support two major projects at the same time, plus the beginnings of Surveyor and other smaller activities. JPL personnel grew from 2,600 in 1960 to 3,500 in 1962; some divisions reported that as many as 60 percent of their professionals had less than two years' experience at the laboratory. Its budget mushroomed from $35 million in fiscal year 1958 to $132 million in fiscal year 1962. Although much of this was funneled to off-lab contractors, the supervision of these business arrangements and their products added many new problems.[18]

Sterilization of the spacecraft presented another problem. When the first satellites circled the Earth, some scientists realized that spaceflight posed a potential hazard. Living organisms from Earth might be inadvertently introduced to other celestial bodies and, if conditions were right, go on to reproduce. This would be a scientific calamity of the first magnitude, for it would forever blot out the chance to determine the existence of extraterrestrial life. To avert this disaster, the International Council of Scientific Unions passed a resolution calling on all nations to sterilize their lunar and planetary spacecraft. NASA complied. Ranger therefore had to be sterilized—not so much because anyone seriously expected to find "moon bugs," as the engineers called them, but because the project was a forerunner of planetary exploration where some scientists thought life might indeed be found. Portions of the spacecraft were heated to temperatures as high as 257° F for twenty-four hours. These measures were controversial. Some persons felt they were unnecessary to start with, and others believed they seriously degraded spacecraft reliability, particularly electronic components. A NASA study in 1962 suggested that sterilization contributed to spacecraft failure and should be abandoned; the JPL failure-review board, on the other hand, virtually ignored sterilization. In any event, sterilization added uncertainty to an already compromised object.[19]

The Jet Propulsion Laboratory's internal problems on Ranger were complicated by difficult relations with NASA headquarters. Most of these focused on Ranger mission objectives, often the role of science. As originally conceived Rangers 1 and 2 would constitute block 1; while carrying some scientific experiments, their primary purpose was to prove out the technology. Obsessed by schedule, Burke was especially adamant that block 1 proceed on time and that anything that interfered with gaining early flight experience should be discarded. He was infuriated, therefore, when the Atomic Energy Commission asked to add an experiment known as Vela Hotel to detect above-ground nuclear explosions just before he froze the final design of Rangers 1 and 2. NASA headquarters—less committed to schedule and perhaps less aware of the engineering problems—acceded to the request. The Vela Hotel episode added "vigor to the technology-science controversy," Burke complained, "and encourage[d] undisciplined efforts by our own [JPL] science people to get Headquarters to order us to wait for them if necessary."[20]

For the block 2 Rangers—flights 3 through 5—NASA had specified that science would be paramount. This block carried added experiments which included a television camera to return close-up photographs, a seismometer to detect seismic activity, and a gamma-ray spectrometer to determine the chemical composition of the surface. JPL engineers continued to insist, however, that development of the technology should take priority, and headquarters eventually agreed.[21]

As JPL carried out the final fabrication and the launches of Rangers 3 through 5, it also battled NASA headquarters over the place of science on block 3, Rangers 6 through 9. The Ranger program had been awarded the four additional flights in 1961 as part of the expanded Apollo program. At first glance the objective seemed clear; block 3 would support manned flight objectives. But Homer Newell, NASA's associate administrator for space sciences and applications (OSSA), was determined to get as much science onto Ranger block 3 as he could. Newell waged a lonely fight for science against the dominant ethos and bureaucratic momentum of the manned program. Some extra weight was available, so he wanted to add eight experiments weighing a total of seventy pounds to Rangers 6 through 9. The trouble with this decision was that the experiments were for atmospheric not lunar science. Many JPL staffers termed these experiments "trinkets" and felt they would jeopardize Ranger's lunar objectives.[22]

Burke balked, raising Newell's hackles. Pickering supported him. "We at JPL are now in favor of a faster-paced and technically simpler program than the ones that we have in the past advocated or at least accepted," he said. "We strongly support the . . . [space science board] recommendation that lunar environmental and engineering data for Apollo design be sought with urgency and even, if necessary, at the expense of data having greater intrinsic scientific value." The director's viewpoint seemed somewhat surprising in view of JPL's later identification with the primarily scientific aspects of the space program, but it was consistent with the outlook embodied in the 1961 laboratory report.[23]

The controversy over the relative merits of pure science as opposed to data for Apollo was finally settled at NASA headquarters in the fall of 1962. The warring NASA offices agreed to coordinate their plans; some of the scientific experiments could be designed to provide the information the manned side wanted. Apollo emerged first among equals. The resolution of the controversy had consumed several months, and it had inflamed relations between NASA and JPL. It had created new design problems and controversies as goals were hammered back and forth. The basic objectives of Mariner, by contrast, were never in doubt. Stretching over most of the period when block 2 hardware moved from fabrication through launch, the controversy diverted energy from a project that was already in serious trouble.[24]

Despite problems that might have suggested a slower approach, JPL confidently pushed the first two Rangers to the launching pad. The hope that an early shot might beat the Russians continually lured the laboratory. Alan Shepard had made the first American manned spaceflight—a fifteen-minute suborbital excursion in May 1961—but it scarcely compared with Gagarin's orbital spectacular. JPL was also influenced by its arsenal experience in building missiles. JPL stopped design work on the ground and began flight-testing missiles earlier than with spacecraft. One expected that several of the early missile flights would fail, some perhaps disastrously; flight tests were an integral part of the final design process. Spaceflight, however, was much more costly and launch opportunities very much rarer. A series of flight tests was an impossible luxury; space machines had to perform successfully from the start. Through Ranger the Jet Propulsion Laboratory would have to unlearn its arsenal experience.

The Ranger spacecraft that JPL trucked to Cape Canaveral in a special air-conditioned van was a sophisticated machine.[25] The aerodynamic shroud that protected the craft during launching gave little hint of the complex systems underneath. The base of the spacecraft was a hexagonal block, five feet in diameter, to which modules containing the sophisticated life-sustaining electronics were bolted. A six-foot tower on which the scientific equipment and a low-gain antenna rode extended above the base. The solar panels and a hinged high-gain antenna were drawn up along the tower and then during spaceflight unfolded like the wings of a butterfly. The scientific experiments on block 1 were in order of priority: solar plasma detector, magnetometer, trapped-radiation detector package, ionization chamber, cosmic-ray telescope, Lyman alpha scanner, and micrometeorite detector. The final hardware for block 1 weighed 675 pounds, which was 164 precious pounds less than could have been accommodated. Difficulties in the development of the launch vehicle had kept JPL guessing on the final weight that could be lifted, and by the time the exact figure was known, the schedule-conscious laboratory had frozen the design. The extra weight could have been put to excellent use in redundant engineering features to insure spacecraft reliability.

As it happened, however, the block 1 spacecraft never got to demonstrate what it could do. An Atlas-Agena two-stage rocket would hurl the spacecraft into its flight path, which, like other aspects of Ranger development, was one step more advanced than a lunar mission required. Developed by General Dynamics-Astronautics in the mid-1950s as the first U. S. intercontinental ballistic missile, Atlas stood five stories tall and developed 360,000 pounds of thrust, equal to that of six Boeing 707 jetliners. Instead of a direct ascent to the moon, Ranger would be launched first into an Earth satellite, or parking, orbit by Atlas. Then the second-stage dual-burn Agena, developed by Lockheed, would provide 16,000 pounds of thrust that would kick Ranger into its deep-space trajectory. As Agena and Ranger circled the Earth together, trajectory planners could compensate for celestial motions and extend the time of the launch window. This added flexibility, which was particularly important for the limited launch intervals of planetary flights, increased the chances of a successful flight if the countdown should be delayed.

After weeks of complicated preflight tests and mating procedures, the ill-starred countdown for Ranger 1 began three days late, on July 28, 1961. Uncertainty clouded the outlook, particularly for Agena, which had had a difficult development process. NASA officials estimated the chances of a successful launch of Atlas-Agena at only 0.5. Two countdowns were aborted because of various problems. The third went smoothly until early in the morning of July 29, when, twenty-eight minutes before launch, a failure of the commercial power in the area plunged the cape into darkness. A day later the fourth countdown began, only to be scrapped when, during a routine test, the spacecraft went into its space act while sitting on the launchpad. The explosive squibs fired, the solar panels unfolded under the shroud, and the experiments began to hum. An errant power discharge from one or two of the scientific experiments seemed to have caused the aberration, although the case was never pinpointed. Hastily removed from

Atlas-Agena and sent back to its hangar, the spacecraft was rewired and its damaged parts replaced. The process took nearly a month. The delay was embarrassing and vexing, particularly to Burke, who took the incident as an unfortunate example of how scientific experiments could interfere with the technological goals that were uppermost to him. On August 22, 1961, the next available lunar opportunity, the fifth countdown proceeded smoothly, and at dawn Ranger 1 roared away.

Before long, however, the tracking stations reported bad news. The Agena second burn had gone badly—a faulty switch had closed too soon and cut off the supply of propellant. The spacecraft's trajectory called for an apogee of about 620,000 miles and a perigree of several hundred miles; instead its actual path reached a high point of only 313 miles and a low point of 105 miles. Designed for deep-space flight, Ranger could not meet the demands of the near-Earth satellite orbit in which it was caught. Every ninety minutes the craft passed into the Earth's shadow and lost solar power and orientation; as the vehicle reemerged into the sunlight, it had to align and stabilize itself anew. Consuming the nitrogen gas of the attitude control system like a drunk with a bottle of cheap wine, Ranger 1 exhausted the gas in a day. The craft began to tumble. The solar panels lost their alignment with the sun, leaving only the battery as a source of power. Telemetry continued to flicker results of the experiments and the performance of the spacecraft system to Earth for three days. But soon the battery was exhausted, and on August 30, Ranger 1, blind and mute, slipped into the atmosphere and was incinerated. JPL engineers considered, however, that the spacecraft's valiant struggle under impossible conditions had proved its basic design was good. They optimistically readied Ranger 2.

But the second flight of Ranger ran into similar problems. An investigation of Agena's hydraulic problems delayed the launch from mid-October to November 17, 1961. Atlas lifted Ranger successfully, but again the Agena second burn went badly. The spacecraft's orbit was even lower than before, and after just twenty hours of flight, the machine cascaded to a fiery demise. Science on Ranger 2 was nearly a washout. Ironically the Vela Hotel experiment, which had been added only over JPL's strenuous objections, was one of the few experiments on either flight of block 1 to return much useful data.

As preparations began for block 2 (Rangers 3 through 5), JPL project managers, particularly Burke, pressed for more flight experience as soon as possible. Block 2 was supposed to have a stronger scientific content, but Agena's failures in block 1 increased JPL engineers' desires to test out the spacecraft—in effect, to continue giving priority to the technological over the scientific goals. The issue came to a head over the trouble-plagued seismometer capsule subsystem, which was designed to detect seismic activity during the course of the two-week lunar day. The delicate instruments of the capsule, under development by Ford Motor Company's Aeronutronic Division, had to operate after being rough-landed on the moon with a residual velocity of 136 miles per hour and a force of 3,000 g. Drop tests in the Mojave Desert cast doubt on the capsule's survivability; the heat sterilization the capsule underwent also seemed to degrade reliability. Oran Nicks, director of the lunar and planetary program office at NASA, argued that Ranger 3's flight should be postponed until the capsule's problems were fixed. To do otherwise for this key experiment, he thought, would distort the objectives of block 2. Pickering and Burke felt, however, that the various in-flight processes and operation of the lunar television system could be determined only by a flight test; even if the capsule subsystem failed on the moon, the flight experience would be invaluable. And besides, the chance always existed that a successful mission would surpass the Russians. In any case two more flights remained in block 2 that could serve science. Edgar Cortright, deputy director of the office of space sciences and applications at NASA, accepted the JPL position and authorized a launch of Ranger 3 on schedule.

The third Ranger thundered upward on January 26, 1962, after last-minute problems with the launch vehicle had run the blast-off to within an hour and fifteen minutes of the time remaining in the launch window. This time the Atlas-Agena performed well. At first the Ranger trajectory looked right. But soon the tracking network revealed that because a sign had been inverted in a computer code, Ranger's path was a mirror image of what it should have been. Although the error would limit the time available for picture taking, some would remain. Meanwhile all other parts of the spacecraft functioned well. On January 28 the spacecraft entered the period known as lunar encounter, and JPL transmitted commands to correct the spacecraft's position as much as possible. But after executing some of the orders, Ranger's signal strength began to fluctuate widely; the antenna was no longer pointing to Earth, as it should have been. The central computer and sequencer on the spacecraft had failed. Its Earth and sun sensors out of commission, controlled only by its gyroscopes, Ranger continued to turn. The television cameras operated, as they were supposed to, but because of the spacecraft's aimless drift about its axis, the pictures did not show the moon, just empty space studded by reference crosses. Ranger rushed past the moon at a distance of 23,000 miles and headed into solar orbit. The flight of Ranger 3 was even more excruciating than the first two. The "near miss" was more tantalizing than the grand failures, and the onus for Ranger 3's shortcoming lay squarely with JPL, particularly its guidance and control engineering. The laboratory scrutinized the possible reasons for the computer failure but without conclusive result.

For Ranger 4 a combination of well-founded optimism and wishful thinking prevailed. The chances of hitting the moon appeared good, and some useful data probably would be returned. But JPL acknowledged privately that the odds of complete mission success were "relatively remote," and it readied a public information plan that was "flexible enough to allow emphasis to be placed on a successful experiment."[26] Ranger 4 scored a direct hit on the far side of the moon on April 26, 1962, but this mission was an even bigger disappointment than Ranger 3. After perfect operation by Atlas-Agena—a mid-course correction had not even been necessary—the spacecraft had failed to operate at all. The master clock in Ranger's central computer and sequencer had failed, which meant that no timed functions could take place and that the machine could not act on commands from Earth. "All we've got is an idiot with a radio signal," said a NASA official.

It was possible to find a silver lining in the direct hit—the first time a U.S. vehicle had succeeded in reaching the moon. Other parts of the space program were going well: John Glenn had orbited the Earth recently, and the Saturn rocket that would power Apollo had just completed a perfect test flight. NASA administrator Webb insisted that the man-in-space program, of which Ranger was an integral part, remained on schedule. But crashing a can of dead electronic gear on the moon offered no support for Apollo or for science. The Soviet Union had deposited a pennant on the moon in 1959, albeit with a less sophisticated spacecraft. Their level of anxiety and embarrassment rising, JPL engineers redoubled their efforts to insure that Ranger 5 worked.

During Ranger's four disappointments, the Mariner program—similar in design but different in organization and execution—made rapid progress. Two Mariner launches interrupted Ranger's schedule in August 1962 and produced JPL's first notable space victory since Explorer 1.

Mariner had originated as a planetary mission that would be propelled by Atlas and Centaur, a rocket under development by Convair, that was more powerful than Agena. But Centaur's development problems accumulated until in the summer of 1961 it became clear that the rocket would not be ready for the Mariner launches the following year. The original fall-back plan had called for launching the first two Mariner As as interplanetary probes in 1963, then firing the next two at Venus in 1964; the first Mariner Bs, which were more sophisticated, would fly to Mars in 1964. Another possibility had been to cancel Mariner A and divert the entire JPL effort to a combined Mars and Venus mission for Mariner B in 1964. Under both plans the 1962 Venus launch opportunity would pass untried. JPL conducted a crash review of Mariner and came up with an imaginative approach that promised to hold losses to a minimum and still achieve some of the program's objectives in 1962. The Atlas-Agena used for Ranger could power a Venus flight, if the spacecraft were lighter. The laboratory proposed stopping work on Mariner A and fashioning a new spacecraft, known as Mariner

R (from Mariner-Ranger), from Ranger, Mariner A, and some new components. The solution had its drawbacks. It entailed a loss of $3 million to $4 million, and, while it promised good interplanetary scientific experiments, the planetary experiments were minimal. Nonetheless, as a way to inaugurate the planetary program and to achieve an American space first, Mariner R had much to recommend it. NASA approved the reprogramming and JPL began working on Mariner R in the fall of 1961.[27]

Although the reorientation first seemed to pose colossal headaches, it turned out to be a blessing in disguise. It forced a design review; coming midway through the project, the review was more comprehensive and took better account of the system as a whole than had happened with Ranger. Mariner Project manager J. H. James also worked with Lockheed to cut 100 pounds from the Agena. Mariner further benefited from a stronger project organization. As problems multiplied in the spring of 1962, James decided he needed a spacecraft systems manager; Dan Schneiderman took on the job full time. James established a matrix organization in which representatives of six technical divisions interfaced with systems personnel who were assigned to the project full-time. Mariner also used more formal written documents, such as flow charts that amounted to promises by one division to supply equipment to another by a certain date, and more rigid quality control. In this way shortcomings tended to come to the attention of someone other than the engineer or group responsible, which increased the chances of getting things fixed.[28]

The imposition of a project organization over the regular division structure posed problems, James acknowledged. He wanted more power. He got "what he needed from the divisions by wrangling." At times he had to rake the division chiefs, but he had to proceed with caution so as not to jeopardize his position with the divisions on whom he depended. Nevertheless, because the technical divisions represented the ongoing work of the laboratory, he did not favor a fully projectized organization. James enjoyed relative freedom from NASA interference. He estimated he spent only twenty-five hours dealing with headquarters, in contrast to Burke's inordinate negotiation. In part this reflected his managerial skill, in part NASA's lesser interest in Mariner than Ranger.[29]

Paradoxically Mariner was a simpler project than its lunar counterpart. James proposed, and NASA accepted, simple objectives. These goals were "to pass near the planet, to communicate with the spacecraft from the planet, and to perform a meaningful Planetary experiment." To carry out these objectives, six relatively simple experiments, weighing 41 pounds, rode on Mariner R. Two were to provide information solely on Venus. They were a microwave radiometer experiment to take the temperature of the planet's surface and an infrared radiometer experiment to gather data on the thermal energy in the Venusian atmosphere. The other four experiments would operate in space and in some cases also near the planet. They included a magnetometer experiment, a charged-particle experiment, a plasma experiment to study the solar corona, and a micrometeorite experiment to measure the density of cosmic-dust particles. The 447-pound spacecraft was based on the hexagonal concept used in Ranger.[30]

Mariner 1, launched from Cape Canaveral on July 22, had the most disastrous flight of any of the Mariner or Ranger series. After a flight of less than five minutes, the vehicle was destroyed by the range safety officer because it took a wildly erratic path. The tiniest of details caused the gigantic error: a hyphen had been omitted from the launch-vehicle guidance equations. Mariner 2 was launched on August 27, 1962, and seemed destined for a similar fate. But the guidance malfunction in the Atlas was overcome just before the Agena second-stage was to separate. A preflight study had estimated the reliability of the spacecraft at 42 percent, but it performed flawlessly. "The spacecraft obediently extended its solar panels and high-gain antenna, acquired the sun and Earth, stabilized in space, and flawlessly executed a necessary midcourse correction maneuver." Some 108 days later, Mariner 2 would pass within 25,000 miles of the surface of Venus.[31]

En route to Venus, Mariner 2 sent back unparalleled scientific data on interplanetary conditions. The spacecraft provided by far the most detailed confirmation of the "solar wind," solar plasma that flowed out from the sun throughout the four-month mission. The cosmic-dust experiment registered only two impacts of particles during the flight. Since spacecraft encountered ten thousand times as much material near the Earth, the findings lent support to theories that meteorites blasted bits of the moon which in turn became trapped in the Earth-moon system. The Mariner 2 flyby of Venus on December 14, 1962, began building the case that Venus, which because of its mass and orbit was sometimes called "the Earth's twin," was in reality quite different. Unlike Earth, Venus exerted no change in magnetic fields or plasma flows near the planet; if Venus had radiation belts, they were less extensive than the Van Allen belts that girdled Earth. The radiometer data revealed that dense, cold clouds surrounded Venus and that its surface temperatures reached at least 800° F.[32]

The scientific returns, while interesting, did not have the dramatic impact other space probes had, such as Explorer's discovery of the Van Allen belts or later landing missions. They tended to eliminate various hypotheses rather than highlight dramatic breakthroughs. The returns, particularly for Venus, were "relatively scant," space science chief Newell acknowledged. "The principal value of the Mariner 2 accomplishment must still be regarded as laying the groundwork for an even more extensive investigation of the planets to come." Newell praised JPL's ingenuity in making an about-face when Mariner 1 met its demise. Three technological achievements drew particular attention. First, Mariner proved that spacecraft could be launched to neighboring planets with accuracy. Second, the spacecraft set a communication record. Using a transmitter that generated only 3.5 watts of power, Mariner 2 communicated with Earth from 54 million miles away. Third, some of the uncertainties of space travel began to fade as Mariner performed satisfactorily for months. And Mariner 2 had put the United States a leg up on the Soviet Union in planetary exploration.[33]

The Mariner interlude gave Ranger personnel a five-month breathing space in which to rework the spacecraft. They made several important changes. Analysis of the Ranger 4 flight indicated that the failure had probably occurred because of short-circuiting in the electronic brain during the few seconds after separation of the spacecraft from Agena; steps were taken to isolate the "hot" lines in the connector. Freed of earlier weight limitations, JPL engineers added a back-up clock and another nitrogen gas bottle to protect against failure. The nagging problem of sterilization was compromised. Rolf Hastrup, the JPL engineer in charge of heat sterilization, argued that the whole program should be abandoned. But the laboratory and NASA decided to keep the heat treatment but waive it for certain critical parts.

Launched into a leaden sky on October 18, Ranger 5 moved easily into its lunar trajectory. But a little more than an hour into the flight, alarms began sounding throughout the space network. The temperature in the power switching and logic unit shot up; electrical power from the solar panels was short-circuited. The craft switched to battery power, but performance remained erratic. In any case, the batteries would be exhausted long before Ranger reached the moon. To make matters worse, the telemetry-to-teletype encoders at the South African and Australian tracking stations had also failed, and the telemetry from the spacecraft was too garbled to be of any use. The scientists' hopes plummeted. Burke and his colleagues decided to salvage what they could by attempting a mid-course maneuver that should make Ranger, although dead, hit the moon. The mid-course maneuver began successfully, but soon further electrical shorting occurred, telemetry blinked on and off, and the maneuver failed. The battery had run down. The radio transmitter went dead, the gyroscopes stopped, and the spacecraft began to tumble. Ranger 5 failed even more dismally than Ranger 4. Turning cartwheels on its way to solar orbit, the fifth Ranger missed the moon by 450 miles. No one found a silver lining. The Ranger project was a shambles.

Both JPL and NASA convened special failure-review boards at once. The six-man committee at the laboratory delivered a strong indictment of

Ranger operations and management to Pickering on November 13, 1962. The board expressed concern about the design process for both Ranger and Mariner. Neither had had sufficient systems design review, which it feared was typical of JPL practice. Burke now felt also that the design erred in placing too much reliance on the central computer and sequencer. Nonetheless the basic design, as the essentially similar Mariner suggested, led the panel to believe Ranger could work. The problem lay in the detailed engineering execution, they stressed. Ranger 5's in-flight failure appeared to be localized in a power switch and logic module; examination of spare units revealed many weaknesses in design and assembly, and the board feared "comparable deficiencies exist[ed] throughout the spacecraft." During systems tests fourteen failures—any one of them serious enough to cause mission failure—proved that engineering excellence was lacking. The rudimentary failure-reporting system relied heavily on personal contact with little follow-up or formal supervision.[34]

The JPL board traced many of these problems to the operational methods of the lunar program office. Drawing on Mariner experience, the committee believed that JPL organization could work, but it demanded "a strong project manager of on-Lab activity." Burke had spent too much time on relations with NASA, the air force, and contractors. He had exercised "little influence on JPL spacecraft project execution," the board found, and attempts to delegate his functions proved ineffective. The board called this style of management "a major hazard to project success and a general underlying cause of the failures experienced." A related managerial problem arose from the nature of the laboratory. It was ill-suited to what was essentially an industrial function: turning out repetitive pieces of equipment. Many persons were attracted to JPL because they liked the challenge of designing new one-shot items and then moving on to design another. Cummings thought Ranger had the "first team" on flights 1 and 2 but that the greener grass of Mariner had drawn them away from flights 3 through 5. JPL quality control chief Brooks T. Morris observed that JPL perhaps suffered from having "too many engineers experienced in *starting* new jobs and not enough experienced in *finishing* them."[35]

A comparison between Ranger and Mariner was instructive. The Mariner R design actually represented attempts to correct Ranger shortcomings more than did the hardware being fabricated for Rangers 6 through 9, the board said. Mariner's failure-reporting system had been stricter. Perhaps of greatest significance, Mariner director James had to spend little time dealing with NASA and could exert the detailed supervision that eluded the Ranger project. His office operated as its own executive without delegating functions to the systems division or some other unit. Mariner felt its project manager's influence at several key points. It further benefited from an influx of top personnel from Ranger, and the very nature of the Venus mission as a one-time possibility encouraged the pursuit of excellence.[36]

The board recommended several stern measures before another Ranger flight was attempted. Of the several managerial changes, the most important were that Burke be replaced by "someone new to the Project, and someone with a Laboratory reputation for successful project management as well as a reputation for dogmatic pursuit of excellence." The panel urged a general tightening of managerial techniques especially in formalizing design and testing procedures and in involving the regular JPL line organization, particularly the section chiefs, more fully. The Ranger 6 spacecraft should be converted into a design evaluation vehicle. Finally, the planning for Rangers 10 through 14 and any subsequent models should be modified in line with the reevaluation of the design of Rangers 6 through 9.[37]

However harsh the JPL board's report may have seemed, the NASA findings were still more grave. Known as the Kelley board after its chairman, Albert J. Kelley, the NASA committee filed its damning report on November 30, 1962. Similar in many respects to the JPL analysis, the Kelley report made two additional points of significance. First, it indicted JPL's emphasis on schedule above all else as a "shoot and hope" approach: "shoot enough and hope that sooner or later one of a series will indeed work." This approach undermined excellence in design and execution and encouraged meeting a flight date instead of slipping schedules for greater reliability. Such a philosophy might work for simpler and relatively inexpensive designs, such as the Sergeant missile, but for sophisticated and costly projects, such as Ranger, the number of launches necessary to produce a successful mission grew very large and prohibitively expensive. Many persons at JPL—Burke in particular—resented the "shoot and hope" characterization and noted that NASA had contributed to the space race atmosphere that encouraged emphasis on schedule.[38]

The report nevertheless struck a vein where the laboratory was vulnerable. JPL had called for an even faster-paced program than had NASA in 1961, and when the national agency had at times wanted to slip the schedule, the laboratory had insisted on shooting soon. The arsenal experience, coupled with JPL's too-confident belief in its ability to meet the severe demands of the new space technology, misled the laboratory.

Second, the Kelley board urged an end to heat sterilization—a subject the JPL committee had all but ignored. The NASA group worried that sterilization degraded the performance of even the best equipment and that on those parts of Ranger that were "marginally designed to begin with" the consequences could be "extremely serious." JPL, the report concluded, had not "applied to Ranger 'buses' the high standards of technical design and fabrication" that were necessary to attain success. The weaknesses were "so extensive" that spacecrafts 6 through 9 were not likely to perform any more successfully than Rangers 3 through 5.[39]

Several recommendations followed. Rangers 6 through 9 should be tested to see whether they could be improved enough to merit launching. An industrial contractor should assume responsibility, under JPL direction, "for system management, including redesign, fabrication, assembly, and test of the spacecraft" on Rangers 10 and following as soon as possible. Laboratory project management should be strengthened with adequate staffing, clear lines of authority, formal design reviews, and strict quality control. The relationship between JPL and NASA also needed reevaluation, and headquarters should not award the laboratory any major new flight projects until the Ranger situation was satisfactorily resolved. Closer NASA monitoring of Ranger and JPL also was suggested. Mission objectives should be clarified and simplified. Finally, heat sterilization should stop at once.[40]

A chastened JPL regrouped. Even though the Kelley report was harsher than JPL staffers had expected or felt warranted, stringent actions could not be avoided. First, the director replaced Burke and Cummings. Their fate seemed to confirm the sardonic observation of veteran NASA project managers that if one wanted to be successful "never be the first manager of a project." Robert Parks, who had run the planetary program, also assumed Cummings's lunar duties. Harris M. "Bud" Schurmeier, took over from his Caltech classmate Burke as Ranger project manager. Pickering also curtailed the "feudal independence" of the laboratory's technical divisions. Section chiefs had to get the consent of project managers before transferring personnel from one project to another; laboratory-wide standards for quality assurance and flight-acceptance testing were laid down. To ride herd on these procedures Brooks Morris was given added authority. And to remove any remaining doubt, Pickering installed Ranger as the laboratory's number one priority.[41]

By mid-December 1962 JPL and NASA officials had hammered out new guidelines for Ranger along the lines of the Kelley report. First, the objectives were simplified. Flying in support of Apollo, Ranger would have one objective: television. As Schurmeier put it: "A few TV pictures of the moon, better than those taken from earth, is the only mission objective. No advanced development experiments or additional scientific instruments will be carried!" Advanced technology for the planetary program became a byproduct, not an objective, of Project Ranger. All the secondary scientific experiments—the notorious "trinkets"—were ditched. Their precious pounds would be devoted to redundant engineering features to make the spacecraft more reliable. Second, heat sterilization was abandoned, as was terminal sterilization of the spacecraft with ethylene oxide gas, and Ranger's sterilized parts were to be replaced. Third, Ranger 6 was postponed indefinitely until JPL and NASA were satisfied the venture had a high probability of success. More than a year would elapse before another shot was tried— January 1964.[42]

Would these measures work? No one knew. Morale had virtually dropped off the charts. The technical and managerial demands remained formidable. If Ranger worked, Apollo would be the beneficiary. Although Homer Newell continued gamely to insist that television pictures of the moon had substantial scientific value, the failure of Ranger block 2 had been a decisive setback for space science. JPL had contributed to that defeat both by its insistence on the primacy of engineering goals and by that very subordination of science to prestige and propaganda purposes that James Killian had warned against. Indeed, without pressure from NASA, the laboratory would have pushed flight schedules even faster and reduced the role of science even more.

Paradoxically, in the midst of Ranger's inglorious streak, JPL's success with Mariner 2 inaugurated the laboratory's sterling series of planetary missions. But at the close of 1962 JPL was still entangled in the prestige race it had helped create. The laboratory had entered the most critical phase of its history to that time. Not only did it have to rework Ranger but the contract with NASA also came up for renewal, and the misunderstandings and accumulated resentments and disappointments that surfaced during the negotiations eventually produced substantial alterations in the character of the laboratory.

9 ★★

JPL, CALTECH, AND NASA:
THE TROUBLED TRIANGLE

The Jet Propulsion Laboratory's unique insider-outsider status was too good to last. The balance of power between JPL and NASA had begun to shift with the escalation of the manned space program in mid-1961. And after Ranger's failures, the laboratory could no longer resist NASA pressure to give up a measure of its independence.

The NASA centers were government organizations with civil service employees and the usual government business regulations. NASA provided JPL's facilities and almost all its budget. But officially it was managed by its parent, the California Institute of Technology. The NASA contract was with CIT; the Institute received a management fee and overhead reimbursement from NASA; and Caltech personnel and purchasing policies governed JPL. The focus of JPL's insider-outsider status was the so-called mutuality clause, which stated that headquarters and the laboratory had to mutually agree on JPL's assignments; NASA could not issue unilateral task orders. This legal arrangement masked the reality that the laboratory more nearly resembled a NASA center than an academic laboratory. JPL had a monopoly on the national unmanned lunar and planetary program. As the key role of Ranger in support of Apollo indicated, this mission assumed crucial importance to NASA. There was nothing to distinguish JPL from either Goddard or Marshall space-flight centers except that "it was not under Civil Service personnel regulations," said a JPL report in 1961. "We are . . . such an integral part of the NASA organization that the nature of our operation is determined by NASA and not CIT."[1]

JPL had received its anomalous position in NASA by virtue of possessing the superior skills the fledgling space agency badly needed in 1958. Even when the Ranger failures gave JPL's critics a field day, NASA continued to have faith in the laboratory's technical competence. "JPL . . . felt they were the best in the world, I think—and they were," said NASA administrator

James Webb. But while the agency consistently ranked the laboratory first technically, it doubted the managerial capability. By 1963 the relative importance of the skills the Pasadena institution could marshal had begun to decline. Other centers, such as Goddard, which recorded twenty-three successes in twenty-six tries with Earth-orbiting satellites by 1963, were coming on strong. Industry too was developing greater prowess in space technology. Meanwhile as JPL also grew, its engineering talent was diluted. When the five Ranger failures cast doubt on the laboratory's technical and managerial practices, NASA found it both possible and necessary to reconsider the aspects of the relationship that had rankled for some time.[2]

Discussions between JPL and NASA took on a thick coloration of the longtime misunderstanding between private and government science. The laboratory had assumed many of the elitist attitudes of Caltech, where the superiority of private over public institutions was a matter of faith. CIT president Lee DuBridge had long argued that the government should not do any of its own scientific research but should contract out all of it. JPL executives from the earliest days of the space program had repeated a litany about NASA incompetence. Having enjoyed a virtual blank check under army funding, JPL officials resented the increasing supervision to which NASA subjected them. The Pasadenans often preferred dealing with technically innocent army officers to justifying their decisions for technically proficient NASA engineers and scientists. Reinforcing the distinction between private and government operations, JPL staffers often enjoyed perquisites such as first-class plane trips and elegant hotel accommodations while NASA civil servants flew coach and pinched pennies on the federal per diem. The laboratory's sense of pride was understandable, but many persons felt it crossed the line into hubris.[3]

An indication of JPL's sense of superiority arose in March 1962 when director William Pickering offered to detail fifteen key staff members to NASA headquarters. The laboratory had not yet produced a successful lunar or planetary flight; planning for several major projects in the future remained incomplete; and the severe personnel shortage appeared likely to get worse. NASA executive Edgar Cortright agreed that the laboratory was "doing an outstanding job," but argued that JPL was too heavily committed to sustain such a diversion of personnel. "May I respectfully suggest," he said, "that you consider providing help . . . in the form of one or two leaders and some bright young lads to work with them, rather than loading the group with top talent which is sorely needed at home." The laboratory needed to learn that its talents, while ample, were not limitless, and that the best and the brightest needed a sense of proportion and humility.[4]

For its part NASA brought to the discussions a sense of federal rights and privileges. Hugh Dryden, deputy NASA administrator whose entire career had been as a federal scientist-bureaucrat, raised hackles at JPL and Caltech when he suggested publicly in 1962 that the laboratory could operate as well under civil service management. Headquarters found the arrangement with JPL cumbersome; it was used to dealing with its own centers directly. As even JPL sometimes acknowledged, its responsiveness to NASA left much to be desired. More geared to project management, headquarters found it hard to understand the research-style operations at JPL. But perhaps as basic as anything else, the national agency reasoned that the Pasadena institution was living off federal funds, and it should therefore approach the same standards of responsiveness and accountability as NASA's other centers.

The dispute was more than simply a power struggle; it also pitted two valid philosophies that could be reconciled only with great difficulty. Pickering believed that the independence and "university atmosphere" of JPL were the keys to its success; this ethos attracted the people whom the space agency praised as the most able in its establishment. NASA had a responsibility for accounting for public funds and a tradition of bureaucratic process with clear hierarchy and points of responsibility. Operating in the glass house of space program politics, JPL could no longer maintain the independence it had enjoyed under the army. But at the same time, if NASA pressed its ideas of laboratory operation too hard, it threatened to destroy the creativity it needed. Converting JPL into another civil service center always had some attraction to NASA, for uniformity appeals to bureaucracy. Having one non-civil service center had strong appeal from the standpoint of diversity and from its yardstick function of measuring the performance of civil service institutions, but if JPL's performance were superior, it might also be embarrassing to the agency.

NASA had been pondering its relationship with JPL for some time before serious discussion opened in 1963. Oran Nicks, flight systems chief in the lunar and planetary programs office, emphasized in 1961 that "the Lab represents a collection of intelligent, well-educated individuals with above-average potential" who were "very energetic, ambitious, and devoted to the JPL cause. . . . They have the kind of spirit and agressiveness [sic] which the space program needs, and . . . with some mellowing and sprinkling of experience from personnel having other than CIT-JPL backgrounds, they can be forged into a very successful team." Nevertheless the laboratory displayed design and management deficiencies. These derived, Nicks felt, from the "academic, relaxed atmosphere that pervades the 'JPL Campus.'" The institution fostered individualism. However conducive that approach might be for research, it did not encourage quick responses and strong team efforts on project-oriented tasks. Many design problems were delegated to junior engineers who worked with little supervision. The experienced personnel who were their nominal supervisors frequently did not exercise their judgment "until complete failure occurs, usually late in the schedule, and drastic action is required." Some supervisors lacked the know-how to improve the designs. Since present JPL management had been reared on the individualistic, academic approach, Nicks doubted that they could provide the "tight engineering control" NASA wanted; outside managers, probably from industry, were needed. The "hands-off" approach carried over in relations with NASA and in lax supervision of contractors, he thought. While he doubted that "any other organization could do a better job than JPL," he thought NASA could get the most out of the laboratory by giving it some competition—specifically, by placing some lunar and planetary projects at other centers. Building up the other NASA centers thus became a way of reducing the organization's dependence on the laboratory and of goading JPL into better performance.[5]

One of headquarters' complaints emphasized the need for firmer day-to-day management. Pickering's management philosophy resembled that of a college president more than a corporation executive or government bureau chief. Although he kept most of the reins in his hands—an organization chart once showed as many as twenty-three boxes reporting to him—neither he nor his immediate staff exercised much day-to-day control over project activities. The postmortems on Ranger showed little evidence of involvement by the director's office; the project offices fought their battles with the divisions on their own for the most part. Like a college president, Pickering was content to set the broad outlines of programs and policies and leave the implementation of them to his deans and department chairmen, unless a crisis required his participation. He also spent much time on community and scientific activities such as the American Institute of Aeronautics and Astronautics (AIAA). Consistent with the academic, individualistic approach Nicks described, this management philosophy suited a research institution. To men with government and industrial backgrounds, this tended to mean, as the first NASA administrator T. Keith Glennan put it, "Bill Pickering was not and, unless I miss my guess, still is not a manager." Since research and advanced development continued to be vital parts of JPL's programs—and in fact indispensable to project success—this philosophy may have had more validity than NASA acknowledged. The space agency noted, for example, that the Lewis and Ames centers, which separated research from projects, faced severe problems in transferring "in-house developed expertise (research) to projectized development management." Nevertheless, since project management demands had come to dominate the Jet Propulsion Laboratory by the early 1960s, nothing less than tighter, more aggressive management would satisfy NASA.[6]

One of the most insistent demands of the space agency was that JPL install a strong general manager to oversee day-to-day operations. Associate administrator Robert C. Seamans, Jr., had recommended such a step in January 1963. Pickering, however, with his firm sense of his role as leader of his laboratory and of prominence in the aerospace fraternity, would resist the appointment of a general manager for eighteen months.[7]

Another NASA concern focused on business operations, which had not kept pace with the demands of an institution whose budget had quadrupled in four years. DuBridge argued that purchasing and subcontracting could be handled more efficiently by the Institute because it was private. But a host of problems in JPL business affairs called this outlook into question. Financial management was so poor that actual costs could not be determined; the reporting systems, moreover, could not, "even in a gross way, be reconciled to match the financial operating plans approved by NASA Headquarters." Various purchasing and subcontracting problems arose, notably potential conflict-of-interest situations in which laboratory employees formed corporations and then influenced the award of JPL subcontracts to their firms. Property management revealed serious lapses. The laboratory did not have a system to account for five of eight of the property accounts, and the systems it used performed poorly. In one case a physical inventory could not be completed during an entire year; nearly one-fourth of the material, worth an estimated $800,000, could not be located. Misappropriation of equipment, particularly hand tools, was a continuing concern, and in 1963 the Federal Bureau of Investigation recovered a freezer and a completely equipped ham radio station that belonged to the government from a private home. Security was so lax that the army threatened in March 1963 to withdraw the laboratory's facilities clearance. NASA learned of "a rash of 'incidents' involving apparent sabotage, security breaches, etc." At three o'clock one morning persons unknown opened a safe that contained the combinations to the approximately six hundred security files and repositories at the institution. All told the space agency taxed JPL management with being "negligent" and remaining "unresponsive to pressure for badly needed improvements."[8]

Some of these charges represented major shortcomings; others were simply different, but not necessarily worse, business procedures than the ones NASA used. Nevertheless, business management was one area where JPL might have yielded more readily to NASA without losing any vital independence, and in so doing it might have countered headquarters' criticism of lack of responsiveness. Caltech had to agree that steps needed to be taken. CIT pointed out in August 1963 that it had made a number of moves to rectify the situation, particularly by having Price, Waterhouse & Company conduct special audits and management studies and by hiring additional business overseers. "One may say that our management improvement programs should have commenced earlier. We agree," said Robert B. Gilmore, vice-president for business affairs at Caltech. "One may say that the programs now in progress should be intensified and accelerated. Again, we agree." The Institute had proceeded cautiously—perhaps too cautiously, he acknowledged—out of a fear of disrupting JPL's ongoing operations. It went without saying also that Caltech and the laboratory had moved as far as they did largely because of pressure from NASA headquarters. Gilmore pledged that the campus would provide leadership in business management as well as in scientific and technical areas.[9]

One of the major questions that had arisen by 1963 was just what leadership Caltech provided the laboratory. NASA continually asked, in effect, what it was getting for the management fee it paid the Institute. Payments for the operation of JPL, which had been important but not crucial to Caltech during the army regime, had by 1963 become a vital part of the Institute budget. The army had paid Caltech $500,000 annually in the mid-1950s to operate JPL; that figure amounted to 5 percent of the Institute's budget. As the laboratory's operations mushroomed under NASA, CIT reaped an ever-larger payment. In fiscal year 1963 the total payment from NASA amounted to $2,200,000. The sum was split in two portions: $950,000 represented reimbursement for allocable indirect expenses; the other segment, $1,250,000, was a special and controversial management fee. The combined figure represented 11.8 percent of the Institute's budget and was slightly larger than the amount the school received from student fees.[10]

Most of the payment for indirect expenses was charged to general administrative overhead. The Institute charged NASA for 78.5 percent of the expenses of the offices of the president, his assistant, assistant treasurer, secretary, safety and security, vice-president for business affairs, audit and JPL consulting, and staff counsel; 72.6 percent of the comptroller's office; and 64.4 percent of the office of the director of nonacademic personnel. NASA overhead payments took care of 78.5 percent of general and administrative expenses related to all activities, and when the category of on-campus activities only was included, the payment met 51 percent of CIT's overall administrative expense. To NASA auditors these figures appeared well in excess of work related to JPL. The comptroller's office, which took the largest single allocatable sum, performed the bulk of its work for on-campus activities, not JPL, the government investigators said.[11] If Caltech administrators devoted as much time to JPL affairs as they were charging for, they were guilty of dereliction of Institute business.

The management fee was the most controversial segment, however. It was not based on any tangible expenses but instead was justified as an arbitrary figure the Institute needed in addition to overhead expenses for operating the laboratory. In 1962 Representative Albert Thomas of Texas, chairman of the House appropriations subcommittee on independent offices, bored in on the question of just what Caltech did to earn its management fee. Thomas had a particular animus against Caltech, which, in his view, raked off an unseemly amount of government research funds. "The more we spend on national defense, the more Caltech gets," he complained. Federal science largess was unfairly concentrated in the Northeast and California, Thomas believed, and he was committed to evening it out. (One of his principal contributions to geographical balance was securing the manned spaceflight center for his home district in Houston.) Thomas's questioning raised the possibility that Congress might end the fee. The Bureau of the Budget was also attempting to tighten up government contracting procedures. NASA officials defended the fee to Thomas and the budget bureau, but their public posture masked their own doubts about the defensibility of the fee.[12]

CIT argued that it received a lower percentage of the total management allowance—about 1 percent of the JPL budget—than other university-operated laboratories. The three laboratories the University of California operated for the Atomic Energy Commission netted the system $2.45 million in fiscal year 1964 on the laboratories' total budget of $264.5 million. The most comparable institution—in both fiscal arrangements and actual university involvement in management—appeared to be the Argonne National Laboratory, which the University of Chicago operated for the AEC. In fiscal year 1964, when Caltech received $2.2 million for JPL, Chicago took in $1.3 million for Argonne, which had a budget of $84 million. For fiscal years 1959 through 1963, CIT enjoyed $6.95 million while Chicago recorded $4.9 million. But turning the yardstick around yielded very different results. If the fee were compared to the university, instead of the laboratory, budget, Caltech was in a class by itself. Chicago's fee accounted for less than 1 percent of the $150-million university budget, and California's for less than 0.5 percent. CIT's payment represented almost 12 percent of the school's total. This was what made the fee such a sensitive issue: The NASA subvention made up an unusually large portion of Caltech's budget, and the Institute had trouble showing what it did directly to earn it.[13]

The Institute revealed an ambivalent attitude toward the laboratory. DuBridge tried to emphasize the closeness between CIT and JPL. He referred to the laboratory as an "arm" of Caltech and suggested that one could not talk about an arm without considering the whole body. But if JPL was an arm of the Institute, it seemed to be a member that might jerk in erratic fashion and bring unpredictable harm to the rest of the body. DuBridge had once described JPL as "a good boy" in the Caltech "family," but it also seemed that the laboratory had some of the attributes of a teenage son who was not quite accepted as a full-fledged family member and whose exploits threatened to humiliate the family. In short, Caltech officials treated JPL as a cost to the school, almost never as a plus. Regular Institute divisions, such as physics or chemistry, were talked about for their contributions to the school—as a positive factor. JPL was cast in the role of a debit, a potential liability for which the California Institute needed reimbursement.[14]

Caltech cited four chief problems in its operation of JPL. First, the laboratory created pressure for higher salaries on campus and thus raised the Institute's operating costs. Caltech salaries ranked among the very top, to be sure; but JPL's role here was uncertain. Since most of the Institute faculty was drawn from the highest-paid academic disciplines, and since many of them were highly distinguished, the school expected to pay high salaries. The limited interchange between the campus and the laboratory probably minimized this salary influence. Moreover, the general demand for aerospace engineers in southern California probably had a substantial effect regardless of the specific JPL presence.[15]

Second, Caltech feared it could suffer heavy losses if the government disallowed costs the laboratory incurred or if subcontractor payments the Institute made were disallowed. This also appeared to be overestimated. NASA pointed out that 70 percent of JPL's costs were subcontracted, most of them on a cost basis. The government audited these contracts before JPL paid them, and disallowances were passed on to the subcontractors. As for its own costs, the laboratory made a practice of clearing questionable items with the contracting officer, which minimized a risk of disallowance. Despite the volume of JPL business, the Institute had suffered hardly any cost disallowance.[16]

Third, Caltech needed the fee as a "buffer" in case the contract were terminated. The Institute claimed to feel a moral obligation to protect some of the JPL staff in the event of termination; it also needed a reserve to ease the period of retrenchment for on-campus personnel who might have to be let go. Although the effects of actual termination were probably overestimated, it was a significant contingency that required some insurance. The Institute began funneling part of the fee into a $5-million contingency fund to guard against cessation of operations. Another usually unstated but nonetheless significant reason was that the school also wanted to have the fund as a sort of income-producing special endowment that would take up some of the slack if NASA no longer paid a fee.[17]

Fourth, Caltech feared that scientific or engineering failures at JPL would adversely affect the school's reputation for excellence. Few schools guarded its image so carefully as the California Institute, and its concern about how that would fare in the glare of international publicity about the space program and the political rough-and-tumble that accompanied it was understandable. Of all the reasons cited for the fee this was the least tangible and least subject to cost accounting. Yet because of the importance of prestige in the world of elite academic institutions, it may well have been the basic fear in Caltech's management of JPL. It was as if the school required an indemnity for the loss of reputation the laboratory arm might produce—a sort of libel payment in advance. If so it was a revealing commentary on the way the Caltech administration looked upon JPL as a tangible loss rather than a potential gain. The Institute managers perhaps did not anticipate that in a few years a successful laboratory might not only produce a monetary windfall for the school but add to its luster as well.[18]

Although Caltech in the early 1960s saw little positive benefit to the Institute from the JPL affiliation, the campus thought the laboratory derived significant—although again largely intangible—benefits from its ties to Caltech. DuBridge argued that JPL's affiliation with an elite technological university enabled it to attract and hold better qualified personnel than would have otherwise been the case. About 12 percent of the professional staff at the laboratory boasted a Caltech pedigree, but the inner circle at JPL was drawn disproportionately from the campus. The laboratory could use various Caltech services, such as the library, seminars, and faculty for consulting work. Upon closer examination, however, the actual contacts were limited. An Institute study found that less than 5 percent of the school's library use came from JPL, and only $11,200 per year was figured into the NASA overhead payment for library services. What faculty consultation there was also was reimbursed by the space agency at prevailing rates. In fact, one of the major disappointments to JPL and NASA was the lack of faculty involvement with the space program in its early years.[19]

The laboratory itself revealed a split personality about the supposed boon of the tie to Caltech. Pickering often contended that the affiliation encouraged an attitude of excellence. Some people, particularly those with CIT degrees, welcomed the aura of being part of the Caltech family, even if they were not full-fledged relations. But the connection also worked the other way. Some JPL staffers resented the campus elitism, feeling with considerable justification that they were cast as second-class citizens. Others felt that the laboratory should jettison the Caltech tie and operate as its own nonprofit corporation; salaries probably would rise, and the laboratory would not be bound by CIT personnel policies, which were sometimes restrictive. The choice NASA might have preferred—civil service status—evoked little enthusiasm, but nonprofit status might have appealed to many at JPL. The Institute claimed that conversion to civil service status would drive away many of the best personnel. The argument was very difficult to assess. Some staff undoubtedly would have left for industrial or academic positions, but the abilities of scientists and engineers at Goddard and other NASA centers suggested that, after a period of transition, civil service status need not have been fatal to the laboratory. The chief problem lay in the laboratory's intensive schedule. Under the pressure of the space race, no one was willing to run the risks involved in à transition to other management unless the provocation became extreme.[20]

JPL had in fact pondered the value of the Caltech connection, especially early in 1961 when the arrival of a new administration in Washington raised the possibility of altered status and when the laboratory's growth was creating an institution "uncomfortably large" for CIT. Interested too in escaping its cramped, smoggy site against the San Gabriel Mountains, JPL studied various alternative locations in an operation known as "rolling green acres." J.D. McKenney, assistant laboratory director, concluded in early 1961 that Caltech offered JPL few advantages. The laboratory would be better off as a nonprofit corporation, such as RAND or MITRE, he thought; it would be forced to sink or swim on its own, and NASA would prefer dealing with it directly rather than through the CIT intermediary. Webb, however, opposed setting up additional contractor or nonprofit organizations within NASA; given that possibility for the Manned Space Center, he chose civil service status. JPL continued under Institute aegis. But McKenney spoke for many at the laboratory—and in NASA—when he said: "CIT must pitch in and earn their [sic] management fee by giving effective support to JPL."[21]

When Caltech opened negotiations for a higher fee in the summer of 1963, a bitter five-year quarrel began over who should be getting what from the ménage à trois. The money was small potatoes to NASA. The agency had poured half a billion dollars into JPL since 1958. "As a practical matter the amount of fee or 'management allowance' paid is of small consequence if we were successfully attaining the objectives of the laboratory," Earl Hilburn, a NASA associate deputy administrator, said. Associate administrator Seamans made the significant admission that, since Caltech operation held down wage costs, NASA probably could not find anyone to run the laboratory more cheaply. But the fee proved to be a useful lever for the agency in exerting pressures on Caltech to make JPL more responsive to Washington.[22]

What gave the controversy its distinctive tone was the personality of the new administrator—the dynamic capitalist cold warrior James Webb. A *Fortune* reporter found him "a stocky, bejowled [sic] man with a florid complexion and an intense manner that gives his blue eyes a permanently pleading, worried look. Webb's trademark is a memorable, gesticulating, humorless volubility." Fifty-seven years old in 1963, he epitomized the post–World War II figure who shuttled between corporate boardrooms and government suites. He learned his way around Washington in the 1930s as an aide to congressmen from his home state of North Carolina. Then he honed his corporate connections at Sperry Gyroscope Company, rising to a vice-presidency. Truman called him back to the capital as director of the Bureau of the Budget, and he later became under secretary of state. During the Eisenhower years Webb built up his personal fortune by running one of Oklahoma Senator Robert Kerr's oil companies. The future NASA administrator also served as a director of Douglas Aircraft, a major aerospace contractor. After Sputnik he increased his exposure to the academic world as the part-time head of Educational Services, a nonprofit corporation trying to improve science education. Though many persons wanted a scientist to head NASA in 1961, Webb's resume proved ideally suited to the direction the space agency would move. He was a confidant of members of the South-Southwest contingent that ran Congress, and his champion, Kerr, held the advantageous position of chairman of the Senate space committee. The new administrator, who portrayed himself as a managerial wizard, reorganized NASA along corporate lines, which drew praise from the business press. As corporate executive and backstage politician, Webb linked capitalist economic growth and the expansion of national power. He found NASA an ideal instrument to do both.[23]

Universities had a responsibility to support the state and free enterprise, he thought. Webb advised historians to read *The City-State of the Greeks and Romans,* an introductory text published in 1893, in which British historian W. Warde Fowler drew maxims from the ancients for readers "whose lot it is" to rule empires. Fowler emphasized internal causes for the fall of Rome, especially the failure of the educational system to instill discipline among its citizens and obedience to the state. Following Bagehot he wrote: "The people that can obey is the fittest to survive." The NASA chief applied the lesson to the United States: "the population not adequately disciplined to carry out large-scale organized efforts, such as are required in wartime, and which are now manifest in the space program, . . . may be subject to the disintegration" that afflicted Rome.[24]

But universities were not meeting their obligations to the country. They were "not bringing all of their available talent to bear on examining major problems," Webb lamented. He envisioned a continuous relationship between universities and government in which academicians would form corps of experts who could be rapidly mobilized to solve contemporary national problems. His supporting universities program made facilities grants available to a multitude of institutions, who, in return, pledged to show "an increased awareness . . . of their societal responsibilities in the attainment of national goals." NASA money could buy, and control, talent. JPL personnel had acquired their skills with public funds on public projects. "They are not, in my view, assets of Caltech so much as they are assets of the United States," Webb said.[25]

What, then, should CIT-JPL be doing? Volubility does not produce precision, and so Webb's desires remained murky. But technical competence, or even virtuosity, was insufficient. He demanded more than "merely meeting the literal terms of their contracts"—an elusive "something extra" that should arise spontaneously from academicians' sense of duty and perhaps gratitude. Contracts ordinarily delimit each party's responsibilities, but Webb wanted to use the documents to establish a floor from which performance would expand rather than to impose a ceiling. He seemed to believe that the Institute's contract with NASA conferred an obligation on faculty members to seek involvement with JPL. CIT had not encouraged "its brightest minds to do advanced research of a basic nature in the field of space, which would complement the advanced applications done at JPL," he complained. He had also hoped that the Institute would spearhead an effort to organize a space research consortium of California universities. After some halfhearted attempts, the idea, which was an administrative nightmare, died quietly. The failure to involve more scientists with JPL left him feeling that NASA had "not derived as much benefit from having CIT as contractor to manage JPL as we should have."[26]

With industry as with the state, universities were falling down on the job. Webb believed the "entrepreneurial mind" provided the machinery for the dissemination of the fruits of science and technology. His high-gain political antennas finely tuned to aerospace firms' clout in Washington, he wooed them with what *Fortune* termed "a bewildering profusion of enormous contracts." Four companies—North American, Grumman, Boeing, and Douglas—basked in NASA contracts worth more than a billion dollars each, and nearly twenty more firms profited from contracts of more than $100 million apiece. "The result," *Fortune* noted happily of Apollo, "is an intimate new sociology of space, a new kind of government-industrial complex in which each interpenetrates the other so much that sometimes it is hard to tell which is which." Webb curbed the growth of JPL and the NASA centers, in order to leave the lion's share for industry. This practice frequently set the laboratory and headquarters at odds, since JPL pressed for in-house tasks. But any flirtation with the "arsenal concept" reduced businesses' profits, restricted their access to new technology, and potentially embarrassed their claims to superior technical prowess. Indeed, Webb thought Caltech-JPL had a peculiar obligation to advance business capability.[27]

There was real doubt that universities could, or should, fulfill the role that Webb envisioned for them. The integration of the university with national power and corporate interests further threatened the already much compromised ideal of the university as an independent institution devoted to the quest for knowledge. Universities were "not merely laboratories qualified to solve current problems," Dael Wolfle, executive officer of the American Association for the Advancement of Science and publisher of *Science*, pointed out. "They must also be independent innovators and stubborn conservators of old values." Even on Webb's terms his program might well have proved self-defeating. Lee DuBridge advised him that researchers needed freedom in their choice of subject and approach; "creative research cannot be significantly directed by external influences." Homer Newell, a scientist, cautioned his chief that experts acquired their knowledge by being freed from the very demands that Webb wanted to put on them. The administrator's performance objectives threatened quickly to consume their slowly acquired endowment of expertise.[28]

The 1963 contract negotiations opened in an atmosphere of tension and distrust. The lavishly complimentary tone which Webb had previously used with DuBridge had given way to formal, even harsh, expression. Webb told one of his intimates: "CIT does not handle its relationship with us on any basis that seems logical to us but rather establishes its own position and then tries to force us to accept it." Caltech might have said the same about NASA. Webb delegated the detailed negotiations to Earl Hilburn, associate deputy administrator for industry affairs who had been vice-president and general manager of Curtiss-Wright Corporation's electronics division. Hilburn later confided to Caltech officials that the NASA chief had originally told him to terminate the contract with CIT. Hilburn, however, developed confidence that some people at the Institute, notably the trustees, understood the gravity of the situation and would make the necessary changes to restore Caltech-JPL to, if not favor, at least tolerance with Webb.[29]

Caltech may have overreached itself in proposing a substantial increase in its fee. The Institute proposed that its fee be upped from $1,250,000 in fiscal year 1963 to $1,610,000 in fiscal year 1964; the school also suggested a more modest increase in the overhead allowance, from $950,000 to $1,105,000. The compensation would total $2,715,000. Considered as a percentage of the JPL budget, the rise in CIT payments did not appear too dramatic. The Institute had received $825,000 in fiscal year 1959, when the JPL budget reached $46 million; the fiscal year 1964 budget was projected to reach $250 million. But much of the budget increase had come from the mushrooming subcontracts. When NASA officials looked at the Caltech allowance in comparison with the number of employees, they were disturbed. JPL personnel had risen from 2,680 in fiscal year 1959 to a projected 4,300 in fiscal year 1964. The payment per JPL employee would double under the Caltech proposal, from $310 in fiscal year 1959 to $630 in fiscal year 1964. The rate per scientist and engineer would increase from $1,270 in fiscal year 1959 to $2,000 in fiscal year 1964. From Caltech's point of view—the increasing size of the contract—the larger payment followed naturally. But to NASA, which thought the payment was too large already and which had not achieved the performance it wanted from JPL and Caltech, the proposal opened the door to imposing its other demands.[30]

NASA prepared a counter position. By September 1963 the space agency hierarchy appeared determined not only to reject the fee increase but to rewrite the contract. As Hilburn pointed out, if the contract were renegotiated to NASA's satisfaction, headquarters would have the leverage "to force management changes and/or any other steps that may be necessary to provide responsive performance from our contractor." If the renegotiations failed, NASA could begin at once to plan "for some other mode of operating the facility."[31]

DuBridge, Pickering, and other CIT-JPL officials presented their case to a bevy of NASA officials on September 16, 1963. One of the central issues concerned the agency's desire to change the fee from a flat sum negotiated in advance to an award, or incentive fee, which would be determined by NASA on its evaluation of the performance of Caltech and JPL during the year. Caltech objected emphatically to an award fee, first, because it would be determined unilaterally by NASA and would be based on criteria that would be difficult to establish. Second, and more important, the Institute found an award fee incompatible with the nature of a university. Such payments might be suitable for an industrial firm, which desired to maximize its profits. University personnel, however, were committed to doing their best because of their devotion to excellence, regardless of specific financial rewards. "The personnel of JPL will best serve the needs of NASA and the nation by having as their sole goal excellence of performance rather than the procurance of extra fees or the avoidance of penalties to the California Institute," DuBridge said. NASA backed off from the award fee, but it surfaced again in an indirect fashion as part of the overall contract renegotiation. The presentation had gone badly; NASA officials even suggested that the previous fee was already too high. A month later DuBridge informed Webb that Caltech would accept the same fee of $1.25 million for the new fiscal year.[32]

Institute officials suddenly realized that losing the JPL contract was a real possibility. The effect would be disastrous. "We are not now prepared to withstand the financial shock of losing JPL," Robert Gilmore, Caltech business vice-president, confided to the chairman of the board of trustees, electronics firm president Arnold O. Beckman. Gilmore thought the Institute had to begin building up a reserve to cushion such a blow, but that would take four years. NASA held the high cards.[33]

An alarmed board of trustees took several actions on November 4, 1963, to reshape the management of JPL. They hoped that, while the steps fell short of what NASA might desire, they would be sufficient for the time being. "Some in NASA would feel more confident of the future success of the relationship if Dr. Pickering were removed from the operation," Hilburn observed. The trustees did not go that far, however, but instead tried to build managerial support around him while curtailing his authority. Of considerable importance to NASA, the board approved the recruitment of a strong general manager who would run the laboratory's day-to-day operations. This appeared to represent a major breakthrough, since Pickering had tenaciously resisted the appointment of a general manager. The trustees required that the CIT staff counsel and business office approve all research and development subcontracts, leases, and construction projects of more than $2,000 and all subcontracts and purchase orders for products or services of more than $25,000. A plan for detailed financial operations at JPL was to be prepared and reviewed with the trustees' executive committee. Before JPL agreed to any NASA task orders, Caltech had to issue its approval. Val Larsen, the laboratory's longtime business head, lost his supervision of financial operations and procurement and contract administration. Although Gilmore had wanted Larsen removed entirely, the trustees allowed him control of the personnel department and some housekeeping functions. A new business manager was to be recruited. These steps encouraged Hilburn, who spoke of "the 'rehabilitation' of JPL."[34]

A series of meetings between CIT, JPL, and NASA officials to renegotiate the contract produced important changes by the first of December. Most of them were favorable to NASA because they trimmed the mutuality clauses. The most important change curbed the laboratory's long-cherished authority to accept or reject assignments from headquarters. Caltech and JPL retained the prerogative of mutuality on determining six major program areas. Within those areas NASA now enjoyed "complete discretion for ordering work." Caltech-JPL negotiators had at first tried to get NASA to accept some limits on the contracting officer's right to issue unilateral task orders. They also wanted a clause by which the Institute could terminate the contract for convenience. NASA rejected both items, however, and CIT-JPL yielded. Along with these substantive changes went a more subtle change of language. The contract originally had authorized the Institute "to manage and operate" the laboratory. The revision specified that the laboratory was a government-furnished facility and could be used by CIT "only as authorized by NASA." These changes worried Caltech officials, and JPL executives disliked giving up their independence. Nevertheless, as CIT staff counsel John MacL. Hunt pointed out, the "practicalities of the situation" limited the risks. It would be shortsighted of NASA to order JPL to turn out lawn mowers, for instance; effective performance still required a mutuality of interest and understanding.[35]

The fee controversy was settled by accepting NASA's desire for incorporating performance evaluation but making it indirect enough to soothe Caltech's feelings somewhat. The fee statement was divided into two parts. One called for evaluation of CIT-JPL management, technical performance, and meeting of schedules. The second clause set up a range of fees related to the annual estimates of the JPL budget; within that range the exact amount would be negotiated each year. The evaluation procedure was separate from the fee negotiation, but in the deliberations, the performance evaluations were one of several factors used to determine where the fee would be placed within a given range. As Hilburn pointed out, "though the contract is not specifically identified as an 'award fee' type, we have the mechanism to make it operate as such." Caltech fared reasonably well in the application of the award fee, although that mechanism sometimes produced serious inconsistencies. But simply going through the evaluation was an "indignity" for Caltech-JPL—and one which none of the other NASA centers had to endure.[36]

Caltech's main success lay in a terminal task order to protect the Institute against liability that might result from a cancellation of the contract. NASA agreed to protect the school from insurance premiums, terminal leave payments, and miscellaneous closeout costs. Although less than the Institute had wanted, the terminal task order mitigated one of the major liabilities in CIT's operation of JPL.[37]

NASA officials were pleased with the direction of the negotiations. As one headquarters position paper observed, the renegotiated contract created "a new relationship with CIT-JPL" that made the laboratory "a special kind of contractor—almost a quasi-NASA Center." Caltech and JPL were less pleased. As Hunt pointed out in December 1963, however, "the collateral benefits which will accrue from our attitude of responsiveness" outweighed the risks. The actual measure of responsiveness would come in the implementation of these agreements, however. Caltech signed the amendment to the contract on February 3, the day after Ranger 6 impacted the moon. NASA decided to wait to sign until it could evaluate CIT-JPL's enthusiasm in carrying out the new provisions. Laboratory officials felt that, ever since the Kelley report in late 1962, they had been "pressed, harassed, and harangued" to make management changes. Nothing would help so much as a successful Ranger flight. As deputy director Brian Sparks confided: "Our future does indeed depend heavily on the success" of Ranger.[38]

Throughout 1963 an army of technical personnel numbering as many as 900 labored on the reengineering of the spacecraft of Ranger 6. The basic design stayed intact, but newly available lifting capacity of the launch vehicle made it possible to make changes that separated and duplicated most key spacecraft functions. Various backup items, such as a battery, transponder, and a duplicate attitude-control gas system, were added. Ranger 6 also profited from Mariner 2, most notably in using the planetary craft's electrically segmented, rectangular solar panels in place of the smaller, trapezoidal panels used on previous Rangers. At RCA, engineers labored over the television system. One of their most vexing problems was in fabricating acceptable vidicon tubes. Despite rigid quality control standards, seemingly identical tubes yielded differing performance; there seemed to be little choice but to fabricate a large number of tubes and then select the most uniform for the television system.[39]

The progress of Ranger 6 continued on schedule until the fall of 1963 when two serious test failures occurred in General Electric guidance components on the Atlas launch vehicle. The culprits proved to be tiny gold flakes which, because of improper bonding, came loose within certain diodes. The size of a grain of rice, these diodes acted as minuscule electrical switches that permitted current to flow in only one direction; if shorted, however, current could move in either direction. The results were potentially disastrous, and hundreds of these diodes made by Continental Devices had already been installed in Rangers 6 and 7. These critical items had escaped notice because ground-testing procedures could not measure the effect of a temporary short and because the tests could not "simulate the zero gravity of outer space, where the gold flakes would float inside the diodes." A JPL investigation concluded in October 1963 that most of the equipment containing these diodes was so contaminated by the gold flakes as to be unfit to fly. Mites laid low an elephant. There was no choice but to replace all the diodes in critical locations in the spacecraft and the launch vehicle. The process cost two lunar months. The launch of Ranger 6 was postponed from early December 1963 to late January 1964.

The Ranger 6 spacecraft that rode from California to Florida in its special air-conditioned van ranked as the most tested spacecraft to that time. Yet the ultimate and finally only meaningful test would come "in the last ten minutes of the sixty-six-hour trip to the moon," when the television cameras would be turned on as the craft careened toward the lunar surface.

Ranger 6's target was the Julius Caesar region in Mare Tranquillitatis, a region within 10 degrees of the lunar equator, which was the area of most interest to Project Apollo. But the Apollonians were no longer watching. Because of the long delays in Ranger, Apollo engineers had already frozen the design of the landing gear. They were banking on a moon with a solid surface; any pictures from Ranger could at most only confirm or deny the design. True to the mission objectives, Ranger scientists nevertheless gave some weight to Apollo's probable landing region. Ironically, Ranger, which had been redefined in October 1962 to support Apollo—a number of its science experiments had been dropped in favor of the television system—

now was largely irrelevant to the manned program. Ranger fell between two stools. On the one hand it was too late for the manned program, for which its mission objectives had been rewritten; on the other, it could not achieve the optimum scientific objectives had those goals remained uppermost. Ranger block 4—flights 10 through 14—which emphasized television similar to block 3 had been cancelled in the summer of 1963. Block 5, where science took precedence, remained alive, but just barely. The Ranger program appeared headed for a dead end. Under the circumstances the question might have arisen whether it made sense to continue with Ranger at all. It was largely a matter of indifference to the Apollo program. As for space science, the soft-landing Surveyor offered many more possibilities. But Ranger 6 had a momentum of its own; many destinies rode with its payload.

Ranger 6 was launched successfully on January 30, 1964. Two minutes into the flight, however, just as the Atlas main-stage engines shut down and began their separation from the Agena second-stage, a startling event took place. The telemetry that monitored the television system turned on by itself, operated for sixty-seven seconds, and then shut itself off. This curious interlude at first alarmed flight officials, who feared the strange operation might have damaged the television system. But tensions eased as the Ranger hewed close to its flight path and as the telemetry showed no malfunctions. Ranger project manager Harris M. Schurmeier pondered turning on the television system to see if it had been damaged. But if the system did not turn off, the battery-powered cameras would run out of power before the craft reached the moon. He and his colleagues decided against the risky test.

For the next sixty-odd hours Ranger sailed closer to the moon, completed a perfect mid-course maneuver, and headed for impact near its selected target. Hopes built. Pickering told the crush of newsmen at the von Kármán auditorium at JPL: "I am cautiously optimistic." Shortly after midnight on February 2 the spacecraft was hurtling toward the lunar surface at nearly 4,500 miles per hour. At eighteen minutes before the scheduled impact, the two full-scan television cameras responded to an automatic command to warm up; in five minutes—thirteen minutes before impact—they should begin to transmit pictures to Earth. The four partial-scan cameras were to begin their photography at impact minus ten minutes. "Thirteen minutes to impact there is no indication of full power video," said mission control announcer Walter Downhower, a JPL senior engineer. The audience began to murmur and shift restlessly. "Ten minutes to impact, we are awaiting transmission from the spacecraft of full power video," he said. JPL officials desperately transmitted last-minute backup commands to the spacecraft. Without result. At 1:24 A.M. PST, Downhower exclaimed: "We have our first report of impact—still no indication of full power video." The unbelievable had happened. After a textbook-perfect flight, the television cameras had failed to turn on in the ultimate system test. An ashen Pickering said: "I never want to go through an experience like this again—never!"

Another pair of review boards—one at JPL, one at NASA—had to be convened at once to investigate the failure. Some wags suggested that the problem was simple: someone had forgotten to take the lens caps off the cameras. Ranger 6 would not be the first disappointed tourist to have only a blank roll of film to show for his travels. But neither JPL nor NASA officials could find even black humor in the situation. Both investigating committees quickly identified the time of the failure—those sixty-seven seconds when the telemetry had unaccountably turned itself on and then off as the vehicle passed through the earth's upper atmosphere. In that critical pressure region, "gaseous breakdown to a state of electrical conduction occurs most readily." The resulting electrical arcing had destroyed the cameras' and transmitters' high-voltage power supplies. The reasons for the turn-on defied simple explanation; however, several varying opinions were advanced. Most critically, the JPL and NASA boards found themselves at odds on what had happened, why, and what to do about it.

The laboratory investigators concluded that the most probable explanation was that the system had been turned on when the command switch moved into its warm-up mode. Then three more movements had returned the switch to position zero, "disconnecting the arcing components from the battery and conditioning the command system for a normal sequence of events." The board recommended several corrective measures. The most important was to modify the television turn-on circuitry to lock out any turn-on signal. Turn-on would now be accomplished when the mechanical separation of the spacecraft from the Agena vehicle activated the circuitry. A second step was to reduce "the number of electrical leads from the Agena nose-fairing umbilical connector through the spacecraft to the television system." Leads that could make the system start up were to be eliminated or to be protected by resistors. The assumption behind the JPL report was that the design was essentially sound; modifications and safeguards within that design—a technical fix—would be sufficient for success.

The NASA review board countered with a severely critical report which questioned the design and testing procedures. Nothing short of a redesign and new intensive testing would suffice, this committee argued. The board had a cast unfriendly to JPL. The committee had been chosen by associate administrator Robert Seamans, who had appointed Earl Hilburn as its chairman. The only Ranger project personnel involved was its ex officio member, NASA Ranger program engineer Walter Jakobowski, whose role was to familiarize the board with details of the project but who cast no vote. Hilburn brought to the committee his conviction that JPL management and technical practices were deficient. The absence of a single "definitive cause" of the failure reinforced his attitude. Ranger project officials might stick to the belief that electrical arcing, caused by a single unknown event, had burned up the television high-voltage power leads. But he thought it equally possible that two or more discrete failures had occurred nearly simultaneously and that they were traceable to design and testing weaknesses. The Hilburn board's final report, filed on March 17, 1964, said: "In view of the evidence that *two or more* failures must have occurred within the spacecraft's TV subsystem, the Board broadened its investigation to include an evaluation of any general weakness in the Ranger design, testing philosophy, and procedures which might have contributed to, or enhanced the possibilities of, in-flight failure."

The board believed it had found several major design deficiencies: (1) "The two video chains and their associated power and control systems were unnecessarily complex. . . . Furthermore, the two TV systems were not entirely redundant; there were many boxes, plugs, junctions, cables, and control circuits which were common to the two chains and in which a single failure would lead to the disablement of both television systems." (2) Unsound design and construction practices, such as the use of a male umbilical connector, exposed terminals that were subject to shorts, and unvented and unsealed boxes, produced hazardous conditions in the spacecraft. (3) Testing procedures were inadequate. For example, the use of some 300 wire electrical connections between the spacecraft and its test equipment could not match operating conditions where only radio communications tied the craft to ground control. The craft's directional antenna was not system tested with the high-power TV transmitters. Finally, prelaunch systems verification was incomplete, taking place twelve days before launch, because JPL feared damage or even destruction of the vehicle if it was tested after being reassembled. The Hilburn report added up to a stinging indictment that strongly implied incompetence on the part of JPL, RCA, and the Office of Space Sciences and Applications in NASA.

Touchy as a live grenade, the report sat in the administrator's office for ten days. NASA stamped the document with a security classification of confidential, even though it contained no military secrets. On March 26, copies were forwarded to Pickering, DuBridge, and Arnold Beckman, CIT board chairman, for their eyes only; no one else at JPL or CIT was allowed to see it. Five days later Webb sent a long letter to the congressional committees charged with NASA oversight in which he said the Hilburn report contained the agency's "present assumptions regarding the Ranger 6 failure and our current plans for future flights." He repeated the board's findings almost verbatim.

Webb's letter was like electrical arcing among the many exposed points in the critical pressure region of the JPL-NASA relationship. Ranger project personnel both at the laboratory and in the Office of Space Sciences and Applications at headquarters united in protest. Newell and his lieutenants had dissented strongly when the Hilburn board had first presented its position orally. Walter Jakobowski had called locking out the television system an adequate preventive measure. But OSSA personnel had registered little impact in toning the report down. Even more serious, they had not seen Webb's letter before he dispatched it to Capitol Hill. Now they prepared a sharp rebuttal in which they criticized the board's technical conclusions, questioned the wisdom of transmitting the disputed findings to Congress, and pointed out the harmful effect on morale at JPL and OSSA. Since Webb had already written to Congress, Seamans advised OSSA not to make their rebuttal public; instead it reposed in the files. Newell's action had at least made top NASA administration aware that the Hilburn report was vulnerable to serious criticism from outside JPL.

The refutation emphasized three points. First, the video chains may have been complex, but that did not mean, as the Hilburn report implied, that any system that was not entirely redundant was badly designed. "The spacecraft itself would have represented a nonredundant series of systems of far greater complexity," they pointed out. "A single failure in the attitude control system," or a booster engine for example, "could result in complete loss of television data." Second, the report's description of design and construction practices implied "the spacecraft was assembled with complete disregard for normal quality control practices." Yet most of these items, such as the venting of unpressurized electronic boxes, were matters of judgment; no Ranger flights had problems traceable to venting. Third, OSSA defended the testing procedures. Many of these were also matters of judgment, and in a number of cases the risks involved in the testing the board recommended were substantial. OSSA and JPL were willing to compromise on some of the Hilburn recommendations and to order additional tests in some cases, but they stopped far short of what the board desired. If implemented, the Hilburn recommendations would require at least twelve months to carry out; if that happened the Ranger project probably would be cancelled. For the moment JPL and the warring NASA factions tried to hammer out a redesign and testing procedure that would produce a reliable Ranger 7 spacecraft by late spring.

Despite these high-level investigations, the reason for the failure of Ranger 6 remained a mystery. Ironically, however, one man working independently came up with the most probable explanation, only to have it buried in the rush of events toward Ranger 7. Suspicions of where the problem lay had switched from the television subsystem's command switch and electronics to the male pins in the external umbilical connector on the Agena nose fairing. The pins were very close together, and a "hot" pin connected to the television's battery stood only one-fourth of an inch from the television's command circuit pin. The battery pin provided twenty volts, but only three volts would activate the television command circuit and step the switch. During ground monitoring, engineers connected the spacecraft to an external power source with a plug and extension cord. At lift-off, however, the spacecraft switched to internal power; the plug was pulled away, and a small door swung over the pins and latched shut mechanically. A special investigative team looked for several months for something that might have bridged the gap between the two pins, but gave up when all its hypotheses remained inconclusive.

Unable to let go of the tantalizing problem, Alexander Bratenahl, a physicist in JPL's space sciences division, continued to examine the sequence of events surrounding the separation of the Atlas engines and the television turn-on. He studied enlarged frames of movie film of the critical seconds. Within the white cloud of liquid oxygen surrounding the rocket, he detected brilliant luminous flashes. During separation the Atlas main-stage engines spilled 250 pounds of oxidizer and 150 pounds of kerosene, and the sustainer rocket engine ignited the vaporized mixture. A flash wave of considerable energy swept over the missile at 600 feet per second. Mechanically latched instead of hermetically sealed, and bowed slightly outward, the door allowed "ample room for the plasma to enter and short the pins." The time sequence suggested this was exactly what had happened. At 140.008 seconds after lift-off the Atlas engines had separated; at 140.498 seconds the television system had turned on, coinciding with the advance of the flash wave. Reluctant to bother Schurmeier in the hectic days before the flight of Ranger 7, Bratenahl recorded his findings in a memorandum on July 30, 1964, that got buried in the space sciences division. The physicist knew in any case that the seventh spacecraft had a positive lock-out mechanism, which should obviate the earlier problem. The implications of Bratenahl's study were momentous. A simple, subtle design error had scuttled Ranger 6. The elaborate theories of the Hilburn board were completely discredited, and with them a key piece of evidence against JPL management practices disintegrated.

Coming when they did, the Bratenahl findings had long since been submerged in the wave of events. Headquarters' actions in the investigation of Ranger 6 in February and March 1964 had further clouded relations between NASA and CIT-JPL. To JPL hands, the choice of Hilburn, who was roundly disliked at the laboratory because of his position in the contract negotiations, was bad enough. But Webb's letter to the congressional committees stung even more. The laboratory received backing from OSSA. "Allowing only limited distribution, such as preventing the Director of JPL from showing the report to his staff, indicates clearly that NASA did not establish the review board for the purpose of feedback to project personnel," observed Oran Nicks, one of Newell's lieutenants. If the purpose of the investigation had been to establish "a basis for a critical letter to Congress," he continued, "we in the Program Office were naively misled initially into supporting it as a constructive endeavor." The use of the report and letter during the delicate negotiations between NASA and JPL suggested that some headquarters executives saw them as providential aids to force the laboratory into making the long-demanded changes. Webb later defended his letter by saying that he had signed it when he was traveling and only learned later that it had not been properly "staffed out"; he had assumed it had been cleared with OSSA. At best this defense was an admission of a serious administrative mistake—and a particularly embarrassing one for a man who advertised NASA's managerial superiority.[40]

There was no avoiding a full-dress congressional investigation, even though Webb now cautioned the investigators that their inquiry might damage the project. NASA and JPL found themselves in "an extremely delicate situation, much like walking down Fifth Avenue in your BVD's," as he put it. Part of that delicacy was of Webb's making. His letter to Congress had raised very serious charges about the management of the project, which, if pressed very far, would reflect badly on NASA supervision. If an inquiry got out of hand, it might prove as damaging to the agency as to the laboratory. Thus NASA and JPL—still dependent on each other—found themselves thrown into an odd and tenuous alliance.[41]

The investigation was chaired by Representative Joseph Karth, a Minnesota Democrat, who earned much respect from JPL officials for the trouble he took to inform himself about the space program. Karth's subcommittee paid some attention to the technical questions; it criticized JPL and NASA for not having run enough tests. But the subcommittee's main interest lay in the JPL-NASA relationship. Pickering conceded that the laboratory had had management problems and that it had moved perhaps too slowly to refurbish the business operations. He pointed out, however, that the laboratory had always been responsive to headquarters' technical direction; on the "trinkets" episode on Ranger block 2, for instance, JPL had yielded despite its strenuous objections. The director also argued that, because of the nature of the research and advanced development carried out at JPL in addition to project management, the laboratory should be allowed more of the freedom associated with a "university atmosphere." Pickering and several of his assistants testified forthrightly and ably in a forum in which they were inexperienced.[42]

But Webb assumed the starring role on the last day of the four-day hearing. His dexterity as "a verbal acrobat of marathon staying power" had seldom showed to better advantage. The Hilburn report notwithstanding,

Webb had not come to bury JPL but to praise it. Most of the laboratory's work was outstanding, he said, "Men there have done and are doing work more technical, more complex, more difficult than is being done in almost any other place by the human race." Nor did he think that threatening CIT-JPL with pulling the contract away unless they put in a stronger project organization would have measurably improved the spacecraft. In fact, a drastic management change might have driven away the best people at JPL. Problems existed, to be sure. NASA, however, had this all but under control. "I think the new contract gives us all the authority that we need," he assured Karth. His agency would wait to sign it, however, until it could see how well CIT-JPL implemented its provisions.[43]

Webb had performed skillfully—so smoothly, in fact, that many observers came away confused. The pro-industrial *Missiles and Rockets* fumed at what "appeared to be almost a conspiracy to soothe the wounded feelings of the Jet Propulsion Laboratory." Surprised and gratified by NASA's support of JPL, the pro-university *Science* mused that Webb, "like the grand old Duke of York in the nursery rhyme, had marched his soldiers up the hill, then marched them down again."[44] Webb had maneuvered out of his dangerously exposed position when he appeared to endorse the Hilburn report; he had also avoided any severe probing of NASA operations. He salved JPL's technical pride but kept the spotlight on JPL's managerial shortcomings. Webb avoided criticism of his agency by stressing that NASA had moved to correct the situation with the new contract.

Congress picked up its cue and handed the administrator an additional club to insure that JPL complied with the contract. The subcommittee's report called for better fabrication and testing procedures but directed most of its artillery at the JPL-NASA relationship. The space agency received some ritual stripes, but Karth laid the onus primarily on JPL. "If there was a single thread which consistently ran through the testimony of NASA officials regarding management of Project Ranger, it was JPL's resistance to NASA supervision," said the report. "These actions cannot reflect anything other than an embarrassing unwillingness on the part of JPL to submit to NASA direction in the past," it continued. The subcommittee considered the laboratory's "extraordinary show of independence" to be "the most significant fact" developed during the investigation. To make JPL more submissive, the subcommittee recommended a general tightening of NASA supervision over the laboratory. For the most part rather general, the recommendations in effect gave NASA the subcommittee's blessing for firmer control but left the implementation to the discretion of the agency. But one specific recommendation handed NASA what it wanted and what JPL had resisted so long. The laboratory, said the subcommittee, should install a strong general manager as deputy director.[45]

The failure of Ranger 6, followed by the impending congressional probe, had stimulated the most intense soul-searching thus far at JPL and Caltech. Pickering appointed an ad hoc committee in late February 1964 to examine the laboratory's current problems, particularly its image. The press and JPL's employees held quite diverse images of the institution, but NASA's was "single-minded." "Briefly, they look upon us as arrogant, uncooperative, and mismanaged." Details of the NASA image were often "badly warped," the committee told Pickering. But it concluded that "as a working hypothesis . . . the NASA image of JPL management is in its broad outlines correct." The laboratory had been guilty of excessive ambition and of overselling its ability to carry out programs. The committee proposed a long list of suggestions on how to improve relations. Most of them involved improving personal relations between JPL and NASA staffs through intercession by third parties, closer working relationships, and more politeness. Personality clashes contributed to bad organizational relations. Webb appears to have been irritated that DuBridge joined the chorus of scientists who criticized the space program for emphasizing manned flight over scientific study. Asked by Representative Karth about personal relations, Pickering declined to answer. But the problems transcended personality clashes, and the suggestions, primarily palliatives, fell short of the concrete steps needed to placate headquarters. In any event little action seemed to result from the study; JPL still seemed stubbornly intent on pursuing its own course.[46]

The inaction at JPL alarmed officials at the campus. "The Institute is in fully as great danger now as we were in September 1963," Robert Gilmore confided to Arnold Beckman. The most important requirement, Gilmore believed, was the item that Pickering opposed the most—"to recruit a top business executive" to serve as general manager. About November 1, 1963, Pickering had promised "Lee [DuBridge] and me *unconditionally*" to do so. Instead the director had elevated a longtime JPL staff member, Brian Sparks, to the new position of assistant laboratory director for technical divisions. Sparks had neither the personal strength nor the authority to perform as a general manager. The five-month delay had "sorely taxed" the confidence of Hilburn and others, Gilmore reported, and it was now imperative to hire a general manager within not months but days. "I believe we must move quickly to protect the Institute and simply let Bill [Pickering] adjust himself to the new situation," Gilmore said.[47]

With the Caltech trustees again aroused and congressional pressure building, Pickering's resistance faded. CIT and JPL intensified their recruitment process, which finally culminated with the announcement on June 29, 1964, that Alvin R. Luedecke would be hired as deputy director of the laboratory. A major general in the air force, Luedecke was retiring as general manager of the Atomic Energy Commission. The choice delighted NASA. Luedecke reported to the laboratory on August 1, 1964, and became in effect director of day-to-day operations. The deputy's role statement made him "responsible for the day-to-day management of its [JPL's] resources and the direction and coordination of its financial, technical, administrative, and service activities." He had broad authority to act on his own, including making organizational and salary changes within his own and subordinate departments and reprogramming budgeted dollars within and between projects. The arrangement, however necessary in 1964, contained the seeds of trouble. For William Pickering, Luedecke represented both factually and symbolically NASA's penetration of his laboratory, and JPL, as it turned out, could not accommodate both of them.[48]

With Luedecke's appointment as the capstone, Beckman reviewed the steps Caltech had taken to restore itself to a state of grace. "The major problems which have come up in the past with respect to JPL are largely behind us," he assured Webb. The changes would become apparent by fall 1964, and he suggested that NASA might want to hold off signing the contract until then.[49]

The agency was in no hurry to sign, for it wanted to see the effects of the changes. In mid-July 1964 Homer Newell, alarmed that Pickering still considered Surveyor a back-burner project, felt compelled to inform him strongly that the project had high priority and required much more attention than JPL was giving it. Surveyor would be one of the prime concerns for Luedecke. Associate administrator Seamans again raised the possibility of switching to alternative management arrangements, despite the "temporarily adverse impact" on NASA programs, if the CIT-JPL relations continued to be "unsatisfactory." He still hoped, however, for "a change in attitude at Caltech and JPL." Webb continued to harbor dark thoughts about the relationship. "We are beginning to receive unsolicited suggestions from several sources as to how an operation like that of JPL could best be conducted over the long pull," he warned Beckman. Attitudes were all-important, the administrator insisted. He wanted to know "whether the attitudes are such that when it is said that no administration of a university can dictate to a faculty, that this ends the matter." "Many things" could still be done, he thought. Webb continued to look for the "something extra" from the Caltech connection. With his government background, Luedecke apparently understood what the NASA chief wanted, but he also cautioned Webb that it would be difficult to procure. Caltech was becoming more responsive to Webb's desires, but until he resigned in 1968 the administrator continued to look for that elusive extra lost in the conflict of two philosophies.[50]

By the summer of 1964 JPL had yielded a great deal to NASA. The articles of confederation had been transformed into a constitution; headquarters had penetrated the shell that had kept JPL an institution apart and could act directly in many instances at the laboratory. Reflecting a movement under way since the Kelley report, JPL's project management had grown stronger.

Business operations had been tightened up and made more compatible with its funding agency's procedures. The appointment of a general manager signified that the laboratory's day-to-day operations would take on a more formal structure. The failures of Rangers 1 through 5 indicated the need for management changes, as even many laboratory staff members recognized. The failure of Ranger 6, however, which eroded the last strata of JPL resistance, belonged more in the category of accident than the sweeping managerial deficiencies contained in the Hilburn report. Whether all the changes improved the laboratory's operations was debatable, but many were simply inherent in the changing situation. The relative decline of JPL's power within NASA by 1963 compared to 1958 made some concessions a foregone conclusion. However desirable the older style of operations might have been, an organization responsible for a quarter of a billion dollars a year in a highly charged political atmosphere could not maintain its one-time independence.

All the same, JPL had rightfully insisted that the changes not go so far as to alter the character of the laboratory fundamentally. Government safeguards could still operate while the laboratory remained free of civil service; the hybrid status of JPL introduced a desirable diversity into government scientific and technological practices. Indeed for the long term, Pickering may have been right to stress the need for autonomy and a "university atmosphere" to enable creative people to do their best work. NASA's preoccupation with projects and the short term could have eventually dried up the springs of creativity necessary for the long haul. For its part NASA had serious managerial shortcomings. The other centers joined JPL in complaining of seeming arbitrariness and high-handedness at headquarters. The demands placed on the centers were often uncoordinated, sometimes contradictory, and at times petty, as when Hilburn insisted that NASA liaison men at JPL have an office on the same floor as the laboratory's top management.[51] Neither JPL nor NASA could emerge from the strained situation completely satisfied.

The years 1963 and 1964 had been an ordeal for the laboratory and for Pickering personally. Brian Sparks spoke for many JPL staff members who felt bewildered by the barrage of managerial advice from NASA and from the campus. "To this day I still don't really understand completely why some of the criticisms have been made, particularly the statement that we need 'hard-headed industrial management,'" he said in May 1964. The laboratory management prayed that relations with NASA had passed their nadir. All eyes turned again to Ranger. "A successful Ranger shot will work wonders," said Sparks. "A few more weeks and we will 'test' the reliability odds again."[52]

10 ★★

MASTERING THE ART
OF BUILDING SPACECRAFT

The Ranger project attracted the most outside attention to the Jet Propulsion Laboratory in 1964, and JPL redoubled its efforts to make it work. But Ranger's problems were complicated by two other projects that reached critical stages in 1964. One was Mariner, the first U. S. flyby of Mars, which presented significant technical challenges by comparison with the 1962 Mariner mission to Venus. The Mariner Mars project would help answer the question whether the success of Mariner 2 had been a fluke. The other project was Surveyor, a second-generation lunar spacecraft that was supposed to make a controlled soft landing on the moon in preparation for Apollo. Surveyor posed not only technical but managerial challenges since the laboratory's role was intended to be limited to supervising an industrial contractor. Taken together, Ranger, Mariner, and Surveyor presented a demanding course in learning to build spacecraft.

In the gloomy early months of 1964 most attention focused on Ranger. For the Ranger 7 spacecraft the three principals—JPL, RCA, and NASA—implemented an elaborate system of tests and double checks. The laboratory increased the number of its engineers assigned to the RCA plant in Hightstown, New Jersey, from three to twenty-five. A special problem–failure reporting system required the signature of both JPL and RCA officials on every problem or failure analysis in the television system. The firm brought in more of its specialists, including a corps from its Princeton research laboratory. NASA dispatched a special team to Pasadena to oversee spacecraft testing; these engineers were instructed to write their own reports and not assign any of their tasks to JPL staff. New testing procedures, which included some of the "no wire" tests the Hilburn board had recommended, were introduced. Confidence slowly built as JPL and RCA tried to make sure they overlooked nothing on the spacecraft. The tension, recalled NASA official Edgar Cortright, "was unbelievable."[1]

161

The confidence was shattered, however, when RCA inspectors opened a sealed electronic module in the television system on March 27, 1964, and found inside a small polyethylene bag containing fourteen screws and a lock washer. Was the bag of screws an accident? The firm's security officers decided it was; they attributed the incident to the pressures of working three shifts seven days a week. Or was it sabotage? The RCA project officers feared the worst; they thought it highly unlikely that the bag of screws could have escaped detection. If it was sabotage, all the television hardware would have to be reopened and inspected. That would cost $500,000 and add another month's delay to the tight flight schedule. JPL project manager Harris Schurmeier dispatched his deputy, Gordon Kautz, for an on-the-scene investigation. Kautz agreed it looked like sabotage. But "I had the inherent and intuitive feeling that we didn't have any saboteurs there," he recalled. He decided the bag of screws incident was "indeed an accident—the people were so fatigued back there that this had occurred." Schurmeier accepted Kautz's momentous recommendation that work proceed without the reinspection.

By the end of July 1964 every failure report had been corrected and all the systems tests completed. NASA headquarters formed a blue-ribbon "buy-off committee" chaired by Homer Newell to make a final determination that the Ranger 7 spacecraft was capable of flight. After a one-day delay because of trouble with the Atlas launch vehicle, yet another Ranger sailed toward the moon on July 28. The flight went without a hitch; the craft would crash almost exactly on target at 6:25 A.M. PDT on July 31, 1964. The television cameras would work "very definitely," Schurmeier boldly assured newsmen. Director Pickering interjected a note of caution, but placed the odds for success at 80 percent.

At 6:07 A.M. two cameras responded to a command and began to warm up. Cheers erupted from the audience. At 6:10 A.M. the other four cameras began to warm up. The flight announcer raced to keep up: "Twelve minutes before impact, excellent video signals continue . . . Ten minutes . . . no interruption of excellent video signals. All cameras appear to be functioning . . . all recorders at Goldstone are 'go' . . . Seven minutes . . . all cameras continue to send excellent signals . . . Five minutes from impact . . . video signals still continue excellent. Everything is 'go,' as it has been since launch . . . Three minutes . . . no interruption, no trouble . . . Two minutes . . . all systems operating. Preliminary analysis shows pictures being received at Goldstone . . . One minute to impact . . . Excellent . . . Excellent . . . Signals to the end . . . IMPACT!"

The hum of Ranger's telemetry gave way to the soft hiss of space static, which, in turn, was flooded out by a surge of cheers from newsmen and JPL employees. Some tossed papers in the air, a few wept. "For . . . those of us who had lived Ranger for so long, it was kind of a spiritual happening," recalled one JPL staff member. Even though Ranger would be superseded by more spectacular and sophisticated projects, for many JPL staffers Ranger 7 represented a climactic experience that no subsequent project could match.

"This is JPL's day," Homer Newell told a news conference a few minutes later. A beaming Pickering responded: "We have had our troubles . . . [but] this is an exciting day." A newsman asked the director about the future of the laboratory. "I think it's improved," Pickering grinned, eliciting laughter and applause from the audience. By the following morning, August 1, Pickering and Newell had flown to Washington, where they briefed President Johnson. Though interested in the photographs, LBJ showed greater concern for Ranger 7's geopolitical implications. "We know this morning that the United States has achieved fully the leadership we have sought for free men," he said. He asked rhetorically: "This is a battle for real existence in the world, isn't it—for survival?"

The photographs were superb—better than anyone had dared hope. Principal scientific investigator Gerard Kuiper, the astronomer who headed the lunar and planetary laboratory at the University of Arizona, exulted: "We have made progress in resolution of lunar detail not by a factor of 10, as [was] hoped would be possible with this flight, nor by a factor of 100, which would have been already very remarkable, but by a factor of 1,000." The pictures boasted 1,132 scan lines per frame, compared to the approximately 500 lines in home television sets. The photographs revealed thousands of craters, ranging in size from a few hundred meters across to tiny indentations less than a meter wide. This was Ranger's biggest surprise for scientists: the moon appeared much more heavily cratered than in Earth-based observations.

But the "remarkable" clarity of the pictures could not resolve the many conflicting theories about the evolution of the moon or even the nature of its surface. There was agreement that the surface appeared smoother and gentler than many had feared, and that was indeed good news for Apollo. But the actual bearing strength of the surface required data from Surveyor. "Ranger's pictures are like mirrors, and everyone sees his own theories reflected in them," noted Cornell physicist Thomas Gold. To Kuiper and geologist Eugene Shoemaker, the ridges and lows appeared typical of lava flows; the fragmented material on the surface would probably be "crunchy," like pulverized lava. Kuiper estimated the depth at not more than five feet, Shoemaker at not more than fifty feet. In either case they thought the findings represented "good news for manned exploration." To Nobel prize-winning chemist Harold Urey, however, the pictures were at best inconclusive. "Earth-based measurements of the thermal conductivity of the outer parts of the moon" were "very low" and could more readily be accounted for "by a soft, spongy, fairy-castle structure for some depth," he said.

The inconclusiveness of Ranger's pictures triggered a growing debate over the project's value. The angriest exchange took place when John Lear, science editor of *Saturday Review,* suggested that scientists were "captured" by government-supported "instant science" which in effect induced them to report favorable findings before they were sure of them. Kuiper denounced the allegations as "complete fantasy," but his spirited defense of Ranger and its implications for Apollo, which went beyond hard data, raised questions about the subtle influences that might work upon experimenters almost unknowingly. More restrained observers also had doubts. The *Christian Science Monitor* observed that, for scientific value, the photographs ranked well below the nonvisual data gathered by the much less expensive Explorers which revealed the Van Allen belts. And historian R. Cargill Hall later pointed out: "Having pushed so long and hard for a Ranger success, neither NASA, JPL, nor the scientists, it appeared, could adequately explain exactly what that success meant."

Ranger's last two flights seemed anticlimactic. For Ranger 8 a landing site was chosen near that of the seventh flight. Scientists had preferred a landing in the highlands, but Newell bowed to the priority accorded Apollo. Ranger 8 operated flawlessly, but the data it returned essentially duplicated its predecessor. For Ranger 9 scientists succeeded in establishing a target in the highlands, but what new findings there were had relatively slight impact. The most spectacular feature of Ranger 9 was technological—the addition of live television transmission. With JPL scientist Ray Heacock describing lunar features, the public had a front-row seat as Ranger 9 hurtled to the surface on March 24, 1965.

The Ranger series ended with a flourish. The project's most important legacy was that JPL had begun to master the complex technological and managerial tasks of developing a spacecraft. The laboratory's problems had been less in design than in carrying out the precision engineering and quality assurance necessary for spacecraft which had to operate nearly perfectly every time. God was in the details—in spotless cleanliness, in thorough testing, and in ruthless follow-up to make sure each failure report was corrected rather than accepted on faith. Like battle-hardened troops, JPL engineers who had gone through Ranger had an unmatched experience to apply to other projects. In the process JPL proved out the basic design for not only lunar but planetary spacecraft. After Ranger JPL was a different organization.

Scientifically, however, Ranger was a disappointment. Not only were the scientific objectives of Rangers 7 through 9 compromised by their role in support of Apollo but a succeeding block of Rangers 10 through 15, which would have carried equipment for more sophisticated scientific experiments, was cancelled as the voracious Apollo consumed a larger portion of the NASA budget. Having spent $267 million to develop Ranger, NASA now decided it could not spend another $72 million or so to use it when it would be most effective.

Building on Ranger's foundation, the Mariner 4 flyby mission to Mars scored an impressive success in 1964. Of most immediate importance to JPL, Mariner 4 represented a landmark in learning to build spacecraft. The mission was also a down payment on a continuing return that would transform understanding of the red planet within little more than a decade.

The Mariner Mars project was authorized by NASA headquarters in November 1962, almost exactly two years before Mariners 3 and 4 would have to be ready for flight, if they were to take advantage of the launch opportunity that occurred every two years. NASA had once envisioned flights to both Venus and Mars in 1964, but budgetary and personnel limitations forced a choice between the two planets. (The success of Mariner 2's Venus flyby made it possible to scrap the return to Venus, which essentially duplicated the 1962 shot, and go for Mars. Subsequent Venus missions would be undertaken with more advanced spacecraft.)[2]

JPL and NASA's new Goddard Space Flight Center proposed competing concepts for the 1964 Mars opportunity. With the planetary program, as with space exploration generally, NASA wanted to promote twin technological objectives which were, to some extent, contradictory. One goal was "the fastest development of the technology necessary for successful planetary landers." The other was "the optimum use of each planetary opportunity to develop the necessary scientific technology." The proper balance between these objectives was hard to achieve, as the conflict over science and engineering on Ranger had indicated. In an extreme case a launch vehicle might be devoted entirely to technical developments, and no scientific experiments would be included until the transport system was perfected; this clearly was undesirable. These constraints were especially critical for the planetary program because of the long flights and long waits between flight opportunities. A conservative approach thus seemed best for Mariner. The primary objectives should be attainable without any technological breakthroughs. The goals, said Oran Nicks of NASA headquarters, "should be based primarily on 'state of the art' at the time of preliminary design."[3]

Since JPL's proposal offered a better blend of both objectives than Goddard's, it received the nod. Headquarters rated the two proposals as approximately equal up until the time of encounter but gave JPL a slight edge. The crucial difference arose when JPL proposed a flyby mission in contrast to Goddard's planetary lander. The flyby required only that the instruments be turned on to achieve success. The lander featured, however, a capsule that had to separate from the spacecraft, enter the Martian atmosphere, deploy a parachute, and land. The scientific returns from both types of missions were ranked about equal, and many of the lander's objectives could be accomplished by Earth-based efforts. Moreover, the risks of contaminating Mars were unknown. Sterilization of the lander posed immense technological problems, as Ranger suggested. Yet landing an unsterilized capsule risked losing Mars for biological study—"a scientific catastrophe of the first order." Accordingly NASA adopted JPL's more cautious strategy.[4]

Mariners 3 and 4 nevertheless posed significant challenges for spacecraft technology. First, flight life. The spacecraft had to operate for 6,000 to 7,000 hours (250 to 290 days), compared with 2,500 hours for Mariner 2. This increased the chances of equipment failure. Second, power. Although Mariner Mars needed less than 200 watts, its source—solar radiation—would decrease by half because it was flying away from the sun. Mariner 2, which gained power as it flew toward the sun, had required only 27 square feet of solar panels; Mariners 3 and 4 needed 70 square feet. (The Mars flight posed a new temperature problem: the spacecraft would grow colder instead of warmer, as on the Venus mission.) Third, communication distance. Mariner 2 had sailed as far as 54 million miles, and its radio waves took nearly five minutes to reach Earth. Mariner Mars would travel nearly three times as far, and communication with the spacecraft would take almost three times as long. Since radio strength decreases as the square of increasing distance, the communications system would have to be nine times better than for Mariner 2. Fourth, the Mars mission was the first that could not use Earth as a reference point for its attitude control. Satellite, lunar, and Venus missions had sighted on Earth or Earth and the sun. But on the Mars flight, Earth would move across the face of the sun and much of the time would appear as "a relatively dim crescent." Mars spacecraft would base their attitude control on the sun and Canopus, "the Yellow Giant," a bright star at a wide angle away from the sun. Fifth, scientific payload. This package would be new and larger than Mariner 2's and required the development of a television camera and the means to point it and to record and transmit its pictures. To meet this complex collection of new technological and scientific demands, JPL engineers could employ only a small increase in weight over the Venus spacecraft.[5]

In engineering Mariners 3 and 4 the laboratory could draw on the learning experience provided by Ranger's troubles and Mariner 2's success. The project entailed a careful blending of design, testing, and scheduling to attain the right balance of conservatism and innovation, rigidity and flexibility.

The design of the spacecraft embodied these approaches. The Ranger and Mariner 2 models had been based on a hexagonal skeleton, to which the instrument packages were fastened, and were topped by a tower for the antenna. To conserve weight on the 1964 project, however, JPL designers turned the packages themselves into the framework. "Eight shallow trays, deriving part of their strength from their close-packed contents, were joined in a ring." Thermal shields were placed over the top and bottom of the large ring. Some equipment that was too bulky to fit between the shields, such as the antennas and spacecraft battery, protruded from the decks. The four solar panels resembled those of Mariner's predecessors and gave the craft their distinctive windmill-like appearance. But a radical approach to the structure of the panels cut the weight to less than half a pound per square foot. The structures used corrugation-stiffened sheet metal for the floor and were supported by stamped aluminum spars "about the gauge of kitchen aluminum foil."[6]

The laboratory first built a prototype, or proof-test, model. This would serve as the final test bed, so that the flight hardware would not be subjected to the rigors of testing plus spaceflight; the proof-test model could also be used for final changes in the overall system testing. After the launch the model could be used for simulating flight situations.

Converting the design into hardware required careful planning and delicate diplomacy in working through JPL's matrix organization. As on other projects, the division managers controlled the allocation of personnel and their activities; representatives from the Mariner project office had influence only over the personnel the division managers assigned to the project. The project office therefore held regular "overlay" meetings with the division chiefs to exchange common problems and receive advice. Such a system had the disadvantage of introducing some redundancy to an already complicated management structure. It boasted the advantage, however, of drawing the division heads into project affairs. When crises arose, they were usually willing to commit their personnel to the project more quickly and effectively.[7]

Top-notch personnel reinforced the project structure. The project manager, J. N. James, had been a division manager and therefore commanded the prestige that had eluded the first Ranger project manager, James Burke. James also exhibited an eye for detail or what he termed "snooping"; unlike some laboratory executives who focused on design concepts, he took little for granted. To test his eye, his engineers once rigged up a defect in a fairly obscure part of the spacecraft, and he found it. Mariner also enjoyed an advantage over Ranger in that it seemed to attract a higher percentage of JPL's better engineers, who responded to the challenge and prestige of working on the more venturesome planetary projects.[8]

The design and hardware process moved through a progressive series of freezes. This required careful evaluation of the trade-offs between allowing enough time for a good design but without delays that would impinge on the system as a whole. The first freeze was handed down fairly early, in March 1963, only four months after the project had received formal authorization. Engineers could change internal designs so long as they did not violate the functional specifications. Designers could still request changes, which occurred frequently, but they now required review and approval of the spacecraft system manager. The final freeze list came out in December 1963. Meanwhile interface documents were placed on the freeze list as rapidly as possible. When the equipment for the proof-test model arrived in January 1964, James laid a freeze over the entire spacecraft. "After that date, it was felt that any change would have a significant impact on the rest of the system," project technicians said. The interface between the spacecraft and ground equipment needed more time for resolution; that freeze was promulgated in May 1964, about five months before the first launch date. After May only such changes as appeared "mandatory for mission success"— which were fairly numerous—were permitted. This much simplified model of spacecraft design and fabrication, from freezes on discrete items through consideration of the interaction of blocks of components to final overall lockup, showed the maturation of JPL's systems engineering, for which it deservedly won high marks.[9]

Concern for extreme reliability of equipment rode throughout the design and fabrication process. Quality assurance was vital. Four elements were emphasized: (1) adequate performance margins (the solar panels, for instance, were designed to generate at least 300 watts of power even though only 200 watts was needed); (2) a rigorous parts qualification and selection program; (3) careful inspection of parts during manufacturing and assembly; and (4) a well-designed prototype and flight qualification testing of assembled flight items. No matter how thorough quality assurance was, however, it could not in itself attain the required standard of reliability. As a summary report said: "For example, if the spacecraft had 30,000 electrical components, each with a mean time between failures of 100 million hours, the probability that at least one component failure would occur by the end of 6,000 hours of operation was 0.84. The spacecraft design had to enable proper operation in spite of failures as well as without them." If a critical component failed, it could not only wipe out a single function, but it could also overtax other components and spawn failures throughout the system.[10]

Redundancy therefore had to be built into the system, especially what was known as "functional redundancy." "Block redundancy," the use of two identical units, would protect against random failures. If, however, the problem was causal (defined as "a design failure or an overstress due to some external perturbation"), both units might well experience the same failure.

By contrast, functional redundancy established "at least two separate and independent paths by which a critical operation could be performed." The cover that protected the scan and television optics offered a good example of functional redundancy. The usual operation involved unlatching the lid with a solenoid, "then allowing the spring-loaded cover to drop." In the back-up scheme the cover was unlatched by a lanyard connected to the cover when the scan platform was turned. In this example two failures would have to occur in the cover itself before both routes would prove inoperative. This imaginative approach required little additional weight, power, or complexity.[11]

No matter how sophisticated and quantitative the engineering, however, some aspects of spacecraft fabrication remained essentially an art. Take the critical process of welding thin-gauge aluminum. Attacking the process mainly by cut and try, experienced welders eventually devised procedures that produced nearly acceptable welds. They followed these techniques "religiously," tried not to change top-quality welders, and maintained scrupulously clean parts. (In this process, as in the assembly of the spacecraft, cleanliness was next to godliness.) Even so the parts usually had to be reworked several times to be finally acceptable.[12]

Throughout the design and fabrication regimen, 55 percent of the schedules were met. The overall slippage averaged slightly under two months—just enough to meet the target date for launch. Mariner 3 blasted off on November 5, 1964, but within minutes problems with the fiberglass honeycomb nose shield doomed the mission. The cylindrical fairing protected the spacecraft as it roared through the atmosphere, later to be jettisoned. But for reasons then unknown, the shroud failed and could not be jettisoned. Two disastrous consequences ensued. The added weight of the nose cone cut the velocity so much that the craft would not reach its target. Nor could the spacecraft unfold its solar panels: no solar cells, no solar power. Repeated commands to deploy the panels met no response. In desperation, flight command prepared to fire the spacecraft rocket motor in the hope of blasting the nose shield loose. But the spacecraft battery ran out of power, and, nearly nine hours after launch, the mission was declared dead.[13]

The spare spacecraft stood ready, but launching it would be pointless without getting to the bottom of the problems with the nose shield. The time remaining in the launch window—just over a month—imposed a severe discipline. The shroud was mainly the responsibility of NASA's Lewis Research Center in Cleveland, which handled the launch-to-injection phase, and Lockheed Missile and Space Corporation, which had built the fairing. But JPL engineers quickly assumed the key role. Exploratory tests were run hurriedly with minimal instrumentation on whatever pieces of the shroud could be spared. They quickly surpassed some of the contractor's initial efforts, which had included the comical scene of executives who drew salaries in six figures crouching inside the shell, tapping it with silver dollars in search of flaws.[14]

Within four days JPL personnel had determined that the problem lay not with a spacecraft malfunction but with a structural defect in the nose shield. The skin separated from the core of the shroud because the honeycomb cells were not vented. Fabrication and handling also tended to inflict local defects inadvertently, and the skin separated most readily at these points. Reliable means of testing the fiberglass sandwich had not been employed—even the "crude coin-tapping inspection method" was bypassed. Most importantly, while the shroud had undergone various tests, it had not been subjected to tests under combined environments such as temperature, vacuum, and time. When JPL tested the unvented specimen in a combined ascent heating-vacuum test, it exploded violently. When a specimen's exterior surface was perforated with small vent holes, the shroud easily passed the same test, even after some parts of it had been deliberately delaminated.[15]

"The remainder of the JPL task," recalled James, "was to convince a great many persons that this evidence and analysis was irrefutable, and then to guide these people towards the optimum solution in the remaining time." The best course appeared to be to abandon the troublesome fiberglass shroud in favor of a metal one. (Ironically, the fabrication of the metal replacement indicated that the supposed weight savings of fiberglass, which had justified its use, was largely illusory.) A Lewis-Lockheed-JPL team worked together to develop a magnesium fairing with an inner thermal liner which was then crafted at Lockheed. The first replacement shroud arrived at Cape Kennedy, as Cape Canaveral had been renamed in honor of the late president, just seventeen days after the failure of Mariner 3. Intensive testing continued on a second specimen. On November 27, the day after the tests were successfully completed, Mariner 4 was readied for launch. The dramatic turnaround in what had seemed like a doomed mission was labeled "brilliant" by some outside observers and showed JPL crisis engineering at its best.[16]

Mariner 4 was launched successfully on November 28, but it experienced some anxious moments on its way to Mars as the spacecraft fumbled for Canopus. Mariner 4 acquired the sun twenty-four minutes after launch. The spacecraft picked up Canopus on November 30, after first locking on several wrong stars. When the mid-course maneuver was attempted on December 4, Mariner prematurely lost its grip and had to go searching again for the Yellow Giant 100 light years, 58 trillion miles, away. The mission completed the mid-course maneuver successfully and reacquired the sun and Canopus without incident. On December 7 the craft lost Canopus again and fixed on Gamma-Velorum. JPL officials allowed the spacecraft to continue this way until December 17, when they broke the lock through ground commands; Mariner locked on Canopus again after a three-minute search. The problems with Canopus were attributed to dust particles that drifted near the spacecraft and reflected a flash of sunlight into the sensor.[17]

As Mariner neared Mars on July 14, 1965, the various experiments went into action. The television camera beamed twenty-one pictures—covering about 1 percent of the Martian surface—back to Earth. The mission included a new experiment that assumed an important role in subsequent planetary exploration: radio occultation measurements of atmospheric density. Conceived shortly before the launch by D. L. Cain of JPL, the device measured the neutral atmosphere by its propagation effects. The experiment required giving up the communications and control links to the spacecraft during the critical encounter period, before the television pictures had been sent. The project manager agonized over this trade-off between a top-notch scientific experiment and technical control but eventually agreed.[18]

The occultation findings reinforced the pictures to produce the "bleak model of Mars" which prevailed for several years. In Schurmeier's summary, Mars appeared as "a rather moonlike object, its surface an old, cold, cratered desert, its atmosphere extremely thin and dominated by carbon dioxide, its magnetic field negligible, and its interior seemingly inert." The "Mars as moon" paradigm surprised and disappointed some observers. It permanently grounded Percival Lowell's flights of fancy about the planet's "veritable cobweb" of canals. Although the trend of some Earth-based observations anticipated Mariner's findings, some scientists had nonetheless expected a more Earth-like planet. Spin rates, obliquity, and seasonal patterns which are similar to those of Earth had raised hopes of finding a twin in the solar system. Some had thought early Martian oceans were possible and had looked for "folded sedimentary mountain belts and other features that might be associated with ancient oceans." But while Mariner 4 ruled out some possibilities, the limits of its observations left its desert paradigm open to major revisions by later Mariners.[19]

Mariner 4 "startled" its proponents and detractors alike with the amount and quality of the data returned, observed Oran Nicks. It was "the first spacecraft to challenge Earth-based planetary exploration and add significantly to our data on another planet," Schurmeier noted. In recognition of these accomplishments, President Johnson awarded Pickering, James, and Nicks the scientific achievement medal at a White House ceremony in August 1965. The Mars mission also gave the United States a leg up on the Russians in the space race. Since 1960 the Soviet Union had attempted at least five flights to Mars before the launch of Mariner 3; two had suffered booster failure, two had not left the parking orbit, and the fifth had failed after 61 percent of its flight. With Mariner 4, planetary spacecraft moved from the pioneering phase to the operating stage. The Mars mission triumph, together with the three successful Rangers, showed that JPL had turned the corner in learning to build spacecraft.[20]

The questions about the lunar surface which the Ranger impact flights could not answer figured prominently in the Surveyor project and made the lunar softlander a much more complicated technical undertaking. Surveyor was also the laboratory's first experience in running a project where the great bulk of the work was done by an industrial contractor. Director Pickering had hoped to avoid this sort of supervisory activity. But given the space agency's desire to utilize industry and to build a power base with aerospace corporations, supervision of industrial contractors loomed ever larger in JPL's future.

For both technical and managerial reasons, Surveyor perhaps ranked as NASA's most troubled project. Edgar Cortright, Newell's deputy, considered Surveyor "probably the greatest technical risk" in the program of the Office of Space Sciences and Applications. "The Surveyor mission has very little margin for error," Cortright said. "Unless virtually all equipment functions within specifications, the flight will fail." By contrast Lunar Orbiter, a series of five spacecraft that would photograph potential Apollo landing sites, was less complex technically and had an unambiguous purpose—to support Apollo. Managed by Langley Research Center and built by Boeing, Lunar Orbiter enjoyed a much easier development.[21]

Surveyor's lunar phase entailed vastly more complicated activities than had Ranger's. Whereas Ranger had impacted the moon and was destroyed in the process, Surveyor was to soft-land on the surface and continue to function throughout the gelid lunar night. When Surveyor approached within 50 miles of the moon, a retro-engine would fire to slow the spacecraft from 9,000 to 350 feet per second. About 5 miles above the surface a three-chambered vernier engine would gradually throttle down the craft to about 15 feet per second. Then, 13 feet above the surface, the vernier unit would shut off and the craft would free-fall to the surface, where its landing would be cushioned by landing-gear shock absorbers, crushable footpads, and crushable blocks on its frame. The process required a new radar altimeter Doppler velocity sensor (RADVS). A difficult development, its success would be crucial to Apollo, whose landing system was patterned after RADVS.[22]

The landing resembled that of a helicopter touchdown on Earth, but without the help of atmosphere or a human pilot. By remote control, a spacecraft had to be slowly backed down to a soft landing 240,000 miles and 66 hours away from its launching site. In some respects the complex process was the reverse of launchings at the cape, where, despite a battalion of technicians and practically unlimited "holds" to fix malfunctioning equipment, failures on the launchpad or early in flight were not uncommon.

Surveyor's troubles were set against the background of the perennial bête noire of early U. S. space projects—development problems in the launch-vehicle system, in this case Centaur. As early as September 1961, Abe Silverstein, director of space-flight programs, warned that Centaur was "an emergency of major proportions." Development problems "could virtually wipe out the unmanned lunar and planetary program until 1965 except for a makeshift effort with Atlas-Agenas." His fears proved true when Mariners 3 and 4 had to fly with Atlas-Agenas. Another potential embarrassment over the launch vehicle was averted when problems with the spacecraft delayed the first Surveyor launch into 1966. Centaur's problems were grave enough that some JPL officials argued in 1962 its development should be abandoned.[23]

Delays and changes in Centaur severely reduced the payload weight, which, in turn, compromised the experiments that could be carried. Centaur builders had promised to produce a vehicle capable of lifting a spacecraft with a total weight of 2,500 pounds; but that slid to 2,100 pounds, then climbed to 2,250 pounds for the first four Surveyors, which were designated engineering test models. The last three Surveyors accommodated a spacecraft weighing 2,450 pounds. As Centaur performance estimates fluctuated, design changes rippled throughout the system. To make matters worse, the weight of the basic spacecraft structure and related hardware rose from an original estimate of 553 pounds to 695 pounds. The combined effect of these changes caused the scientific payload to decline from 345 pounds in the original specifications to just 20 pounds (plus 42.5 pounds of engineering instrumentation) on Surveyors 1 through 4 and only 114 pounds on Surveyors 5 through 7. Once "very ambitious," the experimental payload suffered a series of cutbacks until the first four flights carried a single scanning television camera and the following three flights included but six experiments.[24]

The development of the spacecraft was compromised by four flaws in the project structure which made it, according to a congressional investigation, "one of the least orderly and most poorly executed of NASA projects." First, the project suffered from inadequate preliminary study by everyone involved. Surveyor was conceived in early 1960 when enthusiasm about missions was at a peak but appreciation of the technical difficulties was minimal. William Pickering, Homer Newell, and Hughes Aircraft executives agreed that "we pretty much underestimated the magnitude of this job . . . It is a much bigger job than we originally anticipated." Congress deserved some of the blame. During the investigation into Surveyor which he chaired in 1965, Representative Joseph Karth recalled: "We were in such a sweat to get going that we said, 'let's not think about it, let's do it.' I was on the space committee then, and it's true, we were impetuous." Without adequate early study, Surveyor suffered from a failure to develop an overview of what needed to be done, a lack of understanding of "the major areas of difficulty that need[ed] early work," and an omission of the "breadboard" stage when some problems could have received initial attention. Many difficulties became apparent only in the hardware stage when making changes was harder and costlier.[25]

Second, the cost-plus-fixed-fee (CPFF) contract which NASA negotiated with Hughes opened the project to the legendary abuses of "cost plus" contracting. Devoid of penalty clauses, the CPFF contract virtually guaranteed firms complete recovery of costs and frequently a handsome profit, regardless of performance. Surveyor was but one example of a widespread problem in NASA management, for as much as 80 percent of the agency's contracts through fiscal year 1962 were on a CPFF basis. (By contrast the Department of Defense, plagued with its own overruns, cut CPFF contracting to 21 percent by fiscal year 1963.) NASA officials admitted there was little they could do under this form of contract. "The mistake on Hughes's part is something you necessarily write off as experience from which we can benefit next time; is that right?" asked Representative Charles Mosher of Ohio. "Yes," Newell answered. Not only did the CPFF contract all but eliminate cost discipline, it also allowed top management at Hughes to spend a minimal amount of time on the project until forced to do so by NASA and JPL reviews.[26]

Third, Hughes Aircraft was poorly equipped managerially and technically to handle the project. The firm's first big space project, Surveyor, provided Hughes with a learning experience. JPL had been impressed by the firm's grasp of the Surveyor design and management questions and had awarded it the contract in early 1961 over Space Technology Laboratories, McDonnell Aircraft, and North American Aviation. Before long, however, JPL and NASA officials concluded that, as one Surveyor supervisor put it, the time key Hughes personnel devoted to "advanced planning and sales promotion could be better applied to their current problems." Both JPL and NASA felt the company needed a stronger project organization to replace the matrix setup Hughes continued to use. Systems engineering was less advanced than at JPL. The depth of these managerial and technical problems suggested that the firm needed strong outside supervision.[27]

Finally, neither NASA nor JPL provided the necessary management early in the project. Karth's investigative subcommittee concluded that "communications between NASA Headquarters and Hughes seem to have been virtually nonexistent during the first 4 years of the project." The laboratory's supervision was stronger but still minimal. Until early 1964 fewer than 100

JPL people were detailed to Surveyor full-time. Preoccupied with Ranger and Mariner, the laboratory had little margin to spare for its major outside project. Surveyor suffered at JPL, moreover, because prestige and careers at the laboratory were built on in-house projects.[28]

This concatenation of problems set off alarm bells throughout the Surveyor project organization by early 1964. Technical problems remained unsolved, particularly in the vernier motor. Spacecraft equipment repeatedly failed to meet standards. The first launch date, in mid-1963, had already passed and was now projected for February 1965; even that turned out to be highly optimistic. Costs were climbing "outrageously," NASA officials admitted privately. The original, ludicrously low estimate of $50 million for the entire project had given way to a guess of $190 million, but the end was not in sight. "The Fiscal Year 1965 requirements for Block I have absorbed virtually all funds previously planned for Block II," NASA reported, "and have further required reprogramming into Surveyor of additional funds from other Lunar and Planetary projects." Representative of JPL officials' fears about the project, section chief Charles W. Cole noted that in the several areas where he dealt with Hughes "the equipment was inadequately designed and will probably be inadequately tested." He added: "This may sound like the same old tune . . . but it . . . does represent our continued anxiety over Surveyor."[29]

NASA headquarters finally launched a full-dress design review of Surveyor from March 23 to 27, 1964. A turning point in the project's history, the review pointed up the need for a massive rescue operation. The refrain that ran through the NASA probe was that JPL should step up its monitoring of Hughes but, even more important, should actively move in to right the project. In a number of critical areas, the NASA review board recommended that JPL "bring in the best laboratory talent to assist HAC [Hughes]."[30]

The testing program had suffered from what Nicks termed "a continuing history of poor engineering, poor operational practices, and unsatisfactory management." One of the chief problems was that Hughes considered the test vehicle an "'inexpensive' developmental test bed" and had not applied "flight-quality components, commensurate quality control, and system test procedures" to it. NASA all but insisted that JPL scrupulously review and sign off on all Hughes test plans and operations.[31]

The NASA review board uncovered serious managerial problems at Hughes which it called on JPL to fix. The committee found one critical area to be "so poorly staffed" as to be "shocking"; it expressed alarm at the absence of "real centralized design activity" in another. Surveyor seemed plagued by the same lack of project management that had troubled the early Ranger. Hughes used a strong project organization in some cases, but the firm resisted such a pattern generally. The board argued, however, that "in

176 ★ Mastering the Art of Building Spacecraft

view of the general history of across-the-board technical problems, schedule slippages, and cost overruns on Surveyor, it would appear that considerable improvements in performance might be obtained by projectizing the entire Surveyor operation." Business control was lax. JPL assigned only 5 percent of its procurement staff to handle a contract that represented 30 percent of the division's budget. The Surveyor procurement staff was "grossly overworked," the board said. But the major problem was that JPL could not get accurate cost data from Hughes. The company maintained most of its accounts by division; costs were seldom broken down adequately by Surveyor work packages.[32]

The recommendations of the NASA Surveyor review board recognized that the project desperately needed help from JPL, but they arrived in late March 1964, when the laboratory found it very difficult to respond promptly. Ranger 6 had failed less than two months earlier; the Hilburn board had just leveled its charges at the laboratory; and the congressional probe of Ranger was about to get under way. Relations between headquarters and Pasadena had reached their lowest ebb, and the future status of the laboratory and its director was cloudy at best. A massive effort was under way to make Ranger 7 work, and the Mariners scheduled for launch in late fall 1964 consumed much energy. Nevertheless JPL responded by detailing about twenty people to conduct its own design review of Surveyor in April 1964. Lasting several weeks, the JPL review constituted what the congressional subcommittee termed "an extraordinary measure by the Project Manager to get to the bottom of the difficulties." The laboratory's review board consisted of staffers with an unrivaled perspective—experience on Ranger and Mariner. They could look at Surveyor and say, "'Oh, gee, [do] they have to go through that too?'" The transfer of the laboratory's learning to other institutions became one of the most important contributions of the Surveyor project.[33]

With the first comprehensive look at the Surveyor system, the JPL review board found an alarming number of problems, from small technical design weaknesses to inadequate overall systems engineering. JPL believed the problems stemmed in part from Hughes's lack of spacecraft experience and from the contractor's resistance to the laboratory's supervision. But the board also conceded that JPL had fallen down on its side. "Procedures for relaying JPL experience on Ranger and Mariner to Hughes have been found to be less than adequate," the report said.[34]

The most serious shortcoming lay with the systems engineering, a demanding operation where JPL had learned an immense amount in the school of hard knocks, Ranger. Hughes broke the spacecraft into about one hundred discrete "units" or "control items" instead of eight or ten subsystems, as the laboratory did. In too many cases groups developing a particular unit "showed a surprising lack of information or interest" in the impact their product would have on adjacent subsystems or on the overall system. "The functional specifications tend to be treated as an unalterable document which has been prepared by omniscient system designers," the report said. Even a hurried review brought to light several instances where minor trade-offs between subsystems would have reduced development problems.[35]

The deficient systems engineering had produced, furthermore, a spacecraft of dubious reliability. Hughes hoped to achieve reliability by "employing identical equipment in parallel rather than by providing separate, distinctly different paths to implement a desired function." For instance, timed events could be backed up by commands, and commanded events could have timers as a fallback, but Surveyor had little of this reinforcement. Moreover, most critical spacecraft events were commanded from the ground. The spacecraft employed "parallel receivers and decoders to assure reliable receipt of commands," but each command depended on the successful operation of the entire far-flung Deep Space Network. Many important events also proved to be susceptible to false triggering. The laboratory's review underscored the need for a thorough revamping of the Surveyor design, the Hughes organization, and JPL's supervisory apparatus.[36]

The report had no more than been completed in June 1964 when NASA officials, exasperated that JPL was not moving fast enough, ordered Pickering to give Surveyor higher priority. The agency's alarm about the project was understandable, the indictment of the laboratory less so. NASA officials might have reflected on their own absence of direction which had allowed the crisis to develop in the first place. Moreover, they were telling JPL to make bricks without masons. All the laboratory engineers available under the NASA personnel ceiling were assigned to the desperate effort to make Ranger and Mariner work. The Karth committee suggested that headquarters should have removed the ceiling if more personnel were needed.[37]

With Ranger 7 moving toward the launchpad, the laboratory could respond more adequately. In July 1964 Pickering at NASA's insistence designated Surveyor as the "top priority activity of JPL." The laboratory penetrated deeply into Surveyor. By the fall of 1964 the number of JPL personnel assigned full-time to Surveyor rose to nearly 500—about double the number usually assigned to such a project. In December 1964 the laboratory ordered Hughes to cut its Surveyor work force from 2,000 to 1,700 both to reduce costs and to improve efficiency. It could scarcely escape notice that the reduction in the Hughes work force came on the heels of the buildup of JPL personnel.[38]

The laboratory reorganized its Surveyor management, as well as Hughes's, in response to NASA's desire for a "tight, fast-moving, and responsive projectized team with sufficient number of highly qualified people to properly direct (not just monitor) HAC effort." JPL adopted a "projec-tized" organization with large numbers of people specifically assigned to Surveyor so that they were responsive to the project director rather than to the technical divisions. Then JPL virtually ordered Hughes to follow suit; the company resisted but eventually substantially modified its matrix organi-zation. To improve communication and teamwork, the laboratory moved most of its Surveyor engineers and scientists under one roof and centralized the control functions. To bolster morale both JPL and Hughes held "Sur-veyor Day" rallies at which top executives lavished praise on their project teams and stressed the project's importance in an apparently successful effort to make sure their employees came away "properly motivated."[39]

JPL's assistance took time to become effective, as two disastrous drop tests of the terminal descent guidance and control system showed in 1964. The testing program fell more than a year and a half behind schedule. In the April test the vehicle broke loose from a balloon to which it was attached at 1,200 feet above ground. Recovery efforts were unsuccessful and the vehicle crashed and burned. A second test vehicle was badly damaged in October 1964 when it suffered what was euphemistically termed "a very hard land-ing." The test "turned out to be a tragic comedy of errors which, by all rights, should have resulted in the complete destruction of the test vehicle," said Oran Nicks. He identified at least five separate hardware failures and one operational error, any of which could have been "catastrophic." The vehi-cle's destruction had been averted "only by a fortuitous combination of compensating malfunctions," said Nicks sardonically.[40]

Another serious Surveyor technical problem lay with the vernier motor. By the fall of 1963 it had become the "pacing element" in the project, and the laboratory had stepped in even before the NASA review. Hughes's sub-contractor for the vernier unit, the Reaction Motor Division (RMD) of Thio-kol Chemical Company, had encountered a host of problems, particularly in the motor-cooling system. "Technical disagreements were virtually continu-ous" between Hughes and RMD, and the subcontractor was limited to fund-ing authorizations only for "discrete short-term activities." Increasingly wor-ried, JPL stepped into the project in April 1963 when it awarded a contract to Space Technology Laboratories (STL) for research on a back-up engine. On Saturday, March 14, 1964, JPL shocked everyone involved with a uni-lateral order to terminate the RMD subcontract and upgrade the STL effort to a hardware development program. NASA officials summoned the JPL Surveyor project manager, Walker E. "Gene" Giberson, to Washington for a meeting on Monday, March 16. NASA's Surveyor overseer, Benjamin Mil-witzky, deplored Giberson's "subjective" and "precipitous" decision which, he said, was made without analysis of the latest test results and without consideration of the effects of the decision on spacecraft interactions. The increased costs could be measured in the multimillion-dollar category. Headquarters directed the laboratory to issue RMD a new contract to provide the primary vernier engine system; Space Technology Laboratories would continue as a back-up activity. At the same time, however, NASA recognized that something needed to be done, and it turned to JPL to fix it. NASA called on the JPL propulsion division to assume "full responsibility for vernier engine development and to assign senior engineers to closely monitor and technically direct the program."[41]

Shaken by the termination, RMD adopted many of JPL's suggestions, including a "projectized" organization. The company mounted a serious effort at its own expense to right the project. JPL and RMD worked intensively on the technical bottlenecks. By the fall of 1964 RMD convinced JPL and NASA that its motor would be the best after all. The laboratory then made RMD the prime contractor for the vernier engine, but JPL assumed management of the contract directly without going through Hughes. "The performance of RMD since development has resumed under JPL direction has been exemplary," NASA headquarters reported. By 1965 the vernier engine development, which had once threatened to wreck Surveyor, was finally on the track.[42]

The laboratory's emergency help on the vernier motor demonstrated that, although the activity from which JPL took its name had been overshadowed by new developments, the laboratory's propulsion engineers still ranked in the forefront of their field. They savored the chance to help out the Thiokol company, which had gotten its start in part from JPL's solid-propellant ideas at the end of World War II.

Against the backdrop of these managerial and technical changes, JPL embarked on a "monumental effort" to completely revise the contract, which was hopelessly out-of-date. In some cases documentation lagged two years behind the actual state of the work. Scores of change orders had been applied to the basic contract, some of them of such scope that they more nearly resembled new contracts. The contract thus provided hardly any cost discipline, since overruns were usually buried in the change orders. JPL's new deputy director, Alvin Luedecke, who played a major role in righting Surveyor, hoped eventually to convert the CPFF contract to an incentive form. (Under the latter arrangement the contractor agrees to be responsible for certain specified costs; he receives a fee, or pays a penalty, based on how well he meets standards of quality, schedule, and the like.) When Luedecke began, however, "the contract was still in such disarray that there was, for all intents and purposes, nothing to convert." For a year JPL and Hughes toiled to bring the documentation in line with the work. That "Augean task" completed, JPL and NASA pressed Hughes to adopt an incentive contract. Hughes resisted; its executives were very worried about giving up the sure thing that CPFF represented, particularly on such a troubled project. But eventually Alan Puckett, executive vice-president at Hughes, developed enough confidence in his firm's performance to take the risk. Luedecke "shepherded the contract through the final frenetic stages, flying to Houston to check last-minute details with Cortright and sending the document to Puckett's home early in the morning preceding the day of the first launch."[43]

This expenditure of time and personnel finally brought order to the Surveyor cost picture, although it was too late to establish real control. The project cost totaled $469 million for seven spacecraft, plus launch vehicles. Even granting the complexity of Surveyor, the sum compared badly with the $105 million tab for Mariners 3 and 4 and the $267 million spent on nine Rangers. The long life of and extensive changes in the project were very expensive. Yet despite all these thorns, Hughes plucked a financial rose. The company's engineers bitterly resented JPL's penetration. They chafed under their humiliating demotion in status, the laboratory's advantage in reworking equipment they had begun, and the "interminable" contract negotiations. Given Hughes's track record, however, it seemed clear that only strong intervention by JPL salvaged the project. In the final reckoning JPL treated Hughes fairly, even generously. JPL gave Hughes a 76 percent rating in its performance evaluation, which was good for an incentive fee of more than $17 million, plus a "tractability" bonus of more than $2 million.[44]

Surveyor's balance sheet thus included a substantial profit for an aerospace firm that had been rescued by an academic laboratory which, in turn, had been chastized for not employing enough "hard-headed industrial management" by a government agency that had all but ignored the project for its first four years. This was perhaps the major irony in a project suffused with ironies. There were others, including JPL's imposition on Hughes of the very management techniques which the laboratory had resisted earlier— "projectized" organization, detailed contracts management, and vigorous supervision. It was a further irony that Hughes received more than $20 million in fees on costs of $345 million, or 5.8 percent, while Caltech received fees of about 1 percent for managing JPL; yet NASA and Congress turned much more heat on the Caltech fee than on those of industrial firms. There was some reason for the agency to scrutinize the Caltech-JPL relationship, and some need for improvement. But a comparative perspective was also important. The Surveyor ordeal—coupled with the fumbling when industrial firms tried to grab the baton on Corporal and Sergeant—suggested that NASA was too credulous in the confidence it placed in its aerospace political allies. The Surveyor experience argued strongly for the importance of an independent JPL, both as developer of technology and as yardstick.

With the technology finally proved out and the incentive contract safely couriered to Puckett's home, the first Surveyor was launched on May 30, 1966—almost three years late. Apollo had already advanced to the point where Neil Armstrong and David R. Scott had completed a docking maneuver in space. Surveyor 1 followed a nearly perfect flight path. Without a midcourse correction, the craft would have landed within 250 miles of its target; the mid-course correction brought it within 9 miles of the aim point. Tension ran high at the von Kármán auditorium at JPL as the craft neared the lunar surface and soon would provide answers to the technical and scientific questions of the program. Could a vehicle make a controlled soft landing on another body and operate for an extended period of time? What was the lunar surface really like? Would Surveyor—and after it Apollo—find firm footing or be swallowed up in a bin of dust?[45]

Nearing the crater Flamsteed in Oceanus Procellarum on June 2, 1966, Surveyor's retro-engine fired, followed by the vernier motor, as the craft began to back down to the surface. The three footpads touched the surface nearly simultaneously and penetrated a few inches; the spacecraft rebounded approximately 2½ inches above the surface and then came to rest. For the first time a spacecraft had achieved a soft landing on another celestial body. Surveyor went on to operate impeccably for two lunar days (twenty-eight Earth days); 100,000 commands were sent, verified, and executed without error during the mission; 11,240 television pictures were transmitted to Earth. The pictures yielded the most significant lunar data thus far, and the spacecraft's solid footing radiated confidence for Apollo.[46]

As had sometimes happened to JPL in missile testing, the first Surveyor turned out to be better than its successor. The second flight failed when a vernier motor refused to ignite during the mid-course maneuver, causing the spacecraft to tumble. Surveyor 3, launched on April 17, 1967, three months after the tragic launchpad fire in which three astronauts died, helped restore confidence in Apollo. Despite some erratic behavior, the third Surveyor recorded a highly successful flight. As it reached the moon, the radars lost lock, which prevented the vernier engines from cutting off at 14 feet above the surface. The vernier engines still firing, the craft touched down, lifted off, came in contact with the surface again, lifted off a second time, and touched down for a third time, when the engine was cut off by a back-up command. Surveyor came to rest upright at an angle of about 14 degrees inside a crater. In addition to photographs of Venus, Surveyor 3's cameras chalked up two historic firsts—photographs of Earth from another celestial body and of Earth eclipsing the sun. Surveyor 3 also carried a surface-sampling device that scratched four trenches in the surface. Operating for more than eighteen hours, the surface sampler also performed eight bearing-strength tests and fourteen impact tests of the surface. As successes and failures alternated, Surveyor 4 seemed doomed. In a virtual replay of Ranger 6, the fourth Surveyor operated flawlessly until the last 2½ minutes of flight, when radio signals from the craft ceased abruptly; contact could not be reestablished.[47]

It was with the three successful Surveyors, flights 5, 6, and 7, that the project really came into its own. The flight of Surveyor 5 offered a dramatic example of how a potential disaster was converted into a success. After the mid-course maneuver the vernier motor began to lose helium pressure, which threatened to nullify the soft landing. Flight officials decided to make three additional firings of the vernier motor to reduce weight and to delay operation of the retro-engine from the 30,000-foot elevation originally planned to 4,400 feet. The reprogrammed Surveyor descended as gently as if nothing had gone wrong. Surveyor 5 added an alpha-scattering instrument, which made chemical soil analyses by radioactivity. Using a magnet attached to the landing gear, the craft also looked for the existence of iron. To help Apollo the vernier rockets were fired for two-tenths of a second after the landing; the cameras observed no ill effects from the procedure.[48]

Surveyor 6's operation was textbook-perfect, landing just 2.5 miles from its aim point. Some 30,065 photographs were beamed back to Earth. This craft improved on its predecessors by making a short hop on the surface. On command from Earth, its vernier engines were fired; the craft rose about 10 feet and settled again about 8 feet from its original site. After this maneuver the spacecraft transmitted a 360-decree panorama on which two of three footpad imprints from the original touchdown appeared clearly. The imprints provided additional confirmation of the moon's ability to support the Apollo spacecraft. Defying high odds against surviving a landing in the rugged lunar highlands, Surveyor 7 made a flawless descent on January 10, 1968. This craft continued the series of spectacular photographs and was the first to carry a soil sampler for digging into the lunar surface. All told, the technical and scientific objectives of the Surveyor project were achieved "to a degree far beyond original expectations," NASA reported.[49]

The information from the soil sampler, alpha-scattering device, and magnet test, combined with the more than 65,000 photographs returned from the five successful landings, yielded scientific data of unprecedented value for the study of the moon. The results showed the crust resembled Earth-type basaltic silicate, and the three most abundant elements were the same as the most prevalent on Earth's surface—oxygen, silicon, and aluminum. The surface, which behaved "like fine, damp soil on earth," consisted of fine, granular material in a wide range of grain sizes; rocks and clumps resembling soil clods were strewn over the surface. Thanks to the landing in the highlands, scientists learned that the maria and the highlands were chemically different; the moon apparently was not a uniform planet. It appeared most likely that differentiation had been caused by melting and solidification; "accordingly, portions of the moon's interior were, and may still be, hot." Surveyor's landmark findings contributed importantly to the understanding of lunar origins. They provided "the first direct evidence of a chemical kinship between the moon and the earth," noted NASA scientist Bevan French. "By confirming that the maria soils were similar to terrestrial basalts, the Surveyor experiments proved that the moon was not related to the primitive meteorites; they strengthened the opposing view that it was an evolved planet with a history of chemical change." Yet Surveyor's results, while refining knowledge of the moon, were not comprehensive enough to resolve the competing theories of lunar origins. The three chief rival theories of lunar origin—double planet, fission, and capture—continued to flourish, albeit with much modification in some cases.[50]

JPL's lunar program thus came to a close with mixed—even distorted— scientific results. This outcome derived chiefly from the nature of the lunar race. Ranger, Surveyor, and their launch vehicles encountered serious development problems on their crash schedules which reduced the scientific payload. Then, like Ranger, ten Surveyor flights, which would have made possible a complete mapping of the moon in addition to other important experiments, were cancelled in NASA's budget crunch in the late 1960s. Since Ranger and Surveyor flew in support of Apollo, they were subject to the same scientific compromises which characterized the manned program. Most of the scientific exploration was directed at the near-side equatorial areas because these were the "easiest and safest" for a manned lander to reach. These areas were intensively studied, the polar and far-side regions were not. "In fact, no systematic global reconnaissance of the Moon has ever been made," scientists Bruce Murray, Michael Malin, and Ronald Greeley pointed out. The relatively small investment that would bring lunar studies to fruition after Apollo was not forthcoming.[51] The $30-billion Apollo program and its supporting cast of Ranger, Surveyor, and Lunar Orbiter bought a lot of science but at a very high price and with a distortion of orderly scientific processes. And paradoxically Ranger and Surveyor provided less support for Apollo than they might have since they were going on nearly concurrently with the manned program instead of in sequence. On both the technological and scientific sides the cost of the prestige race was very high indeed.

These limitations could not detract, however, from JPL's technical achievements in the lunar and planetary program from 1964 to 1968. The laboratory's spacecraft were among the most sophisticated machines yet built. Rangers 7 through 9 partially redeemed that troubled project, which had provided the indispensable framework for doing new things. Mariner 4 was especially noteworthy because it showed JPL could meet the very high performance demands of missions in which only one back-up model was possible. Surveyor provided an ironic confirmation of the laboratory's technological eminence. JPL was mastering the course in learning to build spacecraft. As the laboratory concentrated on planetary exploration, the challenge now lay in what to do with them.

11 ★★

THE FLOWERING OF PLANETARY EXPLORATION

"The time is surely here when we must define minimum success in terms not only of 'getting there,' but in terms of scientific accomplishments." With that admonition in 1966 the Ad Hoc Science Advisory Committee of the National Aeronautics and Space Administration argued for a strong commitment to science in the emerging program of planetary exploration. Past decisions had been "excessively dominated" by engineering caution, the panel noted. But if the space program was ever to achieve a rationale other than that of cold war competition or engineering spectaculars, now, as planetary exploration at last came into its own in the mid-1960s, the moment had arrived. The debates over the direction of the space program, and especially over how planetary exploration should be undertaken, had a strong impact on the Jet Propulsion Laboratory. The planetary program, coupled with a resolution of JPL's status within NASA, brought the laboratory to a turning point in the mid-1960s.[1]

JPL staffers, who had long been animated by the desire to do the "final far-out things," had a keen interest in the planetary program. They had strong ideas about how exploration should proceed and the laboratory's role in it. JPL wanted to be the national pacesetter in utilizing space technology for planetary exploration. JPL wanted "to be the first to enter and make measurements" in the Martian and Venusian atmospheres and to have responsibility for "the first instruments that operate on the surface of Mars and Venus." In 1964 the laboratory was already at work on another Mariner-class spacecraft as a follow-up to Mariner 4, and it wanted to manage all the key Mariner missions for the next decade. It also sought to do the surface laboratory of the proposed Voyager mission to Mars. This institutional model would insure JPL's dominance in the planetary program. It was based on the laboratory's long-standing desire to do the most exciting technological work in-house to keep its staff's skills sharp.[2]

But whether these ambitions could be realized hinged on the answers to a question that few generations have a chance to ponder: How does one initiate the exploration of new worlds? The decisions would reflect the interweaving perturbations of science, technology, and—as ever—politics. By 1964 a consensus was forming that planetary exploration should receive a major commitment from NASA. The technological foundation had been laid. When Project Apollo funding crested in the next year or so, it would be possible, and even politically necessary, to adopt the deferred planetary focus. In the summer of 1964 a special study by the president's science advisory committee strongly urged NASA to make a major commitment to scientific planetary exploration. The committee taxed the agency with being "sadly negligent and unimaginative in framing its planetary program," noted Homer Newell, NASA's associate administrator for space sciences and applications. The panel proposed three questions around which to organize space exploration: "Is there life elsewhere in the universe? What is the origin and evolution of the universe? What is the origin and evolution of the solar system?" It was time to tailor technology to science instead of science to technology.[3]

Celestial alignments also argued for a planetary commitment. Mars, the planet generally assumed to be of greatest immediate interest, would be in an optimum position in relation to Earth in 1969, 1971, and 1973. Velocity requirements, lighting conditions, and accessibility of biologically interesting areas would be better at that time than for another twelve to fourteen years. Delays in Mars exploration would be "amplified by nature," Newell pointed out.[4]

Nature's cues were especially dramatic for what was an all but unique space mission: the Grand Tour. "A fantastic case of celestial billiards" would appear from 1976 to 1980 as the outer planets—Jupiter, Saturn, Uranus, Neptune, and Pluto—assumed an alignment more favorable to Earth-launched vehicles than at any other time until the year 2153. It was realized as early as 1963 that, by taking advantage of gravity perturbation during a close flyby of a planet, a spacecraft's heliocentric energy could be boosted enough to reach planets unattainable with the original launch energy. Something like a slingshot, this method could be used to send a spacecraft humming from one planet to another, provided the alignments were right. From 1976 to 1980 a spacecraft which ordinarily could reach only Jupiter could fly by three or four planets, depending on the mission chosen (see figure 3). The Grand Tour offered a first look at these orbs, whose extreme differences from the Earth-like planets—Venus, Mercury, and Mars—posed a major challenge for theories of the origin of the solar system. All of them except Pluto, which was scarcely known, are huge (four to eleven times the size of Earth), low in density (one-eighth to one-fourth Earth's), and obscured in optically thick atmospheres. The elegant, exciting Grand Tour quickly became a favorite of many persons at JPL and Caltech.[5]

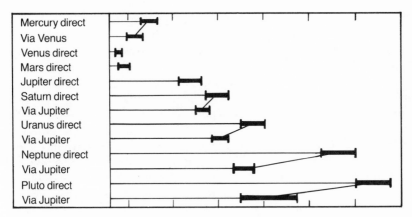

3. U.S. launch-vehicle performance capability and typical planetary launch requirements.

Science was only one consideration, however, for NASA upper echelons. As technology, especially the Saturn launch vehicle, became available, NASA planners escalated their ambitions to take advantage of the biggest systems. Their dream was named Voyager. By late 1964 the Mariner and its 1,250-pound spacecraft envisioned for the 1969 flyby mission seemed too small. A Voyager for 1971, perhaps preceded by test flights in 1969, now loomed on the Martian horizon. Riding on a Saturn 1B Centaur launch vehicle would be a 2,000-pound orbiting spacecraft and a 2,300-pound landing capsule system which would survive for one day on the Martian surface. But in October 1965 NASA planners decided they should use the Saturn 5, the Apollo launch vehicle. A single Saturn 5 would boost two spacecraft, each with an orbiter and a survivable lander; each planetary vehicle (spacecraft, capsule bus and surface laboratory, and propulsion unit) would weigh about 24,200 pounds. The pair, together with the shroud-adapter and an allowance of 5,000 pounds for contingencies, would yield a gross injected weight of 62,700 pounds. Saturn 5's lifting capacity was just short of that estimated to be necessary to send a man to Mars—a possibility for which some NASA figures harbored secret dreams. The huge Voyager would have a long lifetime, return a great deal of scientific data, and lay the groundwork for long-range planetary exploration using a common technology.[6]

If it worked, Voyager was a giant step beyond Mariner and it was a leap in the dark. Within NASA, Oran Nicks opposed Voyager because too little was known about the Martian environment to make sound design decisions and because it entailed too much of a continuing advance in complex engineering. Doubting that an ultimate Voyager could be designed in the mid-1960s, he called for "the evolutionary exploration of Mars, rather than . . . rapid development of large systems."[7]

But technology, and especially politics, remained uppermost at headquarters. Voyager reflected the continuing technological fixation of many executives in the space program. It also offered an extra justification for Apollo. Moreover, the $2-billion Voyager was costly, and therein lay much of its appeal. The giant required that the planetary program, which had been carried at about $50 million per year, be upgraded to $200 to $300 million annually. If expensive biological experiments were incorporated, the figure could rise to $500 million a year. Since Apollo funding would soon decline, this level of expenditure appealed to NASA and its industrial contractors. In the mid-1960s the agency was encouraging industrial firms to invest their own funds heavily to gear up for Voyager. NASA in effect was gambling on a repetition of the Apollo model. In the uncertain times the risks were high, for both NASA and JPL.[8]

Voyager planners had not really tried to balance technology and science. But the question "Technology for what?" received a thoughtful answer from proponents of what might be termed the "opportunity model." The rationale behind this strategy was articulated by Bruce Murray, a young associate professor of planetary science at the California Institute of Technology, whose upward mobility would take him to the directorship of JPL in 1976. "Since this is exploration, he who gets there firstest, gets the mostest," he said. Being second—Murray was still conscious of the Russians—wasn't much fun. "Be opportunistic," he advised, "and . . . maximize the exploratory return on a short-term basis. If there is a chance to go with something exciting now, do it. Don't worry about the future and the long-term evolution of spacecraft and so forth—just go." Murray did not mean missions should be undertaken just because they were possible. He emphasized that they should increase understanding or, of equal but often overlooked importance, "reduce in a dramatic way the enormous range of possibilities." The opportunity model made maximum use of each planetary possibility rather than deferring exploration until a large future assault. The Grand Tour meshed perfectly with the strategy of opportunity, and Murray pushed it every chance he got.[9]

Scientists were generally skeptical of Voyager, as NASA conceived of it, and favored the opportunity model. James Van Allen, now chairman of the space science board of the National Academy of Sciences, expressed it in colorful, albeit sexist, language in 1967: his committee favored "sending a number of well-equipped scouting parties to the several planets before we send out the wagon train with all of our women and children and a full set of household furnishings."[10]

Of the myriad studies and restudies that went into the planning of the planetary program in the mid-1960s, one of the more notable was done by a sixteen-member Caltech-JPL group under Murray's chairmanship in early

1965. Most planetary program studies suffered because they looked at either science or technology to the exclusion of the other. The Murray group combined both. Its comprehensive package also included ground-based observation, which was often overlooked. Besides being an exhilarating chance to map an historic venture in exploration, the study group represented an attempt to meet NASA's desire for more Institute participation and closer contact between the campus and the laboratory.[11]

The Caltech-JPL panel agreed that the space program should aim at the planets, especially Mars, where the search for life should be the primary goal. Secondary, but also of major importance, stood acquisition of general scientific knowledge of the planet. The Pasadenans were particularly concerned with how to get from the level of Mariner 4 to Voyager. "The history of the whole space program demonstrates the necessity of avoiding excessively large steps in progressing from one stage of the program to the next," they argued. Voyager would carry out the real life-detection mission, but it should be postponed until 1973 or later. Meanwhile Mariner-class ventures would make a transition both in scientific knowledge, with simple life-detection experiments, and in technological know-how. In taking the preliminary steps for biological exploration, the Mariners could also yield a wealth of geological, geophysical, and meteorological data "rich enough in all probability to have justified such a flight program in the first place."[12]

Not only was the technological leap from Mariner to Voyager great, it also inhibited efficient utilization of the Voyager payload for science, which was the supposed rationale for the giant. Because so little was known about Mars, "a lander must be designed for environmental extremes far greater than probably really will be encountered there." The lander's payload could easily be halved depending on Martian conditions. This would be the case, for instance, with one design of a lander that incorporated parachutes and a small retro-rocket if it encountered maximum wind velocities of 80 miles per hour. A lander that used crushable material and had no parachutes or retro-rockets could withstand winds up to 100 miles per hour; but the payload of this type of lander was "quite dependent on surface pressure, being twice as great at 40 millibars as at 20 millibars." In sum, the Caltech-JPL group believed "the cumulative cost to resolve the question of life on Mars may well be less if the program includes well-designed preliminary investigations."[13]

The study advanced a possible schedule using the Atlas-Centaur launch vehicle, which could handle a payload about three times the size of the Atlas-Agena employed for Mariner 4. The 1966 opposition was coming up too soon to make a satisfactory mission feasible. For 1969 they recommended a flyby with a simple sterilized impact capsule. For 1971 they suggested flying the same system but with a simple life-detection experiment added. A flyby with sterilized orbiting test body, whose main purpose would be the determination of exospheric density for Voyager, could also be launched in 1971. Certain ground-based observations, particularly with more sensitive radar, and balloon reconnaissance also merited funding. The committee outlined a reasonable but still ambitious program. It provided support for an eventual Voyager yet possessed its own validity.[14]

NASA reviewers praised the report as "excellent" but gave it short shrift. "We are already committed to Voyager," explained one official. The study was "not consistent with current NASA decisions and plans," said another. They minimized the design unknowns and glibly dismissed the omission of the 1969 and possibly 1971 opportunities on the ground that Voyager would gather that data anyway. In this atmosphere Nicks found his arguments ignored. Months later he vented his frustration in a memo to the files: "The Mariner 4 startled both its critics and supporters by the amount of information returned, proving clearly that advancements in knowledge about Mars can be made with modest increases in capability beyond Mariner." Most planners at headquarters were disappointed in the Caltech-JPL report, however, because it was "much more conservative than the thinking . . . when the Ranger and Surveyor programs were . . . initiated." True enough. It would seem that, having toiled on the firing line through those troubled projects, the Pasadenans had learned something about matching appetites to abilities.[15]

But this was not the advice NASA wanted to hear, and the Murray committee was left wondering why it had bothered. "If this is an example of the 'dialogue' that Mr. Webb would like to have with us, we might have more success talking to our Russian friends," aeronautics professor Lester Lees remarked sourly. Bruce Murray seconded that: They were useful "primarily in a critical role rather than in a creative one"; they were "sparring partners" rather than "friends of the court." The group found itself criticizing decisions already made or consequences flowing from them, rather than doing any real long-range planning. Murray found some silver linings—stronger personal ties between Caltech and JPL personnel, enhanced mutual esteem, and the like. But the campus members felt strongly that they should abandon hopes of planning and instead concentrate on experiments and advisory committees for specific projects. The interaction between CIT and JPL that Webb desired proved very hard to pull off, in part because of NASA.[16]

Despite the uncertainties that beclouded Voyager, NASA sold the project to Congress in late 1964. JPL was given responsibility for the capsule segment. The agency decided to drop the follow-up Mariner that JPL had been working on—no missions to Mars would take place between 1964 and 1971. Whatever political appeal the decision had, its scientific and technological rationale was dubious.

The strategy also was short-lived. By the fall of 1965 Voyager was slipping into trouble as Apollo funding continued at a higher rate than anticipated. Once again the manned lunar program impinged on the scientific and planetary side. Trying to save Voyager, NASA chose to stretch its first flight to 1973. Nine years between Mars missions scarcely made for a well-ordered planetary program which would retain the support of the scientific community, especially since two of the optimum chances would slip past. As a result in December 1965 NASA reinstated Mariner missions to Mars for both 1969 and 1971. For once JPL's assignments would have ample lead times. NASA also discovered a "hitherto well-concealed" interest in Venus. It ordered the laboratory to dust off the spare Mariner C and mount a crash program to launch it toward the "earth's twin" in 1967.[17]

Through all these ups and downs, JPL officially supported Voyager, so long as it was preceded by Mariners. Pickering and deputy director Luedecke told the Caltech trustees in early 1966 that the new schedule was "generally desirable." The Mariner-Voyager combination assured in-house projects for three years. If Voyager had to be dropped for fiscal reasons, however, Pickering still wanted the 1971 Mariner to be approved.[18]

But JPL's careful official expressions masked an underlying attitude toward Voyager that sympathetic NASA executives William Rieke and Walter Sohier aptly termed "schizophrenic." That opinion surfaced in various ways. When a survey of the senior staff in early 1967 asked what characteristics the lunar and planetary program should have, first place went to "challenging, technically innovative, pacesetter, significant first." Obtaining "significant, scientific data" scored a close second. In considering how to achieve those goals, Mariner-style projects received nearly twice as much support as Voyager. Another indication appeared when Voyager funding fell short in late 1965. A large percentage of the project's senior engineers transferred off without announcement, and they sometimes left studies half finished which cost many person-months of work. Printed doggerel deriding the mammoth circulated clandestinely. "It was obvious that a large portion of JPL was relieved that Voyager had been put off," D. P. Burcham, the project manager, said sadly. Many hoped that "nothing like it might ever darken the JPL horizon."[19]

The ambivalence about, and outright opposition to, Voyager derived from the "fundamental question" of what the laboratory should be, as Rieke and Sohier put it. Voyager would entail a huge expansion of JPL; its staff would have to grow from the existing 4,200 or so to between 5,500 and 6,500. The sheer size of the project would divert the laboratory from the in-house tasks that Pickering and the senior staff considered vital to its élan and substitute extensive monitoring of industrial contracts. JPL staff were "doers" rather than "managers," and Mariner-type projects allowed them to do what they had come to the laboratory to do.[20]

Moreover, a JPL of 5,500 to 6,500 employees would mean further inroads by headquarters and probably eventual severance from Caltech. Barney Huber, Pickering's executive assistant, warned that, because Voyager bulked so large in NASA's overall program, "headquarters will manage the project through direction . . . and in so doing will manage the Laboratory in virtually every detail." Luedecke and others who favored a big, civil-service type of operation, liked the giant. But Huber and those who advocated "a university-sponsored and managed Laboratory, in which there is a high degree of self-determination" cast a baleful eye on Voyager. Such a large laboratory would "simply overwhelm" Caltech, said Rieke and Sohier. Voyager threatened to "cement the image of the Lab as an engineering factory."[21]

The dangers posed by Voyager failed to materialize in the end, but for reasons beyond JPL's control. The massive project met its demise in late summer 1967 when Congress pared the NASA budget. The space program suffered from the interconnected problems of the escalation of the Vietnam War, the social crisis of the 1960s, and NASA's own diminishing legitimacy. The space program "was once ballyhooed as a benign substitute for war," Daniel S. Greenberg noted in *Science*. "But now no substitute for war is needed; we have a real war." To many people NASA was emblematic of the nation's misplaced priorities, and the agency's romance with technology and management now made it a ready target. The war also made many people question the hard, cold warrior outlook that NASA had once used so effectively to fuel the space race. While some of the antipathy to the space program reflected an antitechnological impulse, the opposition also included many who believed that NASA had lost a sense of proportion. Physicist Ralph E. Lapp proposed, for instance, a scientifically oriented space program which could operate on $1 billion to $2 billion annually.[22]

In September 1967 NASA decided the appropriations were too low to sustain Voyager any longer, and JPL's project office closed up shop. The tragedy of Voyager was that NASA, gambling on a big future program, had passed up good, relatively cheap immediate opportunities. Bruce Murray pointed out that enough money had been poured into Voyager to fund a Mars lander in 1969 or a Mercury mission in 1970. With that money lost, the laboratory regrouped behind a 1971 Mariner to Mars.[23]

The 1971 opportunity at first had seemed to offer the first landing on Mars and the first American touchdown on another planet. JPL planning groups in 1966 and 1967 stressed the desirability of an entry capsule and lander. They proposed a configuration which contained an entry capsule that would send back significant data as it entered the Martian atmosphere. Before capsule impact, a small instrument package would be ejected from the entry capsule and sink to the surface with a parachute. With such a combination the Mariner program would move from "flyby-spacecraft-im-plemented science to devices in direct interaction with the planets." Labora-tory planners believed that the configuration could be justified on its scien-tific merits alone. The drama and prestige attached to the lander was no mean consideration. But they also viewed the entry capsule and lander as "a vital bridge" between past and future ventures. They estimated the cost of the spacecraft at $200 million, the entry capsule and lander at another $75 million.[24]

The lander also raised an important question of institutional politics. JPL lobbied NASA hard to win authorization to build the capsule in-house in-stead of farming it out to industry through a system contract. Concerned over the increasing amount of time devoted to contract monitoring rather than "doing," laboratory officials thirsted for a project they could get their hands on. But besides these institutional concerns, they brought forward other convincing reasons. First, the project would require a quick response to changing conditions, especially since Mariner Mars 69 results would be-come available when the probe fabrication was well under way. JPL believed it could respond to NASA more quickly than if the process involved another link, to industry. Second, the laboratory pointed out that the probe involved a good deal of new technology. When industry had attempted to develop the new technology on previous projects, notably Surveyor, the results had been disastrous. JPL urged NASA to develop the technological base in-house and then turn it over to industry. Third, as the Vietnam War dragged on, it became harder to find industrial firms which were willing to apply their top talent to space work. Well-qualified subsystem contractors would more likely be available. Overall, JPL argued that its in-house plan made the best use of NASA's facilities, assured the best likelihood of meeting the schedule, and offered the most effective transfer of the new technologies to industry.[25]

In the end, however, JPL's hopes went for naught. Not only had NASA's crisis of legitimacy killed Voyager, the Mariner Mars 71 probe was re-oriented in favor of a less costly orbiter mission.

With the flights of Mariners 5, 6, and 7 in the late 1960s, the planetary program at last began to realize its long-promised potential. Mariners 2 and 4 had demonstrated that the Mariner spacecraft provided a sound basis for the evolution of interplanetary spacecraft. The increasing flexibility and sophistication of the Mariner series, which culminated in the spacecraft of Mariners 8, 9, and 10, would make the early models seem almost crude by comparison. But it was in the science results—the Mariners' raison d'être—that the real payoffs appeared.

When NASA suddenly decided to take advantage of the 1967 Venus opposition, it turned to JPL for a hastily designed project. The authorization for Mariner 5 reached the laboratory only in December 1965. The short lead time necessitated working with existing equipment under a schedule that could accommodate only minimal change and scaled down scientific ambitions. JPL turned to the spare Mariner spacecraft that had been left in storage when the perfect flight of Mariner 4 had rendered another Mars mission at that time redundant. Although the equipment had been in storage for months, it remained in excellent condition. Because of the confusion in the Washington decision making, Mariner 5 would not be an optimum project, but it afforded a chance to reach Venus with the first serious scientific experiments and to bridge the technological and scientific gap to the Mariner Mars program at relatively low cost.[26] Except for a few people writing final reports, the Mariner group, which had been in existence since 1961, had been dispersed a few months before the go-ahead came down from NASA headquarters. For the new efforts the core personnel came from the Mariner 4 and Ranger organizations.[27]

While working within the constraints of existing equipment for the Venus mission, the Mariner team made changes in three key areas—the configuration of the spacecraft, the scientific payload, and the Data Automated Subsystem (DAS). The spacecraft design was turned over so that the side containing the solar cells faced the sun during flight. The space devoted to solar panels was cut from 70.4 square feet to 43.6. These changes resulted from the flight path to Venus, which is toward the sun instead of away from it, as in trips to Mars. In other configuration changes, the scan platform was removed, and antennas were added to support the dual-frequency receiver experiment. The DAS was obsolete and limited in capacity. JPL found it easier to redesign the subsystem using integrated circuits and vastly increasing its capacity.[28]

Critical choices, complicated by the intricate terrestrial politics of space science, made the selection of the scientific payload difficult. Responsibility for the decision about which experiments were included rested with Homer Newell. He relied on the advice of the space science board and on JPL's recommendations. In NASA's infancy the laboratory had fought to have the right to decide for itself on the experiments list. But the space agency noted that JPL would often stand in the compromising position of both proposing some of its own experiments and then ruling on their inclusion. There was an unspoken reason as well: NASA did not want to lose control of a critical facet of its relations with the scientific community, especially not to a laboratory which all too often, in the agency's view, did not cooperate with headquarters. The choice of scientific payload thus raised a potential problem area, as JPL had to conform to decisions it disagreed with and sometimes to work with experimenters against its judgment.[29]

In early 1966 a Caltech-JPL study group brought in its recommendations, which would help determine the configuration of scientific experiments. The panel wanted to maximize the scientific return, since it might be nearly a decade before the United States would send another spacecraft for a close-up look at Venus; the group also sought to minimize overlap with ground-based observation. They assigned highest priority to experiments that would answer "one of the major scientific questions about Venus" or reveal phenomena that "could drastically alter our present ideas about it." The "single most crucial datum" they wanted was the surface pressure. The best way to measure that would be with a small sounding capsule. They quickly realized, however, that a lot of engineering stood between the existing designs and a successful mission. The probe—a prominent feature of the Soviet Union's Venus missions—became a casualty of slender budgets and late decision making.[30].

Three of the experiments the board recommended were accepted: the "prime experiment" was the S-band radio occultation experiment. Derived from a similar experiment on Mariner 4, which had scored a "spectacular success" in measuring the density of the Martian atmosphere, the occultation technique probably would determine the surface pressure of the Venusian atmosphere. An ultraviolet photometer ranked next; its measurement of the radiation intensity would make possible a determination of the scale height, density, and temperature, "thus fairly completely defining the exosphere." A third possibility, a celestial mechanics experiment, would refine the knowledge of certain quantities of the solar system, such as the mass of the planet. Newell added a fourth device, a dual-frequency occultation experiment, which JPL had ranked lower. He also approved an ultraviolet spectrometer experiment, which the board feared had too many engineering problems to be feasible then, and added a trapped-radiation detector and a magnetometer.[31]

The most controversial divergence perhaps between Newell and CIT-JPL involved the panel's recommendation that a lightly modified version of the Mariner 4 television subsystem be flown. The other experiments were designed to return specific answers to questions about Venus, the board noted. Television most likely would suggest "what questions we should ask in the future." They pointed out: "It has been characteristic of the study of all the objects in the solar system that our early ideas have turned out to be badly in error." The first close-up pictures of the moon and Mars had brought significant revisions in ideas about those bodies; although photography in the vicinity of Venus would be harder, Venus television might well do the same. Newell liked television also. The problem was that the data automation system did not have enough power to provide storage for both the dual-frequency occultation experiment and television. Photography lost.[32]

The experiment selection process was significant also as a harbinger of a protracted controversy on Mariners 6 and 7. Scientific interest in high-resolution infrared observations ran high, but no one had flight experience, even with balloons, for infrared spectrometers. Nonetheless, George C. Pimentel, a chemistry professor at the University of California at Berkeley, considered his equipment feasible. When one was selected for Mariner Mars, the latent conflict between scientists and engineers erupted.[33]

Launched on June 13, 1967, Mariner 5 enjoyed a relatively untroubled flight to Venus. A little more than four months later, on October 19, the spacecraft encountered the planet for about an hour's worth of measuring. The previous day, the Soviet ship Venera 4, a spacecraft carrier and landing capsule, had arrived at Venus. Mariner's scientific package, in conjunction with Venera 4, made notable contributions to the clouded picture of Venus. The surface of the planet is very hot—about 750° Kelvin or about 900° F. The atmospheric pressure at the surface is 90 times that of Earth. Various refinements of existing knowledge followed, contributing to a fuller, but still highly inconclusive, picture of a planet that is extremely difficult to study. But the 1967 flights confirmed the growing realization that Venus, once considered "Earth's twin," is in fact very different.[34]

The major contribution of the Mariner series came from a more tractable planet: Mars. Mariners 6 and 7 were born in late 1965 when Voyager authorization faltered. The two spacecraft were originally thought of as an interim effort to take advantage of the 1969 opposition; they would be only slightly improved versions of Mariner 4. As 1966 wore on, however, both Voyager's uncertain future and the implications of Mariner 4's success dictated a different approach. JPL reoriented the project to make it a "second generation" flyby mission. "MM '69 should push the Mariner IV design as far as practical," said project manager Harris Schurmeier. More sophisticated experiments would be employed in order to make the missions "as significant as possible."[35]

Helping the laboratory designers were two major improvements external to the spacecraft. The more powerful Atlas-Centaur launch vehicle would be ready, which allowed an increase in weight. And the Goldstone station's network of antennas, which were 85 feet in diameter, were bolstered by the erection of a huge 210-foot addition and acutely sensitive new receivers. Goldstone's desert dishes were integral to the great strides in interplanetary communication that would first become apparent with Mariner Mars 69.[36]

Although Mariner 4 remained the reference point, four major changes were introduced in the spacecraft. First, the scan platform was redesigned to permit movement in both cone angle and clock angle. The platform accommodated both television cameras, both infrared instruments, the ultraviolet spectrometer, and two planet sensors. Second, the data storage subsystem was upgraded markedly with two specially designed tape recorders—one an analog unit, the other a digital device—to meet requirements thirty-five times those of Mariner 4. Third, the telemetry subsystem was boosted from one channel to three, and the telemetry data rate from 8 ⅓ bits per second to 16,200. Fourth, a new central computer and sequencer subsystem was used. This could be reprogrammed in flight—a boon which made possible a major modification of Mariner 7 "almost at the last minute" to benefit from Mariner 6. Instead of two nearly identical flights, the reprogramming feature made possible a significant upgrading of the scientific data returned.[37]

The heart of the project rested with the much more sophisticated scientific experiments. They were designed primarily to narrow the range of questions about the possibility of extraterrestrial life. Mariner 4 had done little to settle that question. Some scientists interpreted its pictures of a moonlike surface to mean that life on Mars was simply impossible. But other investigators thought that Mariner 4's images did not preclude the possibility of life. In any case, the earlier project's twenty-one pictures were scarcely representative. A vast increase in photographic and other data would be required from Mariners 6 and 7 before Mars's secrets would begin to come into focus. Two areas of questions remained open. First, did the surface reflect a condition that had existed for a long time? Or did it develop more recently as the product of changing conditions that may have included a much denser atmosphere and perhaps liquid water on the planet? Second, what explained the difference between the light and dark areas and their seasonal changes in albedo and possibly color?[38]

The major effort went toward a much improved television subsystem that was designed to extend the coverage of the planet's physiography at a resolution sufficient to distinguish "between an episodic and a continuous history." The personnel ceiling NASA imposed on JPL required extensive contracting with industry. The television unit, which was under development by Electro Optical Incorporated, experienced major development problems, which impacted on the rest of the design process. Design delays, coupled with managerial and manufacturing problems, made the delivery of the prototype more than five months late. Insufficient time remained for a thorough prototype evaluation; design deficiencies escaped detection until too late, when they interfered with the spacecraft schedule and testing. The flight units arrived nearly three months late. When the last one was completed, in late June 1968, a special engineering group was formed to iron out the remaining problems on a crash basis.[39]

Quality assurance problems cropped up on many areas farmed out to contractors. One of the most serious involved the radio subsystem under development by Philco Corporation. Observing "out of control" working conditions, combined with numerous deficiencies in workmanship, JPL engineers insisted on a "tear down" of the radio subsystem for inspection.

Laboratory personnel, who had experienced their own and contractor work-manship shortcomings with Ranger, did not want to repeat the experience. During the tear down, 187 deficiencies were found; 143 were reworked and 44 accepted as is.[40]

One of the new scientific experiments on Mariner Mars 69—the infrared spectrometer—became the focus of an embittered, embarrassing, and il-luminating dispute between the laboratory and the experimenter, George Pimentel. The infrared spectrometer (IRS) was a two-channel light analyzer that operated with light beyond the red end of the visible spectrum (the infrared). By measuring the characteristic "colors" transmitted through the Martian atmosphere, the instrument would detect various gaseous substi-tuents, such as carbon dioxide, water vapor, and thus contribute to fuller knowledge of the planet's chemical evolution. JPL nonetheless recom-mended against inclusion of the IRS. Perhaps because of the influence of physicists and geologists, JPL and Caltech emphasized the data that televi-sion would return; they showed less interest in chemical analyses. But NASA's Newell, aware of the political and intellectual need to respond to a diverse scientific clientele, decided to include the IRS on Mariner 69. His decision set the stage for a highly charged encounter between engineers and academic scientists.[41]

JPL professionals often clashed with scientists who, in the laboratory's opinion, did not follow correct construction standards. In one celebrated case James Van Allen's instrument passed all of JPL's tests. But laboratory personnel nevertheless opened the box and then tried to reject the experi-ment because Van Allen had not followed JPL techniques. He was furious. He thought that equipment which passed the laboratory's tests should be accepted. But seldom did the level of conflict rise as high as it did over the IRS. Pimentel and his group at Berkeley operated in the informal manner typical of academic science. They resisted the extensive report writing favored by space program engineers, took an insouciant attitude toward interim deadlines, and counted on ability and resourcefulness to turn out an acceptable product in the end. These methods drove JPL executives to frustration and eventually explosion. Project director Schurmeier engaged in an increasingly acerbic correspondence with Pimentel as he sought re-ports and compliance with JPL schedules and directives.[42]

Pimentel resisted. "A conventional definition of management, as would be used in industry, would draw upon me a very low grade," he acknowledged. "You realize that I use another definition that can be defended only on pragmatic grounds. If you succeed in a difficult enterprise, who is to say that the management is all that bad?" Pimentel repeated the qualifications he and his laboratory possessed—they were among the most eminent in their field in the world—and essentially told JPL to trust them to do the job. The situation was ironic. JPL now found itself assuming the role NASA had taken with it in the early 1960s. The laboratory, which had told headquarters to trust its eminent qualifications, now wanted hard evidence at each step of the process.[43]

The problems of the IRS were real enough, and they drew a sharp reprimand from Newell's successor, John E. Naugle, in January 1968. Of Mariner 69's scientific instruments the IRS was the last to reach completion in prototype form, and it was the only one with major vibration and technical problems. As a result, its projected schedule was the most ominous. "There is a very real risk that your experiment will not fly or that it could jeopardize the mission if it does not meet the test and delivery milestones," Naugle told Pimentel.[44]

But the pattern of conflict continued. In October 1968, Donald G. Rea, deputy director of planetary programs in the Office of Space Sciences and Applications, became irked at the lack of quantitative data on the IRS. "For one molecule of interest, NH_3, the sensitivity of your spectrometer is some two orders of magnitude poorer than the present upper limit established by ground-based observations," Rea noted. He ordered a quantitative analysis of the scientific content carried out—but by the Mariner project office at JPL, not by Pimentel. The experimenter hastened to convince NASA that his instrument's performance would be satisfactory, and the order for testing at JPL was revoked.[45]

As the countdown drew closer, the IRS began to take its place on a sound basis with the other experiments. But conflict, by now endemic, dogged the experiment even through its flight. JPL quarreled with Pimentel over whether a University of California insignia should be left on the equipment and forced its removal; a long conflict over the press release about the IRS that would go into the press kit was eventually resolved when JPL let Pimentel write his own; and the publication of flight data in *Science* was devoid of the usual gentlemanly acknowledgments between experimenters and engineers.[46]

Whatever the unfortunate personal dynamics that colored the IRS, the issue was a significant one. "As the space exploration advances in sophistication of the science experiments, there will be more and more need to accommodate to the research scientist's habitual methods," Pimentel warned. "The only alternatives I see are ever-increasing lead times or much less advanced science. We can afford neither." If something approaching a "cultural adjustment" was being asked of both NASA and JPL in the mid-1960s, the same might have been said of scientists and engineers. The adjustment could develop only through increased exposure by both parties, as the space program continued to evolve.[47]

By early 1969 the complex job of building the spacecraft was finished and three specimens were shipped to Cape Kennedy. The preparations for launch went smoothly until February 14, when the Atlas-Centaur-Mariner combination underwent a simulated launch test. A worn-out relay caused the main valves of the Atlas to open, and the pressure surged out of its 6-inch pipes. Like a deflating balloon, the Atlas sagged alarmingly. Ground crewmen raced to shut off the manual valves inside the rocket. The pressure returned to the tanks, and the Atlas resumed its shape. But a visible scar in the rocket's exterior signaled that another Atlas would have to be used for Mariner 6. The spacecraft that had perched atop the Atlas-Centaur during the harrowing loss of pressure was carefully dismounted and sent back to the JPL hangar for precautionary tests. It had escaped unscathed.[48]

But meanwhile, with the celestial clock ticking a countdown, the spacecraft originally intended for Mariner 7 was placed on a new Atlas-Centaur. Working extra hard, crews cut the prelaunch time from two weeks to one week. On the evening of February 25, 1969, Mariner 6 blasted into the best orbit the Mariner series had achieved. Mariner 7 followed on March 27. For the first time, two U.S. ships were heading for the same planet.[49] With the manned moon landing following in July 1969, the American space program had truly come of age.

Mariner 6 experienced some problems on its way to Mars. Canopus continued to jinx the Mariner project. As with the 1964 flight, Mariner 6 lost lock on the bright star and reacquired it only after much persuasion from ground control. But the Mars encounter worked with astonishing smoothness. (The major flaw was that one channel on Pimentel's infrared spectrometer did not function.) On July 29, forty-eight hours before the closest approach to Mars, the narrow-angle television camera began the series of far-encounter photographs. This sequence provided thirty-three views of Mars, from a distance of 1,241,000 to 725,000 kilometers, as the planet made five-sixths of a revolution. Stored on analogue tape, the pictures were played back to Goldstone. The tapes then were erased so that a second series of seventeen photographs could be made at distances from 561,000 to 175,000 kilometers. Some pictures were good enough to reveal surface features that were 25 kilometers across—six times better than any photographs taken by Earth-based telescopes. The television subsystem followed with a series of twenty-five near-encounter pictures.[50]

But just fifteen minutes before Mariner 6 took its last far-encounter picture, attention was rudely diverted to Mariner 6's sister ship. Alarm bells went off around the world as Mariner 7's signal faltered and, in less than a minute, disappeared. The Deep Space Network searched urgently for the signal, which reappeared intermittently, and the few engineers who could be spared from Mariner 6 controls pored over the evidence. Mariner 7, they concluded "was windmilling through space, torn loose from its line to Canopus, its narrow beam of telemetry sweeping the sky like a searchlight." Having followed a shorter flight path, Mariner 7 was close on the heels of its sister ship; the second spacecraft would encounter Mars only five days later. "The happening," as the Mariner 7 anomaly became known, was an emergency that could scarcely have happened at a worse time. After several hours JPL engineers improvised a way to regain contact with Mariner 7, and its signal reappeared in the space network receivers. The sense of relief was palpable. The spacecraft was still heading for Mars, drawing power from the sun, and orienting itself properly.[51]

But the ship was in trouble. It had slipped off course. What was worse, the camera platform appeared to have rotated a few degrees; but since its pointing angle could be determined only by knowing how far it had moved from its original setting, no one knew exactly where the camera was aiming. Mariner's controllers benefited from both cleverness and luck. The wide-angle television camera was turned on early and gradually moved to locate Mars, then recalibrated with the engineering video. "The mission was resumed with added confidence in the operational capabilities of the spacecraft because of this unplanned exercise," noted experimenter Robert B. Leighton, a Caltech physics professor. Besides the television recalibration, the spacecraft computer, attitude control and power subsystems, and all the scientific instruments had to be rechecked. Although JPL engineers found significant damage in some spots—twenty telemetry channels were out of commission—Mariner 7 had survived its mysterious anomaly surprisingly well.[52]

What had caused "the happening"? Some speculated that the spacecraft had hit a meteorite, others that an inner asteroid belt perturbed spacecraft at a certain distance from the sun. When scientists whimsically proposed the "Great Galactic Ghoul" theory, it became apparent that an answer lay far away. Months after the event, a review panel finally traced the anomaly to an explosive failure of the storage battery. The battery case ruptured and liquid electrolyte sprayed out, pressurizing the spacecraft's interior sufficiently to cause arcing which damaged the electrical equipment. Gas escaping from the spacecraft caused the perturbation in telemetry.[53]

Despite the nearly catastrophic "happening," Mariner 7 recovered to produce results well in excess of expectations. Perhaps the most dramatic operational aspect of the mission was the reprogramming of Mariner 7 to follow up on intriguing leads turned up by Mariner 6 in the southern and western parts of Mars. This was the first time a spacecraft had been reprogrammed in flight to take advantage of data from another flying spacecraft. Mariner 7's flexibility, made possible by the new central computer and sequencer, enhanced the payoff of the dual mission. The spacecraft sent back ninety-three pictures from its far encounter, and thirty-three (an increase of eight over the original plan) from its near encounter. The mission photographed about 10 percent of the surface. Some anxious moments remained when the infrared spectrometer began operation. Since its operation depended on a one-time expenditure of tanks of nitrogen and hydrogen, mission control had not turned them on when the other scientific experiments were tested. But the IRS performed handsomely, collecting more than double the spectral pairs called for in the project requirements.[54]

Mariner Mars 69 forced some reconsideration of the ideas which Mariner 4 had encouraged about the planet. "The new surprise," said Leighton, "is that Mars is not just an oversized moon but has distinctive features of its own—features unknown elsewhere in the solar system." Where Mariner 4 had revealed a heavily cratered surface, the 1969 mission showed some regions, such as the desert of Hellas, that had hardly any craters. Scientists also observed terrain which geologists term "chaotic," or made up of "short, jumbled ridges and valleys." Since craters had probably existed in both the desert and chaotic regions at one time, scientists puzzled over what had caused them to be erased. The chaotic regions' jumbled ridges did not appear on the moon and were not duplicated on Earth on so large a scale. As Mariner 4 data had suggested, the Martian polar covering was frozen carbon dioxide (dry ice), and CO_2 dominated in the atmosphere. All told, the dual mission of 1969, by revising the lunar model of Mars, moved the conception of the planet into an anomalous position. It was neither moon nor Earth, and it had its own unique properties. But just what those were awaited the major revision dictated by the Mariner 9 orbiter in 1971.[55]

The changing fortunes of the space program which determined the shape of the Jet Propulsion Laboratory's program in the mid-1960s contributed eventually to a clarification of the Caltech-JPL-NASA triangle. A resolution of the conflict-ridden relationship between Washington and Pasadena seemingly was possible only as NASA grew weaker and its top administrators changed in the twilight of the Johnson administration.

NASA pressure on JPL in the mid-1960s aroused fears among some outside observers. An important indicator of this trend surfaced when Henry O. Fuchs, a professor of mechanical engineering at Stanford University, appealed to President Johnson and administrator Webb to ease off on JPL. Fuchs's particular concern was that the agency was going too far in converting the laboratory into a monitoring facility rather than a creative organization. But by implication he raised the larger issue of JPL's role. Based on two summers of observation from inside the laboratory, Fuchs argued that its personnel were motivated primarily by "the discipline of very critical self-satisfaction." The profit motive might work in industrial firms, but the "intangible incentives [that] have traditionally spurred the search for knowledge" accounted for JPL's success. "We have only one JPL," he concluded.

NASA's changes risked "the almost certain destruction of this unique resource."[56]

When Fuchs's letter was circulated at NASA headquarters it drew emphatic endorsements from second-level managers. Benjamin Milwitzky, who had worked closely with JPL as headquarters' Surveyor liaison, said: "I agree with the Prof. wholeheartedly. I just hope it is not already too late." William O'Bryant, manager of advanced programs and technology, agreed: "The effects of current policy are already beginning to show. I personally would like to get on the bandwagon to reverse the trend." Glenn Reiff, NASA's Mariner overseer, concurred: "I strongly endorse the letter and the [above] comments."[57]

A still more significant indicator of the dissent from Webb's position emerged in a study done for the administrator in 1966 by William Rieke, assistant administrator for industry affairs and administration, and Walter Sohier, general counsel. "Progress by both JPL and Caltech was much better than is understood or appreciated," they concluded. To suggest otherwise was to do the leadership of both institutions "a grave injustice." Pressure from the space agency had been necessary and beneficial in the past. The three organizations had "indeed created an immensely capable engineering laboratory which can and will undoubtedly perform to our exacting technical specifications in the future," they said. There was still room for improvement, of course, particularly in the involvement of the Institute in JPL affairs, but the difficulties of bringing those possibilities to fruition made it doubtful that continued pressure would be productive. They advised NASA to end "the high-frustration mode" it had followed with CIT and JPL and "work quietly at establishing a more receptive environment for some of the returns still in embryo."[58]

Rieke and Sohier devoted much of their attention to Webb's preoccupation with getting that "something extra" from the California Institute. This relationship had not lived up to expectations in part because project management had become "the dominant theme at JPL to the virtual exclusion of other considerations," they noted. Hostile environments and inflexible timetables imposed unavoidable constraints if missions were to succeed. To the laboratory "the Campus may always be an ivory tower out of touch with engineering realities," Rieke and Sohier wrote. Conversely, the very conditions that were indispensable for the success of flight projects tended to drive away outside scientists. University researchers usually did their work with one or two colleagues and several graduate students, and if a project was not finished one year, it could be continued the next. To them flight opportunities seemed "few and far between and [were] not absolutely essential to the orderly progress of their own research." What was worse, the demands of flight schedules seemed too often to overwhelm ground-based investigation. Many of the researchers whom NASA wished to attract to JPL projects dreaded or detested the "highly disciplined regime" attractive to the space agency. Rieke and Sohier concluded: "In some ways, we are asking almost cultural adjustments from both parties."[59]

Their findings echoed the concerns of practicing space scientists. Bruce Murray noted that the original intention to build a strong capability in planetary science at JPL had been "shattered by the realities of a project-oriented organization." The laboratory's scientific capacity had been thereby diminished and its reputation tarnished within the scientific community. Homer Newell of NASA had also admonished Webb that the process of creating an on-call scientific facility was incompatible with the creativity the administrator wanted to foster.[60]

Rieke and Sohier went on to observe that, in addition to these problems, NASA had not been able to express "in reasonably specific terms just what kind of 'added ingredients' it wanted from CIT-JPL." Although Caltech had at times been overly resistant to NASA's wishes, the Institute's lack of responsiveness stemmed also from a genuine puzzlement at what Webb expected. And some of Webb's ideas threatened the proper role of the university. For the most part Caltech's involvement with JPL rested perforce on "traditional themes of intellectual mutuality of interests," Rieke and Sohier said. The Institute might have expanded those interests, but Rieke and Sohier correctly circumscribed the area in which academic participation in the JPL program was realistic to expect. They sympathized with the "mystification" that JPL and Caltech personnel might feel when their hardware performed brilliantly, but NASA nevertheless continued to talk about "'total' responsibilities." Rieke and Sohier ventured a bold conclusion: "One could argue that successful execution of part of the overall technical program is all that NASA should expect from Caltech and JPL and that anything beyond this should be considered primarily a governmental obligation."[61]

This trenchant critique of the NASA position made unwelcome reading in the administrator's office. Webb and some of his aides continued to be vexed by their relationship with Caltech, as their hard line in negotiations over the renewal of the Institute's contract in the fall of 1966 demonstrated. Their attitude came across in a one-line memorandum from associate administrator Robert Seamans in 1965: "Aren't we obtaining *any* identifiable returns from our large annual investment in CIT?" Caltech officials argued their performance merited a higher fee. They also protested what they perceived as a continuing erosion of the earlier mutuality between JPL and NASA; the revision of the contract in 1963 to 1964 was a "harsh" agreement that had been negotiated during a period of duress. NASA negotiators rejected CIT's complaints. There was little hope of arresting headquarters' continuing inroads into JPL administration.[62]

Much of the controversy in the negotiations focused on the space agency's evaluation of CIT-JPL performance. The overall size of the laboratory's budget determined the range of Caltech's fee; the exact amount within that range was based on how NASA filled out the report card. As Earl Hilburn had noted when the scheme was introduced in 1964, the evaluations amounted to an award fee procedure, in effect if not in name. Offended by the very idea of an award fee, Caltech officials also contended that NASA misused it. They argued that, under the 1964 contract revision, performance in previous years was to be considered in establishing the level of fee; in practice, however, NASA used the performance evaluation for the current fiscal year. "For all practical purposes this has converted Amendment 10 into a cost-plus-award-fee type contract—the very thing we were seeking to avoid," complained Robert Gilmore, the Institute's business vice-president. But since the agency had wanted an award fee all along, it gave Caltech's objections little serious consideration. The Institute's staff counsel, John MacL. Hunt, felt frustrated enough to suggest that CIT bow to the facts of life and openly accept the award fee, but Gilmore and DuBridge demurred.[63]

The evaluation mechanism was not unfair by itself, but it inevitably became tangled in the whole web of CIT-JPL-NASA relations. The ratings were determined by a board, chaired by Homer Newell, which relied on reports submitted by headquarters officials who dealt extensively with the laboratory. So long as the board rated flight projects, especially completed ones, the criteria were usually clear and the interpretations noncontroversial—a mission succeeded or it didn't. Thus the Mariner project, with the brilliant success of Mariner 4, drew a rating of "outstanding." Mariner 4 had operated on a continuous basis for more than a year in a nearly flawless manner," the evaluators said. "The scientific results have been widely acclaimed." Similarly, the Ranger project, with its last three flights successful, merited an "outstanding."[64]

But the system's inconsistency became apparent when NASA rated JPL's performance on Surveyor. Before its successful flights, Surveyor usually received marks of "marginal" or even "unsatisfactory." But when Surveyor 1's successful flight followed on the heels of that rating, NASA turned around and gave Hughes the maximum incentive fee payment for its performance. Granted that Surveyor's early problems could be traced in part to JPL's weaknesses, the eventual success of the flights was traceable to a large dosage of the laboratory's assistance. The situation was anomalous: an industrial firm in the end reaped a windfall in large part because of JPL's assistance, which had been rated marginal or unsatisfactory. The evaluation scheme was another mechanism NASA could use to reward its politically powerful industrial contractors but keep JPL responsive to headquarters.[65]

Business procedures usually received ratings of "good," but included continued criticism that JPL did not follow NASA procedures exactly. These reflected substantial improvement since Luedecke had become deputy director in 1964. DuBridge objected, however, to the agency's insistence on following its specifications to the letter; the procedures were largely matters of judgment and had little effect on the government's risk. "Caltech's reputation is at stake here and you have my personal assurance that our ultimate goal is to see that the very best job of procurement, under all the circumstances, is done," he said. DuBridge was probably right. Yet CIT-JPL had done badly here in the past, and conformity to NASA wishes could have been accomplished with little compromise of any essential university or laboratory interests. Gentlemen's assurances belonged to a different world than that of a federally funded laboratory handling nearly a quarter of a billion dollars a year.[66]

The elasticity of the yardstick became evident in the category "supplemental benefits of CIT management." In June 1965 the board rated this area "somewhere between marginal and good." It noted that some Institute scientists had begun to participate in JPL projects, though on an individual not an institutional basis. It applauded the long-range planning study of the exploration of Mars in 1964 and 1965. But the board overlooked the damage done to NASA-Caltech relations when the agency gave the study short shrift because it did not conform to NASA's predilections. The board nevertheless concluded: "For an institution of the competence, reputation, and established leadership in other fields, the performance of CIT during the current evaluation period is considered to be far less than could have been achieved or should have been expected." What might have been expected? Webb did not feel that was NASA's obligation. As he once told his intimates: Caltech needs "to cooperate with us . . . rather than to put the problem up to us to solve it for them in their way."[67]

The NASA board had trouble being specific, too, because chairman Newell was ambivalent about Webb's ideas, insofar as he understood them. The board apparently was dissatisfied that the participation of Caltech faculty was on an individual basis, and hence little different from that of other universities. "More than the normal participation by scientists in other universities is to be expected from CIT," the board argued. It suggested the "emergence of a distinct and vigorous leadership by CIT in space science and engineering, comparable to that established by the Institute in such fields as aeronautics and aerodynamics, astronomy, and engineering." This was an intriguing vision. Implementation would be difficult, however. The agency had hoped Caltech would enlist other universities in JPL's work, but one possible vehicle for this, the California Universities Council of Space Sciences, had been stillborn. For Caltech to do it alone would have taken more money than NASA seemed likely to provide and required giving space science a primacy that the Institute's established divisions probably would have opposed.[68]

DuBridge replied that Caltech had never imagined that the JPL contract entailed this degree of change in the campus scientific program. Faculty members were free to pursue their own research interests without dictation from the administration. The Institute had no extra funds with which to initiate a large space science program, and Caltech's smallness would always limit such a program. After CIT's protest, the board raised the rating to "good." But Caltech leaders had again demonstrated that they would do the minimum necessary for the fee. On the other hand, NASA officialdom continued to expect Caltech to uncover the unspecified extra that the agency itself could not articulate. The "high-frustration mode" continued.[69]

The Institute got nowhere with NASA. The school's fee proposal was rejected with the advice that CIT "quit while we are ahead." The negotiations ended in late 1966 with a fee of $1,650,000 for Caltech. The figure was well above the minimum but below the $1,691,000 CIT thought it merited. The sum was compatible with the overall rating of "good." The contract remained essentially unchanged and would run through 1968 when Webb, in his swan song as administrator, made a last attempt to extend NASA's control.[70]

The pattern of conflict between Pasadena and Washington was played out at another level in 1966 and 1967, in the executive suites on the top floor of JPL administration building 180. The simmering dispute between Pickering and Luedecke moved toward a showdown. Pickering had acceded to the appointment of a strong deputy in 1964, only when pressure from Congress, NASA, and Caltech in the wake of the Ranger failures left him no choice. Luedecke was a de facto general manager and virtual alter ego of the director. The former general manager of the Atomic Energy Commission had done a great deal to shape up JPL's business operations and to improve relations with NASA headquarters. He had played a key role in getting to the bottom of Surveyor's problems, and he provided an on-the-scene resolution of problems that some laboratory personnel believed had been lacking previously. These contributions were prized by NASA headquarters personnel, who repeatedly praised the retired general. Indeed, it was Luedecke's ability to empathize with NASA that proved his undoing.[71]

Luedecke's penetration into the organization, coupled with his ties to headquarters, created a situation which was threatening to the director personally and, Pickering believed, to the proper role of the laboratory. In mid-1966 Pickering began taking a more active part in JPL's day-to-day operations. In September he issued new job descriptions that severely curbed the deputy's power. Many of the actions the deputy had been able to take on his own now required the director's concurrence or were reduced to nothing more than recommendations to the director. Pickering also attempted to reassert his own authority in contract negotiations, which had been part of Luedecke's job description. As a counter to the deputy director, Pickering augmented the power of the assistant directors.[72]

A showdown loomed. Luedecke bitterly protested the revisions. He wanted the director to set policy and handle relations with outside entities, but the implementation should be left to the general manager, who would have an "organization . . . accountable to him for that purpose." The situation continued to deteriorate. When Pickering and Luedecke clashed in the summer of 1967, the general apparently called NASA headquarters to enlist support. Edgar Cortright, Newell's deputy, relayed Washington's support for Luedecke to Caltech officials. Newell, as chairman of the Caltech-JPL performance evaluation board, expressed concern that the weakening of the deputy's role would cause a return to the "less than satisfactory" situation of the early 1960s. Newell warned DuBridge: "The Board believes this *must* be resolved."[73]

Pickering now felt that Caltech had to choose between him and Luedecke. He asked DuBridge to dismiss Luedecke at once. If not, "I believe I will be put into a position where I will be unable to continue to function as Director." The director acknowledged his deputy's contributions to business affairs and to improving relations with headquarters, but he omitted any evaluation of his performance on the technical side. The main issue to Pickering was loyalty. Because of various actions and "attitude," Pickering had doubted Luedecke's allegiance to JPL; the deputy's recent appeal to headquarters confirmed his suspicions. Newell and Cortright considered Luedecke to be "their most important asset at the Laboratory," the director said, "and . . . they will humor him in any way necessary to insure that he stays here." If Caltech yielded, Luedecke would be "in fact running the Laboratory" and would be "NASA's man." Before long JPL would become "merely a 'job shop' for NASA, serving as a convenient means of getting additional staff and hiding under a cloak of respectability by using the Caltech name," Pickering continued. "If this occurs, I would recommend that the Institute withdraw from the contract."[74]

At a meeting of the Institute's board of trustees in mid-August 1967, the Caltech family closed ranks behind Pickering. Luedecke tendered his resignation "for personal reasons." His short letter, devoid of the flourishes of happy departures, said in part: "Performance in this position has been a real challenge. I can look back with gratification upon what I believe to have been substantial achievements toward established objectives of the Laboratory." Luedecke moved to Texas A & M University as a vice-president.[75]

NASA officialdom was alarmed over the firing. It was somewhat mollified, however, when the laboratory hired Rear Adm. John E. Clark as deputy director. A less rigid figure than Luedecke, Clark lightened the atmosphere at the laboratory, many JPL personnel felt. The military tradition continued when Charles Terhune, like Luedecke a retired air force general, replaced Clark several years later. The presence of a military figure as second in command evidently was one of the ways the laboratory cultivated good relations with NASA.[76]

In the aftermath of Luedecke's dismissal, James Webb decided on a new move to put pressure on Caltech-JPL. One day in September 1967 the NASA head was listening to concerns expressed by two old friends, Willard Libby, a former member of the Atomic Energy Commission, and Chauncey Starr, dean of the college of engineering at the University of California at Los Angeles (UCLA), about declining NASA support for universities. Instead of responding to their anxieties, he shifted the conversation to JPL, what was wrong with it, and what ought to be done about it. Then, to the astonishment of both Libby and Starr, he asked them to chair a task force investigating JPL. They temporized and returned to Los Angeles, where they found a letter from Webb—soon followed by a second—pressing them to launch the study.[77]

Webb planned to put pressure on CIT-JPL from two fronts. First, he apparently wanted to use the UCLA study as a weapon against Caltech when the contract negotiations resumed in 1968. He explained to DuBridge that the study would examine "the resources we have paid for at JPL, what we might do with the reduced resources likely to be available to us in the future, and the possibility of alternative management arrangements that will overcome some of the deficiencies we have experienced." The linkage of "reduced resources" and "alternative management arrangements" suggested that scarcity might accomplish what abundance had failed to do in the past. CIT-JPL would have to yield more to NASA.[78]

Second, Webb laid plans to appoint an assistant administrator for special contract negotiation and review who would orchestrate "all of the skill, requirements, and subsidiary endeavors necessary to end up with a proper relationship if possible" with Caltech. If that proved impossible, he continued, "we should end up in a position that we have done all we could in that direction and will then consider alternative arrangements." The negotiator should conduct himself with an eye toward justifying his actions inside and outside the government.[79]

In the end, however, Webb found himself hoist by his own petard. The overture to Starr did not produce ammunition to use against Caltech but instead encouraged the university people to close ranks. Before accepting Webb's assignment, Starr talked to chancellor Franklin Murphy of UCLA, who at once relayed information of the maneuver to DuBridge. The Caltech president was "very much astonished, and also concerned." Starr had assured the chancellor he would "approach the issue in a constructive and positive fashion," and Murphy pointed out that the study might reduce Webb's "disquiet." Before long DuBridge and Pickering came to the same conclusion. Starr and Pickering, who had known each other for a long time, held some friendly conversations. Various other committee members talked informally and sympathetically with Pickering before the official meetings of the "boarding party," as the Starr committee was known around the laboratory. "In a general way, I think the committee will be sympathetic and constructive," the director concluded.[80]

The formal recommendations of the Starr committee in late summer 1968 were mild. They repeated well-worn themes. NASA should clarify what it wanted from JPL, modify the personnel ceiling that irritated the laboratory, study different contractual arrangements, and "maintain and strengthen" the JPL-NASA relationship. JPL should maintain its proven capabilities, modify its "mission orientation" in favor of "multiple objectives," be more flexible in university relations, and improve its cost-effectiveness. Caltech should remove restrictions that tended to impede faculty and graduate students working at JPL. Who could object to such good intentions? With that series of admonitions to all concerned, the Starr committee disbanded.[81]

Even though Starr had not given Webb what he wanted, the NASA hierarchy ventured into contract negotiations with new demands in September 1968. Webb sought to achieve more integration through three measures. First, NASA proposed to sharply diminish Pickering's authority and JPL's autonomy by creating an executive committee; the panel would be similar to a corporate board of directors with a powerful chairman. The board would consist of four to seven members, and the chairman would be a member of the CIT board of trustees. All members would be expected to devote approximately 20 percent of their time to JPL affairs and would be paid $10,000 a year, except for the chairman, who would receive $20,000. Both NASA and Caltech could nominate members, but the space agency would have a veto on membership. (The Starr committee had proposed a JPL board of directors, but its power would have been far short of this executive committee.) Second, Washington wanted the power to veto appointments at the level of assistant director and higher. Under the 1966 contract, CIT-JPL informed headquarters of personnel actions for anyone making $20,000 or more, but JPL could and did hire persons against the agency's verbally expressed wishes. Third, NASA thought Caltech should hand over one-third of its fee to the director of JPL for independent research and development at the laboratory as approved by the executive committee primarily for work at JPL by faculty and students from the Institute and other universities.[82]

Caltech and JPL intensely disliked these ideas, which all but gutted the concept of a university-managed laboratory, and they were able to resist most of them. NASA's power was declining, signified by the budget cuts of 1967 and 1968. But of particular importance for CIT-JPL, the agency's top administrators changed. Associate Administrator Seamans had left in late 1967. In October 1968 Webb retired from NASA. He was succeeded by Thomas O. Paine, the agency's deputy administrator since January 1968. A Stanford Ph.D. in physical metallurgy, he had spent nineteen years in industrial research. The manager of General Electric's TEMPO think tank in Santa Barbara before joining NASA, Paine was more receptive to an academic style of operation than his predecessor. He was also, said *The Economist*, "unusually sensitive" to others for a "Washington man."[83]

Webb's departure was crucial. Whatever the merits of his stance toward CIT-JPL in the early 1960s, by 1966 it had become counterproductive—as many of his own second-level managers now believed. The Caltech-JPL relationship still needed improvement. But most of Webb's negotiating points of 1968 had less to do with increased effectiveness than with assertion of control over the laboratory.

Under Paine the negotiating climate improved markedly. An agreement was reached on December 11, 1968, which attempted to set up mechanisms for increased cooperation but in a framework more acceptable to Caltech. The executive committee emerged as a shadow of its proposed self; the new model was styled a "visiting committee" and possessed only vague consultative powers. The personnel action provisions were modified. Two potentially important new positions were created, in line with NASA wishes. One was a science director, who would build up JPL's scientific prowess, coordinate scientific activities on flight projects, and provide a link with academic institutions and the scientific community at large. The other was a technology transfer director, who would foster the dissemination of space technology to universities and industry. The science director proved to be effective, the technology transfer officer mostly ineffective. The discretionary research funds took on a new coloration. NASA provided a fund of $400,000 to the JPL director to sponsor independent research. Caltech set up a second account, of $175,000, which the agency matched, also to fund independent work at the laboratory. Thus a total of $750,000 would be made available for academic work at JPL, of which CIT put up $175,000. The Institute's contribution was far short of the $500,000 or more NASA wanted the campus to make available, but mechanisms for greater university involvement were at last being set up.[84]

NASA and CIT-JPL agreed on two items that forecast new directions. One clause reflected a modus vivendi that had finally been reached after a decade of conflict. It read: "To achieve the mutual objectives sought, it will be appropriate, on the one hand, that CIT regard its stewardship not only as a contract but as a public trust and that NASA, for its part, exercise the restraint in those administrative matters which is consistent with a recognition of CIT's function as a trustee for the university community." Caltech recognized, as NASA wished, that it had an obligation to provide something beyond simple fulfillment of the contract. NASA conceded, as the Institute desired, that it should temper its administrative penetration. The sentence was vague, elastic, and subject to infinite interpretation in day-to-day performance. But it was nonetheless a harbinger of better relations between NASA and CIT-JPL which would not have been possible a few months earlier. As relations warmed between Washington and Pasadena, Paine agreed to a 75 percent increase in Caltech's fee, which brought it close to $3 million a year.[85]

The second clause carried much substantive importance. It allowed the laboratory to seek funding from agencies other than NASA, so long as the space administration concurred. This latitude was vital to JPL, for with space budgets declining, some diversification of effort was necessary to avert a sharp decline in budget and personnel. In 1967 the laboratory had formed a civil systems division and was starting projects in various terrestrial areas, particularly police administration. This move reflected in part NASA's own much-ballyhooed attempt to revive support for the space program by demonstrating presumed technological spin-offs on Earth. For Pickering and most other JPL personnel, civil systems would never possess the glamour of the space program. But since institutions rarely volunteer for major surgery, JPL soon moved into civil systems, especially energy, and by the early 1980s increasingly sought military support.[86]

By the end of 1968 JPL stood at a contradictory point. Its most notable space exploration missions were unfolding smoothly, although they did not have the character JPL would have preferred. The laboratory had successfully defended its primacy in NASA's planetary exploration plans, although it had not won the promises of in-house projects Pickering had sought. But the space program's aura of legitimacy was eroding, and with it, money. The challenges of the early 1960s had been technical and administrative; the challenges of the late '60s and the '70s would be to diversify and preserve the institution.

The changes that lay ahead threatened to undermine the extraordinary morale that suffused the JPL staff. Many observers found that JPL in the early and mid-1960s had that high esprit and cohesiveness that mark extra-performance institutions. Iowa scientist James Van Allen, who had plenty of experience with the laboratory both positive and negative, compared the laboratory's élan to that of the marines—and found it equally offensive. JPL's arrogance—laboratory managers were quite capable of being conde-scending toward not only NASA bureaucrats but world-renowned scien-tists—received frequent comment. There was no doubt that the laboratory's arrogance made it all too often unnecessarily hard to deal with and overcon-fident of its abilities. JPL's swagger played a part in NASA's sometimes understandable efforts to cut the laboratory down to size and in the resent-ment scientists, contractors, and other laboratories directed at the Pasadenans.[87]

But JPL's arrogance was also a measure of the pride that pervaded the staff. Such pride grew out of the quality of the institution. Director Pickering always stressed that the laboratory's program played a key role in attracting and retaining talented staff. This conviction lay behind his efforts to insure that the institution always had at least one major flight project underway and that his staff actually carried out the advanced engineering themselves rather than merely supervise outside contractors. At JPL engineers had a chance to do true technological pioneering. Ed Chandler, an engineer who left the laboratory in disillusionment, nonetheless recalled the sense of pride he still felt when he looked at the moon and remembered that a piece of Surveyor equipment he had worked on lay there. The challenge to be first in a meaningful program galvanized individuals' efforts. Homer Newell once said that there is nothing like working at the frontiers to bring out people's best abilities. As Chandler's observation indicated, it was not merely associa-tion with a pioneering effort that counted, it was also the chance to get one's hands on the equipment—a sort of old-fashioned craftsmanship ethic—that attracted talent.[88]

But even for many of those who never touched an antenna, entered a clean room, or tracked a Mariner, working for JPL made them feel they were making a contribution beyond that of an ordinary job. Secretaries and file clerks were fond of recalling the excitement of the 1960s when they felt special, as if their activities fit clearly into one large cohesive enterprise. Much of that élan dissipated as the years wore on and space exploration became more routine and less of a national priority. By the 1970s the rank and file found JPL "just a job."

Program also meant pressure. The JPL atmosphere appeared conducive to ulcers, heart attacks, and nervous breakdowns. The stakes were high. The cold war ethos pervaded the laboratory, and any failure seemed to inflict serious wounds on American prestige. If nothing else, the sheer amounts of money involved would have produced tension. If something had gone wrong on Surveyor, for instance, and the launch had been delayed for a month, the added cost would have reached $25 million. The pressure grew intense as launch dates approached. Work weeks of seventy to eighty hours were common. At the cape engineers could recall working more than twenty-four hours straight or going back exhausted to their motel, only to be awakened after two hours' sleep and called back to the assembly area to work on something.[89]

Pickering and the top brass attempted to maintain an institutional setting which they believed was conducive to effectiveness under high-pressure demands. JPL's much-touted effort to offer some of the autonomy and amenities of a university was integral to their strategy. JPL claimed to offer the advantages of a university without the disadvantages of industry or civil service. Unlike industry, where scores of engineers might be herded together in a bullpen, most JPL engineers enjoyed a private office. They could sign for expenditures of $2,500 (or more, depending on position) without a countersignature. One engineer recalled how good that felt after being employed by a firm "where the general manager called you on the carpet and raised hell when you wanted to spend five dollars." Since the professional staff worked in divisions which resembled university disciplines, they had somewhat more control over their work environment and whom they worked with than in an institution organized along project lines. And in the 1960s if one survived the first six months, one in effect had tenure.[90]

An important intangible was the connection with Caltech. For most JPL professionals the connection was more apparent than real. Relatively few laboratory employees, except for the very top echelons, set foot on the campus in any guise other than that of general public, and if they thought that JPL's being a part of Caltech bestowed on them any claims for special consideration, they were quickly disabused of the notion. If outsiders resented JPL's condescension toward them, many JPL employees chafed under the campus's snobbery. Nonetheless many JPL professionals took pride in being employees of the Institute and basked in the added prestige CIT bestowed. That allure began to dim, however, in the 1970s as civil service salaries rose steadily. The middle echelons at the laboratory became increasingly restive as they realized that the Caltech connection, which had once enabled JPL to outbid civil service, now sometimes placed a ceiling on salaries below government figures. A sense of insecurity also crept across the laboratory as budget cuts and personnel ceilings reduced employment levels. The absence of civil service red tape also meant that safeguards against arbitrary firing were fewer.[91]

Taken together these attributes of JPL made its employees feel they were part of an international elite. Yet even in the laboratory's heyday, the early to mid-1960s, anxiety grew that it was losing its edge. This was in part probably correct and also in large measure unavoidable. The laboratory's personnel grew rapidly, from approximately 2,300 in 1958 to 3,600 in 1962—an increase of more than 50 percent in four years—and then coasted upward to a range around 4,400 in 1964, which continued for several years. It was impossible to grow both quickly and well; that was one of the contradictions of a crash program. Some engineers cited their perception that JPL as an organization was declining in technical competence as a reason for switching to other jobs as early as the mid-1960s. Top management echoed these fears. As the first tremors of budget cuts reached Pasadena in 1966 and 1967, the sense that the laboratory's program had peaked contributed to a growing malaise. This perception was inaccurate in that some of JPL's best endeavors—the sophisticated Mariners, Viking, and Voyager—still lay ahead. But this view was correct in the sense that by the late 1960s JPL growth had crested and now began to slip downward.[92]

The JPL personnel buildup peaked in the late 1960s with a NASA-imposed ceiling of 4,650 employees. That number declined to the neighborhood of 4,000 by the early 1970s. The most significant change in the composition of the staff was an increase in the percentage of engineers and scientists, from about 22 percent of total employees to about 40 percent by 1970 and to 54.5 percent in 1980. This change took place largely as the category of technician/technical aide diminished accordingly. The combined administrative and office/clerical staffs held steady at slightly under 30 percent of the work force. Another noteworthy development was an increase in the percentage of engineers and scientists holding Ph.D.'s from 13 percent in 1968 to 23 percent in 1980. Master's degrees, which had always been strongly in evidence at the laboratory, held at 30 percent from the mid-1960s onward. By 1980 JPL fielded an engineering and scientific staff with more than 50 percent boasting advanced degrees.[93]

The laboratory remained through the '70s a white male preserve. Women and minorities together generally filled about 30 percent of the jobs at JPL. But they were virtually unrepresented in the upper echelons of the laboratory. The key body of personnel—the top 75 people, who composed the senior staff—contained 1 minority male and no women in 1972. At the second level—senior section managers—only 3 minority males and no women were found among the 118 employees. Thus the top two tiers were solely male and had only 2 percent minority representation. The profile improved only slightly in the next two ranks. The top third of the laboratory, with a total roster of 1,405 souls in 1972, included only 68 minority members, or 4.8 percent, and just 14 women, or barely 1 percent. But in the lower two-thirds of the pay scale, women made up one-fourth and minority personnel one-seventh of the staff. An internal study concluded: "Present participation by minorities and females in upper professional levels, both line and staff, is far short of any desirable, eventual participation."[94]

Even more than the rest of society, JPL and the space community were worlds run by white males. The reasons were complex and had to do with the relatively small numbers of women and minorities attracted, or encouraged, to engineering, as well as historic patterns of discrimination whether subtle or overt. JPL undertook an affirmative action program in the early 1970s and tried in particular to target minority groups in southern California. But the situation was further complicated by the declining number of job openings at JPL. The laboratory could report some success. By 1980 some 7 percent of its engineers and scientists were women. But most women still found jobs on the support staff, where they represented 40 percent of the employees. Only an aggressive affirmative action program could open the top third of the laboratory to women and minority groups.[95]

In the mid-1960s JPL's physical environment began to change from what looked like a haphazard collection of leftover buildings to a steady-state laboratory. As the laboratory grew, the overcrowding in its two- and three-story, vintage army-base buildings became acute. JPL's roughly triangular site was bounded by the San Gabriel Mountains, the Arroyo Seco, and the upper-middle-class residential community of La Cañada. It could only build up. The first high-rise, the nine-story marble and glass-sheathed central engineering building better known as building 180, which housed the administrative staff, began to take shape in 1962. As the laboratory came more into the public eye, a master plan for beautification of the main part of the laboratory was implemented. A central mall adorned with a fountain stretched from the gate into the main working area of the laboratory. It was flanked on the north by building 180 and on the southwest by the new von Kármán auditorium, which appropriately honored JPL's early guiding spirit. The auditorium became the scene of triumphant news conferences and other public events as the lunar and planetary missions captured international attention.

Eugene Pierce, the architect who had supervised JPL's physical plant since 1943, was amazed at the transformation. In the 1950s he had struggled to get anything green for the laboratory and was often reduced to buying discarded grass and ice plant from the city of Pasadena. Now even trees and flowers were available. The landscaping was limited to the public areas. One writer compared the look of JPL to a junior college that ran out of money halfway through a building program. If one penetrated into the back yards along the arroyo and against the mountains, the rough-hewn character of the 1940s laboratory remained. Trailers which had been squeezed into any available corner in the early '60s were still there. JPL administrators found it as hard as college presidents to phase out "temporary" buildings.[96]

But like marines who didn't trust equipment unless it was leaking hydraulic fluid, some engineers found the landscaping a sure sign of institutional decadence. When the trees and flower pots appeared, "we knew it was all over for this organization," said one sardonic engineer. "When the landscaping goes in, the organization has reached its peak and will eventually go the other way." Indeed, trying to maintain the health of the laboratory in the face of changing national priorities posed a major institutional problem for JPL in the late 1960s and 1970s.[97]

12 ★★

THE END OF THE BEGINNING

JPL's planetary missions reached maturity in the 1970s both technically and scientifically. Yet paradoxically at the very time the laboratory was carrying out its most exciting projects, it faced a mounting institutional crisis.

Mariner Mars 71 (Mariners 8 and 9) ranked as the most stunning planetary science mission to date. The mission single-handedly brought about a startling reinterpretation of the moonlike Mars that had emerged from Mariners 2, 6, and 7. It also played a major role in broadening planetary understanding from what Cornell astronomy professor Carl Sagan termed "a strange kind of Earth-moon parochialism" to the solar system.[1]

Mariner Mars 71 had originally been planned as a landing probe. Budget and time constraints forced JPL, however, to limit the mission to an orbiter, which in any case proved to be a sensible stepping-stone from flybys to a lander. In line with the general objectives of planetary exploration—the search for life and inquiry into the origins of the universe—the project had several specific goals. They included mapping a large part of the Martian surface at much higher resolution than was possible from Earth, studying the Wave of Darkening (which some scientists believed varied according to biota), and making measurements related to the temperatures, composition, and thermal properties of the surface, including in particular the polar caps. Other activities included gathering data on the atmosphere and the internal activity, mass distribution, and shape of Mars. Three of the four scientific experiments—television, infrared radiometer, and ultraviolet spectrometer—had flown on the 1969 mission. The fourth, which was new to Mariner, was an infrared interferometer spectrometer designed by Rudolf Hanel of Goddard Space Flight Center. The visual imaging team featured two figures who were destined to become well known—Sagan and Bruce Murray.[2]

The development of the spacecraft went relatively smoothly, in large measure because the orbiter was less complicated than a lander. "The importance of a high inheritability cannot be overemphasized in optimizing reliability, cost, and schedule," JPL's final report on the project pointed out. One of the major changes required was a propulsion subsystem to inject the spacecraft into orbit when it reached Mars. Most of the components of the 300-pound-thrust engine had been used previously, but the subsystem represented a new design. The data storage subsystem was wholly new and boasted larger capacity and more flexibility. Major changes also showed up in the television and attitude control subsystems. In such areas as command, telemetry, and antennas, the changes were minor.[3]

JPL personnel had high confidence in the 1971 spacecraft. But they received a reminder that planetary exploration had not yet become routine when the Centaur failed to boost Mariner 8 into orbit after its launch on May 5, 1971. Mariner 9, however, enjoyed a successful launch and injection on May 30, 1971. Since the original plans had called for complementary missions on the order of Mariners 6 and 7, a hybrid approach had to be devised to accomplish as much as possible with the one spacecraft.[4]

By late September 1971, as Mariner 9 moved into the last third of its journey, a bright yellow cloud began developing over Noachis, in southern Mars. In about two weeks the cloud spread over the rest of the planet, and the entire globe disappeared from telescopic sight. A giant Mars dust storm—beyond the worst imaginings of any Okie in the 1930s—was brewing up. When the storm peaked in its fifth week, it had outstripped all previously observed Martian storms for obscuration, area, and duration. The phenomenon excited some scientists, who wanted a chance to observe it close up, but it posed headaches for Mariner 9 mission control. Although the storm began to subside by the time the spacecraft was inserted into orbit around the planet on November 14, the surface remained almost totally occluded. Only five distinct features could be made out—the south polar cap and four dark spots, including the giant volcano Olympus Mons which poked above the storm. "It was apparent," the project's scientists observed dryly, "that Mars was not the same planet for which this mission had been planned."[5]

The original mapping sequence had to be abandoned because of the dust. But the programmable computer proved to be a mission-saver; it could be told to wait for three months until the dust settled before doing its number. (By contrast the Soviet Union's Mars 2 orbiter had a fixed program and film-recording system, which went through their preset motions before the surface was completely visible.) Mariner scientists switched to a new plan, "the reconnaissance mode," which included global coverage on each revolution, followed by zeroing in on "specific targets in relatively clear areas." Augmenting the programmable computer were the capabilities of the digital television system and sophisticated computer-processing techniques which made it possible "to bring out contrast detail invisible to the eye in the raw pictures." Mariner 9 operated for more than a year—well in excess of the ninety days JPL promised.[6]

Its observations revolutionized the interpretation of Mars. From the vast amount of data the spacecraft returned, including the first surface photographs of Mars's two moons, the visual images of the surface of the planet awakened the greatest interest. The southern half of Mars, on which the earlier Mariners had focused, continued to appear moonlike. But the northern hemisphere fairly blossomed with evidence of recent geological and meteorological activity, some of which was analogous to that on Earth. An instant focus of attention was the largest volcano, Olympus Mons. This awesome giant dwarfed anything on Earth. Towering 25 kilometers above the surrounding terrain and measuring 600 kilometers across, Olympus Mons is three times larger than Mauna Loa on Hawaii, the closest terrestrial competitor. Olympus Mons stands in a huge field of volcanoes. Interestingly, unlike Earth, the volcanoes were not formed by the constant shifting of a series of plates. Some scientists believed the absence of plate motion might explain why Mars's shield volcanoes are so large.[7]

Of even greater moment for most was the surprising discovery of "winding, braided channels" which resembled terrestrial river valleys. The largest such channels were as much as 1,500 kilometers long and 200 kilometers wide. Quite different in appearance from channels which were formed by flowing lava, they seemed to have been carved by running water when Mars was warmer and wetter. They most resembled the "channeled scablands" of eastern Washington, which were formed when "a natural dam holding the water in a large ice-age lake gave way." The name Valles Marineris, or "Valley of the Mariners," was aptly bestowed on the most spectacular system of canyons. Its scale is enormous—2,700 kilometers long and as much as 500 kilometers wide and at points 6 kilometers deep. Superimposed on the United States, Valley of the Mariners would span almost the entire continent.[8]

Mariner 9 demonstrated that Mars, once considered geologically dead, had in fact an "active geological history." To be sure, conditions are at present unfavorable for life. But Mars had a denser atmosphere in the past. And supposing it had been "warmer and wetter" and had not changed too rapidly, life forms might have gotten started and had time to adapt. Carl Sagan opined that Mariner 9 suggested "Mars may be much more habitable for terrestrial microorganisms than many had suspected possible." He thought there might even be forms of life big enough to see, what he called "macrobes."[9]

Most scientists, geologists in particular, still doubted that life exists on Mars, at least in any form resembling that on Earth or amenable to science's present interpretation of life processes. Bruce Murray, for one, thought that scientists as well as laymen were beguiled by the notion of extraterrestrial life and that this collective "wishful thinking" actually distorted scientific data and priorities. "We *want* Mars to be like the Earth," he said. "There is a very deep-seated desire to find another place where we can make another start." Reflecting his own theoretical bias, Murray thought the evidence from Mariner 9 made life on Mars even less probable. For that matter most members of the biological experiment team for Viking put the chances of finding life on the order of 1 or 2 percent at best. That remote possibility should not overshadow the continuing importance of a balanced approach that would address the many other important scientific questions about Mars. Still, as Murray, Michael Malin, and Ronald Greeley later put it: "The possibility of alien life is so significant that the question must be asked scientifically each time a possible new habitat is encountered." Pulses quickened in anticipation of the Viking orbiter-lander, which would provide the best answer for a generation.[10]

With the flight of Mariner 10, the last of the series, in 1973 to 1975, JPL engineered the first visit to the perplexing world of extremes, Mercury. Because of its proximity to the sun, Mercury is exceptionally difficult to study from Earth. Telescopes reveal "only a few vague markings." Such elementary information as the planet's rate of rotation continued to be disputed into the 1960s. Mercury thus ranked as an obvious candidate for exploration by spacecraft. But the launch energy required—almost as much as for a trip to Jupiter—put Mercury beyond Mariner's normal reach. In 1973 and 1974, however, celestial alignments made possible a gravity assist from Venus. A lesser version of JPL's Grand Tour fantasy, this "exquisite celestial billiards shot" used the slingshot effect of a close passage of Venus to bend the spacecraft's trajectory toward the orbit of Mercury. Mariner 10 therefore registered three firsts; besides making the initial visit to Mercury, the mission was the first to visit two planets and to use the gravity-assist technique.[11]

Mariner 10 was significant also for a managerial advance—what was probably the most effective cost management of any major NASA space project to that date. The 1973 Mariner budget totaled $98 million, which was by space program standards very tight. (Some estimates for the project ran as high as $146 million.) Mariner Mars 69 had cost $126.9 million, Mariner Mars 71 $133.5 million; but if the rapid inflation of the early 1970s were taken into account, Mariner 10's budget was actually about 50 percent lower than the two Mars predecessors. NASA insisted that the $98 million could not be exceeded. If a cost overrun loomed, performance capabilities should be cut back to stay within the budget. The agency had never imposed a similar cost discipline. John R. Biggs, a senior official in NASA's space science divisions, and Walter J. Downhower, a senior engineer at JPL, observed that this cost attitude was "the more unusual since NASA had previously stressed technical performance and schedule requirements over cost as a discipline." Prominent space administrators rarely made such a revealing admission, for it tended to confirm a frequent criticism of the space program. NASA officials prided themselves on their ability to build high performance systems to meet deadlines, but they tended to overlook the huge resources they employed to bring about these managerial successes. Only in the late 1960s when NASA faced a budget crunch did cost become an object of discipline, and the scientific program bore the brunt of its first demonstration.[12]

Significantly, the new attitude toward cost did not degrade performance but may even have enhanced it. The Mariner 10 team managed to produce a spacecraft with substantially greater capabilities than anticipated. The JPL final report ranked this achievement second only to the successful mission in significance. Some problems developed during the flight, but, as Biggs and Downhower pointed out, they did not seem to be the result of the cost regimen.[13]

The successful blending of cost and performance goals could be credited to several factors. First, a long period of planning. Although JPL had the most experience in complex planetary missions, the Goddard Space Flight Center proposed an alternative design concept. The competition between the two centers forced JPL to work out an unusually thorough conceptual design. Once JPL won authorization for the project, the schedule called for a longer-than-usual period of planning before major contracts were let. Biggs and Downhower believed that this approach, "unprecedented in launch-critical planetary programs, may have been the single most important factor in meeting cost goals." The postponement of contracts alarmed some people, who feared the schedule was being shaved too close. But the admittedly greater risks were offset by the more detailed design and better planning of the spacecraft fabrication. "The greatest number of people worked on the project for the shortest period of time," Biggs and Downhower wrote. The time required for fabrication and testing and spacecraft assembly was about the same as for Mariners 69 and 71—sixteen or seventeen months in each case. The system design period, however, was cut from seventeen months for the 1969 Mariner to fourteen months for the 1971 Mariner to just eleven months for the 1973 Mariner. Biggs and Downhower proposed an axiom: "The shorter the schedule, the less the cost."[14]

The planning, in turn, benefited from a second factor: high inheritability from previous Mariners. The development plan emphasized "maximum use of existing designs, hardware, and software"; in this way perhaps 50 percent of design and development costs and 15 percent of hardware costs was saved. The relatively low level of innovation made it easier to turn the project over to industry. Boeing was selected as systems contractor over three competitors. Boeing operated under a cost-plus-award-fee contract, which contained strong cost incentives accompanied by a process of evaluation and award. A particularly noteworthy aspect of the contract was its attempt to deal with overhead costs, one of the thorniest problems in systems contracting. The contract included a negotiated ceiling on overhead, but because of Boeing's effective management, the company's overhead costs did not scrape the ceiling.[15]

Third, all parties were imbued with the cost doctrine. "Do only the essential" became the watchword. A "single thread" concept was adopted. Choices were analyzed and one selected for development, in contrast to earlier projects where costly parallel developments might be carried on. Changes were minimized. JPL had to learn restraint. It monitored construction of the scientific instruments "only at the interface level." The Pasadenans no longer reached back into the scientific laboratory to redesign equipment that met tests for airworthiness. Management meetings sought to instill a new cost consciousness; attitudes were augmented by incentives and contract requirements.[16]

Some changes from previous Mariners proved necessary, of course, chiefly because the Mercury flight took it nearer the sun than any previous spacecraft. Mariner 10 sported a foldable sunshade, made from a Teflon-coated, glass-fiber fabric known as beta cloth, which billowed open to protect the spacecraft. The craft's solar panels could be turned so that the maximum temperature of the solar cells never went above about 115°C (239°F). Thermal blankets and surface coatings were used extensively throughout the craft. In fact the insulation proved to be almost too good. The temperature of the television cameras dropped so low during flight that engineers and scientists feared the quality of pictures might be degraded. But when they tried to warm the cameras from the spacecraft, they found that the cameras were so well protected from heat that they simply had to endure the low temperatures. Fortunately, picture quality did not suffer from the cold. The only real failure of the scientific mission occurred when the protective door on the plasma detector failed to open completely and the plasma experiment remained partially inoperative.[17]

On November 3, 1973, the first multiplanet and cost-disciplined spacecraft blasted off. As Mariner 10 swung past Venus, about 500 kilometers above the surface, it returned significant data on the nature, composition, and circulation of the planet's upper atmosphere. But this was a secondary objective. The gravity-assist maneuver worked, changing the spacecraft velocity by more than a kilometer per second. Parasol unfurled, the new planetary belle made three flybys of Mercury. The spacecraft encountered more than its share of malfunctions. Ever-troublesome Canopus was lost again and then recovered. Mysterious malfunctions wasted some of the critically short supply of attitude-control gas. At one point JPL controllers had to interrupt the German Helios tracking because they needed access to a big antenna. But Mariner 10 survived these anomalies, and a treasure house of data streamed to Earth.[18]

Taken together the data made for a surprising planetary paradox. Mariner 10 confirmed and refined Earth-based radar measurements of Mercury's gross characteristics. They suggested a planet similar to Earth. The spacecraft's radio occultations confirmed the planet's diameter at 4,878 kilometers, or about three-eighths the mean diameter of Earth. Scientists made a more precise measurement of the planet's mass by analyzing Mercury's attraction on the motion of the spacecraft, which was tracked by Mariner's range-Doppler signals. The mass of the planet registered about half that of Earth. This meant that Mercury has an unexpectedly high mean density, just a little less than that of Earth. Since the red sphere is little compressed, it ranks as the intrinsically densest planet. The relatively high mean density suggests that Mercury has an interior iron core, which appears to extend for approximately 1,800 kilometers, or about 75 percent of the planet's radius. The silicate mantle "floating" on top would then be only about 600 kilometers deep. Mariner 10 indirectly confirmed the presence of the iron core when measurements from a magnetometer revealed a dipole magnetic field, which is much stronger than those of the moon, Venus, or Mars, but much weaker than Earth's.[19]

The discovery of the magnetic field was "completely unexpected and very exciting," said James A. Dunne and Eric Burgess. Clearly of internal origin, the field gave rise to two competing theories. One held that it was presently generated, the other that it was "a relic of a previous field." Both interpretations had major problems, however, and fed a growing scientific debate over the formation of Mercury and what the planet indicated about the solar system.[20]

In contrast to data that suggested similarities to Earth, Mariner 10's pictures showed that the surface resembled the moon's. The spacecraft's 2,300 visual images covered about half the surface and provided "really our first 'solid' information about Mercury's surface," wrote Harvard astronomer Fred L. Whipple. "We may conclude that Mercury is covered with fine soil, compacting with depth, as should occur on an airless body whose upper layers have been gardened by impact cratering for some three or four aeons." The small planet seemed to have experienced the same sequence of events as the moon: "a period of early heavy bombardment," which formed huge basins, and then was followed by "widespread volcanism," which was detectable in the plains materials. Although Mercury exhibited a strong chemical similarity to the moon, its greater density suggested that it must be a chemically differentiated planet. Three bodies—the moon, Mars, and now Mercury—displayed large basins but striking other differences. The Mercury data provided new fuel for the blazing debates over the origins of the terrestrial planets.[21]

Mariner also provided additional evidence of Mercury's very harsh environment. Analyzing its data, scientists determined that the planet has a tenuous atmosphere, composed largely of helium. Earth-based calculation of Mercury's extreme heat was borne out. During the long day—equal to 176 Earth days—the temperature rises to 430°C near the subsolar point, hot enough to melt tin, lead, and even zinc. Mariner recorded the first night temperature, −173°C, making the surface of Mercury almost as cold as the moon's. With a temperature variation of 600 degrees, Mercury was truly a planet of extremes.[22]

Mariner 10 plucked Mercury from obscurity. This single flight had brought forth a transformation in the state of knowledge about Mercury comparable to the several Mariner missions to Mars. On a relatively lean budget, Mariner 10 painted an object lesson in how to use spacecraft to advance understanding beyond Earth-based observation. "We have viewed a new world," said Bruce Murray. "Mariner 10's long reach across space has magnified our view of Mercury's surface five-thousandfold and transported us back in time to the very formation of the terrestrial planets."[23]

Mariner 10 completed JPL's reconnaissance of the inner solar system and closed out the Mariner series. The technological advance could be measured in many ways. Mariners 1 through 5 had managed a mass of 200 to 260 kilograms, Mariner 10 of 630 kilograms; the payload had risen from the range of 15 to 27 kilograms on the first five to 70 kilograms on the last two. The spacecraft's solar power jumped from 150 to 200 watts on the first half to 505 on Mariner 10. The telemetry rate underwent a veritable explosion, from 8⅓ bits per second to 22,000–118,000 per second. The television pictures returned were originally numbered in the tens, eventually in the thousands, and they were increasingly returned in real time instead of recorded for later playback. Guidance, once problematic, was assuming the accuracy of William Tell (see figure 4). In 1962 and 1964 Venus and Mars flybys still struck some people as requiring luck's helping hand; by 1973 and 1974, orbits of other planets and even gravity-assist trajectories were reliable operations.[24]

These technological feats made possible a vast increase in knowledge of the solar system. Whatever illusions about Venus—"this hellhole of a planet," in Sagan's words—as the Earth's twin had been incinerated.[25] Bare-

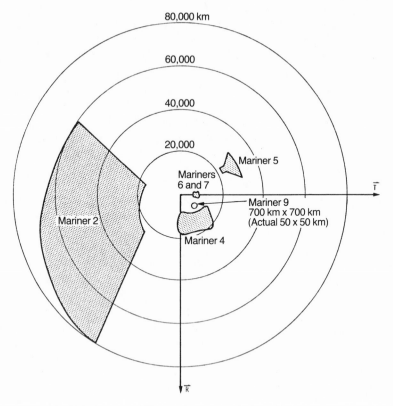

4. Relative size of interplanetary mission aiming zones.

ly known Mercury had been thrust into the center of the debate over the origins of the solar system. But it was ever-alluring Mars which attracted the most attention, and all eyes turned to Viking.

When the money ran out for the giant Voyager in 1967, NASA found an alternative Mars lander project in Viking. This combined orbiter-lander for 1973 had a projected bargain-basement price tag of $364 million. Congress bought the project in 1968. But it soon became apparent that NASA had either underestimated the cost of what it wanted to do or had shaded its estimates to win congressional authorization, or both. In any event a more precise project definition in 1970 returned a cost estimate of $750 million. Opposition was rising in the scientific community where a significant segment thought that kind of money would produce greater returns if parceled out among several smaller missions. Under pressure from the Office of

Management and Budget, NASA administrator James C. Fletcher ordered
Viking stretched out from 1973 to 1975.[26]

The stretch-out had mixed results. On the one hand, it added to the
project's cost. On the other, it made for a more sophisticated mission in the
end, even though 1975 was a more difficult opportunity than 1973 because
Mars was farther away. Indeed, the postponement may have been a godsend, for the tighter schedule made the 1973 mission considerably riskier.
When Representative James Symington, Jr., of Missouri, inquired whether
NASA could have flown in 1973, Edgar Cortright confessed: "We often ask
ourselves that question, Mr. Chairman, and the answer we come up with is,
we think we could have flown a mission in 1973 . . . but it would have been
tight, very tight." These retrospective assessments would seem to have vindicated those scientists and engineers who doubted that "an ultimate Voyager"
could or should have been built for the early 1970s.[27]

JPL's role in Viking was much curtailed from Voyager. The laboratory
was limited to the design and fabrication of the orbiter and mission support
with the Deep Space Network. By the late 1960s NASA had many mouths to
feed and a smaller purse. The systems management contract went to
NASA's Langley Research Center in Virginia. The most glamorous part of
the mission, the lander, was assigned to an aerospace firm, Martin Marietta,
which won a competition with Boeing and McDonnell-Douglas. JPL's limited role in its special domain—planetary exploration—forecast an increasingly uncertain future for the institution.[28]

Within the limits of its Viking assignment, however, JPL performed nobly.
The orbiter proved to have the best cost record of any portion of the project.
Despite inflation and increased performance, the laboratory managed to cut
the cost of the orbiter from an estimated $124 million in 1970 to $103 million
or approximately 17 percent. The lander, by contrast, rose in cost by more
than 50 percent, from $360 million in 1970 to $545 million. The lander
called for more advances in the state of the art than did the orbiter, but this
represented a significant cost overrun, particularly in view of the claims that
industry and NASA headquarters made for business efficiency. Support
costs rose slightly, from $133 million in 1970 to $138 million. Taken together, the components which were largely JPL's responsibility, the orbiter
and support, declined from $257 million in 1970 to $241 million. Had the
lander system been managed in similar fashion, the project would have come
in somewhat under the $750-million figure instead of gliding upward to the
$1-billion range.[29]

The Pasadenans were helped greatly by inheritability from Mariner. But
while the orbiter was from the same family as the Mariners, it had its own
distinct personal traits. JPL engineers had hoped that the orbiter could be

basically a scaled-up version of Mariner. The orbiter's different functions, however, dictated some fairly important modifications from the design for a flyby. Since the lander hibernated through the ten-month flight to the Martian neighborhood, the orbiter provided the spacecraft stabilization, telemetry, and command links with Earth, and electrical power for the lander. Near Mars the orbiter's engine fired to slow the spacecraft enough for it to be captured and to initiate the process of orbiting the planet in search of a suitable landing site. Once that was located, the automatic lander went through its separation and entry phases and settled on the surface. During the descent the orbiter provided the only communication link with Earth, and after the landing the orbiter continued to relay most of the lander data to the Deep Space Network. Then the orbiter went on with its three experiments—television mapping, atmospheric water detection, and infrared thermal mapping.[30]

The most obvious design change these functions made necessary was a tripling of the propellant capacity in order to decelerate the spacecraft. Viking also needed more solar power; 15 square meters of its panels provided 620 watts compared with 505 watts for Mariner 10. Because the orbiter had to provide contiguous coverage of a landing site, it snapped pictures on a 4.5-second cycle, compared to Mariner's 42-second cycle. Viking orbiter also boasted an upgraded tape recording system so that it could handle the vast discrepancy between the rapid acquisition of data and the slower transmission to Earth. Improved communications and computer functions were also included. Within the familiar but now larger X-shaped silhouette and hexagonal core, JPL built a spacecraft weighing 2,325 kilograms, contrasted with Mariner 10's 630 kilograms.[31]

Viking 1 was launched on August 20, 1975, its identical twin on September 9, 1975. Inserted into Martian orbit on June 19, 1976, the first Viking began searching for a suitable landing site in the Chryse Planitia, the Plains of Gold. This area seemed to satisfy the demand for a spot that was both a live prospect for biological findings and smooth and hard enough for safe landing. The orbiter's visual imaging, combined with Earth-based radar observations, showed the first choice to be of great scientific interest but too ambiguous as a landing field. And so mission control ordered the spacecraft to "walk" westward in search of a better site. "It seemed as if we were doomed to some sort of orbital purgatory," said Thomas A. Mutch of Brown University, leader of the lander imaging team. But finally, a month after Viking 1 achieved orbit about Mars, the project manager concluded that a new site on the Chryse plain was suitable. The relatively smooth area was punctuated by low ridges, but these formations resembled ridges found in the maria regions of the moon, where Surveyor 5 had landed safely.[32]

Accordingly, on July 19, 1976, the lander was commanded to start going through its warm-ups. At 1:15 the next morning (Pasadena time) the lander separated from the orbiter and began its descent to the surface, in the process acquiring much new data on the atmosphere. If all went well the lander settled to the surface shortly before 5 A.M. with a small jolt—about like the jolt a person receives in jumping off a foot-high stool on Earth. But since it took the lander's signal about twenty minutes to traverse the 360-million kilometers from Mars to Earth, the capacity throng at the von Kár-mán auditorium could only speculate nervously. By 5 A.M. the room was engulfed in an "overwhelming silence." Mission control announced each stage in the flat, objective, yet emotion-laden voice which had become famil-iar to observers of the space program.

5:05 A.M.   "400,000 feet."
5:09 A.M.   "74,000 feet."
5:11:43 A.M. "2,600 feet."
5:12:07 A.M. "Touchdown. We have touchdown."

The crowd erupted with cheers, applause, handshakes, embraces. But re-membering Ranger, mission controllers knew the elation was premature. The moment for celebration was at least forty minutes away, when the first picture from the surface would appear. Finally at 5:54 A.M. the first narrow slivers of light flickered in the blankness of the television monitor. The picture grew. Rocks and sand could be made out, and then the spacecraft's footpads, "a symbolic artifact that stamps our accomplishment with the sign of reality," said Mutch.[33]

The lander continued to beam back spectacular pictures via the orbiter. The reddish-hued, rock-strewn plain looked almost like a landscape of the American Southwest. Some rocks resembled the lava produced by volcanoes on Earth; sand dunes appeared in some spots. The second lander settled on a site in the Plains of Utopia which was more rolling but less varied than at Chryse. From the photographs of marks, trenches, and clods on the ground, scientists concluded that Martian soil is "about as firm as good farming soil on Earth."[34]

The greatest attention was attracted to the biological experiments which would make the long-awaited analysis in the pursuit of extraterrestrial life. All three—the pyrolytic, gas exchange, and labeled release experiments—yielded active results. But most scientists concluded that the results were explicable in chemical terms and did not substantiate biological hopes. In-terestingly, the molecular analysis experiment, which was not specifically directed to the biological questions, drove one of the biggest nails in the biologists' coffin. This experiment revealed that, although quantities of water were evolved in the analysis of the soil samples, no evidence of organic compounds indigenous to the samples could be found. As the scene of analysis shifted to laboratories on Earth, some scientists still strained for a biological explanation—proving a negative is always difficult. Some previously hopeful analysts admitted that they had given up on the Martian deserts as abodes of life, but, drawing on the evidence of an earlier abundance of water, they were loath to close the door on the "oases" or the depths of the great canyons.[35]

Norman Horowitz of Caltech, one of the principal biology investigators, confessed that the results were "undeniably disappointing" but pointed out that they had to be faced squarely. Viking had, if anything, decreased the chances of finding life on Mars. It was, in that sense, a confirmatory mission rather than a revolutionary one.[36]

Although largely eclipsed by the lander, JPL's orbiter continued methodically to go about its rounds. The orbiter snapped nearly 52,000 pictures, more than mission planners ever dreamed possible. They covered 97 percent of the Martian surface, at a resolution of 1,000 feet; this promised maps with several times the detail of Mariner 9. Among the orbiter's last sequence were color views of Tharsis Ridge, which contains three huge volcanoes with an average elevation of 17 kilometers, as well as two smaller ones. The atmospheric water detector found that water vapor content, nearly zero near the south (winter) polar cap, increased dramatically in the northern (summer) hemisphere. The total quantity of water vapor in the Martian atmosphere appeared to remain constant at about 1.3 cubic kilometers of water, but the issue of seasonal water-vapor migration remained moot. The orbiter's infrared thermal mapper provided more complete and more accurate temperatures; the mean temperature of Mars at the surface is $-23°C$ compared with $22°C$ for Earth. This type of data, combined with similar evidence from the lander, was less glamorous than the search for microbes, but they also made a major contribution to planetary understanding.[37]

Indeed, unmanned spacecraft exploration of the terrestrial planets, capped by Viking, had produced an intellectual revolution. Understanding of Earth, its geological history and its relationship to the rest of the solar system, was transformed in little more than a decade. Limited to Earth-based observations, planetary studies had been moribund. Now, thanks to a technological breakthrough, the amount of data on the planets almost exceeded the capacity of theory to make sense of it. The dramatic turnabout in the comprehension of Mars was one of the best indices of the change. Before the space age, Mars had seemed similar to Earth. Comparable seasonal patterns and evidence of water spawned optimistic theories. But virtually every bit of evidence for similarity came to be disproved by the Mariners and Viking. The comparable spin rates and obliquity turned out to be "completely fortuitous." "The brilliant white caps that migrate seasonally" were composed not of water ice but carbon dioxide. Early Martian oceans had been considered possible, but the survival of moonlike craters rendered them impossible for at least the past three or four billion years. The Martian atmosphere was thought to be similar to Earth's, but in fact it is extremely thin—only 0.5 percent of Earth's. The seasonal variations of light and dark markings are not a cycle of plant life but are caused by dust storms.[38]

More generally the evidence from spacecraft exploration contributed to a major shift in the theory of planetary origins, "from a cold birth to a hot one." Older notions held that the planets had accumulated while cold and that they were homogeneous, becoming differentiated later. Space-age theory turned that on its head. Now it is believed that the planets accumulated while hot and that their differentiation occurred during the accretion period. Thus planets' internal temperatures have been gradually cooling throughout geological time rather than registering an increase. Instead of Earth's geologic history being studied in isolation, scientists have gained a new appreciation of its relationship to the other planets of the inner solar system. As Murray, Malin, and Greeley put it: "New insights are developing that link Earth, including the very atoms that compose its sentient beings, with the origin and evolution of those other four planets . . . [in] a common planetary environmental history."[39] This intellectual revolution represented the most profound achievement of the space program and provided its most cogent rationale.

The present reconnaissance of the inner solar system drew to a close in mid-August 1980 as Viking 1's orbiter literally ran out of gas. (Its sister ship, plagued by a gas leak, had gone dead in 1978.) JPL had promised an orbiter that would operate for at least ninety days after insertion into Martian orbit, but Viking 1's orbiter stayed alive for four years. Since 1978 the orbiter had been running on little more than fumes, and finally the last bits of attitude-control gas ran out. On its 1,489th trip around Mars, the orbiter was commanded to cease operations. Its electrical system shut down, no longer steerable, the orbiter sinks slowly until it crashes into the Martian surface sometime after the year 2019.[40]

For JPL the Viking project had been bittersweet. The laboratory had to content itself with the orbiter and with mission support. Both were important, of course. But someone else was doing the "final far-out things" on the Martian surface. What was more, there was a disturbing parallel between the winding down of Viking and the American planetary space program. "This space effort, such a conspicuously successful part of American science for the last two decades, is now beginning to drop toward the 'E' mark on its gauge of programs and funds," observed George Alexander, the *Los Angeles Times* science writer. "Like Viking Orbiter 1 giving out the last of its stabilizing helium and nitrogen gases in little puffs, the U.S. planetary program is now putting out the few remaining bursts in its inventory of deep-space projects." This outcome was ironic; now that the technology was fully in hand, there seemed little inclination to use it. The cool professionals were "not unmoved" at the orbiter's end, for they were witnessing one of the milestones of a vanishing era. As Bruce Murray said sadly, planetary exploration was reaching "the end of the beginning."[41]

The decline of the planetary program, which had been JPL's raison d'être, imperiled the laboratory's future. NASA's budget woes brought a series of cutbacks at JPL through the early 1970s. The laboratory's budget peaked at $247 million in 1967 and then dropped precipitously to $144 million in fiscal year 1969. (This drop did not hurt quite so much as the stark figures suggested, since a large percentage of the budget went to outside procurement. Total employees gradually fell by about 12 percent. The budget nonetheless served as an indicator of declining activity.) For fiscal years 1972 through 1975 the budget reached an average of $210 million annually. Only in fiscal year 1976 did the overall obligation surpass the 1967 record, at $257 million; but ten years of inflation left the budget still significantly below the 1967 peak in real terms.[42]

The decline in flight projects accounted for most of the drop. At its peak in the mid-1960s JPL flight projects took up about two-thirds of the laboratory's activity. Thereafter a gradual decline set in, which was altered only temporarily by Viking. By 1976, flight projects accounted for about half of JPL's personnel time and, by 1980, only about 40 percent. What was more, there seemed to be no end in sight to the downward curve. During this time two other space functions held fairly steady; these were technology and space program development, and telecommunications and data acquisitions, which had broader support missions than JPL's immediate flight projects. The one growth item on the laboratory's budget charts was the civil systems division, the merest sliver in 1967 but a sizable wedge composing 18 percent of the $277-million budget ten years later. Perceived institutional necessity more than a clear vision of program coherence pushed JPL to diversify. Without civil systems the laboratory would have faced a wrenching retrenchment or perhaps partial funding by the military.[43]

JPL's diversification paralleled NASA efforts to brake its descent by stressing the space program's spin-offs. The more questioning that arose about the value of NASA programs, the more the agency stressed technology transfer. Instead of justifying the space program on its own terms, its advocates stressed its side effects. Once this process began, virtually any technological undertaking could be justified through its by-products. Robert Seamans even found a long list of spin-offs to excuse the notorious Mohole, a project to drill through the Earth's crust which was abandoned as an expensive boondoggle after $125 million had been spent. But contrary to

NASA's assertions, the spin-offs were dubious. Raymond A. Bauer concluded that the agency was not able to exert much influence over the transfer of space technology in part because NASA thought in terms of discrete, countable items that could be passed directly to industry. In reality, he said, the process was much more complex. T. Keith Glennan, NASA's first administrator, dismissed the spin-off argument as having "little substance." "Certainly, there is nothing to justify the tremendous expenditures from which some of these minor industrial applications have been derived," he said.[44]

A related second-order defense was what might be termed the "management magnificence" notion. NASA, particularly Webb, advanced this argument frequently. The actual project might be dubious, but the managerial techniques at least were transferable. If its management processes could be put to use on other tasks, Apollo would be "a splendid bargain," said *Fortune*. "This is potentially the most powerful tool in man's history."[45]

These attempts to shore up NASA's defenses left Senator William Proxmire of Wisconsin bemused. "One would think that the purpose of the space program is primarily to provide fallout," said the baldish bestower of the golden fleece. "We could spend $5 billion on a cure for baldness—and sometimes I wish we would—I am sure there would be a great deal of fallout from that; but it seems to me that the program should stand on its own feet."[46]

Undaunted JPL moved into the civil systems field. William Pickering wanted to show that the $40-billion space program had produced things that would "impact the seething ghetto" at home not just leave "a few corrugated footprints near Hadley Rille." The JPL director admitted that "technologists" did not understand politics, but they should nonetheless seize the initiative. Systems management teams should be transferred "bodily" to government agencies. There the technologist would "clearly identify a problem, a need for his product, and then attempt to educate the decision makers into accepting his solution." He concluded: "We must learn to satisfy the human condition with technological means."[47] In other words, social problems were essentially engineering problems.

But technology's greatest contribution could be realized only if it was designed to foster social change rather than merely reinforce existing power relationships in society. The troubled field of urban transportation serves as an example. Lack of technology was not the problem. The urban transportation tangle has more to do with such nontechnological factors as inefficient land use, energy inefficiency, unequal access to transportation depending on one's location in the social structure, ineffective planning, and deterioration of existing public transportation systems. Moreover, some of these problems were exacerbated by recent technological developments, such as the automobile. Urban transportation was primarily a political problem having to do with levels of funding, the impact of taxation on various sectors of society, and the economic interests served by particular modes of transportation. Technology would meet the most pressing problems of urban transportation only if the political process directed it toward the goal of widespread equality of access to transportation. But the space program's technology and systems management, which was centralized and capital-intensive, failed to address the truly important questions of urban transportation.

The problems of transferring aerospace technology to the civilian sector surfaced dramatically in one of JPL's first major civil systems activities, the Morgantown, West Virginia, Personal Rapid Transit (PRT) project. The laboratory served as the systems manager for the project, which was funded by the Urban Mass Transportation Administration. PRT was designed to combine the advantages of fixed guideway transit systems and the flexibility of automobiles. Some one hundred computer-controlled small vehicles would move over an extensive network of elevated guideways and then deliver passengers close to their destinations by going "off-line." The Morgantown project had many of the hallmarks of space technology development: it was complex, costly, capital-intensive, and subjected to a tight development schedule. Whatever the validity of the concept, PRT bogged down in cost overruns several times the original estimates and a development schedule several years longer than promised. JPL bailed out in frustration and desperation once the initial development was on the track. But the Morgantown project gained notoriety in urban transportation literature as "overdesigned, overbuilt, and overpriced." Finally in operation, PRT worked well. But its high cost, particularly for the "off-line" capability, made it one of a kind.[48]

A different approach to technology diffusion, but with at best ambiguous results, characterized JPL's California Four Cities program, a pilot project in aerospace-to-urban technology application. A senior engineer from each of four aerospace companies was detailed to one of four cities—Anaheim, Fresno, Pasadena, and San Jose—to serve as a science and technology adviser. Each engineer studied the process of technology transfer, attempted to acquaint the city governments with new technologies, and watched for new technological opportunities; in turn the engineer gained greater awareness of local government problems. A major objective also was to look for new market opportunities for their firms. The results were ambiguous. The most tangible benefit came in the cities' adoption of some software and managerial techniques, such as "management by objectives." The latter was scarcely dependent on aerospace managers, however, since a wide variety of institutions were experimenting with such techniques by the 1970s.[49]

The negative findings were perhaps more significant and, had they received more attention, might have tempered expectations about aerospace civil systems applications. The JPL report on the project concluded that "aerospace hardware technology found little application." The companies discovered there was no market to go after. One commercial product emerged—Probeye, an infrared viewer that helped firemen see through smoke. But "company benefits, beyond generalized market research, were limited." The engineers and city officials involved in the four-cities project all attested to enhanced mutual understanding, and few would object to this sort of cross-cultural exchange. But the decidedly ambiguous results of the project cast doubt on the technology transfer argument the space establishment was selling.[50]

If the grander dreams of technology transfer dimmed, JPL nonetheless found ample scope for the application of its talents in hardware development for civil systems. One of its main areas of work was in what was loosely grouped as "public safety." As the California Four Cities report observed, civilian activities most related to military operations had been especially receptive to the adoption of federally funded military and aerospace research and development techniques and hardware. "Urban law enforcement has seen the greatest technical advance in this period, with improvements including aviation support, communications, tactical training, and weaponry," the report noted. "Aspects of this area of transfer have proved controversial at the very least."[51]

Despite such controversy, JPL found its technology readily adaptable to "public safety" applications. This effort had two focuses in the early 1970s. The laboratory designed visual aid systems to make helicopter surveillance by the Los Angeles Police Department more effective. By day, observers could use a magnified full-color display; by night, an infrared search light coupled to an image intensifier. Surveillance in schools also received space-age technology as JPL designed such items as pocket-size devices which teachers could use to summon help in the event of emergencies. Tested in Pasadena and Sacramento high schools, the system drew strong endorsements from school officials for its use in warning of potential disorders. Whatever their beneficial results, these systems also demonstrated how aerospace technology could be used to heighten surveillance of citizens and to increase centralized control.[52]

Originally sponsored mostly by NASA, JPL's medical activities soon attracted the bulk of their funding from medical sources. The laboratory's approach blended with the dominant trend of post–World War II American medicine with its application of high technology to catastrophic disease, particularly cancer and heart-related illnesses. Several studies examined the occlusion of vital arteries. In one a miniature force transducer, which had been developed for solid-propellant stress analysis, was modified for implantation in the myocardium during in vivo animal tests. Other aerospace technologies adapted to medical uses included clean room techniques to reduce operating-room contamination and mass spectrometry and image processing devices for diagnosis.[53]

JPL also branched out into environmental and then energy work as those issues attracted funding in the 1970s. The laboratory developed new techniques of wastewater purification and sophisticated mapping techniques for natural resources and sources of pollution. Solar energy seemed a logical focus for JPL because of its experience with solar-powered spacecraft functions. Set up in early 1975 under Energy Research and Development Administration sponsorship, the Low-cost Silicon Solar Array (LSSA) Project quickly became the largest single civil systems effort. LSSA issued more than eighty contracts for research, development, and production and carried out a variety of theoretical studies and performance tests at JPL. The project's goal was to achieve large national production of silicon solar array modules at greatly reduced cost. Related energy activities included work on solar-thermal-electric power systems for small communities and solar systems for water heating. Solar energy was probably the most promising civil systems activity, but it was ominously vulnerable to budget cuts under the Reagan administration.[54]

JPL's experience in civil systems thus seemed to undermine rather than strengthen the case for civilian spin-offs from the space program. The suspicion grew that most of the applications from space were military. JPL's civil systems effort was a diffuse collection of relatively small projects which had veered from transportation to environment to energy as federal funding fashions changed. When civil systems were threatened in the 1980s, technology transfer boomed, but in the direction of the military. Civil systems, like the hard times on which flight projects had fallen, underscored the institutional crisis that beset JPL at the close of its fourth decade.

JPL's institutional malaise aroused continuing concern at parent Caltech. Throughout the 1960s a substantial body of opinion among Institute faculty members held that the campus should divest itself of JPL. During the Ranger agony in early 1962 two extraordinary faculty discussion groups were convened to explore the situation. But the decisions to initiate and to continue campus management of the laboratory had been made by the administration with narrow faculty consultation. DuBridge never wavered in his belief the affiliation should continue. When he left in 1969 to become Nixon's science adviser, however, one of the main institutional supporters of the connection was gone. His successor was Harold Brown, a physicist turned science administrator whose background symbolized the intertwined relationship between big science and the national security state. Brown had run the Livermore Laboratory, where the hydrogen bomb was developed. Then he became the air force's science chief and, from 1965 to 1969, secretary of the air force. After eight years at Caltech, where he was much less of a presence than his predecessor, Brown resigned to serve as Jimmy Carter's secretary of defense.[55]

The changeover from DuBridge to Brown, taking place against the backdrop of ferment in higher education generally, made early 1969 an appropriate time for Caltech to conduct an institutional self-study. The relationship with JPL figured prominently in the "aims and goals study" conducted by an ad hoc faculty committee. They noted that the faculty's animosity toward JPL had cooled with the laboratory's successes. But "it has certainly not been replaced by a faculty-wide, warm, paternal feeling toward JPL," the committee said. The group identified three "well defined negative feelings" on the part of the faculty. First, they feared that Caltech was hurt in the competition for research dollars because funding agencies lumped the JPL budget with the campus's. Second, they thought CIT scientists might be at a disadvantage because "JPL (and/or NASA) appears to be overcompensating for nonexistent favoritism." Third, they worried that as the laboratory ventured into new fields, particularly civil systems, the Institute's reputation might suffer.[56]

There appeared to be some merit in the third anxiety, for the general public tended to conflate JPL and Caltech. The first two objections seemed illusory, however; CIT remained awash in research dollars, and Institute scientists were well represented as experimenters in JPL flight projects. Perhaps most serious was the intangible but real concern that JPL might compromise what the committee saw as Caltech's real mission—teaching and pure research. The panel saw few benefits in campus management. Indeed, it concluded that "most of the alleged advantages are contentious or *are not contingent upon Caltech actually running JPL, but rather that JPL be in the immediate vicinity of Caltech.*" Interestingly, the study skirted discussion of the Institute's management fee. (Disregard of institutional finance is one way faculties retain their self-esteem and illusions of innocence.)[57]

The study concluded that continuation of the CIT-JPL link should be reviewed. Although this was not an explicit call for severance, the negative tone was unmistakable. Brown responded by creating a special committee, chaired by Norman Brooks, professor of civil engineering, to study the CIT-JPL relationship. Despite considerable sentiment for divorce, the committee eventually decided that the relationship should be maintained. Two old arguments—Caltech's fee and the difficulty of disengagement—remained strong. But a new point also surfaced: The 1968 memorandum of agreement between Caltech and NASA had eased tensions and possibly opened the door to more fruitful cooperation between the laboratory and the campus.[58]

The Brooks report devoted much of its attention to ways that interaction could be fostered in the context of JPL's continuing planetary program and its accelerating diversification. The study's key assumption was that Caltech management made sense only so long as the laboratory's "scope and style of work" was appropriate to a university affiliation and so long as "meaningful interactions with the campus exist." This suggested that the substance of JPL's work needed clarification through heightened campus involvement. The report chided JPL management for diversifying simply as a means of maintaining institutional size in the face of cuts in space program funding. As a result JPL's activities outside space lacked a focus. There was a plethora of small, sometimes unrelated projects, and all too often the laboratory had moved into areas, especially civil systems, where its engineers had little expertise. To correct these problems, the Brooks committee argued, "diversification . . . should proceed only in search of new missions, or to fill a need for interactions with the university community." The laboratory needed to broaden its staff, particularly with social scientists, for its civil systems work. In place of the haphazard diversification, JPL should concentrate on a few missions at a time; they should be clearly related to its capabilities, at the forefront of their fields, and of interest to campus faculty. The study emphasized: "Long-range planning for JPL must be part of the Institute's planning, with active involvement of faculty." An unexceptional recommendation, surely, except that little action of this sort had been tried.[59]

To encourage interaction with the campus, the Brooks committee proposed various procedural changes. All were geared toward more openness on the part of the laboratory. The report commended JPL for having largely abandoned classified work. In 1958 some 62 percent of its publications were classified, in 1970 less than 1 percent; the one remaining classified project was being phased out. All JPL work should be unclassified, the report said, "except for highly unusual cases of national urgency." Procedures to facilitate Caltech students' work at JPL were suggested. And finally the committee recommended a change in a small but symbolic barrier to cooperation. Caltech faculty, like others, had to sign in and be verified by laboratory personnel before they could pass through visitor control. Henceforth, said the report, a Caltech faculty member should be able to enter the laboratory simply by showing the university identification card. The JPL hierarchy concurred and soon CIT professors could avoid the time-consuming and demeaning processing at visitor control along with vendors and other outside personnel.[60]

The committee had sketched a reasonable, even bland, plan to foster the interaction which everyone claimed to want but which nonetheless never quite materialized. "The Brooks report did not produce much of a response from either the JPL or the campus administration except for a few items that were more cosmetic than substantive," recalled economics professor Roger G. Noll, a member of the committee. "While it was easier for faculty and students to get onto the lab grounds, it was not any easier to affect lab policy, to find out what it was doing and why, or to engage in collaborative work between the campus and the lab."[61]

By 1975, however, business as usual no longer sufficed. The mid-1970s was as critical a period for the laboratory as any since the dark days of Ranger or the immediate post–World War II transition. The future of unmanned space exploration looked increasingly uncertain. After Viking the laboratory had only one flight project—the revamped Voyager, which, quite different from the earlier Mars project, aimed flybys at Jupiter and Saturn. JPL would also have a new director on April 1, 1976. William H. Pickering, who had served as director since 1954, and who had outlasted his detractors at NASA headquarters, would leave JPL upon reaching age 65, the Institute's mandatory retirement age for administrators. Pickering had been successful in forging a dynamic role for JPL in the space program and in attracting and molding a skilled technical team, in part because of the autonomy he allowed them. His mode of administration had been frustrating for NASA and at times may have left project organization too weak, but his belief that the health of the laboratory depended on strong technical disciplines was vindicated in the end by JPL's successes. But Pickering, like many other administrators of his generation, knew and operated best while missilery and space moved on a seemingly unending upward curve. When the curve turned downward, they were disheartened and ill-equipped to deal with the austerity of the 1970s.

Faced with the transition in the laboratory's program and directorship, Harold Brown convened a new committee in mid-1975 for yet another probe of the Caltech-JPL relationship. The distinguished twelve-member group, composed equally of CIT and JPL representatives, was chaired by Rochus Vogt, professor of physics. Its report was generally known as the "orange report," from its vivid orange covers, and JPL management referred to implementing its hard-hitting recommendations as "biting the orange."[62]

The Vogt committee returned to many of the themes of the Brooks report but with new intensity and lofty urgency. Although ostensibly a study of relations between the laboratory and the campus, the Vogt report focused much of its attention on JPL's internal affairs. It raised penetrating questions about the recent operation of the laboratory. The Vogt panel feared JPL was losing its technical preeminence. "At one time JPL was an undisputed leader in the fields in which it generally practiced," the report said.

In some areas, such as very-long telecommunications, this was still true. But in other fields "many authoritative individuals" believed JPL was lagging. Industry was considered ahead of the laboratory in advanced solid-state components and microcircuit technology. The NASA center and industry combinations had outstripped JPL in the design of atmospheric entry, spin-stabilized spacecraft and landing systems, and in some advanced mission studies and key scientific instruments. The committee attributed JPL's decline to increased contract monitoring as opposed to hands-on engineering, more conservatism in its undertakings, and less innovative engineering research. The decline of innovation at JPL, in turn, made the laboratory less interesting to the Caltech engineering division. This authoritative critique of JPL's engineering prowess was the most fundamental that could be directed at the laboratory, for, whatever managerial deficiencies JPL might admit, it always claimed technical preeminence.[63]

To compound the problems, the orange report criticized JPL for circumscribing the role of science. "Scientists at the Laboratory rarely have an opportunity to participate in mission planning, do not have well-defined roles and responsibilities, and are not accorded a status equal to that of their Campus counterparts," the committee found. Although JPL had some good scientists, a number of "first-rate scientists" had left "in frustration." By contrast, Goddard Space Flight Center, a civil service organization, was "highly attractive to scientists" and had built a scientific staff "comparable in many areas to the best university research groups." The consequences of JPL's inability, or unwillingness, to modify its structure to give scientists a truly important role came back to haunt the organization in this invidious comparison with Goddard, its chief rival inside NASA. Moreover, science's low profile at JPL was especially inhibiting to the promised interaction between the campus and laboratory. A strong scientific component would have been particularly useful in bridging the gap between the laboratory, which was primarily an engineering organization, and the campus, which was mainly scientific. The laboratory's scientific capability needed strengthening in all areas. "Nevertheless, the main objective should be to acquire international leadership in the scientific aspects of planetary exploration, at least for as long as this is the main mission of JPL," the report said. Among the institutional changes proposed was creation of the position of chief scientist, who would be the focal point for scientific activities at the laboratory. When that position was created in 1977, its first occupant was Vogt.[64]

The failure to achieve joint planning for space missions drew particular criticism. It was highly anomalous, as the report pointed out, that "the Campus, a leader in the space sciences, and JPL, the major technological contributor to lunar and planetary exploration, have not established effective methods of cooperation in handling strategy, tactics, and implementation of space missions." The experience of the Murray committee in 1965 lingered as an example of the barriers to planning, some of which were beyond JPL's control. The absence of Caltech assistance in the early stages of mission planning seemed particularly unfortunate. "That such a condition exists and has been allowed to exist is not justifiable." The orange report urged the formation of a joint mission-advisory group to advise JPL on both space science exploration and Earth-oriented programs.[65]

A related issue concerned JPL's diversification. Despite the Brooks report's recommendations, financial stability rather than program coherence continued to characterize the laboratory's approach. JPL ran certain risks as it moved away from its traditional focus on lunar and planetary exploration. (Even here, the orange report observed, JPL's leadership would have been significantly strengthened had it chosen to bring scientists into its program.) While the skills of laboratory personnel were relevant to other tasks than space, those talents seldom were sufficiently broad to insure success, particularly in civil systems. "In those instances where JPL's qualifications were deficient, the performance has not been up to Caltech standards." The laboratory therefore needed the campus's help, the committee believed. But in many cases the Institute's small faculty would be inadequate, and a broadening of staff would be required. These arguments applied with particular force to the energy field, where the report suggested a comprehensive effort to unite JPL and the several Caltech operations concerned with this problem. Although specific mechanisms were lacking, the committee clearly intended closer cooperation with the campus on diversification.[66]

In addition to these programmatic issues, the Vogt committee listed among its twenty recommendations various mechanisms to increase cooperation. They included such items as arrangements for postdoctoral appointments at JPL, several joint appointments with the campus, and some laboratory personnel teaching on campus. They also suggested that JPL professional staff be allowed to devote 10 percent of their workweek to their own research without having to charge it to a specific project or account. This minimal discretion, which many civil servants enjoyed, would enhance the research talents and professional standing of JPL personnel. Finally, the Vogt report strengthened the admonition to eschew classified research except in times of "universally recognized national emergency."[67]

The orange report was filed on April 2, 1976, a day after a member of the Vogt committee took over as the new director of JPL. He was Bruce Murray, aged 44, the distinguished geologist and frequent experimenter on JPL planetary missions. Murray kept intact the tradition of finding a director from Caltech. But unlike previous directors he came from a scientific division rather than the engineering division. He was a man of strong opinions about the value of planetary exploration and the way it should be carried out, and he was a sophisticated salesman for a scientific space program. He was also short on administrative experience. Before becoming director of JPL, his biggest administrative job had been running a campus geology project that employed six persons on a budget of $200,000 a year. But he could rely on Pickering's deputy director Charles Terhune, who continued to serve. Certainly Murray's JPL would not lack for direction. Murray was, in the words of the *New York Times*, "a tall, square-jawed man more comfortable giving orders than listening to advice [who] brought to the lab an aggressive—some would say abrasive—style of leadership." Committed to the increased interaction the Vogt report called for, Murray as a personal example spent part of each week at his campus office. Although implementation of some of the committee's recommendations would be difficult, they seemed to have their best chance with a committee member as director of the laboratory.[68]

Ironically, no sooner had Murray established himself at JPL than the scientific and planetary program entered the most ominous decline in its twenty-five-year history. The scientist who might have devoted his directorship to bolstering science and to improving interchange with the campus instead found himself confronting a challenge to the very survival of the institution.

EPILOGUE: JPL AND THE FUTURE OF THE AMERICAN SPACE PROGRAM

In the early years of Bruce Murray's directorship JPL crowned the first quarter century of space exploration with the brilliant Voyager missions. Having overcome a crisis in software development that threatened to limit data return, JPL managed the first major visits to Jupiter and Saturn. Photographs of the gigantic volcanoes of Io and the multihued rings of Saturn were only the most spectacular returns from the outer reaches of the solar system. For the next stage of exploration JPL planning focused on three dramatic projects: Galileo, an orbiter and probe to Jupiter in 1985; a mission to intercept Halley's comet in 1986; and the American spacecraft for the International Solar Polar Mission.

But the future of planetary exploration was imperiled by the hemorrhaging in the NASA science budget since 1974. Two processes placed planetary exploration in extremis by the 1980s. The first was a sharp overall decline in the NASA budget. The agency's funds peaked at close to $6 billion in fiscal year 1966. After a decline to about $3 billion in appropriations in the early 1970s, the budget rose again to nearly $6 billion in fiscal year 1981. But because inflation reduced the purchasing power of the 1981 budget to merely one-third that of the 1966 budget, NASA employees slipped from 36,000 in 1967 to 14,000 in 1981.[1]

The second was NASA's choice of programs within those tighter appropriations. James C. Fletcher, administrator from 1971 to 1977, decided on the space shuttle as the device with which to rebuild his budget. The reusable shuttle had the appeal of commercial flights and, most importantly, military clout. NASA decided to reestablish the alliance with industry and the military which had worked in the 1960s with Apollo. But the shuttle's promise was illusory. Its development took much longer and cost much more than anticipated, and the number of missions it could fly was severely reduced, casting doubt on its economic feasibility.[2]

243

What was worse, the shuttle increasingly was paid for out of the science sector. "NASA mortgaged nearly everything—science, space exploration, the development of new technologies—to build the space shuttle on what was a shoestring budget, as big Government projects go," said John Noble Wilford, the *New York Times* science writer. The planetary budget, adjusted for inflation, was slashed by a factor of four from 1974, when Viking expenditures topped out, to 1977. From then through 1982 the planetary slice floated between $200 million and $300 million (in 1982 dollars). That sum had to carry all the planetary activities, including Voyager, the Pioneer Venus mission, Galileo development, and the Deep Space Network. There were no scraps for new missions.[3]

Some NASA officials argued, to be sure, that the shuttle would eventually benefit planetary exploration. But William Pickering, like most people involved in space science, was dubious. He preferred launching from "a good, solid launching site in Florida" to blasting off from "a moving platform in space." So long as spacecraft continued to weigh about a ton, booster technology was adequate. Eugene Levy of the University of Arizona, chairman of the National Academy of Sciences' subcommittee on lunar and planetary exploration, noted that existing technology could reach the comets and asteroids, which "we haven't even approached yet." Their "primitive, undisturbed material" assumed great importance for understanding not only the origins of the solar system but all stars. In the face of the Reagan administration's budget cuts in 1981 and 1982, however, NASA chose what Wilford termed "bureaucratic triage." It saved the shuttle "by killing off most other projects." When the shuttle Columbia attained orbit in November 1981, it rose "from the ruins of the nation's civilian space program." Whatever value the shuttle might eventually have for science, its immediate effect was to all but end planetary exploration.[4]

The budget cuts occasioned much soul-searching at NASA headquarters. Space missions could still galvanize public attention but not consolidate political support. The reasons behind this paradox were no doubt complex, but NASA was in part reaping the tares of its salesmanship of the 1960s. "The space program was sold to the public as both a circus and a response to a foreign danger," pointed out Daniel Greenberg, publisher of *Science & Government Report*. "But it is difficult to build a durable political base on repetitious entertainment and exaggerated fear." T. Keith Glennan and the Eisenhower administration had tried to downplay the circus atmosphere in favor of a steady, long-range space program based on its own merits. Indeed Glennan worried that the feverish environment of the Apollo program could "in the long run . . . work strongly to our detriment." The growing disillusionment with the space program in the 1970s and '80s bore out his contention.[5]

In this atmosphere the future of JPL's planetary program hung by a thread. The Halley's comet mission—a truly once-in-a-lifetime occasion—died on the budget room floor. Readers of Forest Ray Moulton's astronomy text in 1933 would probably have been astonished to learn that the United States, having developed the technology to greet this great celestial visitor, would forgo the opportunity. The United States also pulled out of the solar polar project. For a time it even looked as if the budget cutters might pull the plug on the Deep Space Network, leaving Voyager to sail on to Uranus and telemeter its data back to a deaf Earth. The one major project to survive was Galileo. It had already had a narrow escape in 1979, when a House of Representatives appropriations committee recommended against it, but in a rare move it was restored on the floor of the House. Targeted for extinction by budget director David Stockman, Galileo narrowly managed to survive as the last major planetary mission in the 1982 budget. With that decision rode 1,200 jobs at JPL and continuation of the laboratory's planetary role.[6]

Facing drastic cutbacks, JPL eyed military support. At first the laboratory saw Defense Department funding as a way to fill a relatively small gap in the budget and thereby keep its space team intact. In the spring of 1980 a laboratory study team concluded that JPL's principal commitment should remain solar system exploration. But the panel also recommended that JPL, although not again becoming a military laboratory, should acquire "a limited number of defense tasks which would both sustain and strengthen JPL's ability to perform NASA programs." A new assistant laboratory directorate was formed to handle Defense Department tasks, and Murray set a provisional limit of 8 percent on Defense Department staffing in relation to the JPL total. Classified work was limited initially to one project—the air force's Autonomous Spacecraft Project, which was designed to make satellites "less dependent on ground control and more survivable." Realizing the troubling problems a turn to Defense Department work might entail, a special Caltech faculty committee was established to monitor these activities. "As long as there is an opportunity for a substantial solar system exploration program for the nation and for JPL, defense work will be acquired by JPL primarily for the purpose of bolstering the solar system exploration skills, not to create a large stand-alone DOD activity," JPL management insisted.[7]

Caltech faculty expressed varying degrees of anxiety about military funding. One of the strongest expressions of opposition came from physicist Kip Thorne, who was "unalterably opposed" to JPL staff members doing classified work on-lab, "except in times of severe national need." A team might be lent to the air force for work off-lab. "Or let the team disintegrate if that is the price of keeping JPL fully open," he said. "Openness is crucial to a university and its research facilities."[8]

These reservations went for naught, however, in the wake of further ax-wielding on the budget in early 1982. Ankle-deep in military funding in 1981, JPL now intended to wade into the military stream up to its knees. Following consultation with the campus, Murray announced plans for a "major, carefully planned, and well-executed effort" to secure long-term commitments to raise the level of military funding to about 30 percent of the budget. Murray thought the institution had three choices. One was to continue with minimal Defense Department funding on a short-term basis. He believed, however, that this course would reduce the technical challenges and thereby "undermine the enthusiasm" of key staff members. JPL would, in turn, become "a much less distinguished and important laboratory." A second possibility was to become a Defense Department laboratory, which would entail a drastic mission reorientation and increase in secrecy. This course would sever the NASA connection and radically diminish relations with Caltech. Significantly, he did not rule out this possibility for the future. Murray moved to the third model—retention of the NASA and Caltech ties with 30-percent Defense Department funding, perhaps half of that remaining unclassified. He expected the NASA-Defense Department activities combined with such energy, transportation, and health projects as could be procured, to maintain JPL as "a laboratory of excellence and importance." Murray wanted the institution to continue as a major national laboratory. Perhaps not coincidentally, JPL was also conscious of the NASA payments to Caltech, which exceeded $6 million annually in the 1980s.[9]

By 1982 JPL's clear identity as a space laboratory was fading. Space exploration had given the institution instant recognition, clarity of purpose, and unique appeal for two decades. But the inroads of military activities, whose future proportions might be very large, would, at the least, compromise institutional objectives and possibly distort the laboratory into something unrecognizable in its vintage years of space exploration. The looming changes disturbed some of the people who had been attracted to JPL in the 1960s and '70s, and it remained to be seen whether military programs—however technically challenging—would retain such staff members. But at the same time it was not clear where they might go, in view of the slashes in nonmilitary research funding. JPL, its program, and staff were part of a process by which the Reagan administration moved to recapture a larger portion of research and development funding and personnel for military purposes.

JPL's changing orientation in the early 1980s sharpened the perspective of its relationship with the national security state throughout its first forty years. Space technology provided a classic example of the double-edged nature of much post–World War II scientific and engineering research. This technology offered human beings their first chance to explore the solar system, but its peaceful and intellectual purposes could easily be diverted to weaponry and propaganda.

JPL's space program rested on a military foundation. Responding to military interest, the GALCIT researchers made fundamental breakthroughs in both solid- and liquid-propellant motors which enabled it to be called the seedbed of American rocketry. JPL was created from the shell of the GALCIT project to work toward the development of weapons systems and to stake the army's claim for an ongoing rocket project when the shooting stopped. After the war the permanent JPL shifted its emphasis to basic research but in the context of missile systems. The most important question—what type of basic research to do—was answered by the army. Almost all of JPL's work, whether basic or applied, quickly became classified. The intimate connection between research and applications was underscored when the laboratory converted the Corporal research vehicle into a weapons system and, indeed, went on to supervise industrial contractors and even helped to train troops. To its credit, JPL leadership realized in the mid-1950s that continuation of such activities would leave the institution little more than a job shop for the army. Pickering vowed to make Sergeant the last weapons project. But even when JPL moved into the potentially nonmilitary space program, it continued its national security orientation for some years.

Mission-oriented institutions such as JPL were a notable feature of the merger of research interests and the national security establishment after World War II. These interests were reinforced by an ideology which subsumed questions of the appropriateness of university involvement in classified research and management of military laboratories under the assumption that such activities were purely in response to an inherently expansionist Soviet system. As Lee DuBridge put it: Weapons development was "not the fault of Caltech or of the military services but the fault of one Joseph Stalin." Since the United States lacked a policy of directing scientific research and advanced development toward a broad range of national needs, the Defense Department and military-related agencies usually underwrote at least four-fifths of the federal research budget in the 1950s, and in 1953 accounted for 93 percent of it. Not all of this research had direct military bearing, of course, but the national security domination of federal research was nonetheless clear. The university-managed national laboratory, such as JPL, was a key component of the national security research structure. On the few occasions when questions were raised about this pattern, as in 1956 by the chairman of the Caltech Board of Trustees, the issues received little more than pro forma discussion. Lacking a strong institutional ethic, the science and research engineering communities allowed the organization and agenda of research to be determined disproportionately by military funding. The dream of Edward Bowles, science adviser to Secretary of War Henry Stimson, to integrate top research talent with national security objectives had largely succeeded.[10]

To be sure, the United States faced a dangerous world after 1945, and scientists and engineers would perforce play an important role in national security. But because of their usually uncritical embrace of the state—the source of funds for sweet research projects—they contributed to a self-perpetuating paradigm that helped fuel the arms race. As some participants in the dance of military technology realized, America was not simply reacting to events but was also encouraging the arms spiral. Herbert York, onetime director of the Livermore Laboratory and the Defense Department's chief scientist, believed that the United States bore a major responsibility for the arms race. In most areas of weapons development it was ahead of the Soviet Union, and in those where it was behind, the scope and pace of the American response triggered a new round of escalation. John Foster, director of Defense Department research and engineering, candidly observed that two forces drive American research and development: "Either we see from the fields of science and technology some new possibilities which we think we ought to exploit, or we see threats on the horizon, possible threats, usually not something the enemy has done, but something we have thought of ourselves that he might do, we must therefore be prepared for." War-born institutions such as JPL contributed to these self-sustaining processes.[11]

Paradoxically it was through JPL's military technology that a window opened to peaceful exploration of space when interest in a scientific satellite program burgeoned in the mid-1950s. The Eisenhower administration initiated a deliberately paced civilian space program that tried to keep scientific and manned objectives in balance. But a sizable constituency, which was never reconciled to Sputnik's first, still pressed for a space race. The sense of desperation reached its climax when, in less than a week, Yuri Gagarin orbited the Earth, and the Bay of Pigs invasion ended disastrously. Despite the misgivings of important members of his administration, John F. Kennedy launched a hastily conceived project that aimed to place a man on the moon by the end of the decade.

JPL eagerly endorsed the Apollo decision—the Pasadenans had chafed under the Eisenhower administration's pace. And yet this reorientation of NASA set in motion a train of events that would bring major changes to the laboratory. Some of them were institutional. There was no doubting JPL's technical competence. Many people ranked the organization in its heyday as the world's premier space laboratory. Oran Nicks, seconded by his boss Homer Newell, considered the laboratory staff the most competent organization in NASA. Even James Webb, for all his disputes with CIT-JPL management, acknowledged: "JPL . . . felt they were the best in the world, I think—and they were."[12]

It was not the laboratory's ability but rather its independence that rankled at headquarters. Although NASA held the purse and hence ultimate control of programs, JPL's Caltech affiliation gave it enough autonomy to propose programs at variance with headquarters and to attract staff outside government lines. Greater compliance with NASA was no doubt politically necessary in the early 1960s and may have improved management. By the mid-1960s, however, Webb's continuing pressure on JPL struck even NASA middle managers as unjustified and counterproductive. JPL represented for NASA in the 1960s not so much a technical or managerial liability as a political problem. The laboratory's independence, which in the end was crucial to its excellence, threatened NASA's political alliances with the aerospace industry and their congressional supporters. Ironically, NASA needed JPL, and never more so than in 1964 when the Pasadenans were called on to right the Surveyor project at Hughes Aircraft. The laboratory had its share of problems, particularly in the management arena in the early 1960s. But the disparity between its performance and that of leading industrial firms on the Corporal, Sergeant, and Surveyor projects challenged an ideology of business superiority.[13]

The strains of the Apollo era also changed Caltech's relationship with JPL. CIT had to modify its expectation of minimal relations with JPL for a maximum fee. Leadership and active involvement, not merely a corporate shell, were necessary. But the Institute rightly resisted NASA's attempted encroachment on research. Some of Webb's ideas about the manipulation of academic activities—in particular the cadres of on-call intellectuals—threatened the already compromised ideal of academic independence.

Apollo also affected JPL's programs. The technological achievements were undeniably impressive. Beginning with Explorer 1, the small "Rube Goldbergish" Earth-orbiting satellite, JPL went on to design some of the most sophisticated machines ever built. By the 1970s the laboratory's spacecraft could move through variable orbits of Mars while acting as the mother ship for a landing craft; they could use the gravity-assist technique to visit several planets in one mission; and they could sail to the dimmer reaches of the solar system—Jupiter, Saturn, and Uranus. From a distance of a billion and a half miles, a radio signal with power equivalent to that of a 10-watt refrigerator light bulb could return data to Goldstone.

But this technological virtuosity would have been sterile without scientific content. The manned program—particularly the way in which it was carried out in the 1960s—epitomized the distortion of the space program for political and propagandistic purposes. Both Ranger and Surveyor fell short of their scientific potential, in large measure because of Apollo. When the NASA budget could no longer sustain both the manned and unmanned programs in the mid- to late-1960s, Apollo won out. Ranger's last seven missions and Surveyor's final ten flights were jettisoned. Moreover, the comprehensive scientific objectives of Ranger and Surveyor were curtailed in favor of landing-site surveys for Apollo. NASA bought a lot of science, to be sure. The real question was whether the agency achieved a sound balance of activities.[14]

Through the planetary program JPL made its greatest contribution. The Mariners, Viking, and Voyager confirmed James Killian's contention that the "really exciting discoveries" in space would be made by instruments, not by men.[15] JPL provided the technological key for the intellectual transformation of understanding of the solar system. At the beginning of the space era the planets were largely realms of mystery. By the 1980s, knowledge had increased dramatically. Many questions remained, of course, but they could be framed with a precision and refinement that placed them in a category wholly different from previous questions.

The planetary explorers revealed astonishing diversity. The most interest centered on Mars. Once considered Earth's twin, Mars turned out to be in fact very different. Extensive biota had seemed possible to some and even the existence of oceans in the not-so-distant geologic past. But the red planet is in reality "a desert locked in an ice age." Not that it is uninteresting. Its geological features alone are astounding, notably the giant shield volcanoes and Valley of the Mariners, which would span North America from coast to coast. The evolution of Martian perceptions was a sort of metaphor of intellectual endeavor. First samples from the early Mariners suggested a moonlike planet; as knowledge became more complete, Mars ceased to be an analogy and emerged as its own distinct, complex world. Venus, too, had once been considered, if not Earth's twin, then perhaps a sister. But with surface temperatures ranging as high as 900°F and an atmosphere 90 times denser than Earth's, cloud-shrouded Venus is a "hellhole of a planet." Mercury, extremely difficult to study from Earth, stood out in a surprising new form by virtue of Mariner 10's three passes, which gave scientists their first really solid data about the little planet. A puzzling combination of Earth-like and moonlike features, Mercury aroused great interest among some scientists.[16]

These discoveries cast the solar system in a new light. The geologic history of Earth was no longer interpreted in isolation. Instead, as Murray pointed out, scientists began to grasp that the humans' home—and indeed "the very atoms that compose its sentient beings"—is linked with the other terrestrial planets in "a common planetary environmental history."[17] Not only scientists were affected. Growing numbers of the educated public began to assimilate the wonders of planetary exploration.

The impending end to an era of space exploration was thus more than an institutional tragedy. The United States, which had pioneered in the scientific study of the solar system, now appeared ready to relinquish its leadership to other countries and thereby damage its international prestige. But the greatest loss lay in the destruction of the challenge, excitement, and expansion of knowledge for a generation. Some opportunities, such as Halley's comet, would be lost for a lifetime. Whether American space exploration had a future beyond Galileo was uncertain at best. In the early 1980s JPL and the space science community recognized that austerity, if not bareness, was in store for a long time and began searching for ways to slash the cost of spaceflight. By using standardized parts and scaling back scientific capacity, the cost of a mission could be reduced from approximately $500 million spent on Voyager and Galileo to perhaps $150 million. Such costs were trifles by comparison with Apollo and Columbia, but the political climate dictated that space science do the economizing.[18]

The civilian NASA took on an increasingly military cast. Air force officers assumed key positions in the agency. The cooperative space programs between the United States and the Soviet Union lapsed. Military use of the shuttle grew. The Defense Department, which originally was limited to 30 percent of the shuttle's projected flights, claimed nearly half of them through 1994. Moreover, DOD got its flights at a 32 percent discount from the commercial rate through 1986, even though NASA had developed and tested the shuttle at little charge to the Pentagon. Senator Harrison H. (Jack) Schmitt, the former astronaut and chairman of the Senate subcommittee on space, complained that the Defense Department was "getting a free ride on the space shuttle." But in the cold war reprise of the 1980s, space, which for a time offered an arena of international cooperation and peaceful exploration, began to look like hostile territory.[19]

JPL, like NASA, was partially recaptured by the military. Satisfied that he had secured a lifeline for the laboratory from the Defense Department, Murray resigned abruptly, effective on July 1, 1982. In a marked departure from tradition, the directorship went to Gen. Lew Allen, the recently retired air force chief of staff. Allen, a research physicist with a Ph.D. from the University of Illinois, ran air force space programs before becoming chief of staff in 1978. He was also made a vice president of Caltech, the first JPL director to hold other than professorial rank in the university.[20]

The transition in program and directors placed in high relief the uneasy relationship of space technology, scientific exploration, and military purposes in the national security state. If the space program had a justification beyond political manipulation, it lay in the new horizons of understanding made possible by the scientific and planetary programs. In the early 1980s the first era of space exploration—a unique and fruitful one despite its compromises—drew to a close. Whatever the outlook for the American space program, the Jet Propulsion Laboratory's first quarter-century in space had established a rich endowment—the great explorations that transformed our understanding of the solar system.

ABBREVIATIONS USED IN NOTES

acc	accession
CITArchives	archives of the California Institute of Technology, Pasadena, California
DDEL	Dwight D. Eisenhower Library, Abilene, Kansas
FRC	Federal Records Center, Laguna Niguel, California
HSTL	Harry S. Truman Library, Independence, Missouri
JFKL	John F. Kennedy Library, Boston, Massachusetts
JPL Foothill D RSC	Records Storage Center
JPLHF	Jet Propulsion Laboratory History File
JPL Lyons	Jet Propulsion Laboratory, Lyons Records Storage Center, Pasadena, California
JPLVC	Jet Propulsion Laboratory Vellum Center
NA	National Archives (General Archives Division)
RG	Record Group
WNRC	Washington National Records Center, Suitland, Maryland

NOTES

Preface

1. William Sims Bainbridge, *The Spaceflight Revolution: A Sociological Study* (New York, 1976), p. 12.
2. Ironically Bainbridge's book is an example of this oversight. He points out that "military missiles should always have used solid propulsion" and attributes the fascination with liquid propulsion to the V-2s and their "propaganda impact" during World War II (Ibid., pp. 91–92). But he goes on to discuss missile technology without mentioning JPL and its breakthroughs in solid propulsion.
3. James R. Killian, Jr., *Sputnik, Scientists, and Eisenhower* (Cambridge, 1977), p. 247.
4. Daniel Yergin, *Shattered Peace: The Origins of the Cold War and the National Security State* (Boston, 1977).

Chapter 1

1. Forest Ray Moulton, *Astronomy* (New York, 1933), p. 296.
2. There are many overviews of the development of rocketry; a useful summary is found in Homer E. Newell, *Beyond the Atmosphere: Early Years of Space Science* (Washington, D.C., 1980), chap. 3.
3. On Goddard see Milton Lehman, *This High Man: The Life of Robert H. Goddard* (New York, 1963). On others see various pieces in R. Cargill Hall, eds., *Essays on the History of Rocketry and Astronautics: Proceedings of the Third through the Sixth History Symposia of the International Academy of Astronautics* (Washington, D.C., 1977).
4. Theodore von Kármán with Lee Edson, *The Wind and Beyond: Theodore von Kármán, Pioneer in Aviation and Pathfinder in Space* (Boston, 1967), pp. 236–37.
5. Frank J. Malina, "The GALCIT Rocket Research Project, 1936–1938," in F. C. Durant and G. S. James, eds., *First Steps Toward Space: Proceedings of the First and Second History Symposia of the International Academy of Astronautics* (Washington, D.C., 1974), pp. 113–14.
6. Ibid.
7. Ibid.
8. Ibid.

9. Ibid., p. 117; Kármán with Edson, *Wind and Beyond*, pp. 240–42; Esther C. Goddard and G. Edward Pendray, eds., *The Papers of Robert H. Goddard* (New York, 1970), 2:1012–13, 1089–91.
10. Malina to his parents, June 29, 1936, JPLHF 3–7. Because of the dearth of primary sources on the early years of GALCIT, Malina's letters home are a particularly important source.
11. Ibid., Nov. 1, 1936.
12. Ibid., Nov. 15 and 29, 1936; Malina, "The GALCIT Rocket Research Project," p. 119.
13. Malina, "The GALCIT Rocket Research Project," p. 119; Malina to his parents, Nov. 29 and Dec. 14, 1936.
14. Malina to his parents, May 22, 1937.
15. Ibid., Apr. 17, 1937; Kármán with Edson, *Wind and Beyond*, p. 240.
16. Frank J. Malina and A. M. O. Smith, "Flight Analysis of the Sounding Rocket," *Journal of the Aeronautical Sciences* 5 (1938): 202; Malina to his parents, Jan. 21, 1938.
17. Malina to his parents, Jan. 26, Feb. 6 and 12, Apr. 10, May 7 and 22, June 25, July 5, 1938; Associated Press story by E. H. Tipton, April 1938, JPLHF 3-94a; *Time* 31 (Feb. 7, 1938): 30.
18. Malina, "The GALCIT Rocket Research Project," p. 124.
19. Kármán with Edson, *Wind and Beyond*, p. 243.
20. Frank J. Malina, "Report on Jet Propulsion for the National Academy of Science Committee on Air Corps Research," Dec. 21, 1938, JPLHF 3-86.
21. Malina to his parents, Oct. 24, 1938; Kármán with Edson, *Wind and Beyond*, p. 244; Frank J. Malina, "The U.S. Army Air Corps Jet Propulsion Research Project, GALCIT Project No. 1, 1939–1946: A Memoir," in Hall, ed., *Essays on the History of Rocketry and Astronautics*, p. 158.
22. Kármán with Edson, *Wind and Beyond*, p. 244.
23. Malina, "GALCIT Project No. 1," p. 163.
24. Kármán with Edson, *Wind and Beyond*, p. 245.
25. Goddard and Pendray, eds., *Papers of Robert Goddard*, 3:1353; Newell, *Beyond the Atmosphere*, pp. 30–31.
26. Summerfield to Pickering, Oct. 7, 1968, JPLHF 3-209; Malina to his parents, Sept. 3, 1940; Malina, "GALCIT Project No. 1," pp. 159–60.
27. Malina, "GALCIT Project No. 1," pp. 169–70.
28. Ibid.; Kármán with Edson, *Wind and Beyond*, p. 250; Report No. 1–9 regarding Ercoupe tests, n.d. (about Aug. 30, 1941), JPLHF 3-64.
29. Same sources as note 28.
30. Malina, "GALCIT Project No. 1," pp. 170–72.
31. Ibid., p. 174.
32. Ibid.
33. Ibid., p. 178; author's interview with Summerfield, Princeton, N.J., May 5, 1975.
34. Kármán with Edson, *Wind and Beyond*, p. 252; Malina, "GALCIT Project No. 1," pp. 178–80.
35. Same sources as note 34; *Collected Works of Theodore von Kármán* (London, 1956), 4:94–106.

36. Malina, "GALCIT Project No. 1," pp. 178–79; James H. Wilson interview with Powell, JPLHF 3-732.
37. Malina to his parents, Mar. 22, Apr. 29, 1942; Kármán with Edson, *Wind and Beyond*, p. 254.
38. Author's interview with Pierce, Pasadena, Calif., Feb. 17, 1975.
39. Ibid.; author's interview with Seifert, Stanford, Calif., Dec. 29, 1975.
40. Malina to his parents, Sept. 3, 1940, Sept. 3, 1942; author's interviews with Pierce, Seifert, and W. Duncan Rannie, Pasadena, Dec. 3, 1974.
41. Kármán with Edson, *Wind and Beyond*, p. 256; Malina to his parents, Mar. 22, 1942; Malina, "GALCIT Project No. 1," pp. 194–95.
42. Same sources as note 41.
43. Same sources as note 41.
44. Newell correctly assesses the importance of JPL contributions to American rocketry in *Beyond the Atmosphere*, pp. 30–31. Representative of the many treatments which overestimate the Germans' importance is Bainbridge, *Spaceflight Revolution*.

Chapter 2

1. Kármán with Edson, *Wind and Beyond* pp. 263–64; Theodore von Kármán, "Memorandum on the Possibilities of Long-Range Rocket Projectiles," Memo JPL-1 Nov. 20, 1943, JPLHF 3-61.
2. Same sources as note 1; H. S. Tsien and F. J. Malina, "A Review and Preliminary Analysis of Long-Range Rocket Projectiles," Memo JPL-1, Nov. 20, 1943, JPLHF 3-61.
3. Same sources as note 2.
4. Frank J. Malina, "America's First Long-Range Missile and Space Exploration Programme: The ORDCIT Project of the Jet Propulsion Laboratory, 1943–1946," *Spaceflight* 15 (Dec. 1973): 445; author's interview with Staver, Dec. 29, 1975; R. C. Miles, "History of the ORDCIT Project," pp. 26–31, JPLHF 3-526.
5. Same sources as note 4; Bush to Bowles, Sept. 25, 1944, Division 14-Radar, Director's Files, Office of Scientific Research and Development records, NA.
6. Malina, "America's First Long-Range," p. 445; Army-CIT contract, Jan. 16, 1945, JPLHF 3-522; Minutes, CIT Board of Trustees, Feb. 1944.
7. Minutes, CIT Board of Trustees, Jan. 31, Aug. 2, 1944.
8. Malina, "America's First Long-Range," p. 446; Wilson interview with Stewart, May 1973, JPLHF 3-635; Malina to section chiefs, JPL, Aug. 18, 1944, JPLHF 3-57; author's interview with Pierce, Feb. 17, 1975.
9. C. B. Millikan to CIT Executive Committee, Oct. 12, 1945, JPLHF 3-40b; Miles, "History of ORDCIT," pp. 17–18.
10. Minutes, JPL Executive Board, Dec. 22, 1944, JPLHF 3-539; Frank L. Wattendorf and Frank J. Malina, "Theodore von Kármán, 1881–1963," *Astronautica Acta* 10 (1964): 85; Frank J. Malina, "America's First Long-Range Missile and Space Exploration Program: The ORDCIT Project of the Jet Propulsion Laboratory, 1943–1946: A Memoir," in Hall, ed., *Essays on the History of Rocketry and Astronautics*, pp. 346–47.

11. Army-JPL contract, JPLHF 3-522; Kármán with Edson, *Wind and Beyond*, p. 265.
12. S. J. Goldberg, "Firing Tests of Private A at Leach Spring, Camp Irwin, California," JPL Report 4-3, Mar. 14, 1945; Alan E. Slater, ed., "Research and Development at the Jet Propulsion Laboratory, GALCIT," *Journal of the British Interplanetary Society* 6 (Sept. 1946): 48–49.
13. Malina, "America's First Long-Range," pp. 448–49.
14. Ibid., pp. 449–52; Wilson interview with Stewart, JPLHF 3-635.
15. Same sources as note 14; Frank J. Malina and Homer Stewart, "Considerations of the Feasibility of Developing a 100,000 ft. Altitude Rocket (The WAC Corporal)," JPL Report 4-4, Jan. 16, 1945, JPLHF 3-121.
16. Louis Dunn, W. B. Powell, and Howard Seifert, "Heat Transfer Studies Relating to Rocket Power Plant Development," Proceedings of Third Anglo-American Conference, 1951, pp. 271–328.
17. Same sources as note 16.
18. Barnes to Robert Millikan, Sept. 26, 1945, Millikan Papers.
19. Leslie E. Simon, *German Research in World War II* (New York, 1947), pp. 206–07; Daniel J. Kevles, "Scientists, the Military, and the Control of Postwar Defense Research: The Case of the Research Board for National Security, 1944–46," *Technology and Culture*, 16 (Jan. 1975), 23–27; Michael S. Sherry, *Preparing for the Next War: American Plans for Postwar Defense, 1941–1945* (New Haven, 1977), p. 120; Charles E. Wilson, "For the Common Defense: A Plea for a Continuing Program of Industrial Preparedness," *Army Ordnance*, 26 (March–April 1944), 285–88.
20. Report of War Department Equipment Board, Feb. 23, 1946, box K2698, RG 156, WNRC; Forrestal quoted in Clarence G. Lasby, *Project Paperclip: German Scientists and the Cold War* (New York, 1971), p. 93.
21. Bowles to DuBridge, Dec. 10, 1946, Lee A. DuBridge Papers, CIT Archives; James B. Conant, *My Several Lives: Memoirs of a Social Inventor* (New York, 1970), p. 245; author's interview with DuBridge, Pasadena, March 8, 1976; James R. Killian, Jr., "MIT Redeploys for Peace," in John Burchard, *Q.E.D.: MIT in World War II* (New York, 1948), 313–15; Dorothy Nelkin, *The University and Military Research: Moral Politics at MIT* (Ithaca, N.Y., 1972), pp. 16–17.
22. Minutes, Committee on Government Contracts, May 14, 1945, folder 1.2, C. C. Lauritsen Papers, CIT Archives; author's interviews with Fred Lindvall and W. Duncan Rannie, Dec. 2, 1974; Albert B. Christman, *Sailors, Scientists, and Rockets: Origins of the Navy Rocket Program and of the Naval Ordnance Test Station, Inyokern* (Washington, 1971), p. 238.
23. C. B. Millikan to CIT Executive Committee, March 1946, JPLHF 3-40b; Daniel J. Kevles, "Millikan: Spokesman for Science in the Twenties," *Engineering and Science*, 32 (April 1968), 17–22.
24. Frank J. Malina, "Memorandum on the Future of Jet Propulsion Research at the California Institute of Technology," Nov. 1945, JPLHF 3-541; Malina, "America's First Long-Range," p. 443.
25. Minutes, JPL Executive Board, Mar. 22, 1946, JPLHF 3-539; C. B. Millikan to JPL Executive Board, Mar. 21, 1946, JPLHF 3-546.

26. Minutes, CIT Board of Trustees, Apr. 1, 1946; Minutes, Committee on Government Contracts, Apr. 25, 1946; JPLHF 3-658; Kevles, "Control of Postwar Defense Research," p. 43.
27. Miles, "History of ORDCIT"; Philip Morrison, "The Laboratory Demobilizes . . . ," *Bulletin of the Atomic Scientists* 2 (Nov. 1, 1946): 6.
28. Joseph Haberer, *Politics and the Community of Science* (New York, 1969), pp. 321–23.
29. Steve J. Heims, *John von Neumann and Norbert Wiener: From Mathematics to the Technologies of Life and Death* (Cambridge, Mass., 1980).

Chapter 3

1. Author's interviews with Summerfield, Malina, and Rannie; Wilson interview with Malina, June 8, 1973, JPLHF 3-710.
2. Milton Viorst, "The Bitter Tea of Dr. Tsien," *Esquire* 68 (Sept. 1967): 125–29, 168.
3. Author's interview with Malina; Wilson interview with Malina, June 8, 1973.
4. Author's interviews with Dunn, Mountain Ranch, Calif., Dec. 30, 1975, Seifert, Dec. 29, 1975, and Hibbs, Dec. 15, 1975; *New York Times*, Feb. 1, 1958.
5. Minutes, JPL Executive Board; author's interview with Dunn, Dec. 30, 1975; V. Larsen to Dunn, July 7, 1948, JPLVC roll 614-5.
6. JPL director's annual report, Sept. 7, 1950, Sept. 28, 1951, JPLVC roll 614-12; July 1, 1949, JPLVC roll 614-10.
7. Author's interviews with Seifert, Dec. 29, 1975, Pickering, Mar. 1976, and Cliff Cummings, Apr. 1976.
8. Army-JPL contracts, JPLHF 3-522; Green to DuBridge, Oct. 19, 1948, DuBridge Papers, CIT Archives.
9. Same sources as note 8; Green to DuBridge, Mar. 14, 1949, JPLHF 3-976.
10. Author's interviews with Dunn, Dec. 30, 1975, and Hibbs, Dec. 15, 1975; Army-JPL contracts, JPLHF 3-522; William H. Pickering, "The Corporal: A Surface-to-Surface Guided Missile," JPL Report 20-100, Mar. 17, 1958, p. 311.
11. Louis Dunn, "Jet Propulsion Laboratory Activities, 1946–47," JPL director's annual report, 1947–48, JPLVC roll 614-10; M. A. Tuve to E. R. Gilliland, Mar. 27, 1946, Minutes, Propulsion Panel, Guided Missiles Committee, Joint Committee on New Weapons and Equipment, War Department, Feb. 8, 1946, JPLHF.
12. Howard Seifert, "Twenty-Five Years of Rocket Development," *Jet Propulsion* (Nov. 1955): 596.
13. Seifert, "Twenty-Five Years of Rocket Development," p. 596.
14. Howard Seifert, "History of Ordnance Research at the Jet Propulsion Laboratory, 1945–1953," JPL Pub. 22, pp. 3–7; DuBridge to Dunn, Apr. 23, 1949, DuBridge Papers.
15. Howard Seifert, "The Jet Propulsion Laboratory and Its Work," JPLHF 3-167.
16. Louis Dunn, W. B. Powell, and Howard Seifert, "Heat Transfer Studies Relating to Rocket Power Plant Development," Proceedings of Third Anglo-American Conference, 1951, pp. 271–328.

17. Pendray quoted in P. Thomas Carroll, "Historical Origins of the Sergeant Missile Powerplant," unpub. paper, JPL History Report 3.
18. Ibid.
19. Ibid.
20. Ibid.
21. Ibid.; M. Summerfield, J. I., Shafer, H. L. Thackwell, Jr., and C. E. Bartley, "Applicability of Solid Propellants to High-Performance Rocket Vehicles," JPL Memo 4-17, reprinted, *Astronautics* (Oct. 1962): 50–56; Dunn to B. H. Sage, Feb. 6, 1951, JPLVC roll 614–10.
22. Toftoy speech, U.S. Military Academy, Dec. 1, 1947, box 1, entry 68S-2853, Records of the Office of the Chief of Ordnance, RG 156, WNRC; Wilson interview with Stewart, May 24, 1972, JPLHF 3-637.
23. Pickering, "The Corporal," Chap. 2; Seifert, "The Jet Propulsion Laboratory and Its Work."
24. William H. Pickering and James E. Wilson, "Countdown to Space Exploration: A Memoir of the Jet Propulsion Laboratory, 1944–1958," in Hall, ed., *Essays on the History of Rocketry and Astronautics*, vol. 2, pp. 392–93; Frank G. Denison, Jr., and Chauncey J. Hamlin, Jr., "The Design of the Axial-Cooled Rocket Motor for the Corporal E," JPL Progress Report 4-112, Aug. 29, 1949; author's interview with Dunn, Dec. 30, 1975.
25. Same sources as note 24.
26. Pickering and Wilson, "Countdown to Space Exploration," p. 387.
27. Ibid., pp. 392–93; Pickering, "The Corporal," chap. 2.
28. Malina, "America's First Long-Range," p. 375; Newell, *Beyond the Atmosphere*, pp. 34–39.
29. Wilson interviews with Stewart, May 24, June 7, 1972, JPLHF 3-637, 3-639; James Gavin, "Tactical Use of the Atomic Bomb," *Combat Forces Journal* 1 (Nov. 1950): 9, 12; James Gavin, *War and Peace in the Space Age* (New York, 1958), pp. 112–16; Robert E. Osgood, *NATO: The Entangling Alliance* (Chicago, 1962), pp. 66, 68; Richard G. Hewlett and Francis Duncan, *Atomic Shield, 1947/1952* (University Park, Pa., 1969), pp. 178–79; Dean Acheson, *Present at the Creation* (New York, 1969), p. 308.
30. George F. Kennan, *Memoirs, 1925–1950* (Boston, 1967), pp. 472–73. On the nuclear basis of NATO and American policy in Europe, see the exchange of views between Harold Brown and Daniel Seligman in *Fortune* 105 (Feb. 8, 1982): 19–20.
31. Gregg Herken, *The Winning Weapon: The Atomic Bomb in the Cold War, 1945–1950* (New York, 1980), pp. 303, 314; Executive Secretary, National Security Council, Report to National Security Council on "United States Objectives and Programs for National Security," NSC-68, Apr. 14, 1950, file 381.02, Records of the Air Force, RG 341, NA.
32. Minutes, "Conference on Corporal E Program," JPLVC roll 614-30; Louis Dunn, Paul J. Meeks, and Frank G. Denison, Jr., "Present Status of the Corporal E Development," JPL memo 4-59, Mar. 17, 1950, p. 2; author's interview with Dunn, Dec. 30, 1975; Pickering and Wilson, "Countdown to Space Exploration," p. 400.

Chapter 4

1. Toftoy to Dunn, Feb. 8, 1950, file 14.4, box K2254, Records of the Office of the Chief of Ordnance, Department of the Army, RG 156, NA; Simon to Army Chief of Staff, Oct. 31, 1950, acc. 68A2853, box 22, RG 156, NA; James W. Bragg, *Development of the Corporal: The Embryo of the Army Missile Program*, 2 vols. (Redstone Arsenal, Ala., 1961), 1:121–22; "Ordnance Guided Missile and Rocket Programs, vol. 3, Corporal," Technical Report, June 30, 1955, acc. 68A2853, box 18, RG 156, NA; Dunn, Meeks, and Denison, "Present Status of the Corporal E Development," pp. 7–9.

2. Executive Secretary, Report to National Security Council NSC-68; K. T. Keller, Final Report of the Director of Guided Missiles, Sept. 17, 1953, Keller Papers, HSTL; Pickering, "The Corporal", p. 6; David S. McLellan, *Dean Acheson: The State Department Years* (New York, 1976), pp. 270–72.

3. "Corporal," Technical Report, p. 3; Wilson interview with Stewart, JPLHF 3-641.

4. Howard S. Seifert, "History of Ordnance Research at the Jet Propulsion Laboratory, 1945–1953," July 29, 1953, p. 25, JPLHF 3-97; Pickering "The Corporal," p. 6.

5. "Corporal," Technical Report, pp. 14–17; Senate subcommittee on the air force, committee on armed services, "Study of Airpower," (84th Cong., 2nd Sess.) 9:715–16; Willie Ley, *Rockets, Missiles and Men in Space* (New York, 1968), p. 206.

6. "Corporal," Technical Report, pp. 14–17; Pickering, "The Corporal," pp. 89–92, 227.

7. Same sources as note 6; Wilson interview with Stewart; Seifert, "History of Ordnance Research," pp. 26–27.

8. Keller, Final Report; Bragg, *Development of the Corporal*, p. 174; H. B. Bishop, Jr., G-4, to Chief of Ordnance, May 4, 1950, file 471.94, box A1454, Asst. Chief of Staff, G-4, to Chief of Ordnance, Oct. 5, 1951, file 471.9, box A1676, RG 156, NA.

9. Pickering to Dunn, Dec. 28, 1950, JPLVC roll 614-30.

10. Pickering, "The Corporal," pp. 6–10.

11. Author's interview with Dunn, Dec. 30, 1975; Wilson interview with Stewart, Aug. 23, 1972, JPLHF 3-643.

12. Administrator's report, Jan. 1, 1950 to June 1951, JPLVC roll 614-1.

13. Ibid.; Administrator's report, Jan. 1, 1953 to December 1953, JPLVC roll 614-9; Parsons to Toftoy, June 5, 1951, file 14.2, box K2254, Toftoy to District Chief, Los Angeles Ordnance District, June 11, 1951, file 471.9, box A1676, RG 156, NA; Wilson interview with Stewart, JPLHF 3-641.

14. Parsons to Toftoy, June 5, 1951; Parsons to Office, Chief of Ordnance, May 16, 1951, file 471.94, box 1499, RG 156, NA; Minutes, CIT Board of Trustees, Sept. 10, 1956.

15. Alfred Millard to DuBridge, May 29, 1949, West Altadena Improvement Association to DuBridge, Apr. 11, 1951, James Fiedler to DuBridge, Aug. 6, 1951, DuBridge to Gibson, July 25, 1951, DuBridge Papers, CIT Archives; R. C. Hall interview with Larsen, JPLHF 2-759; author's interview with Pierce, Feb. 17, 1975.

16. DuBridge to Newman, Sept. 26, 1951, Ford to DuBridge, Aug. 11, 1951, resume of press conference with Simon, Sept. 10, 1951, DuBridge Papers, CIT Archives.

17. Dunn to DuBridge, Feb. 21, 1952, DuBridge Papers, CIT Archives; minutes, CIT Trustees Contract Committee, Oct. 13, 1952; author's interviews with Dunn, Dec. 30, 1975, and Pickering, Mar. 3, 1976.

18. Minutes, JPL board, Aug. 28, 1950, DuBridge Papers, CIT Archives; DuBridge to Ford, Mar. 31, 1950, file 14.4, box K2254, Ford to DuBridge, Apr. 19, 1950, file 14.4, box K2254, RG 156, NA; Lee DuBridge, "Science and Government," *Chemical and Engineering News* 31 (April 6, 1953): 1384–90; author's interview with DuBridge, Mar. 8, 1976.

19. Minutes, Trustees Contract Committee, Oct. 13, 1952, minutes, CIT Board of Trustees, Dec. 1, 1952; Hall interview with Larsen; author's interview with Dunn, Dec. 30, 1975.

20. E. S. Gruver to District Chief, Los Angeles Ordnance District, Aug. 25, 1952, Dunn to DuBridge, Dec. 7, 1953, JPLVC roll 614-9.

21. DuBridge to Cummings, Dec. 18, 1953, Simon to DuBridge, Aug. 24, 1954, DuBridge Papers, CIT Archives.

22. Resident Ordnance Officer's Report, Dec. 18, 1950, file 471.9, box A1677, RG 156, NA.

23. Robert Lusser to Col. Gillon, Sept. 29, 1953, file 471.9, box A1537, RG 156, NA; Pickering, "The Corporal," p. 352.

24. William Pickering, "Management Techniques for the Management and Development of Weapon Systems" (Address at Industrial College of the Armed Forces, Washington, D.C., Jan. 22, 1958), JPLHF 3-655.

25. Memo regarding Corporal to Keller, Mar. 21, 1951, file 14.4, box K2254, RG 156, NA; Dunn to Lt. Ledford, June 26, 1951, box I140, P. S. Irvine to Office, Chief of Ordnance, Jan. 26, 1951, Broberg to Ford, Jan. 19, 1951, file 471.9, box A1676, RG 156, NA.

26. Resident Ordnance Officer, JPL to Procurement Division, Redstone Arsenal, Mar. 28, 1952, box I141, "Comments on Integrated Army Program for Development of Short-Range Guided Rockets," n.d., file 14.4, box K2254, RG 156, NA; Seifert, "History of Ordnance Research," p. 28.

27. W. S. Broberg to Cummings, Apr. 25, 1952, Cummings memo regarding Gilfillan, May 1, 1952, Corporal Project Report, May 16, 1952, box I141, W. B. Palmer to Cummings, Nov. 26, 1954, Cummings to Palmer, Dec. 10, 1954, file 471.9, box A1592, D. E. Noble to Charles Eifler, June 15, 1953, file 14.2, box K2254, RG 156, NA; Eifler to Dunn, June 26, 1953, JPLVC roll 614-25; Pickering, "The Corporal," p. 138; Bragg, *Development of the Corporal,* p. 160.

28. Pickering, "The Corporal," pp. 341–47.

29. Ibid., chap. 8; Wilson interview with Paul McGiven, Aug. 10, 1971, JPLHF 3-521.

30. Same sources as note 29; Wilson interview with Pickering, JPLHF 3-786. The intermediate-range ballistic missile Redstone, produced by the army later in the 1950s, was dubbed by military personnel as "the world's most expensive roadblock." See Mark Schneider, "Nuclear Weapons and American Strategy, 1945–1953" (Ph.D. diss., University of Southern California, 1974), pp. 277–78.

31. "Corporal," Technical Report, p. 4; Pickering, "The Corporal," pp. 99–100.
32. Pickering, "The Corporal," p. 317; Army Field Forces Liaison Office, JPL reports, Mar. 31, 1952, file 471.9, box A1677, Mar. 2, 1953, file 471.9, box A1678, Nov. 23, 1953, file 471.9, box A1679, "Current Status of the Corporal Program," acc. 68A2853, box 9, RG 156, NA; "Corporal," Technical Report, pp. 50–51.
33. "Corporal," Technical Report, pp. 4–5.
34. William Pickering, "History of Ordnance Research at the Jet Propulsion Laboratory," June 1, 1953, through December 31, 1954, JPL Pub. No. 45, pp. 6–7; Pickering, "The Corporal," p. 11.
35. Notes on Ordnance-Contractor Technical Committee, Investigation of Type 1 Corporal System, June 29, 1954, JPLVC roll 614–30.
36. Pickering, "The Corporal," pp. 360–61; Corporal Progress Report, May 21, 1952, JPLVC roll 614–25.
37. "Deployment of Corporal Battalions," acc. 68A2853, box 9, James M. Gavin to Asst. Chief of Staff, G-4, file 471.9, box A1698, RG 156, NA; Robert E. Osgood, *NATO: The Entangling Alliance* (Chicago, 1962), pp. 158–60.
38. J. McGee to Pickering, June 16, 1956, Nov. 16, 1956, JPLHF.
39. Patrick W. Powers, "Missile Away!" *Army Combat Forces Journal* (Aug. 1956): 39–41.
40. "Corporal," Technical Report, pp. 17–19; Schneider, "Nuclear Weapons and American Strategy," p. 182.
41. Wheelock to all concerned, Dec. 9, 1955, JPLVC roll 21-8; F. W. Mulley, *The Politics of Western Defence* (London, 1962), p. 77; "Report on the Corporal Guided Missile Deployed in Europe," n.d. (about July 22, 1956), JPLVC roll 614-24; Eddy to Chief of Ordnance, Jan. 23, 1953, file 14.06, box K2255, RG 156, NA.
42. Pickering, "The Corporal," pp. 371–73; Bragg, *Development of the Corporal*, p. 176; P. N. Haurlan to Pickering, Sept. 27, 1956, JPLVC roll 614-29.
43. Pickering and Wilson, "Countdown to Space Exploration," p. 401.

Chapter 5

1. Toftoy to District Chief, Los Angeles Ordnance District, Feb. 9, 1951, box A1499, file 471.94, Records of the Office of the Chief of Ordnance, RG 156, NA; R. B. Power, Toftoy, and H. G. Jones to Simon, Jan. 21, 1952, box A1500, file 471.94, RG 156, NA; JPL memo, "Plans for the Development of a Solid-Propellant Loki Rocket," Mar. 19, 1951, JPLHF.
2. William Tier to Asst. Chief of Staff for Research and Development, Feb. 29, 1952, box 1677, file 471.9, RG 156, NA; Hall interview with Hibbs, JPLHF 3-595; Dunn to Simon, Jan. 27, 1954, JPLHF; Pickering, "History of Ordnance Research" p. 7.
3. Louis Dunn, "The SERGEANT Surface-to-Surface Guided Missile System," JPL Report 20-76, Apr. 15, 1954.
4. "The Objectives and Responsibilities of the Ad Hoc Evaluation Committee on a Solid Propellant Surface-to-Surface Guided Missile System," May 13, 1954, JPLVC roll 614-97; C. M. Hudson, W. H. Pickering, A. K. Thiel, W. S. Carlson, P.

W. Newton, and W. W. Berning, "Report of the Sergeant Evaluation Committee," Aug. 1954, JPLVC roll 614-97.

5. Dunn, "The SERGEANT Surface-to-Surface Guided Missile System."

6. Hudson, et al., "Report of the Sergeant Evaluation Committee."

7. Dunn, "The SERGEANT Surface-to-Surface Guided Missile System," p. 67.

8. Author's interview with Dunn, Dec. 30, 1975; Herbert York, *Race to Oblivion: A Participant's View of the Arms Race* (New York, 1970), pp. 85–88; Steve J. Heims, *John von Neumann and Norbert Wiener: From Mathematics to the Technologies of Life and Death* (Cambridge, Mass., 1980), p. 247.

9. Author's interviews with Dunn, Dec. 30, 1975, and DuBridge, Mar. 8, 1976.

10. Author's interviews with DuBridge, Mar. 8, 1976, and Pickering, Mar. 3, 1976; William Pickering and James H. Wilson, "Countdown to Space Exploration: A Memoir of the Jet Propulsion Laboratory, 1944–1958," in Hall, ed., *Essays on the History of Rocketry and Astronautics*, pp. 399–400.

11. Mary T. Cagle, *History of Sergeant* (Huntsville, Ala., 1963), pp. 98–99.

12. "Radio-Inertial Guidance Program IRBM #2," n.d. (about Dec. 1955), "Proposed Supplement to Laboratory Proposal 20-8: Jupiter Radio Guidance Development," n.d. (about Jan. 1956), JPLVC roll 21-14; Michael H. Armacost, *The Politics of Weapons Innovation: The Thor-Jupiter Controversy* (New York, 1969), chaps. 1–2; John B. Medaris with Arthur Gordon, *Countdown for Decision* (New York, 1960), pp. 118, 123; Pickering to author, July 10, 1981.

13. York, *Race to Oblivion*, p. 99; Pickering and Wilson, "Countdown to Space Exploration," pp. 411–13.

14. Minutes, CIT Board of Trustees, Sept. 10, 1956; CIT annual reports, 1955–1958. The figures cited are actual expenditures; the budget projected for fiscal year 1956 was $29 million.

15. Ruddock to DuBridge, Sept. 24, 1956, Ruddock notes, n.d. (about Oct. 1, 1956), DuBridge Papers, CIT Archives.

16. DuBridge to Ruddock, Sept. 27, 1956, DuBridge Papers.

17. DuBridge to Ruddock, Oct. 1, 1956, DuBridge Papers.

18. Ibid.

19. Ibid.; DuBridge to Trustees, Oct. 3, 1956, DuBridge Papers.

20. Sames sources as note 19.

21. Same sources as note 19; author's interviews with Dunn, Dec. 30, 1975, and Pickering, Mar. 3, 1976, and DuBridge, Mar. 8, 1976.

22. Lyon statement, Oct. 5, 1956, DuBridge Papers; Minutes, JPL board, Sept. 21, 1956, DuBridge Papers; Minutes, CIT Board of Trustees, Sept. 10, Oct. 8, 1956.

23. For representative ordnance comment see Ford to DuBridge, Sept. 24, 1956, DuBridge Papers.

24. Author's interview with Pickering; Pickering, "Management Techniques," address, Jan. 22, 1958, JPLHF 3-655.

25. Cagle, *History of Sergeant*, chap. 3; P. N. Haurlan, "Status of Sergeant Program, Presentation for General Osborne," Oct. 21, 1957, JPLVC roll 21-14.

26. Pickering, "The Sergeant Co-Contractual Relationship," Mar. 28, 1956, JPLVC roll 21-14; Cagle, *History of Sergeant*, pp. 41–64.

27. Frank E. Goddard, Jr. to Richard E. Horner, Apr. 18, 1960; Pickering and Wilson, "Countdown to Space Exploration," pp. 411–13.
28. Same sources as note 27.
29. William Pickering, "Sergeant Final Report," JPL Report 20-137, 1960, pp. 3, 124–29.
30. F. G. Denison to distribution, June 15, 1955, unsigned (probably Denison), "Sergeant JPL-Thiokol-RCA Considerations," Apr. 8, 1957, JPLVC roll 311-58.
31. Pickering, "Sergeant Final Report," pp. 1–3, 124–29.
32. Ibid., pp. 49–50; Pickering and Wilson, "Countdown to Space Exploration," pp. 405–06.
33. Cagle, *History of Sergeant*, pp. 131–34.
34. Kenneth F. Gantz, ed., *The United States Air Force Report on the Ballistic Missile* (Garden City, N.Y., 1958), pp. 210–11; Denison to Pickering, Aug. 28, 1956, JPLHF.
35. Toftoy to Chief of Ordnance, May 2, 1953, box A1677, file 471.9, RG 156, NA.
36. Cummings to McKenney, Jan. 12, 1956, McKenney to Cummings, Jan. 16, 1956, G. Neiswanger to McKenney, Jan. 4, 1956, JPLHF; J. E. Densmore to Parks, Jan. 3, 1958, JPLVC roll 311-53; Pickering, "Sergeant Final Report," chap. 4.
37. W. E. Giberson conference report, July 5, 1957, B. P. Huber to Parks, May 20, 1959, Parks and Paul Vestigo, "Suggestions to Improve SUEL Sergeant Program Participation," May 21, 1959, James B. Densmore and C. W. Cole, "An Estimate of the Sergeant Situation," May 29, 1959, Densmore to Cole, Apr. 30, 1959, unsigned, "Proposed Party Line for Sergeant (Shinkle) Meeting, Monday, November 23," Nov. 20, 1959, JPLVC roll 311-55; "Sergeant R & D Program Status Review for General J. G. Shinkle, 28 October 1959," JPLVC roll 311-52; Pickering to Shinkle, Nov. 23, 1959, JPLVC roll 614-95; Cagle, *History of Sergeant*, p. 55.
38. Hall interview with Larsen, May 28, 1968, JPLHF 2-759; Cagle, *History of Sergeant*, pp. 118–19.
39. Pickering to Medaris, June 11, 1959, JPLVC roll 311-53; Medaris to Pickering, July 6, 1959, JPLVC roll 311-54; Cagle, *History of Sergeant*, pp. 85, 152–54, 215; Goddard to Horner, Apr. 18, 1960.
40. Pickering to Shinkle, May 17, 1960, Pickering to Hinrichs, May 20, 1960; Cagle, *History of Sergeant*, p. 80.
41. Cagle, *History of Sergeant*, pp. 169–70, 199.
42. John Lewis Gaddis, *Strategies of Containment: A Critical Appraisal of Postwar American National Security Policy* (New York, 1982), p. 174; Osgood, *NATO: The Entangling Alliance*, p. 37; Henry Kissinger, *Nuclear Weapons and Foreign Policy* (New York, 1957), p. 292.

Chapter 6

1. Malina, "America's First Long-Range Missile: A Memoir," p. 375; Pickering and Wilson, "Countdown to Space Exploration," pp. 408–11; H. S. Seifert, M. M. Mills, and M. Summerfield, "Physics of Rockets: Dynamics of Long-Range Rock-

ets," *American Journal of Physics* 15 (1947): 255; Wilson interview with Stewart, Aug. 30, 1972, JPLHF 3-644. See also Newell, *Beyond the Atmosphere,* chap. 4.

2. S. P. Johnston et al., "The Scientific Exploration of Outer Space," Mar. 12, 1958, Records of the Office of the Special Assistant for Science and Technology, White House Office, DDEL; R. Cargill Hall, "Early U.S. Satellite Proposals," *Technology and Culture* 4 (Fall 1963): 410–34.

3. Stewart to Pickering, Apr. 19, 1955, JPLVC roll 10-3.

4. "Report of Ad Hoc Advisory Group on Special Capabilities," Aug. 1955, and related materials, JPLVC roll 10-3; R. Cargill Hall, "Origins and Development of the Vanguard and Explorer Satellite Programs," *Aerospace Historian* 11 (1964): 106–09.

5. Pickering and Wilson, "Countdown to Space Exploration," p. 414; Constance M. Green and Milton Lomask, *Vanguard: A History* (Washington, 1971), pp. 53–56.

6. Pickering and Wilson, "Countdown to Space Exploration," p. 416.

7. Green and Lomask, *Vanguard: A History,* pp. 22–32.

8. Ibid., pp. 33–40; G. Robillard, "Explorer Rocket Research Program," *American Rocket Society Journal* 29 (July 1959): 492–96.

9. George Kistiakowsky, *A Scientist at the White House: The Private Diary of President Eisenhower's Special Assistant for Science and Technology* (Cambridge, 1976), p. 97; Allen E. Wolfe et al., *Juno I,* (JPL Report, 1959), pp. 38–40; Medaris with Gordon, *Countdown for Decision,* pp. 119–24.

10. Medaris with Gordon, *Countdown for Decision,* pp. 122–24; Stewart to W. M. Holaday, June 12, 1957, JPLVC roll 10-3.

11. Minutes, satellite proposal meetings, Sept. 6, 20, 1957, JPLVC roll 211-5; J. D. Burke, "JPL Research & Development Programs 1958–1960," Aug. 6, 1957, JPLVC roll 211-2.

12. Author's interview with Pickering, June 9, 1977.

13. Medaris with Gordon, *Countdown for Decision,* pp. 155–56.

14. Memoranda of conferences with the president, Oct. 9, 1957, box 22, Oct. 31, 1957, box 16, Staff Notes, Dwight D. Eisenhower Papers as President, DDEL; *Public Papers of the Presidents: Dwight D. Eisenhower, 1957* (Washington, D.C., 1958), pp. 789–99.

15. Robert D. Lapidus, "Sputnik and Its Repercussions: A Historical Catalyst," *Aerospace Historian* 17 (Summer–Fall 1970): 88–93; Homer Boushey, "Who Controls the Moon Controls the Earth," *U.S. News and World Report* (Feb. 7, 1958): 54; *Los Angeles Times,* Dec. 18, 1957; Pickering to J. I. Shafer, Nov. 2, 1957, JPLVC roll 211-2.; Killian, *Sputnik, Scientists, and Eisenhower,* p. 8.

16. Pickering to DuBridge with summary of Red Socks proposal, Oct. 25, 1957, JPLHF 2-581.

17. Author's interview with Pickering, June 9, 1977.

18. Medaris with Gordon, *Countdown for Decision,* pp. 159, 165–79; Green and Lomask, *Vanguard: A History,* p. 220.

19. Author's interview with Pickering, June 9, 1977; Pickering and Wilson, "Countdown to Space Exploration," p. 417.

20. *Washington Star,* Feb. 5, 1959, JPLHF 3-152b; "Explorer I," JPL external publication no. 461, Feb. 28, 1958.

21. "Explorer I," pp. 7–12.
22. Ibid.
23. Robillard, "Explorer Rocket Research Program," p. 493.
24. Wolfe et. al., *Juno I*, pp. 56–57.
25. Medaris to Pickering, Dec. 24, 1957, Froehlich to Medaris, Dec. 30, 1957, JPLVC roll 614-217.
26. Teletype messages between Cape Canaveral and JPL, Jan. 31, 1958, JPLVC roll 614-217.
27. Ibid.; "Up There—At Last," *Newsweek* (Feb. 10, 1958): 27–29.
28. Pickering and Wilson, "Countdown to Space Exploration," p. 417.
29. Cape-JPL teletypes.
30. Wilson interview with Stewart, Aug. 30, 1972; Wolfe et. al., *Juno I*, p. 70.
31. *Time* (Feb. 17, 1958): 25; *New York Times*, Feb. 1, 1958.
32. Wolfe et. al., *Juno I*, pp. 72–73.
33. Ibid., pp. 73–74; James A. Van Allen, "Radiation Belts around the Earth," *Scientific American* 200 (March 1959): 39–47.
34. Van Allen, "Radiation Belts"; *Science* 129 (Apr. 10, 1959): 949–51.
35. Allen E. Wolfe, "Juno Final Report, vol. 2, Juno II: Space Probes," JPL Technical Report no. 32-31, pp. 1–5, 53–57, 73–74.
36. Ibid.
37. Ibid.

Chapter 7

1. Hall interview with Small, Dec. 6, 1968, JPLHF 2-1392.
2. Medaris to Chief of Research and Development, Office of the Chief of Ordnance, Feb. 5, 1958, JPLVC roll 614-217, Eberhardt Rechtin to Medaris, Apr. 29, 1958, JPLVC roll 614-218, J. D. Burke, "Narrative for Juno IV ARPA Discussion," Apr. 30, 1958, JPLVC roll 614-93.
3. Pickering to Medaris, May 13, 1958, Medaris to Froehlich, May 14, 1958, JPLVC roll 614-218.
4. Parks to Froehlich, Aug. 8, 1958, JPLVC roll 614-218.
5. Rechtin to Parks, June 16, 1958, JPLVC roll 34-6.
6. McGarrity to Pickering, June 20, 1958; author's interview with Cummings, Arlington, Va., Apr. 27, 1976; J. H. Wilson interview with Stewart, Sept. 20, 1972, JPLHF 3-646.
7. Cummings to Pickering, June 19, 1958, JPLVC roll 211-2.
8. Ibid.
9. Ibid.; Parks to Pickering, July 2, 1958; Wilson interview with Stewart, Sept. 20, 1972, JPLHF 3-646. The first NASA administrator, T. Keith Glennan, sensed some of the same weaknesses. The NACA management staff, "although composed of reasonably able people had very little depth," he said, "and even these had relatively little experience in the management of large affairs." (T. Keith Glennan Diary, p. 6, DDEL).
10. Pickering draft, "The Jet Propulsion Laboratory and the U.S. Space Program," n.d., (about June 1958); Pickering to Killian, July 9, 1958, box 15, White House Office, Office of Science and Technology, Eisenhower Papers, DDEL.

11. Glennan to McElroy, Oct. 15, 1958, JPLHF 2-617; NASA staff document, "Suggested Program for Implementation of Proposal Made to the Honorable Neil H. McElroy," Oct. 15, 1958, JPLHF 2-618; "NASA Takes Over Jet Propulsion Lab," *Aviation Week* (Dec. 8, 1958).

12. Wilber M. Brucker, "Army Position Paper," n.d., (about Oct. 15, 1958), JPLHF 3-394; William M. Holaday and Roy W. Johnson to McElroy, Oct. 28, 1958, JPLHF 3-551; NASA memos for record regarding transfer of JPL, Nov. 12 and 15, 1958, JPLHF 3-588, 3-599, 3-656; Wesley Hjornevik, "Summary of our Position on the Remaining Unresolved Issues re the Transfer of JPL from the Army," Nov. 24, 1958, JPLHF 3-715; R. O. Piland to Killian, July 11, 1958, box 15, White House Office, Office of Science and Technology, Eisenhower Papers, DDEL.

13. Minutes, CIT Board of Trustees, Dec. 8, 1958; [Hugh Dryden?] "Possible Statement of Mission for Jet Propulsion Laboratory," Oct. 10, 1958.

14. "Proposal for Space Flight Program Study," JPL proposal to NASA, Nov. 7, 1958, JPLHF 2-620c.

15. Minutes and related memos of NASA program study committee at JPL, October 1958 through January 1959, esp. Nov. 19, Dec. 12, 17, 18, 23, 1958; McKenney to distribution, Jan. 16, 1959, JPLVC roll 211-2.

16. A. R. Hibbs, ed., "Exploration of the Moon, the Planets, and Interplanetary Space," JPL Report No. 30-1, April 1959, JPLHF 2-12.

17. J. D. Burke, "Vehicles for Deep Space Exploration," Dec. 31, 1958, JPLVC roll 211-4; teletypes between Pickering and Medaris, Jan. 5, 1959, JPLVC roll 614-218.

18. McKenney to distribution, "Minutes of meeting of NASA Program Study Committee and JPL Senior Staff with Abe Silverstein, Homer Stewart, Homer Newell, and Milton Rosen," Jan. 16, 1959, JPLVC roll 211-2.

19. Newell notes on meeting at JPL, Jan. 12, 1959, box 28, Newell Files, NASA History Office, Washington, D.C.; Newell, *Beyond the Atmosphere*, chap. 16.

20. Pickering to Glennan, Mar. 24, 1959, JPLHF 2-831; Pickering to Glennan, Silverstein, and Cummings, Feb. 20, 1959; J. H. Keyser, "JPL-Convair Vega Management Meeting," May 6, 1959, JPLVC roll 311-65.

21. Minutes, Vega staff meeting, May 25, 1959, JPLVC roll 311-65; R. Cargill Hall, *Lunar Impact: A History of Project Ranger* (Washington, D.C., 1977).

22. "Addendum to Lunar Program, Spacecraft Development Program," August 1959, JPLVC roll 211-4; "Vega Spacecraft Experiment Planning," Oct. 14, 1959, JPLVC roll 211-4.

23. Memorandum, Glennan and Dryden conference with the president, July 15, 1959, box 27, Eisenhower Papers as President (Ann Whitman File), DDEL; Vega Letter Report No. 1, July 31, 1959, JPLVC roll 614-93; Cummings to Vega distribution list C, Nov. 30, 1959, JPLVC roll 311-65.

24. Stewart to Glennan, Sept. 28, Oct. 14, 1959, box 7, acc. 70A5793, Records of the National Aeronautics and Space Administration, RG 255, WNRC; Paul Means, "Vega-Agena B Mix-Up Cost Millions," *Missiles and Rockets* (June 20, 1960); Evert Clark, "Vega Study Shows Early NASA Problems," *Aviation Week* 72 (June 27, 1960):62–68; Kistiakowsky, *A Scientist at the White House*, p. 129.

25. "Edited Notes on Phone Call to Horner in NASA," Dec. 8, 1959, JPLVC roll 311-64.
26. Ibid.; Horner to Pickering, Dec. 16, 1959, JPLVC roll 211-4; author's interview with Pickering, June 9, 1977.
27. Silverstein to Pickering, Dec. 21, 1959, JPLVC roll 614-167; Pickering interoffice memo No. 16, Dec. 16, 1959, Burke memo, Jan. 1959, JPLVC roll 211-4; Hall, *Lunar Impact*, pp. 46–49.
28. "Jet Propulsion Laboratory: Its Objectives, Organization, and Programs," May 6, 1960, JPLHF 3-630.
29. Ibid.; House of Representatives subcommittee on NASA Oversight, Committee on Science and Astronautics, "Investigation of Project Ranger," (88th Cong., 2nd Sess., Apr. 29, 1964), p. 143.
30. Same sources as note 26.
31. McKinsey & Co. to Glennan, Dec. 18, 1958, JPLHF 3-194; Glennan to Dryden, et al., Oct. 19, 1959, box 16, acc. 70A5793, RG 255, WNRC.
32. Same sources as note 28; Glennan to DuBridge, Aug. 10, 1959, DuBridge Papers.
33. Glennan to Dryden, et al., Oct. 19, 1959; Pickering to Glennan, May 17, 1960, JPLHF 3-947.
34. "NASA-JPL Relationships," Aug. 2, 1960, JPLHF 2-963; Hall, *Lunar Impact*, chap. 4.
35. Glennan Diary, p. 17, DDEL; author's interview with Glennan, Washington, D.C., Apr. 23, 1976; "Major Problems in the Management of JPL," n.d. (about Nov. 16, 1959), box 16, acc. 70A5793, RG 255, WNRC.
36. Author's interview with Glennan, Washington, D.C., Apr. 23, 1976; Glennan to DuBridge, Nov. 12, 1959, DuBridge Papers; Newell, *Beyond the Atmosphere*, p. 260.
37. Pickering to Newell, Mar. 22, 1960, file 38.2, Bacher to DuBridge, Apr. 14, 1960, file 33.7, DuBridge Papers; Newell, *Beyond the Atmosphere*, pp. 264–65.
38. Seamans interview with Walter Bonney, Feb. 23, 1973, JPLHF 5-664; Mose L. Harvey, "Preeminence in Space: Still a Critical National Issue," *Orbis* 12 (Winter 1969): 964.
39. Glennan Diary, pp. 37, 396, and "Thoughts on the Nation's Space Program as it has Developed since January 1961," [Nov. 12, 1963], Glennan Diary.
40. Glennan, "Thoughts on the Nation's Space Program"; Glennan Diary, p. 238.
41. Glennan, "Thoughts on the Nation's Space Program"; Kistiakowsky, *A Scientist at the White House*, p. 100; Newell, *Beyond the Atmosphere*, p. 396.
42. Pickering to Glennan, May 17, 1960, JPLHF 3-947; Glennan to Pickering, June 17, 1960, JPLHF 3-948; Pickering speech reprinted in *Astronautics* (Jan. 1960): 83–84; Pickering to senior staff, Jan. 13, 1960, JPLVC roll 211-5.

Chapter 8

1. L. D. Jaffe, R. R. McDonald, and W. J. Schimandle, "Preliminary Study of a National Space Effort," May 9, 1961, JPLHF.
2. James R. Killian, Jr., "Making Science a Vital Force in Foreign Policy," *Science* 33 (Jan. 6, 1961): 24–25.

3. Bell to Kennedy, n.d., (about Mar. 25, 1961), box 82, President's Official File, JFKL (emphasis in original).
4. Bush to Webb, Apr. 11, 1963, box 84, JFKL.
5. Theodore Sorensen, *Kennedy* (New York, 1965), pp. 524–25; Webb speech at NASA-Industry Conference, Feb. 11, 1963, in *NASA-Industry Program Plans Conference* (Washington, D.C., 1963), p. 4. On credibility see generally Jonathan Schell, *The Time of Illusion* (New York, 1976), esp. pp. 133–34.
6. Sorensen, *Kennedy*, p. 608; Webb to Kennedy, Aug. 9, 1963, box 84, President's Official File, JFKL. Frederick Seitz, president of the National Academy of Sciences, said that while individual space missions probably had negligible military value, the overall effect was significant. "The protection of the Free World requires that we remain in the forefront of nations concerned with the technology needed for the exploration of space," he said. See Seitz, "Science and the Space Program," *Science* 152 (June 24, 1966): 1721. For an insightful study of Kennedy's missile programs see Desmond Ball, *Politics and Force Levels: The Strategic Missile Programs of the Kennedy Administration* (Berkeley, 1980).
7. Webb to Kennedy, Aug. 9, 1963.
8. John M. Logsdon, *The Decision to Go to the Moon: Project Apollo and the National Interest* (Cambridge, Mass., 1970), p. 112; Johnson to Kennedy, Apr. 28, 1961, box 30, President's Official File, JFKL. In recent years some writers have tried to foreshorten the chronology of events leading to the Apollo decision and place the decision on April 14, 1961. This has the advantage of giving Apollo an immaculate conception. If the decision were made at this point, the man-on-the-moon program would be solely in response to Gagarin's flight since it was decided on *before* the Bay of Pigs disaster became apparent. (See Eugene M. Emme, "Presidents and Space," in Frederick C. Durant, III, ed., *Between Sputnik and the Shuttle: New Perspectives on American Astronautics* [San Diego, 1981], American Astronautical Society History Series, vol. 3, pp. 53–55, 78.) Contemporary sources do not substantiate this chronology. Hugh Sidey, presidential correspondent for the Henry Luce publications, was brought in for part of the meeting on April 14—indeed, the event appears to have been a reprise of an earlier session which was staged for his benefit. Sidey reported at the time only that Kennedy was "determined to get an answer" to what should be done. If the president made the decision to go to the moon at that time, as Sidey recalled nearly twenty years later, Sidey missed the scoop of the decade. (See Hugh Sidey, "How the News Hit Washington," *Life* 50 [Apr. 21, 1961]: 26–27. Sidey repeats basically the same account in his *John F. Kennedy, President* [New York, 1963], pp. 110–23.) In short, Logsdon's intuition that both the Gagarin flight and the Bay of Pigs were linked in an important, if imprecise, manner seems justified.
9. Pickering to senior staff, Apr. 25, 1961, file 31.2, DuBridge Papers, CIT Archives.
10. Jaffe, McDonald, and Schimandle, "Preliminary Study."
11. Meghreblian to Pickering and Goddard, May 3, 1961, JPLHF 3-1090; William Pickering, "Acceleration of the U.S. Space Program," n.d. (about May 1961), JPLHF 3-1107.
12. *Public Papers of the Presidents: Kennedy, 1961* (Washington, D.C., 1962), pp. 396–406; Cummings quoted in Hall, *Lunar Impact*, p. 120.

13. Burke to author, Mar. 10, 1981; [Burke?], "BEAT THE RUSSIANS: A 'First' at Something with Public Recogniz," JPLVC roll 211-4; Hall, *Lunar Impact*, p. 65.
14. Packard to Executive Secretary, National Aeronautics and Space Council, Apr. 24, 1963, box 84, JFKL.
15. Hall, *Lunar Impact*, pp. 46–49; Rechtin to Sparks, Feb. 20, 1963, Ranger 5 Failure Investigation Board interview with John Small, Oct. 30, 1962, box 3, shipment 1427, JPL Foothill D RSC.
16. Interview summaries, Ranger 5 Failure Investigation Board.
17. Ibid., esp. interviews with Burke, Nov. 2, 1962, Cummings, Nov. 6, 1962, Small, Oct. 30, 1962, and James, Nov. 2, 1962.
18. Ibid., esp. interview with Cummings, Nov. 6, 1962.
19. Ibid.; Hall, *Lunar Impact*, pp. 72–74, 124–27.
20. Hall, *Lunar Impact*, pp. 74–77. The subordination of scientific experiments to engineering was apparent in a memorandum Burke wrote in March 1960: "Scientific experiments are an integral part of the planned program. By setting up scientific objectives for each round, we force ourselves to consider system interactions that would not otherwise be apparent, and we develop kinds of equipment needed in the future. *Scientific experiments, as such, are carried on a basis of non-interference with engineering measurements,* but engineering development of scientific instrumentation is as important as other engineering developments in the spacecraft" ("Mission Objectives and Design Criteria for Ranger flights 3, 4, 5," Mar. 9, 1960, JPLVC roll 211-5, emphasis added).
21. Hall, *Lunar Impact*, p. 57.
22. Ranger 5 Failure Investigation Board interview with R. Heacock, Oct. 30, 1962, JPL Foothill D RSC; Hall, *Lunar Impact*, pp. 130–37.
23. Hall, *Lunar Impact*, pp. 162–63.
24. Ranger 5 Failure Investigation Board interview with James, Nov. 2, 1962.
25. This section is based substantially on Hall's indispensable *Lunar Impact*, primarily chaps. 6 and 9.
26. NASA, "Final Report of the Ranger Board of Inquiry," Nov. 30, 1962, p. 5, JPLHF 2-2463.
27. Burke to Parks and Cummings, May 19, 1960, JPLHF 8-101; Silverstein to Seamans, Aug. 30, 1961, Homer Newell Files, NASA History Office; Parks to Schurmeier, and others, Sept. 6, 1961, JPLHF 8-46.
28. Ranger 5 Failure Investigation Board interview with James, Nov. 6, 1962, JPL Foothill D RSC.
29. Ibid.
30. Ibid.; *The Mariner Mission—1962* (Pasadena, 1963), pp. 5, 10–11.
31. *Mariner Mission*, p. 3; Planning Research Corporation, "Reliability Assessment of the Mariner Spacecraft," Dec. 17, 1962, JPLHF 8-12; Hall, *Lunar Impact*, p. 160.
32. Newell to Frank R. Hammill, Jr., May 8, 1963, Newell Files, NASA History Office; Newell to Joseph E. Karth in House of Representatives subcommittee on NASA Oversight, Committee on Science and Astronautics, "Investigation of Project Ranger," (Washington, D.C., 1964), p. 5.
33. Hall, *Lunar Impact*, pp. 163–70.
34. Report of JPL Failure Investigation Board, "Ranger RA-5 Failure Investigation," Nov. 13, 1962, JPL Foothill D RSC.

35. Ibid.; Morris to Pickering, Nov. 14, 1962, in Report of JPL, Failure Investigation Board (emphasis in original).
36. Report of JPL Failure Investigation Board.
37. Ibid. W. K. Victor, who felt that "the Mariner project was successful in spite of the management tools provided by the Laboratory organization rather than because of it," dissented from the recommendation to replace Burke (Victor to JPL Failure Investigation Board, Nov. 13, 1962).
38. NASA, "Final Report of the Ranger Board of Inquiry," Nov. 30, 1962, JPLHF 2-2463.
39. Ibid. See also the discussion of the two investigating boards in Hall, *Lunar Impact*, chap. 11.
40. NASA, "Final Report of the Ranger Board of Inquiry."
41. Hall, *Lunar Impact*, pp. 176–82. The project managers' observations are from Richard L. Chapman, *Project Management in NASA: The System and the Men* (Washington, D.C., 1973), p. 112.
42. Hall, *Lunar Impact*, pp. 176–82.

Chapter 9

1. J. D. McKenney, "Discussion Paper—CIT-JPL-NASA," Jan. 9, 1961, file 34.12, DuBridge Papers, CIT Archives.
2. Hall interview with Webb, Oct. 26, 1972, JPLHF 2-2308; "NASA-Caltech-JPL Position Paper," Feb. 14, 1964, box 16, acc. 70A5793, RG 255, WNRC.
3. Lee DuBridge, "Science and Government," *Chemical and Engineering News* 21 (Apr. 6, 1953): 1384–90; Hall interview with Larsen, May 28, 1968, JPLHF 2-759.
4. Cortright to Pickering, Mar. 7, 1962.
5. Nicks to Silverstein, Oct. 6, 1961.
6. Glennan to Walter Bonney; NASA staff document, "Some Questions to be Considered Concerning JPL," Jan. 17, 1963, box 17, Hilburn to Beckman, Mar. 27, 1964, box 16, acc. 70A5793, RG 255, WNRC.
7. Cortright to Seamans, July 19, 1963, box 9, acc. 72A3070, RG 255, WNRC.
8. NASA staff document, "Administrative Weaknesses at JPL," Sept. 10, 1963, box 16, acc. 70A5793, RG 255, WNRC; DuBridge to Pickering, July 25, 1962, file 31.2, DuBridge Papers.
9. Gilmore to Walter L. Lingle, Jr., Aug. 2, 1963, file 38.5, DuBridge Papers.
10. Hilburn to Seamans, Aug. 1, 1963, box 17, acc. 70A5793, RG 255, WNRC.
11. Raymond Einhorn and Robert B. Lewis to Hilburn, Oct. 20, 1964, box 9, acc. 72A3070, RG 255, WNRC.
12. Thomas quoted in *Science* 151 (March 4, 1966): 1065; Albert F. Siepert to Webb, May 2, 1962, box 17, acc. 70A5793, RG 255, WNRC. On Thomas and Houston see Glennan Diary, pp. 19–20.
13. Hilburn to Seamans, Aug. 1, 1963; Einhorn and Lewis to Hilburn, Oct. 20, 1964; American Council on Education, *American Universities and Colleges* (Washington, D.C., 1964).
14. CIT, "A Prepared Statement Regarding the FY 64 Fixed Fee to Be Negotiated Under Contract No. NAS7-100" and "Analysis and Justification for the

$1,440,000 Fixed Fee Proposed for FY 64 Under Contract No. NAS 7-100," both Sept. 6, 1963, with marginal notations by Hilburn, Sept. 12, 1963, box 17, acc. 70A5793, RG 255, WNRC; transcript, "Presentation by Caltech and JPL on Justification of Contract Fee," Washington, D.C., Sept. 16, 1963, box 12, acc. 72A3070, RG 255, WNRC; DuBridge to Ruddock, Oct. 1, 1956, file 33.6, DuBridge Papers.

15. Transcript, "Presentation by Caltech and JPL on Justification of Contract Fee," Sept. 16, 1963.

16. Ibid.

17. Ibid.

18. Ibid.

19. Einhorn and Lewis to Hilburn, Oct. 20, 1964; author's interview with Pickering, July 19, 1978.

20. Same sources as note 19.

21. Same sources as note 19; McKenney to Pickering and Sparks, Jan. 17 and 20, 1961, box 5, shipment 1427, JPL Lyons.

22. Hilburn to Seamans, Aug. 1, 1963.

23. John Mecklin, "Jim Webb's Earthy Management of Space," *Fortune* 76 (Aug. 1967): 86. Citing medical advice, Webb politely declined the author's requests for an interview. He assured the author that the issues around the JPL-CIT-NASA triangle were amply documented in archival materials and in interviews with other historians, notably with Hall, JPLHF 2-2308.

24. Webb to Emme, Jan. 29, 1965, box 165, Webb Papers, HSTL; W. Warde Fowler, *The City-State of the Greeks and Romans* (London, 1893), chap. 10, esp. p. 270.

25. Thomas W. Adams and Thomas P. Murphy, "NASA's University Research Programs: Dilemma and Problems on the Government-Academic Interface," *Public Administration Review* 27 (Mar. 1967): 12; Webb to Chauncey Starr, Oct. 19, 1967, file 34.6, DuBridge Papers.

26. "Highlight Notes, Visit of Mr. James Webb to JPL," Mar. 28, 1963, file 31.2, DuBridge Papers; materials on California Universities Council on Space Sciences in file 32.7, DuBridge Papers; Webb to Hilburn, Aug. 19, 1963, box 9, acc. 72A3070, RG 255, WNRC; author's interview with Newell, Washington, D.C., Apr. 21, 1977.

27. James Webb, "Science and Technology—Keys to Economic Progress" (Commencement address at Northeastern University, Boston, June 17, 1962); Webb to Lingle, Aug. 15, 1962, Webb Papers, HSTL; James E. Webb, *Space Age Management: The Large-scale Approach* (New York, 1969); Mecklin, "Jim Webb's Earthy Management of Space," p. 86; Tom Alexander, "The Unexpected Payoff of Project Apollo," *Fortune* 80 (July 1969): 117.

28. Dael Wolfle, "The Support of Science in the United States," *Scientific American* 213 (July 1965): 25; "Highlight Notes, Visit of Mr. James Webb to JPL," Mar. 28, 1963; author's interview with Newell, Apr. 21, 1977.

29. Webb to Seamans, Aug. 19, 1963, Webb to Hilburn, Aug. 19, 1963, box 9, acc. 72A3070, RG 255, WNRC; Webb to DuBridge, Aug. 29, 1961, file 32.7, Gilmore to Beckman, Mar. 5, 1964, file 34.2, DuBridge Papers.

30. Hilburn to Seamans, Aug. 1, 1963.

31. Hilburn to Seamans, Sept. 11, 1963, box 17, acc. 70A5793, RG 255, WNRC.

32. DuBridge to Webb, June 28, 1963, file 32.10, Oct. 29, 1963, file 38.5, DuBridge Papers; Webb to Lingle, June 27, 1963, box 9, acc. 72A3070, RG 255, WNRC.
33. Gilmore to Beckman, Mar. 5, 1964, file 34.2, DuBridge Papers.
34. Hilburn to Seamans, Nov. 6, 1963, box 16, acc. 70A5793, RG 255, WNRC.
35. NASA staff document, "Summary of Improvements Resulting from Renewal Agreement with the California Institute of Technology for Performance of Research Utilizing the Jet Propulsion Laboratory (Contract NAS7-100, Modification No. 10)," Dec. 27, 1963, box 17, acc. 70A5793, RG 255, WNRC; John MacL. Hunt to record, Dec. 13, 1963, file 32.10, DuBridge Papers.
36. Same sources as note 35.; Hilburn notes, May 2, 1964, box 17, acc. 70A5793, RG 255, WNRC; Newell, *Beyond the Atmosphere*, p. 271.
37. Hunt to record, Dec. 13, 1963.
38. NASA, "Summary of Improvements," Dec. 27, 1963; Sparks to Medaris, July 12, 1963, box 3, shipment 976, JPL Lyons.
39. The following sections on the technical development, flight, and subsequent investigation of Ranger 6 are based in large part on Hall, *Lunar Impact*, chaps. 15 and 16.
40. Hall interview with Webb, Oct. 26, 1972, JPLHF 2-2308.
41. Hall, *Lunar Impact*, p. 254.
42. House of Representatives Committee on Science and Astronautics, "Investigation of Project Ranger," (88th Cong., 2nd Sess., 1964), pp. 139–82; author's interview with Pickering, July 19, 1978.
43. "Investigation of Project Ranger," pp. 211–46, esp. pp. 214, 218, 226; "Pitchman for NASA's Trip to the Moon," *Business Week* (May 27, 1967): 71.
44. Hall, *Lunar Impact*, p. 254.
45. House of Representatives Committee on Science and Astronautics, "Project Ranger," (88th Cong., 2nd Sess., report no. 1487, 1964), esp. pp. 30–31. H. L. Nieburg uses the Ranger investigation as the centerpiece of his discussion of JPL-NASA relations in his study of the "contract state." (See his *In the Name of Science* [Chicago, 1966], chap. 12.) Lacking access to internal documents when he wrote, Nieburg necessarily is somewhat incomplete and may underestimate some of the internal problems at JPL and the clouded role of Caltech. There is much merit, nonetheless, in Nieburg's idea of JPL as a "yardstick."
46. Pickering to JPL Executive Council, Feb. 26, 1964, Report of Ad Hoc Advisory Group, Mar. 16, 1964, JPLHF; "Investigation of Project Ranger," p. 169; see also W. S. Shipley to Pickering, Nov. 15, 1962, box 3, shipment 1427, JPL Lyons.
47. Gilmore to Beckman, Mar. 5, 1964, emphasis in original.
48. Gilmore to DuBridge, May 13, 1964, file 34.2, DuBridge Papers.
49. Beckman to Webb, July 31, 1964, file 35.10, DuBridge Papers.
50. Seamans to Webb, July 15, 1964, box 17, acc. 70A5793; Webb to Beckman, March 27, 1964, Aug. 18, 1964; Webb to Hilburn, Sept. 8, 1964, Hilburn to record, Sept. 1, 1964, box 16, acc. 70A5793, RG 255, WNRC.
51. Hilburn to Gilmore, Oct. 17, 1963, box 12, acc. 72A3070, RG 255; Newell, *Beyond the Atmosphere*, chap. 16.
52. Sparks to Medaris, May 22, 1964, box 3, shipment 976, JPL Lyons.

Chapter 10

1. This section is substantially based on Hall, *Lunar Impact*, esp. chaps. 15–17. The author is, however, less sanguine about Ranger's scientific rewards than Hall (see p. 309).
2. Nicks to Newell, Oct. 9, 1962, Mariner Files, Records of the National Aeronautics and Space Administration, RG 255, WNRC; Parks to senior staff, Jan. 8, 1963, JPLHF 8-253.
3. Same sources as note 2.
4. G. L. Hobby to Fred Kochendorfer, Oct. 2, 1962, Mariner Files, RG 255, WNRC.
5. H. M. Schurmeier, "Planetary Exploration: Earth's New Horizon," *Journal of Spacecraft and Rockets* 12 (July 1975): 391; James H. Wilson, "Report from Mars: Mariner IV 1964–1965," JPL Report, 1966, pp. 10–11, 24.
6. Wilson, "Report from Mars," pp. 14–15.
7. "Mariner Mars 1964 Project Report: Mission and Spacecraft Development," NASA Technical Report No. 32-740, 1966, p. 31.
8. Author's interview with James, Jan. 24, 1979; Hall, *Lunar Impact*, p. 307.
9. "Mariner Mars 1964 Project Report," pp. 31–32.
10. Ibid.
11. Ibid., pp. 83–84.
12. Ibid., p. 630.
13. Wilson, "Report from Mars," p. 21.
14. N. E. Johnson, and others, "Evaluations and Recommendations Pertaining to Mariner C Fiberglass Honeycomb Shroud," JPL Section Report No. 352-6, 1965, pp. 2–3, JPLHF 8-25; author's interview with James, Jan. 24, 1979.
15. Same sources as note 14; "Mariner Mars 1964 Project Report," pp. 46–47.
16. Same sources as note 15; James to Pickering, Luedecke, and Parks, Feb. 18, 1965, JPLHF 8-406; Bruce C. Murray and Merton E. Davies, "A Comparison of U.S. and Soviet Efforts to Explore Mars," *Science* 151 (Feb. 25, 1966): 947.
17. Thomas L. Branigan, "Mariner-IV Nears Mars," *Engineering Opportunities* (July 1965): 9–16.
18. Schurmeier, "Planetary Exploration," p. 393.
19. Ibid., p. 391; Wilson, "Report from Mars," p. 5; Bruce Murray, Michael C. Malin, and Ronald Greeley, *Earthlike Planets: Surfaces of Mercury, Venus, Earth, Moon, Mars* (San Francisco, 1981), p. 15.
20. Oran Nicks, "Recommendation for an Evolutionary Planetary Program," RG 255, WNRC; Schurmeier, "Planetary Exploration," p. 391; Murray and Davies, "A Comparison of U.S. and Soviet Efforts to Explore Mars," p. 946.
21. Cortright to Seamans, Mar. 17, 1967, box 3, acc. 69A7258, RG 255, WNRC.
22. House of Representatives Committee on Science and Astronautics, "Project Surveyor," (89th Cong., 1st Sess., Committee Print, Serial J, 1965), pp. 12–14.
23. Silverstein to Seamans, Sept. 6, 1961, Milwitzky to Director, Lunar and Planetary Programs, "JPL Presentation to Dr. Seamans on September 24 Regarding the Laboratory's Viewpoints on Centaur and Saturn," Sept. 26, 1962, Surveyor Files, RG 255, WNRC; see also telexes between Giberson and Hans Hueter, Sept. 1961, JPLVC roll 614-219.

24. House Committee, "Project Surveyor," pp. 15–21, 30; "Surveyor Project Final Report, Part 1, Project Description and Performance," JPL Technical Report 32-1265, 1969, vol. 1, p. 27.
25. "Surveyor Project Final Report," p. 30; *Space/Aeronautics* (December 1965): 18.
26. Mosher-Newell colloquy quoted in House Committee, "Project Surveyor," p. 34; Herman O. Stekler, *The Structure and Performance of the Aerospace Industry* (Berkeley, 1965), p. 83. Stekler notes: "The salient features of the aerospace industry are: a high concentration of sales; the absence of competition; a failure on the buyer's part to impose economic incentives on the sellers; and high entry barriers. One would theorize that the performance of the industry with such a structure would not be outstanding. This, indeed, is the case" (p. 204). Specific problems he cites include excessive development, "lack of enthusiasm for value engineering," and erratic product quality (p. 196).
27. Milwitzky to Cortright, Mar. 27, 1963, Surveyor Files, RG 255, WNRC; Minutes and related documents of JPL Surveyor Soft-Landing Spacecraft Source Evaluation Board, Jan. 4 and 5, 1961, box 1, acc. 73-695, JPL Records, RG 255, FRC.
28. House Committee, "Project Surveyor," pp. 31–33.
29. NASA performance evaluation, file 35.3, DuBridge Papers; Cole to Parks, Giberson, and H. H. Haglund, Jan. 14, 1964, JPLHF 6-195.
30. Summary minutes, Surveyor Design Review, Mar. 23–27, 1964, box 1, acc. 73-695, JPL Records, RG 255, FRC.
31. Newell to Seamans, Dec. 28, 1964, box 5, shipment 1427, JPL Records, RG 255, FRC.
32. Surveyor Design Review, pp. 9, 18, 19, 31, 33, 47–49; Erasmus Kloman, "Surveyor," unpub. ms., Aug. 12, 1970, box 126, Webb Papers, HSTL.
33. Transcript of Conference of the House Space Science and Applications Subcommittee held at JPL, Sept. 2, 1965, box 1, acc. 73-695, p. 25, JPL Records, RG 255, FRC; House Committee, "Project Surveyor," p. 25.
34. Surveyor Design Review Task Team Report, pp. 9–10, JPLHF 6-255.
35. Ibid., pp. 3, 9–10; House Subcommittee transcript, p. 25.
36. Surveyor Design Review Task Team Report, pp. 9–10; see also "Surveyor Project Final Report," pp. 411–24.
37. Newell, *Beyond the Atmosphere*, p. 270; House Committee "Project Surveyor," pp. 34–35.
38. Pickering to Cortright, July 14, 1964; "Surveyor Project Final Report," p. 53.
39. Milwitzky memorandum, "Surveyor Problem Areas," Nov. 1963, Surveyor Files, RG 255, WNRC; NASA Office of Space Sciences and Applications Surveyor Review, Feb. 9, 1965, box 6, acc. 69A1504, RG 255, WNRC.
40. Nicks to Luedecke, Nov. 3, 1964, box 5, shipment 1427, JPL Lyons.
41. Milwitzky to Giberson, Mar. 14, 1964, Milwitzky to F. A. Zihlman, May 6, 1964, box 3, acc. 68A6337, RG 255, WNRC; D. A. Mahaffy and R. E. Sears, "The Surveyor Vernier Engine Subcontract with Thiokol Reaction Motors Division," July 20, 1964, box 1, shipment 604, JPL Lyons.
42. Milwitzky to Giberson, "Surveyor Vernier Propulsion Program," Mar. 4, 1965, JPLHF 6-206; "Surveyor Vernier Propulsion Program Chronology of Events," n.d. (about Feb. 1965), JPLHF 6-177.

43. Contract data and quotations are drawn from chapter 5 of Kloman's "Surveyor," box 126, Webb Papers, HSTL. The study by Kloman, a senior research associate of the National Academy of Public Administration, is an illuminating source not only for Surveyor but for NASA and aerospace contracting generally. Regrettably the published version omits much of the insightful material. See Erasmus H. Kloman, *Unmanned Space Project Management: Surveyor and Lunar Orbiter* (Washington, D.C., NASA Sp-4901, 1972).

44. Contract data from Kloman, "Surveyor," chap. 5, esp. pp. 19–21; House Committee, "Project Surveyor," pp. 26–29, 33; Parks to Nicks, Sept. 22, 1964, with "JPL Response to NASA Headquarters Surveyor Project Review of March 23–27, 1964," Nicks to record, Oct. 19, 1964, box 3, acc. 68A6337, RG 255, WNRC; House Subcommittee transcript, pp. 44, 48. Its mission presumably accomplished, JPL reduced its work on Surveyors 3 through 7. But continuing problems at Hughes—particularly a series of more than twenty human errors from mid-1965 through 1966—caused NASA to register a strong protest with the firm. The errors rendered at least one spacecraft unflyable, necessitated extensive rework and revalidation of hardware, drove up costs on Surveyor and other projects, and fouled flight schedules at Cape Kennedy. Homer Newell found some of the errors to be "particularly inexcusable" because they repeated known problems from Surveyors 1 and 2. Hughes had not "as yet properly instilled the discipline" the effort required, he told the firm's president, L. A. Hyland. "The number and frequency of human errors occurring during this operation seem to be greater than those normally encountered on similar projects by other contractors, and also seem to represent little, if any, improvement over the Surveyor 1 and 2 experiences" (Newell to Hyland, Jan. 9, 1967, box 9, acc. 69A1504, RG 255, WNRC).

45. "The Surveyor Project," JPL Report, 1968, p. 9.

46. Ibid. The Soviet Union's Luna 9 landed, somewhat less softly than Surveyor, in February 1966 and sent back the first pictures from the surface of the moon.

47. *Surveyor Program Results* (Washington, D.C., 1969), p. v.

48. "The Surveyor Project," pp. 10, 14.

49. Ibid., pp. 17–18; *Surveyor Program Results*, pp. 13–17.

50. Same sources as note 49; Bevan French, *The Moon Book* (New York, 1977), pp. 82–83, 60, 78–79, 247–48. See also the reports by Homer J. Stewart and Albert Hibbs in "Lunar Exploration: The Impact of Ranger and Surveyor Results," NASA Technical Report 32-1399.

51. Murray, Malin, and Greeley, *Earthlike Planets*, pp. 227–28.

Chapter 11

1. NASA Ad Hoc Science Advisory Committee, Report to the Administrator, Aug. 15, 1966, box 1, shipment 976, JPL Lyons.

2. Hall interview with Small, Dec. 6, 1968, JPLHF 2-1392; Pickering to senior staff, June 23, 1967, box 1, shipment 976, JPL Lyons.

3. Newell to Seamans, Sept. 25, 1964, box 8, acc. 68A6256, Records of the National Aeronautics and Space Administration, RG 255, WNRC.

4. Ibid.
5. Bruce C. Murray, "A New Strategy for Planetary Exploration," Aug. 16, 1968, box 5, shipment 976, JPL Lyons; James E. Long, "To the Outer Planets," *Astronautics & Aeronautics* (June 1969): 32–47.
6. Newell testimony before House Subcommittee on Space Sciences and Applications, n.d. (about Mar. 4, 1965), box 8, acc. 68A6256, RG 255, WNRC.
7. Oran Nicks, "Recommendation for an Evolutionary Planetary Program," Sept. 27, 1965, box 8, acc. 68A6256, RG 255, WNRC.
8. Voyager project development plan, Aug. 1967, box 6, acc. 68A6256, RG 255, WNRC; *Science* 157 (Aug. 11, 1967): 658–60; Bruce C. Murray, "The U.S. Planetary Program, Midstream in 1966," June 3, 1966, and "Problems of U.S. Planetary Program and the Role of Hypothetical Institutes," box 5, shipment 976, JPL Lyons.
9. Murray, "New Strategy for Planetary Exploration."
10. *Science,* Aug. 11, 1967, p. 659.
11. Murray to DuBridge, Feb. 23, 1965, with "Suggestions for Martian Exploration Following Mariner IV," JPLHF 3-467.
12. Same sources as note 11.
13. Same sources as note 11.
14. Murray to DuBridge, Feb. 23, 1965.
15. Donald P. Hearth to Nicks, Robert F. Fellows to Nicks, O'Bryant to Nicks, all Mar. 9, 1965, JPLHF 3-466; Nicks, "Recommendation for an Evolutionary Planetary Program," box 8, acc. 68A6256, RG 255, WNRC.
16. Lees to Murray, Mar. 22, 1965, Murray to DuBridge, Sept. 24, 1965, box 5, shipment 976, JPL Lyons.
17. Murray, "The U.S. Planetary Program, Midstream in 1966."
18. Minutes, CIT Board of Trustees, Jan. 10, 1966.
19. Rieke and Sohier to Webb, Sept. 10, 1966, box 12, acc. 72A3070, RG 255, WNRC; minutes, JPL Executive Council, Mar. 6, 1967; D. P. Burcham, "Voyager notes," Jan. 23, 1966, JPLHF 3-270.
20. Rieke and Sohier to Webb, Sept. 10, 1966.
21. Ibid.; Huber to Pickering, Aug. 1, 1966, box 5, shipment 976, JPL Lyons; see also James to Luedecke, Sept. 15, 1965, JPLHF 8-260.
22. Daniel S. Greenberg, "Space: Caution Prevails on Post-Apollo Commitments," *Science* 153 (Sept. 9, 1966): 1222; Ralph Lapp, "But What Comes After the Moon," *New Republic* 155 (Nov. 19, 1966): 10–12.
23. Minutes, Voyager Board of Directors, July 12, 1967, box 7, acc. 68A6256, RG 255, WNRC; Murray, "A New Strategy for Planetary Exploration," box 5, shipment 976, JPL Lyons. As late as early November 1967 Webb still wanted a big Voyager, with two spacecraft in orbit of Mars in 1973 and with two orbiters and two softlanders in 1975. (The latter would use the Saturn 5, which was ten times more costly than the Titan 3C.) NASA's own lunar and planetary missions board had differed with the administrator. They proposed (1) a Venus and Mercury flyby in 1970, instead of 1973, as Webb wanted; (2) a Mariner-class atmospheric probe of Mars in 1971, but not the more costly one Webb called for; (3) a galactic probe and flyby of Jupiter in 1974 in preparation for the Grand Tour; and (4) skipping Voyager 1975 as premature in terms of the state

of both technology and the knowledge of Mars. The board's ideas were on the same order as Murray's. See *Science* 158 (Nov. 24, 1967): p. 1026.

24. JPL Mariner Mars 71 Proposal, August 1966, JPLHF 8-174.
25. Pickering to Cortright, July 27, 1967, file 38.8, DuBridge Papers; Pickering to Newell, Mar. 7, 1967, JPLHF 8-184; Pickering to Newell, Apr. 14, 1967, JPLHF 8-232; James to Pickering, May 9, 1967, JPLHF 8-220; JPL position paper on Mariner Mars 71 in-house, May 31, 1967, JPLHF 8-233.
26. Homer J. Stewart notes on planetary program planning, JPLHF 8-95; James H. Wilson, "Return to Venus," JPL Technical Memorandum 33-393, 1968, p. 13.
27. Same sources as note 26.
28. JPL Project document No. 70 (n.d., about February 1966).
29. Newell, *Beyond the Atmosphere*, p. 264.
30. Conway W. Snyder to Dan Schneiderman, Jan. 14, 1966, JPLHF 8-79; Donald P. Hearth to James and Robert Crane, Jan. 25, 1966, JPLHF 8-103. JPL continued to study a possible Venus probe for 1972. But in November 1967 that essay was halted by what a laboratory engineer termed "the untimely Russian success" (Venera 4). See C. R. Gates to Parks, Nov. 7, 1967, JPLHF 8-133.
31. Pickering to Newell, Jan. 17, 1966, Feb. 15, 1966, Newell to Pickering, Feb. 4, 1966, all JPLHF 8-79.
32. Snyder to Schneiderman, Jan. 14, 1966, JPLHF 8-79.
33. Murray to Robert P. Sharp, Oct. 1, 1965, file 34.13, DuBridge Papers.
34. Wilson, "Return to Venus," pp. 29–32.
35. Schurmeier to MM 69 Preliminary Design Review Board members, Nov. 29, 1966, JPLHF 8-211; Schurmeier, "Mariner Mars 69 Project," Jan. 21, 1966, JPLHF 8-212.
36. N. A. Renzetti, ed., "A History of the Deep Space Network," JPL Technical Report 32-1533, Sept. 1, 1971, pp. 72–73.
37. "Mariner Mars 1969 Project Final Report, Development, Design, and Test," vol. 1, JPL Technical Report 32-1460, Nov. 1, 1970, part 2.
38. Urner Liddel to Naugle, Dec. 6, 1965, box 6, acc. 69A1504, RG 255, WNRC; "Mariner Mars 1969 Project Final Report, vol. 3, Scientific Investigations," JPL Technical Report 32-1460, Sept. 15, 1971, pp. 3–4.
39. "Mariner Mars 1969 Project Final Report," vol. 1, pp. 182–89; Newton W. Cunningham to record, Apr. 25, 1966, RG 255, WNRC.
40. "Mariner Mars 1969 Project Final Report," vol. 1, pp. 524–29.
41. Schneiderman to Reiff, Jan. 27, 1966, JPLHF 8-79.
42. Newell, *Beyond the Atmosphere*, pp. 266–67. The controversy between JPL and Pimentel generated more than two score letters which are preserved in JPLHF; only the most important are cited here.
43. Pimentel to Schurmeier, Mar. 4, 1969, JPLHF 8-143.
44. Naugle to Pimentel, Jan. 5, 1968, JPLHF 8-139.
45. Rea to Pimentel, Oct. 14, 1968, N. William Cunningham to Schurmeier, Oct. 9, 1968, JPLHF 8-152; Pimentel to Cunningham, Oct. 25, 1968, Pimentel to Rea, Oct. 25, 1968, JPLHF 8-153.
46. Pimentel to Schurmeier, May 6, 1969, Schurmeier to Pimentel, May 26, 1969, JPLHF 8-162; Pimentel to Schurmeier, Nov. 11, 1968, JPLHF 8-154; Rea to Cunningham, June 2, 1969, JPLHF 8-163; Kenneth C. Herr and George C.

Pimentel, "Evidence for Solid Carbon Dioxide in the Upper Atmosphere of Mars," *Science* 167 (Jan. 2, 1970): 47–49.

47. Pimentel to Schurmeier, Jan. 5, 1968, JPLHF 8-139.
48. James H. Wilson, "Two over Mars: Mariner VI and Mariner VII, February to August 1969," JPL publication, 1969, p. 13.
49. "Mariner Mars 1969 Project Final Report, vol. 2, Performance," JPL Technical Report 32-1460, Mar. 1, 1971, p. 69.
50. Ibid., pp. 100–10.
51. Ibid., pp. 110–25; Wilson, "Two over Mars," p. 23.
52. Robert B. Leighton, "The Surface of Mars," *Scientific American* 222 (May 1970): 35; same sources as note 51.
53. Same sources as note 52.
54. Leighton, "The Surface of Mars," pp. 35–41; N. W. Cunningham and H. M. Schurmeier, *Mariner-Mars 1969: A Preliminary Report* (Washington, D.C., 1969). Eleven journal articles on Mariners 6 and 7 science results are reprinted in "Mariner Mars 1969 Project Final Report, vol. II, Scientific Investigations."
55. Leighton, "The Surface of Mars," p. 27.
56. Fuchs to Johnson, July 19, 1965, box 9, acc. 72A3070, RG 255, WNRC.
57. NASA routing slip attached to Fuchs letter, ibid. As early as January 1965 none other than Earl Hilburn, who had dealt harshly with JPL over Ranger, had urged Webb to "ease our pressure on CIT" (see Hilburn to Webb, Jan. 6, 1965).
58. Rieke and Sohier to Webb, Sept. 10, 1966.
59. Ibid.
60. Murray to Sharp, file 34.13, DuBridge Papers; author's interview with Newell, Apr. 21, 1977.
61. Rieke and Sohier to Webb, Sept. 10, 1966.
62. Seamans to Sohier, Aug. 18, 1965, box 16, acc. 70A5793, RG 255, WNRC, emphasis in original; Gilmore to Earle J. Sample, May 11, 1966, Sample to Gilmore, June 17, 1966, box 32.11, DuBridge Papers. The situation was touchy enough in 1966 that Webb threw cold water on a proposal to write a history of JPL. Relations among NASA, CIT, and JPL were so "delicate," he said, that "a history might upset the current situation." Such a study, he said, would have to bring out the Caltech fee and the resistance of the Institute and JPL to closer cooperation. "If this becomes widely known through some authoritative history, it will react to the disadvantage of CIT, and I would much rather straighten out our relationships and get moving in the right direction than I would . . . generate a new wave of criticism. However, I may be wrong in the implications that are involved." He concluded: "At the proper time and with the prospect of a capable historian doing the job, I would certainly want to encourage the writing of this history" (Webb to Col. Vogel, Oct. 17, 1966, file 34.1, DuBridge Papers). Indicating the importance he attached to this issue, he even left a special file of documents on the NASA relationship with Caltech-JPL in his papers, specially culled for historians.
63. Gilmore to Sample, Nov. 8, 1966, Hunt to Gilmore, Dec. 15, 1966, file 32.11, DuBridge Papers. On the evaluations see also Newell, *Beyond the Atmosphere,* p. 271.

64. JPL performance evaluation for period July 1, 1965, to Dec. 31, 1965, file 35.3, DuBridge Papers.
65. See various performance evaluations, especially for fiscal year 1965, in file 35.3, DuBridge Papers.
66. Various performance evaluations and DuBridge to Newell, May 24, 1966, file 35.4, DuBridge Papers.
67. Gilmore to DuBridge, June 11, 1965, Newell to DuBridge, Sept. 27, 1965, file 35.3, DuBridge Papers.
68. Same sources as note 67. See also materials on California Universities Council on Space Sciences for 1960–61 in file 32.7, DuBridge Papers.
69. DuBridge to Newell, May 24, 1966, file 35.4, DuBridge Papers.
70. Gilmore to DuBridge, Dec. 1, 1966, file 32.11, DuBridge Papers.
71. W. J. Harmeyer to Hunt, Nov. 10, 1966, Webb to DuBridge, Sept. 18, 1967, Newell to DuBridge (not signed), n.d. (about Aug. 14, 1967), file 34.3, Du-Bridge Papers.
72. Gilmore to DuBridge, May 13, 1964, file 34.2, Gilmore to DuBridge, Nov. 8, 1966, DuBridge to Pickering, Nov. 22, 1966, Jan. 20, 1967, file 34.3, DuBridge Papers.
73. Luedecke to Pickering, Mar. 21, 1967, Pickering to DuBridge, Aug. 7, 1967, file 34.4, Newell to DuBridge, July 24, 1967, file 35.5, DuBridge Papers, emphasis in original.
74. Pickering to DuBridge, Aug. 7, 1967, file 34.4, DuBridge Papers.
75. Luedecke to DuBridge, Aug. 16, 1967, file 34.4, DuBridge Papers.
76. Webb to DuBridge, Sept. 18, 1967, file 34.3, DuBridge Papers; Wilson interview with Clark.
77. Murphy to DuBridge, Oct. 24, 1967, file 34.6, DuBridge Papers.
78. Webb to DuBridge, Oct. 19, 1967, file 34.6, DuBridge Papers.
79. Webb to Harold Finger, Nov. 6, 1967, box 12, acc. 72A3070, RG 255, WNRC.
80. DuBridge to Webb, Nov. 2, 1967, DuBridge to Murphy, Nov. 1, 1967, file 34.6, DuBridge Papers; Pickering to William Zisch, Apr. 23, 1968, Huber to Pickering, Apr. 25, 1968, box 1, shipment L3202, JPL Lyons.
81. Starr committee recommendations, Sept. 30, 1968, box 2, shipment L3202, JPL Lyons.
82. Draft memorandum of understanding, Sept. 17, 1968, file 34.11, DuBridge Papers.
83. *The Economist* (Aug. 1, 1970): 43–44; *Science* 163 (Mar. 14, 1969): 1182.
84. The negotiations may be followed in files 34.10 through 34.13 in DuBridge Papers; see especially DuBridge to Bernard Moritz, Nov. 14, 1968, file 34.11.
85. A. O. Beckman to JPL Trustee Committee, Sept. 26, 1968, file 34.10, DuBridge Papers; Clark to JPL senior staff, containing "memorandum of understanding," Mar. 17, 1969, JPLHF 3-343a.
86. Same sources as note 85.
87. The "tactile" sense of the laboratory in this section is built up in large measure from the author's impressions gathered from a wide variety of persons who worked at JPL. Only the more salient comments are specifically identified. Newell, *Beyond the Atmosphere,* pp. 266–67.

88. Author's interviews with Pickering, Pasadena, June 9, 1977, and Ed Chandler, Pasadena, Sept. 1, 1977, and Newell, Washington, D.C., April 21, 1977.
89. For a sense of the tension see Hall, *Lunar Impact*, pp. 138–43; author's interview with Chandler.
90. Phyllis Langton Stewart, "Organizational Change in an Advanced Research and Development Laboratory: A Study of Professional Attrition" (Ph.D. diss., University of California at Los Angeles, 1968), p. 75. Although Stewart identifies the organization in her study only as "Space Flight Laboratories," internal evidence persuasively suggests it is JPL. Author's interview with Fred Scheuer, Pasadena, Sept. 1, 1977.
91. Author's interview with Newell, Apr. 21, 1977.
92. G. E. Nichols, Jr., "Manpower Trends at JPL Since 1961," Apr. 1, 1966, box 2, shipment F3164, JPL Lyons; Stewart, "Organizational Change in an Advanced Research and Development Laboratory," p. 87.
93. Data provided from JPL employee compensation services and records section in Leo Lunine to author, Apr. 17, 1981.
94. R. E. Covey to Terhune, Sept. 28, 1972, Terhune to Earle J. Sample, Dec. 3, 1971, box 2, shipment F3164, JPL Lyons.
95. Data in Lunine to author, Apr. 17, 1981.
96. Author's interview with Pierce, Feb. 17, 1975.
97. Stewart, "Organizational Change in an Advanced Research and Development Laboratory," p. 195.

Chapter 12

1. Ray Bradbury et al., *Mars and the Mind of Man* (New York, 1973), p. 89. The first part of this book contains the transcript of a panel discussion held in November 1971 at the California Institute of Technology in which scientists Carl Sagan and Bruce Murray, science fiction writers Ray Bradbury and Arthur C. Clarke, and *New York Times* science writer Walter Sullivan discussed what they expected Mariner 9 to reveal about Mars. The second part includes the panel members' ruminations on what they thought the Mariner 9 data actually told them. The book, particularly in the Sagan and Murray segments, provides a fascinating look at the interaction of hope and hard data as scientists go about their work.
2. James to distribution, "Mariner Mars 1971 Orbiter Study," Dec. 29, 1966, JPLHF 9-198; Orbiter study, late 1966, JPLHF 8-227; Mariner Mars 1971 Preliminary Project Development Plan, Mar. 10, 1967, JPLHF 8-190; R. H. Steinbacher and N. R. Haynes, "Mariner 9 Mission Profile and Project History," *Icarus* 18 (1973): 64–74; R. H. Steinbacher and S. Z. Gunter, "The Mariner Mars 1971 Experiments: Introduction," *Icarus* 12 (1970): 3–9.
3. "Mariner Mars 1971 Project Final Report, vol. I, Project Development Through Launch and Trajectory Correction Maneuver," JPL Technical Report 32-1550, Apr. 1, 1973, p. 4.
4. Ibid., pp. 513–54.

5. "Mariner Mars 1971 Project Final Report, vol. 5, Science Experiment Results," JPL Technical Report 32-1550, Aug. 20, 1973, p. 5.
6. H. M. Schurmeier, "Planetary Exploration: Earth's New Horizon," *Journal of Spacecraft and Rockets* 12 (July 1975): 393.
7. "Mariner Mars 1971 Project Final Report," vol. 5; Zdenek Kopal, *The Realm of the Terrestrial Planets* (New York, 1979), p. 139; William K. Hartmann and Odell Raper, *The New Mars: The Discoveries of Mariner 9 and Satellites of the Solar System* (Washington, D.C., 1974).
8. Same sources as note 7; Fred L. Whipple, *Orbiting the Sun: Planets and Satellites of the Solar System* (Cambridge, Mass., 1981), pp. 223–24.
9. Bradbury et al., *Mars and the Mind of Man*, p. 103; Henry S. F. Cooper, Jr., "The Search for Life on Mars, I—Important, Unique, and Exciting Things," *New Yorker* 54 (Feb. 5, 1979): 47; Norman Horowitz, "The Search for Life on Mars," *Scientific American* 237 (July 1977): 53.
10. Bradbury et al., *Mars and the Mind of Man*, p. 22 (emphasis in original); Murray, Malin, and Greeley, *Earthlike Planets*, p. 51.
11. Bruce C. Murray, "Mercury," *Scientific American* 233 (September 1975): 59–62.
12. John R. Biggs and Walter J. Downhower, "A Strategy of Cost Control," *Astronautics & Aeronautics* (June 1974): 51.
13. Ibid., p. 53; "Mariner Venus-Mercury 1973 Project Final Report, vol. I, Venus and Mercury 1 Encounters," JPL Technical Memorandum 33-734, Sept. 15, 1976, p. 3.
14. Biggs and Downhower, "Strategy of Cost Control," p. 50.
15. Ibid., p. 52.
16. Ibid., pp. 50–51.
17. James A. Dunne and Eric Burgess, *The Voyage of Mariner 10: Mission to Venus and Mercury* (Washington, D.C., 1978), pp. 16–17, 32–38, 46–47. This volume includes an extremely rare picture of a woman working on a spacecraft—she is running beta cloth through a sewing machine (see p. 39).
18. Ibid., pp. 55, 72, 90, 96.
19. Whipple, *Orbiting the Sun*, p. 178; Kopal, *Realm of the Terrestrial Planets*, pp. 102–08.
20. Dunne and Burgess, *Voyage of Mariner 10*, pp. 101–02.
21. Whipple, *Orbiting the Sun*, pp. 173, 178.
22. Ibid.
23. Bruce C. Murray et al., "Mercury's Surface: Preliminary Description and Interpretation from Mariner 10 Pictures," *Science* 185 (July 12, 1974): 178.
24. Schurmeier, "Planetary Exploration: Earth's New Horizon," p. 399.
25. Bradbury et al., *Mars and the Mind of Man*, p. 109.
26. House of Representatives subcommittee on Space Science and Applications, "Viking Project," (93rd Cong., 2nd Sess., 1974), pp. 13–15.
27. Ibid., p. 165.
28. Ibid., pp. 101–02.
29. Ibid., pp. 101, 167.
30. William R. Corliss, *The Viking Mission to Mars* (Washington, D.C., 1974), pp. 40, 45–51.

31. Thomas A. Mutch, "The Viking Lander Imaging Investigation: An Anecdotal Account," in Viking Lander Imaging Team, *The Martian Landscape* (Washington, D.C., 1978), p. 26.
32. Ibid., p. 3.
33. Ibid.
34. *Viking I Early Results* (Washington, D.C., 1976), pp. 19–24; N. A. Holmberg et al., *Viking '75 Spacecraft Design and Test Summary, Engineering Test Summary*, vol. 3 (Washington, D.C., 1980), p. 63.
35. Bevan French, *Mars: The Viking Discoveries* (Washington, D.C., 1977), p. 12.
36. Whipple, *Orbiting the Sun*, pp. 229–30. For a blow-by-blow account of the biological investigation, see Cooper, "The Search for Life on Mars, I—Important, Unique, and Exciting Things," and "II—A Residue of Doubt," *New Yorker* 54 (Feb. 12, 1979): 48–87; Horowitz, "Search for Life on Mars," p. 61.
37. Whipple, *Orbiting the Sun*, pp. 210–13; *Science News* 118 (Aug. 9, 1980): 3–4.
38. Murray, Malin, and Greeley, *Earthlike Planets*, pp. xi, 2–17.
39. Ibid.
40. "Farewell to the Red Planet," *Time* 116 (Aug. 18, 1980); *New York Times*, Aug. 5, 1980.
41. *Los Angeles Times*, Aug. 11, 1980, Jan. 28, 1982.
42. From data provided by JPL employee records and compensation division in Lunine to author, Apr. 17, 1981.
43. Ibid.
44. Glennan, "Thoughts on the Nation's Space Program," Glennan Diary; Raymond A. Bauer, *Second-Order Consequences: A Methodological Essay on the Impact of Technology* (Cambridge, Mass., 1969), pp. 162, 178.
45. Mecklin, "Jim Webb's Earthy Management of Space," pp. 114, 156. Webb's *Space-Age Management* is a revealing statement of his views on management.
46. Greenberg, "Space: Caution Prevails on Post-Apollo Commitment," p. 1222.
47. William H. Pickering, "Some Practical Considerations in Technology Transfer," AAS 72-033, JPLHF.
48. Sumner Myers, "Public Policy and Transportation Innovation: The Role of Demonstration," in Alan Altshuler, ed., *Current Issues in Transportation Policy* (Lexington, Mass., 1979), pp. 176–77. Whatever the presumed need for technological innovation in transportation, NASA seemed to have little direct effect, despite its mandate to further innovation. Myers notes some indirect effects but concludes that the technological utilization program "appears to have had little success, given its huge budget" (p. 180n4).
49. H. L. Macomber and James H. Wilson, "California Four Cities Program," 1971–1973, JPL, May 15, 1974, pp. 1–3, 13.
50. Ibid., pp. 8–9, 14.
51. Ibid., p. 1.
52. JPL annual report, 1972–73, pp. 36–37.
53. Ibid, pp. 31–32.
54. JPL annual report, 1976–77, p. 27.
55. "Aims and Goals of the Institute," preliminary report from the Ad Hoc Faculty Committee on Aims and Goals, April 1969, chap. 7, pp. 7, 19, 20, Caltech Archives.

56. Ibid., pp. 10–11.
57. Ibid., pp. 8–10 (emphasis in original).
58. "The Jet Propulsion Laboratory and the Caltech Campus," report of the JPL Study Committee to President Harold Brown [Brooks committee], Mar. 11, 1970.
59. Ibid.
60. Ibid.
61. Roger Noll to author, July 21, 1981.
62. Bruce Murray semi-annual report to the laboratory, Apr. 1977.
63. "A Study of Relations Between the Jet Propulsion Laboratory and the Campus of the California Institute of Technology," report of the Ad Hoc Study on JPL/Campus Interactions to President Harold Brown, Apr. 2, 1976, vol. 1, pp. 34–35.
64. Ibid., p. 36.
65. Ibid., p. 20.
66. Ibid., p. 22.
67. Ibid., p. 44.
68. Timothy Ferris, "Navigators who Probe the Mysteries of Deep Space," *New York Times Magazine* (April 1, 1979).

Epilogue

1. *New York Times*, Nov. 1, 1981; J. Kelly Beatty, "NASA and the Selling of Space Science," *Sky and Telescope* 63 (March 1982), 243–45.
2. *Los Angeles Times*, July 2, 8, 1981; *New York Times*, Nov. 17, 1981; Newell, *Beyond the Atmosphere*, pp. 387–91; Jerry Grey, *Enterprise* (New York, 1979); and Henry S. F. Cooper, "The Space Shuttle—I," *New Yorker* 56 (Feb. 9, 1981): 43–105, and "The Space Shuttle—II," *New Yorker* 57 (Feb. 16, 1981): 65–113.
3. *New York Times*, Nov. 1, 1981; M. Mitchell Waldrop, "Planetary Science *in extremis*," *Science* 214 (Dec. 18, 1981): 1322.
4. Same sources as note 3; *Chicago Sun-Times*, Aug. 30, 1981.
5. Daniel Greenberg, "Why Space Agency Finds Itself in a Void," *Los Angeles Times*, Dec. 21, 1981; Glennan, "Thoughts on the Nation's Space Program," Glennan Diary.
6. Waldrop, "Planetary Science *in extremis*," p. 1322; *Pasadena Star-News*, Feb. 18, 1982; "The NASA Budget: Planetary Panic," *Science News* (Oct. 24, 1981).
7. Murray to senior staff, Dec. 16, 1980.
8. Minutes, Caltech faculty meeting, Dec. 15, 1980.
9. Murray to senior staff, Oct. 30, 1981.
10. DuBridge to Newman, Sept. 26, 1951, DuBridge Papers; Kenneth M. Jones, "The Government-Science Complex," in Robert Bremner and Gary Reichard, eds., *Reshaping America: Society and Institutions, 1945–1960* (Columbus, Ohio, 1982). See also Liebe F. Cavalieri, *The Double-Edged Helix: Science in the Real World* (New York, 1981). On the institutional ethic see Joseph Haberer, *Politics and the Community of Science* (New York, 1969), pp. 321–23. The Nobel prize-winning physicist I. I. Rabi explained the symbiotic relationship between science and the military as follows: "It is also necessary for the military services to

develop close contacts with civilian scientists, not only for the information and developments it may obtain from them but also to maintain at all times a strong scientific reserve—civilians who know the military area and thus are more readily useful and available when there is special need or emergency. A knowledge of military requirements by civilian scientists helps them recognize the military importance of scientific developments and to call them to the attention of the military." See Rabi, chairman of the Office of Defense Mobilization Science Advisory Committee, to Gordon Gray, July 19, 1957, Official File 133-Q (1), box 674, DDEL.

11. Herbert York, *Race to Oblivion* (New York, 1970). Foster quoted in Graham T. Allison and Frederic A. Morris, "Armaments and Arms Control: Exploring the Determinants of Military Weapons," *Daedalus* 104 (1975): 120.

12. Hall interview with Webb, Oct. 26, 1971, JPLHF 2-2308; Newell, *Beyond the Atmosphere*, p. 272.

13. Admiral Hyman Rickover, father of the nuclear navy, indicated similar problems with shipbuilders for the navy and called for government plants as yardsticks. See reprinted testimony in *New York Review of Books* 29 (Mar. 18, 1982): 13.

14. A detailed examination of this question awaits a much needed interpretive history of the space program. A few points about NASA's budget might be made here, however. (See Newell, *Beyond the Atmosphere*, p. 394, for figures by fiscal years.) The space sciences research and development composed almost 20 percent of the NASA budget from 1958 to 1963. During the peak of Apollo funding from 1964 to 1966, the science component dropped to about 12 percent. As the manned program continued and the overall NASA budget was slashed from 1967 to 1969, science funding was particularly hard hit; it fell to just 9 percent of the agency's budget in 1969. In current dollars science funds had dropped from $664.9 million in 1966 to $356.5 million just three years later. Significantly, however, while the NASA budget continued to decline, from $3822 million in 1969 to $2758.5 million in 1974, science funding recovered to some extent. By 1973 and 1974 science funding had regained its share of 20 percent or more of the agency budget. In 1973 the science figure of $672 million topped the previous record. Although NASA's budget has increased since 1974, the planetary science slice has fallen both in absolute and relative terms. These funding patterns raise the interesting possibility that science was able to "justify its budget on its own merits" (Newell, p. 384). Apollo provided at best an artificial boost and may actually have hurt science funding. Apollo did what space science could not do—generate funding demands large enough to satisfy the aerospace industry and its political allies and provide enough technological reinforcement for the military's interest in near-Earth technology. These considerations have an echo in the space shuttle.

15. Killian, "Making Science a Vital Force in Foreign Policy," p. 25.

16. John Noble Wilford, "A Rich Era in the Study of Planets Draws to a Close," *New York Times*, Aug. 25, 1981; Bradbury et al., *Mars and the Mind of Man*, p. 109.

17. Murray, Malin, and Greeley, *Earthlike Planets*, p. xi.

18. Waldrop, "Planetary Science *in extremis*," p. 1322.

19. *Washington Post*, May 8, 1982; *New York Times*, June 15, 1982.

20. *Pasadena Star-News*, Feb. 18, May 13, June 2, 1982.

A NOTE ON SOURCES

The most important sources for this history are the internal files of the organizations concerned. Those of the Jet Propulsion Laboratory are, of course, central. The starting point for JPL history is the JPL History File (JPLHF), a collection of several thousand items, ranging from single letters to multivolume reports, which was organized by R. Cargill Hall and is now housed in the JPL library. The bulk of JPLHF is devoted to the Ranger project, but a random collection of documents from many aspects of the laboratory's history is preserved here. Each item is listed in a computerized finding aid.

After JPLHF a warehouse of records remains. Some of the records, from the laboratory's Central Files of 1944–1962, were microfilmed and are housed in the JPL Vellum Center. After 1962 no central file exists; the records consist of files transferred, and in most cases still controlled, by the originating office or person. Finding aids are minimal and in some cases nonexistent. By comparison with the usual archival research, the historian must shovel through huge quantities of material before locating key items to sift.

In a recent pilot project which examined the files of the Brookhaven laboratory, the history office of the American Institute of Physics concluded that both preservation and usability of the records of federal laboratories are major problems. The JPL experience corroborates that.

The files of three other organizations are also vital. The records of JPL's two chief funding agencies are found in the Washington National Records Center in Suitland, Maryland; they are the Army Ordnance Corps (record group 156) and the National Aeronautics and Space Administration (record group 255). Various records of the California Institute of Technology pertaining to JPL are found in the Caltech Archives. Particularly important are the JPL materials in the Lee A. DuBridge Papers. The NASA History Office has a collection of materials on the space program, with the Homer Newell files being particularly important for space science. Presidential libraries contain materials on the overall missile and space programs. The Dwight E. Eisenhower Library is especially useful and includes the revealing diary of T. Keith Glennan, first NASA administrator.

Published works fall into three categories. First, the reports by JPL and NASA were important sources for some aspects of projects and at times of policy. Second, periodicals, memoirs, and secondary works illuminated national policy and historiographical controversy at certain points. The footnotes provide a guide to the most important of such works. Third, although scholarly historical work on the space program is still sparse, two books are of particular importance to JPL and space science. They are R. Cargill Hall, *Lunar Impact: A History of Project Ranger* (Washington, 1977) and Homer Newell, *Beyond the Atmosphere: Early Years of Space Science* (Washington, 1980).

NAME INDEX

Alexander, George, 231
Armstrong, Neil, 181
Arnold, H. H. "Hap," 8
Arnold, Weld, 5–7

Bacher, Robert F., 110
Bainbridge, William Sims, x
Barnes, Gladeon M., 22, 24, 27
Bartley, C. E., 36
Bauer, Raymond, 233
Beckman, Arnold O., 147
Bell, David, E., 114
Berkner, Lloyd, 83
Biggs, John R., 222
Bollay, William, 3
Boushey, Homer: JATO tests, 11–12; Sputnik's impact, 84
Bowles, Edward L., 25, 28, 247
Bratenahl, Alexander, 155
Brooks, Norman, 237
Brown, Harold: Caltech president, 236–37
Brucker, Wilbur, 73
Burcham, D. P., 191
Burgess, Eric, 224
Burke, James D., 101, 117–18; Ranger project's shortcomings, 120; dismissed, 132
Bush, Vannevar, 19, 25, 67; on Apollo, 114

Cain, D. L., 171
Chandler, Ed, 213
Chidlaw, Benjamin, 9
Clark, John E., 209
Cole, Charles W., 175
Conant, James, 26
Cortright, Edgar, 125, 135, 172, 227

Cummings, Clifford I.: aerospace industry characterized by, 96–97, 115–16; dismissed, 132
Cummings, E. L., 50

Dane, Paul H., 14
Downhower, Walter, 151, 222
Dryden, Hugh, 135–36
DuBridge, Lee, 25, 31; JPL location controversy, 48; JPL /Caltech ties, 67–70, 140, 142, 147, 206–07; private and government science, 135; Webb's relations with, 146; leaves Caltech, 236. *See also* California Institute of Technology; Jet Propulsion Laboratory; National Aeronautics and Space Administration
Dulles, John Foster, 57
Dunn, Louis, 21; described, 31–32; Corporal as nuclear weapon, 42; White Sands experience, 46–47; resigns, 64–65
Dunne, James A., 224
Duwez, Pol, 36

Eddy, G. C., 59
Eimer, Manfred, 117
Eisenhower, Dwight: nuclear war, 77; peaceful uses of space, 79; reaction to Sputnik, 83–84; manned lunar landing, 111

Fletcher, James C., 227, 243
Ford, E. L., 48
Forman, Ed, 3
Forrestal, James, 25
Foster, John, 248

289

SUBJECT INDEX

Advanced Research Projects Agency, 95
Aerobee, 24
Aerojet: formation of, 16–17; constructs Aerobee, 24
Aerospace industry: characterized, 96–97, 115–16, 276n26
Affirmative action, 216
Agena: failure in Ranger, 123–24
Agena B: rivals Vega, 105
Aircraft: rocket-assisted takeoffs, 8–9. *See also* JATOs
Allegheny Ballistics Laboratory, 37
All-inertial guidance system: development, 63, 65–66; described, 74. *See also* Radio-inertial guidance system
Alpha-scattering device, 182
American Institute of Aeronautics and Astronautics, 137
Aniline: as liquid fuel, 14, 23; advantages and disadvantages, 34–35
Apollo program: value debated, 114, 115; as crash program, 118; effects, 248–49. *See also* Ranger; Surveyor
Argonne National Laboratories, 140. *See also* California Institute of Technology
Argus experiment, 91–92
Arming. *see* Corporal; Warhead
Arms race, 247
Army Ballistic Missile Agency: Project Orbiter, 79; reentry test vehicles, 79–80; JPL alliance, 79–94 passim; renamed, 105
Asphalt: as solid fuel, 12–13; in Private A, 22; substitute for sought, 36
Atlas: early development, 64
Atlas-Agena rocket: described, 123

Atlas-Centaur launch vehicle, 189
Atomic Energy Commission, 54–55, 96,140
Autonomous Spacecraft Project, 245
Axial-cooled engine, 39–40

Bay of Pigs invasion, 116, 248
Bell Laboratories, 24
Black powder: as solid fuel, 10, 12
Boeing: NASA contracts, 145; Lunar Orbiter, 172; Mariner *10*, 223; Viking, 227. *See also* Aerospace industry
Brooks report on CIT-JPL relationship, 237–39
Budgets: GALCIT project, 15, 19–20; JPL, 33, 47, 67–69, 120, 232; Caltech, 139–140, 146–49; Mariner flights, 221; NASA, 243–44, 286n14
Bumper-WAC, 40–41
Burnouts: Corporal E, 39

California Four Cities program, 234–35
California Institute of Technology (Caltech or CIT), 2–17 passim; guided missile research by, urged, 19–20, 27; postwar military research question, 26–29; JPL ties debated, 32–34, 48–50, 67–70, 140–42, 236–37; management fee for JPL, 32–34, 68, 139–40, 146–49, 212, 246; JPL location controversy, 48–50, 143; Caltech/JPL joint appointments, 49; Rieke-Sohier study, 203–04; Brooks report, 238–39; Orange report, 239–41
Canopus: Mariner Mars flights, 166, 170–71, 200; Mariner *10* Mercury flight, 224

293